The Politics of Multiculturalism in the New Europe: Racism, Identity and Community

edited by

TARIQ MODOOD AND
PNINA WERBNER

Zed Books Ltd
LONDON & NEW YORK

The Politics of Multiculturalism in the New Europe: Racism, Identity and Community was first published by Zed Books Ltd, 7 Cynthia Street, London N1 9JF, UK, and Room 400, 175 Fifth Avenue, New York, NY 10010, USA in 1997.

Copyright © the contributors, 1997

Cover designed by Andrew Corbett
Set in Monotype Garamond by Ewan Smith
Printed and bound in the United Kingdom
by Biddles Ltd, Guildford and King's Lynn

The rights of the contributors to be identified as the authors of this work have been asserted by them in accordance with the Copyright, Designs and Patents Act, 1988.

A catalogue record for this book is available from the British Library

US CIP data is available from the Library of Congress

Distributed exclusively in the USA by St Martin's Press, Inc., 175 Fifth Avenue, New York, NY 10010, USA.

ISBN 1 85649 421 7 cased
ISBN 1 85649 422 5 limp

Contents

Preface

Europe has become a novel experiment in multiple, tiered and mediated multiculturalisms, a supranational community of cultures, subcultures and transcultures inserted differentially into radically different political and cultural traditions. The consequences of this re-imagining and re-making of a new Europe are seen variously to be threatening or utopian. In a post-communist and allegedly a post-national era, multiculturalism has been theorised as a paternalistic, top-down solution to the 'problem' of minorities, a dangerous reification of 'culture', or a new way forwards towards a politics of 'recognition' and 'authenticity'. But is multiculturalism simply a novel project of social engineering, devised for the twenty-first century by well-meaning liberals or communitarians? The present volume rejects this view by demonstrating that multiculturalism is the political outcome of ongoing power struggles and collective negotiations of cultural, ethnic and racial differences. These are currently reshaping the public spheres and civil societies of the new Europe. Consequently, multiculturalisms are multiple, fluid and continuously contested – a negotiation and transcendence of difference and otherness at different scales, from the communal and local to the national and supranational.

This book, which is a companion volume to *Debating Cultural Hybridity: Multi-Cultural Identities and the Politics of Anti-Racism* edited by the same authors, brings together a new generation of promising European anthropologists, sociologists and political scientists. The chapters contain a wealth of fresh theoretical and ethnographic insights into the practice of multiculturalism and the racist challenges it faces throughout the new Europe, from eastern Europe, Scandinavia and southern Europe to the contested heartland of the European Union.

The two books result from a European Workshop convened in Manchester in December 1994. It was generously funded by the Economic and Social Research Council, UK, and by the European Union through its COST A2 Migration Programme on 'Multiculturalism, Democracy and European Integration'. Altogether, forty scholars from Europe and the United Kingdom were supported by the two funding bodies. The editors would like to thank the ESRC and the Economic Union, as well as their own institutions, the International Centre for Contemporary Cultural Research (ICCCR), Universities of Keele and Manchester, and the Policy Studies Institute (PSI), London, for their generous support.

Thanks are due to several people who made the project possible. Laura Turney helped prepare the manuscript for publication, and gave unstintingly of her time and good will. Gabriele Schroter, Kingsley Purdam and Katherine Tyler, postgraduate students at Keele and Manchester, all worked tirelessly to make the workshop a success. Michel Arens, Secretary of COST A2, sorted out all the administrative complexities with great skill. John Hutnyk and Bobby Sayyid, postdoctoral fellows at the ICCCR, gave support, encouragement and labour. Finally, Richard Werbner, Director of the ICCCR, helped make it all possible.

Tariq Modood and
Pnina Werbner

Contributors

Gideon Ben-Tovim is reader in sociology at the University of Liverpool and director of the Race and Social Policy Unit. He is the author or co-author of various studies in the field of race and local politics, and race and education including *The Local Politics of Race* (Macmillan), *The Racial Politics of Militant* (Runnymede Trust) and *Black Youth in Liverpool* (Giordano Bruno). He is the former chair of Merseyside Community Relations Council and former secretary of Merseyside Anti-Racialist Alliance. He is now an elected member of Liverpool City Council, where he has served as chair of the Education Committee and the Equal Opportunities Committee. He is currently co-chair of the Toxteth Local Partnership, chair of the Liverpool Standing Council for Religious Education, and chair of the City of Liverpool Community College. He is a member of the Council of Europe Working Party on Cities and Education, and has been involved in ethnic minority policy development in local government in eastern Europe.

Tore Bjørgo is a research fellow at the Norwegian Institute of International Affairs. A social anthropologist by training, he is conducting research projects on right-wing violence and terrorism in Scandinavia, and on responses to racist violence. His main works in English include *Conspiracy Rhetoric in Arab Politics* (1987), *Maritime Terrorism* (1991), and several articles on racist violence and neo-Nazism. He has co-edited *Racist Violence in Europe* (1993) and edited *Terror from the Extreme Right* (1995), and co-authored (in Norwegian) books on terrorism and political communication.

Christopher Brewin was educated at Grenoble, Oxford and Harvard universities. He is a lecturer in international relations at Keele University and course tutor of the European studies programme. He has written extensively on the institutions and policies of the European Union, has a particular interest in Turkey, and also writes on international ethics.

Ayse S. Caglar is an assistant professor at the Institut für Ethnologie, Freie Universität, Berlin. She received her BA in sociology from Bosphorus University, Istanbul, and her MA and PhD in anthropology from McGill University, Montreal. She has worked on ethnicity, nationalist discourse and migration. Her current work focuses on consumption, popular culture and immigrants' incorporation into German society. Her research has been published in several books and journals, including *Turkish*

State, Turkish Society, Marketing in a Multicultural World, New Community, and *Zeitschrift für Turkei Studien*.

A. Moustapha Diop is maître de conferences (senior lecturer) at the Institut National des Langues et Civilisations Orientales (INALCO) in Paris. He has conducted extensive research among Senegalese and Muslim settlers in France and is author of *Rapport sur le mouvement islamique en Île-de-France* (Paris CERi/FNSP, 1990), and *Société manjak et migration* (Thise-Besançon, Imprimérie Jacques et Demonstrond, 1996).

László Kürti received his PhD in anthropology from the University of Massachusetts, Amherst, in 1989. Currently, he is associate professor at the Eotvos Lorand University in Budapest and professor in the Department of Political Sciences at the University of Miskole. His publications include *Beyond Borders* (Westview 1997), and *Nations and Relations* (forthcoming, SUNY Press), as well as many articles in various professional journals. He has conducted fieldwork in North America, among east European diaspora communities, in Hungary, Romania and among the Hanty-Mansy people of Siberia, Russia.

Philip Lewis is the Inter-Faith Adviser for the Anglican Bishop of Bradford and Lecturer in Theology and Religious Studies at Leeds University. He represents the Archbishop of Canterbury on the Advisory Council for the Centre for the Study of Islam and Christian–Muslim Relations in Birmingham. Dr Lewis's extensive writings on race, religion and ethnicity include his book, *Islamic Britain: Religion, Politics and Identity among British Muslims* (IB Tauris 1994). He is currently a commissioner for the Runnymede Trust inquiry into British Muslim communities and Islamophobia.

Wenonah Lyon is a research fellow in the Centre for Social Anthropology and Computing at the University of Kent. She has done extensive fieldwork in Lahore, Pakistan, on lower-income groups, in the Cook Islands on popular cultural festivals, and in the UK on women and popular culture among Asian immigrants.

Umberto Melotti is full professor of political sociology at the Faculty of Sociology of the University of Rome 'La Sapienza', where he also teaches the cultural anthropology of migration. Among his published works are *Marx and the Third World* (Macmillan 1977), 'In-group/Out-group Relations and the Issue of Group Selection' in *The Sociobiology of Ethnocentrism* (Croom Helm 1987), and *L'immigrazione: una sfida per l'Europa* (Edizioni Associate, Roma 1992). He is the editor of the quarterly journal *Terzo Mondo*.

Tariq Modood is a programme director at the Policy Studies Institute. He has held fellowships at Nuffield College, Oxford, and the University of Manchester, and lectureships in political theory at several universities. He has worked at the Commission for Racial Equality and served as chair of the Oxford Council for Community Relations. He is a regular contributor to journals and newspapers, and his publications include *Not Easy Being British: Colour, Culture and Citizenship* (Trentham Books for the Runnymede Trust 1992), *Racial Equality* (Institute for Public Policy Research 1994), *Changing Ethnic Identities* (co-authored 1994), *Asian Self-Employment: The Interaction of Culture and Economics* (co-authored 1996) and *Britain's Ethnic Minorities: Diversity and Disadvantage* (co-authored 1997)

Yunas Samad is a lecturer in the Department of Social and Economic Studies, Bradford University. He is the author of *Nation in Turmoil: Nationalism and Ethnicity in Pakistan, 1937–1958* (Sage, Delhi 1995) and co-editor (with Terence Ranger and Ossie Stuart) of *Culture, Identity and Politics* (Avebury 1996). He has conducted research on Asian voluntary associations in Bradford and Birmingham, and is currently collaborating on an ESRC project on 'Globalisation, Ethnic Minority Media and the Representation of Islam'.

Werner Schiffauer studied social anthropology at the Free University of Berlin and in Ankara. He currently holds the Chair of Comparative Social and Cultural Anthropology at the European University Viadrina in Frankfurt/Oder. His fieldwork in Turkey and in Germany has focused on religious anthropology with particular reference to Islam, migration and urban anthropology. His major publications include *Die Gewalt der Ehre* (Frankfurt/Main, Suhrkamp 1983); *Die Bauern von Subay* (Stuttgart, Klett Cotta 1986); *Die Migranten aus Subay* (Stuttgart, Klett-Cotta 1991); *Kultur and Differenz* (Frankfurt/Main, Suhrkamp forthcoming).

Pnina Werbner is a reader in social anthropology at Keele University and research administrator of the International Centre for Contemporary Cultural Research (ICCCR) at the universities of Manchester and Keele. Her publications include *The Migration Process: Capital, Gifts and Offerings among British Pakistanis* (Berg 1990), *Black and Ethnic Leaderships in Britain: The Cultural Dimensions of Political Action* co-edited with Muhammad Anwar (Routledge 1991), *Economy and Culture in Pakistan: Migrants and Cities in a Muslim Society* (Macmillan 1991) co-edited with Hastings Donnan, and *Debating Cultural Hybridity* (Zed Books 1996) co-edited with Tariq Modood. Her forthcoming book, *Diaspora and Millennium: Islamic Narrations, Identity Politics and the Aesthetics of the Religious Imagination*, is on the political imaginaries of British Pakistanis. She is director of an ESRC-funded research project on 'South Asian Popular Culture: Gender, Generation and Identity'.

Lale Yalçın-Heckmann studied sociology at Bogazici University, Istanbul, and social anthropology at the London School of Economics. Her doctoral research was on Kurdish tribes and kinship in southeastern Turkey and, more recently, on Muslims and Turks in Germany and France. She lectured at the Department of Sociology of the Middle East Technical University, Ankara, and has been a research fellow at the Chair of Islamic Studies, and later the Chair of Turkish Studies, at the University of Bamberg. Her publications include numerous articles on Kurdish ethnography and ethnicity, the monograph *Tribe and Kinship among the Kurds* (Frankfurt; Peter Lang, 1991), and articles on Islam and Turks in Germany and Europe.

CHAPTER I

Introduction:
The Politics of Multiculturalism
in the New Europe

Tariq Modood

Inclusion and exclusion

The 'new Europe' that this book is primarily concerned with is one of ethnic heterogeneity inserted into a multicultural suprastate. This follows several decades of immigration and utilisation of so-called guest-workers mainly from outside Europe: from the Caribbean, various parts of Africa, Turkey, the Middle East and Asia. From the late 1940s through to the 1970s, the economic reconstruction and development of western Europe attracted skilled and unskilled people from less developed economies to meet its labour shortages. The demand for labour ceased with the recession that began in the mid-1970s, but by then many of the migrants had settled in the region, where their families were joining them, and which remained a magnet for economic migrants, refugees and asylum seekers. These movements of people, often from former colonies, whether welcome or not, have created a multiculturalism that is qualitatively different from the diversity of personal lifestyles or cultural differences of historic, territorially based minorities that already characterise some western European countries. It is the fears, challenges, dialogues and exclusions that this new multiculturalism has given rise to, and the developments that it intimates for the future, that are the central concerns of this book. Nevertheless, we appreciate that there are at least two other contemporary events that connect with these, and which are just as critical to any use of the phrase 'the new Europe'. One is the development of a European Union (EU) which already has created a European citizenship that some, including Christopher Brewin in this volume, hope will transform western European nation-states from the top down, as multiculturalism may be transforming them from the bottom upwards.

The other development that has led to the making of a new Europe has been the ending of the Cold War which for nearly fifty years divided Europe into two, each half being a junior, protected partner in a trans-continental military alliance opposed to the other. The collapse of the Soviet Union has meant, amongst other things, the shifting of boundaries as new politics were born, new states were created (sometimes leading to appalling barbarities, as in the former Yugoslavia), and the peoples of central and eastern Europe began to reconstruct and reconceptualise those regions and their relation to each other and to western Europe. In Chapter 2, Lázló Kürti examines the discourse of 'Europe' in post-1989 eastern and central Europe. He looks at the call to rejoin 'Europe' being made by various intellectuals and polemicists, usually on the democratic wing of politics, in a number of countries in that region. He documents the pre-1939 and nineteenth-century lineage of this modernising ideology and its discursive ideas and tropes, arguing forcefully that despite what may be of value in such politics, it deploys old canards and stereotypes about various peoples and groups in the region, usually peoples who are to the south and/or the east of the ideologues. Thus Czechs, for example, are viewed as democratic, liberal and belonging to European civilisation, contributors to a distinctive 'Central European' ethos, while by contrast the Slovaks are characterised as illiberal, intellectually and politically backward, mired in ethnic hostilities, half-Asian, at best 'East European'. Whatever the truth about particular peoples and countries, this is essentially a polar, black-and-white discourse in which progressives and modernists define themselves in relation to a negative 'otherness'. The portrayal of self-virtues and aspirations depends upon negative, indeed racist, images of others, so that, as Kurti says, the fashioning of 'Central Europe' is at the same time a re-making of 'Eastern Europe'.

For centuries eastern and central Europe have been a battleground and frontier between Christian peoples and rulers, and Muslim peoples and rulers. Muslims are indeed very much part of 'the otherness' in the self-definition of the various peoples of the region. If a theme of Croatian nationalism has been its Catholicism in contrast to the 'eastern' Orthodox Christianity of the Serbs and beyond, a leitmotif of Serbian nationalism is of the Serbs as the bulwark against the Muslim Turks. An interesting contemporary by-product of this process has been the way Bosnian Muslims, of the same Slavic descent as their Serbian neighbours, have been 'racialised' or 'ethnicised', so that they are now universally regarded (and regard themselves) as an ethnic rather than simply a religious group. This racialisation of Muslims, which parallels the experience of another faith community, the Jews, is not confined to Bosnia. For Muslims are now emerging as the critical 'other' in various nationalist discourses and in definitions of Europe in western Europe too. This, of course, is connected to the decades of immigration from outside Europe into western Europe (detailed by Melotti in Chapter 4), in which Muslims formed a majority of immigrants. Yet the anti-Muslim discourses are not only prevalent where there are large Muslim settlements or where there is a historical antipathy, of a Crusader or colonial sort, to Islam. As Tore Bjørgo shows in his analysis of extreme right-wing nationalist discourse in Scandinavia, even though this region is amongst the furthest of any in Europe from Muslim territories, and thus is marked by an absence of any historical encounter with Muslims, Muslims feature centrally as 'the invaders' in that discourse now. In particular, he argues that while neo-Nazis still make a symbolic use of the Jews as the arch enemy, in some Norwegian and Danish right-wing discourse an anti-Islamic conspiracy theory (Muslim immigrants are part of a coordinated plan to conquer Europe for Islam) serves as a substitute for classical anti-Semitic conspiracy theories.

Bjørgo in fact goes further and notes that the problematising of Muslims is not confined to racists. He suggests that among western political elites Islam has replaced communism as the main threat to what is conceived of as Western civilisation. This has now become a familiar argument, but it is worth drawing out one important implication. Discourse that sees Muslims as a problem or a threat is not confined to an extreme fringe, nor to popular prejudice, but is prominent in certain elite discourses. Nor are these discourses confined to the right wing. Just as in central Europe progressive politics can use, consciously or unconsciously, a negative 'otherness' in order to project itself, so similarly an anti-Muslim bias can be implicit or explicit in progressive discourse. For example, at the height of *The Satanic Verses* controversy in Britain, one of the most emotive polemics against multiculturalism in general and Muslims in particular came from a prominent liberal feminist (Weldon 1989). John Rex has recently noted, not for the first time, that in Europe 'Islam is now a focus of "racist" hostility at least as important as colour', evidenced in an indiscriminate description of Muslims as 'fundamentalists'; this hostility rests on attitudes 'shared not merely by minorities of racists but by commentators in the quality media and many social scientists' (Rex 1996: 8). It is a bias which, for example, can reveal itself in the simple, careless factual errors that theorists of multiculturalism of the stature of Charles Taylor, Will Kymlicka and Stephen Macedo make when writing about Muslims, and more fundamentally, in how Muslims are excluded from their conception of multiculturalism, as in the case of Taylor's 'politics of recognition' (see Modood 1993; 1996). For example, in an otherwise stimulating essay, Taylor argues, rightly I believe, that liberalism is not a 'neutral ground on which people of all cultures can meet and coexist' (Taylor 1994: 62). The only example he gives of where 'one has to draw the line' is 'incitement to assassination'. So far there is likely to be no conflict. He reaches this conclusion however by arguing that the controversy over *The Satanic Verses* shows that '[f]or mainstream Islam, there is no question of separating politics and religion the way we have come to expect in Western liberal society' (ibid.). My objection is that it is far from obvious that this is what the controversy showed or needs to show in order for anyone to reach the conclusion that liberalism ought not to tolerate incitement to murder. Taylor offers no evidence that 'mainstream Islam' involves an acceptance of incitement to assassination; nor that if you hold that politics and religion do not have to be separated (in the way that Taylor himself argues that politics and culture do not have to be separated), then you have no argument against incitement to assassination. The reference to mainstream Islam is in fact a *non sequitur*, but the impression is created that liberalism cannot accommodate mainstream Islam, that mainstream Muslims are not to be included in 'the politics of recognition'.

The term 'Islamophobia' may, however, be somewhat misleading. The contemporary prejudice against Muslim immigrants is based on an anxiety about (what are perceived to be) features of values and practices derived from Islam, but it is not at all clear that these attitudes represent, as some Muslim writers contend, a historical continuity with the ideology of the Crusades (Akhtar 1989; Kabbani 1989). For the Islamophobia in question is more like anti-semitism than anti-Judaism. It is more a form of racism than a form of religious intolerance, though it may perhaps be best described as a form of cultural racism, in recognition of the fact that the target group, the Muslims, are identified in terms of their non-European descent, in terms of their not being white, and in terms of their perceived culture, and that the prejudice against each of these aspects interacts with and reinforces the prejudice against the others. Moreover, at least in Britain, committed Christians are less likely to express prejudice against Muslims than are nominal Christians and agnostics/atheists (Modood et al. 1997: 134).

If, as in Scandinavia, it is possible to identify related but different forms of racism (anti-Semitism, Islamophobia, white supremacism), these are, as Bjørgo shows, related to national histories and national political cultures. The Nazi invasions of Denmark and Norway in the 1940s make it close to impossible to be a Nazi nationalist in those countries today in the way that it is possible in Sweden. So, similarly, there are different forms of anti-racism, different conceptions of racial equality and different forms of multiculturalism across Europe. That multiculturalism is conceived differently in different countries and is given varied institutional expression depending upon the local and national political culture is a pervasive theme of this book. Umberto Melotti, for example, gives an overview of aspects of post-war immigration into western Europe, comparing the situation in different countries, especially in relation to their immigration policies and the political responses to the presence of large numbers of migrants, naturalised citizens and their families. He focuses on four of the larger countries – France, Britain, Germany and Italy – and shows that while Italy has only recently become a country of net immigration, in the other three countries the period of immigration has been long enough to display the consequences of their different responses.

Melotti argues that while France has a long tradition of welcoming immigration and of extending full citizenship to the immigrants and their children, this egalitarianism is premised on an unashamed assimilationism. He contends that however well this has worked in the past, and it does seem to have worked very well when the immigrants were from other Latin and Roman Catholic countries, ethnocentric assimilation does not seem to be working in the case of the non-Europeans. Not only is the cultural difference between the natives and the immigrants greater than in the past, but at the present time respect for cultural differences has emerged as a value, and the assimilationist project is perceived by many as lacking legitimacy and is generating an ideological crisis. If the French approach has been based on an egalitarianism that is intolerant of cultural loyalties that may compete with loyalties due to the French republic, the British approach, based on a different colonial history and conception of nationhood, is more tolerant of cultural difference, more relaxed about the formation of ethnic minority communities but is not committed to equality of membership in the national community. Despite the anti-discrimination measures that have been taken in the UK, racial discrimination persists; and Melotti argues that it is unclear whether racial inequality can really be eliminated within the approach used to date.

The German approach, once again reflecting the distinctive political history of that country, is different again. For decades Germany denied its status as an host immigrant country. Incoming ethnic Germans were not immigrants because, regardless of where in the world they were coming from, they were embraced as rediscovered members of the German nation and automatically granted citizenship. All other incomers, such as the Turks, were not immigrants because they were 'guest-workers' and were expected to return to their country. To this day, adult Turks born in Germany find it difficult to acquire German citizenship. This state of affairs is now widely perceived as unsatisfactory and has generated a debate about the reform of German citizenship. Hence, Melotti argues, all three of the main policy approaches to non-European migration in western Europe have led to an impasse and have given rise in each of the three countries to a debate about a new, multicultural model of integration.

From immigrants to citizens

These broad differences disguise further differences in the way multi-culturalism operates locally. It is only through specific case studies that we can analyse how integration and multiculturalism are worked in different ways in different local and national settings, or explore what a new politics of multiculturalism looks like. The difference between the German and French approaches to multiculturalism is evident in Lale Yalçın-Heckmann's contrasting study of the associations of Turkish migrants in a small

Bavarian town and a small Alsatian town. In the German town, it was initially taken for granted that Turks were not only not German citizens but that they did not belong in Germany, and so it was considered appropriate to give them separate educational classes in Turkish language and culture. Yet latterly there have also been moves by the local government to give some recognition to the local alien population. A feature of this recognition is that it is group-based, as the local state co-opts those individuals who can demonstrate that they speak for a community and encourages institutionalised representation in the form of a so-called Foreigners' Council. By contrast, in the French town of Colmar, while there is no less evidence of migrants' politics, with its rivalries and intra- and inter-ethnic alliances, the multiculturalism that emerges is fostered by a stronger grassroots movement with virtually no state backing. Yet the Turks are more marginal to multiculturalism in Colmar than in Bamberg. This may be partly due to the relative numbers within various minority groups, but perhaps the top-down Foreigners' Council approach, whether intended to contain multiculturalism or not, has in the Bavarian case continued the particularistic tendencies that have made Turks politically marginal in Colmar. Ironically, then, the top-down approach is not necessarily inimical to multiculturalism. What Yalçin-Heckmann's comparative study also shows is that whatever the differences in the local political contexts, the associations in each town are partly shaped, especially in terms of their internal divisions and rivalries, by the politics, or at least the political rhetoric, of Turkey. At the same time forms of cooperation and unity are developing amongst migrants from different countries, especially in terms of their resistance to their subordinate status.

Chapters 6, 7 and 8 focus on attempts to include Muslims into the civic culture in three different countries. They continue to illustrate how policies of inclusion are shaped by pre-existing civic cultures, and additionally affirm how central Muslims and religious identity are to the new multiculturalism in western Europe. Moustapha Diop carries forward the discussion of immigrants' associations, but this time at a national French level. He shows how Muslim associations in France date back to student organisations at the beginning of the twentieth century, and gives a brief outline of their history and the views of the current leaders on what Islam should mean in France today. He concludes by offering some general thoughts of his own. It is interesting that the language he uses is not a language of rights or of equality but of 'mutual respect'. The ultimate goal for Muslim associations, he thinks, should be the establishment of a respected French Islamic civilisation, and he believes that this requires Islam to be legitimised and recognised by French society and the French state. In his reflections on how Muslims in France might achieve this, he emphasises the dual strategy of increased group consciousness and increased national consciousness.

Diop's advice to Muslims is to forget their internal differences and rivalries and work to achieve solidarity amongst Muslims in France regardless of their national origins. At the same time he favours weakening links with the international Muslim community, the *ummah*, and especially with the more militant ideologies circulating in parts of the Muslim world. As we shall see below, either aspect of this strategy might be objected to by other multiculturalists. For them multiculturalism is not about institutionalising group differences but about individuals crossing group boundaries and becoming conscious of their hybridity. Again, many multiculturalists would emphasise the cultivation of international networks. Diop on the other hand believes that Muslims in France, suffering from 'a narcissism of minor differences', need to increase their social cohesion if they are to speak with a single voice, which they must do if they are to negotiate with the government and other bodies to achieve a place for Islam in French institutions. This certainly is not a ghettoised approach, for Diop emphasises the importance of reaching out and cooperating with the wider French society. On the contrary, it is clear that the focus is on the French state and society, and what is being sought is accommodation within that through a fusion of the collective identities French and Muslim. What this suggests is that in those societies where strong national identities exist, the process of social inclusion, of converting immigrants into citizens, is likely to take the form not of challenging the national identity but of prising it open to allow for insertions and new syntheses.

How elements of the state and/or the religious establishment are attempting to assist in the incorporation of Muslims in Britain and Germany is explored by Philip Lewis and Werner Schiffauer respectively. Lewis focuses on one city, Bradford, which with its high profile in several political controversies has been dubbed 'the Muslim capital of Britain'; he is aware of the national setting too, however, about which he makes some important general points. He astutely recognises that Bradford City Council played a part in encouraging Muslim mobilisation (as opposed to other minority politics that Muslims are part of, such as Asian or 'black' politics). In this sense the 'recognition' of identities and communities is a political process in which state agencies and others play an active part. Lewis notes also that when events like the Rushdie affair and the Gulf War radicalised Muslim opinion, making it unacceptable to the city authorities, they withdrew support from institutions such as the Council of Mosques; latterly they have sought to resurrect an 'Asian' identity in order to have (so they hope) more cooperative bodies to work with. It is because the public recognition of community identities is so deeply political that it is itself a source of political activity and conflict. Both Diop and Lewis argue that one of the spurs to Muslim community activism in France and Britain respectively was the recognition of secular anti-racism as the authentic voice of immigrant, black and ethnic minority groups. The

defining of immigrant groups without reference to religious identities –
largely a consequence of the view of religion as a matter of private life,
not collective action or public policy – certainly has generated the charge
amongst some Muslims in Britain that secular multiculturalism seeks to
deliberately emasculate Muslim communities (Muslim Parliament 1992).
Muslims in Britain, for example, feel particularly aggrieved that while
racial discrimination and incitement to racial hatred are unlawful, religious
discrimination and incitement to religious hatred is unlawful only in
Northern Ireland (UKACIA 1993). Additionally, there are a number of
ways in which Muslims do not enjoy the same rights as members of some
other religions. The single most persistent controversy concerns the failure
of all applications to date by Muslim schools to win public funding on
the same basis as Christian and Jewish schools. The situation in Britain
can be contrasted with the Netherlands where there are many state-funded
Islamic schools (Dwyer and Meyer 1995), and where the Islamic Broadcasting Association is given thirteen hours of state TV and fifty-two hours
of state radio time a week (Slomp et al. 1988: 9). In Belgium as early as
1974, Islam was recognised as one of the official religions of the country
with rights to various state disbursements (Rath et al. 1991).

Lewis cites a historical precedent that suggests that the British government is being particularly short-sighted. He suggests that a measure of
state funding for their schools has been enormously important in allowing
Catholics, especially Irish Catholics, eventually to feel accepted and become
a part of British society. If the central government has been reluctant to
extend equality of treatment to Muslims, Lewis argues that the religious
establishment, especially in Bradford, has been active in assisting the Muslim
organisations to participate in public debates and at times to feel less
rejected and besieged than they otherwise might. Certainly at the time of
the Rushdie affair, especially in the weeks following Ayatollah Khomeini's
famous *fatwa* when Muslims felt desperately cornered, the churches were
more supportive than most, possibly any other, element in British society.
Lewis describes how, in Bradford, the Anglican Church has at critical
times taken a lead in creating institutions to give expression to the multiracial and multi-faith character of the city, rather than wait upon the local
state to do so. Perhaps its confidence to do so, and its sense of responsibility, comes from the fact that being the Established Church it feels
part of the state. As Lewis notes, its actions can perhaps also be seen to
be continuous with the highly ecumenical character of English Christianity
(Hastings 1992). As active worship has progressively and drastically declined
in Britain, especially in England, the churches have not aggressively sought
to increase their market share, but instead have sought to cooperate with
each other over their common interests. It may be that this ecumenicism
of mutual solace is in some ways being extended to cover the non-Christian
faiths (Modood 1997). A sign of the times could thus be the declaration

in a television interview by Prince Charles, who, if and when he becomes the monarch, will inherit the title Defender of the Faith, that as king he would not wish to identify exclusively with one faith and would prefer to be a defender of faith in general, of all faiths.

Were the British monarch's duties to be so revised, a form of multi-culturalism would be expressed in a core symbol of the state. Werner Schiffauer in his chapter in this book argues that at least some elements of the German state apparatus are looking beyond the temporary *Gastarbeiter* policy and are beginning to design policies on the assumption that Germany will permanently have a Muslim population. Schiffauer's interest is in how the German state tradition will respond to this challenge. The decision of the provincial government of North Rhine-Westphalia (Nordrhein-Westfalen) to establish Islamic religious education in its schools is perhaps not that unusual. What is more unusual is that the designers of the appropriate curriculum should set themselves the goal of creating a vehicle that demonstrates that the principles embodied in the Qur'an are ones that most Germans would recognise as broadly compatible with the norms and principles of contemporary German society. Even this is not a particularly bizarre goal, given the discussion of Diop's vision of a French Islamic civilisation. What is most unusual and the main focus of Schiffauer's analysis is that the task of curriculum design should be in the hands of non-Muslim German civil servants. In this, Schiffauer argues, is displayed the distinctive German state tradition. There is a sense that if Muslims are to be part of a new national German culture then it must be demonstrated that their values do not jar with the ethos of the German state, that there is no ethical tension between being a good Muslim and a good German. Moreover, if the state is serious about this, it must undertake the task itself lest some radical sect should hijack the project or its success be prevented through dissension, lack of expertise or vision. So while the incorporation of Islam into state curricula or, even more generally, the goal of nationalising Islam is not peculiar to German multiculturalists, the reliance on the state does seem to be. I have already noted that several western European states are working to allow space for Islam within national symbols and national institutions, and have con-sidered the example that state funding of Catholic schools in England played in integrating Irish immigrants and their descendants. Yet in at least the British case the method involves delegation of power and funds downwards, not the state taking charge. The contrast can be directly seen by comparing North Rhine-Westphalia with Bradford, where too a new religious education syllabus was introduced as part of the city's institu-tionalising multiculturalism. From Lewis's account, it can be seen that though the syllabus was created within a national framework, it was a local creation, the product of the participation of communities, and was done on an interfaith basis.

The politics of plural identities

I have so far considered ethnic groups, religious communities, national cultures, multiculturalism and so on as if these were unproblematic terms. However, there is a powerful current of argument in contemporary social science that argues that most uses of these terms, especially in political contexts, are based on a flawed understanding of culture. The criticism is that 'multiculturalism' and related discourses assume that for each identifiable group there is a single culture, that it is homogenous, that it has always been the same, that wherever the group is found or travels to the same culture is found, so that one can talk about a group and its culture without any reference to context, to contact or interaction with other groups, to economic circumstances, political power and so on. The key term that expresses these related points is 'essentialism'; commonsense discourse about cultures assumes that each culture has a unique, fixed essence that can be grasped independently of context or intercultural relations, and which makes an ethnic group act the way it does. While anti-essentialism is a relatively recent position, the position it attacks, however much it may be assumed in our unreflective moments, is so manifestly absurd that few would want to defend it. In fact, it has recently been said that 'opposition to essentialism is a near-universal characteristic of the debate on identity' (Kirton 1995: 5).

In Chapter 9 Ayse S. Caglar offers a powerful critique of our unreflective as well as some of our political and intellectual discourse about culture and multiculturalism. She argues that the assumption that a culture is a self-contained, unified construct that belongs to spatially bounded, separate social entities or 'communities' is extremely pervasive and is implicit even in some attempts to oppose such essentialist ideas. She examines a number of attempts in anthropology and cultural studies to come to terms with migration and transnational cultural processes, and with the fact that many people now define themselves in terms of multiple national attachments and are comfortable with fluid and plural identities; she argues that these attempts actually employ the same flawed concept of culture that they are opposing. For example, some analysts have developed a concept of 'hybridity' to capture the complexity of the lives and subjectivities, the cultural syntheses and practices of those whose family background and home upbringing may be very different from the wider societal cultures that are as much a part of their personal identity, and which they combine in new creative ways. Caglar points out, however, that while theorists of hybridity are able to show how cultures can mix, the presumption is that prior to the mixing there were two different cultures à la essentialism. Moreover, even if hybridity theory shows the crassness of the idea of 'one nation, one culture' and allows for fluidity and change, the cultures that it speaks of are still anchored in territorial ideas, for the underlying assumption is that 'one space, one culture' is the norm to which hybridity is the exception. Caglar believes, in any case, that in practice even those who speak of hybridity in fact treat cultures as bounded and closed, and that it is not at all clear how the notion of hybridity can be helpful to a politics of multiculturalism. For what prevents true multiculturalism are cultural and other forms of domination, and hybridity is unable to destabilise existing hierarchies.

It cannot be denied that Caglar has a point. In talking about other people's cultures we often assume that a culture has just the kind of features that anti-essentialists identify. When non-Chinese people, for example, talk of 'Chinese civilisation' their starting point often is that it has a coherence, sameness over centuries and a reified quality. Sometimes, as Caglar notes of minority intellectuals, one slips into such a mentality when talking of one's own cultural traditions. One is particularly prone to this when one is producing a systematic summary or ideological justification for those traditions. Hence rich, complex histories become simplified and collapsed into a teleological progress or a unified ideological construct called 'French' culture or 'European' civilisation or the 'Muslim' way of life. In cases where we essentialise or reify someone else's culture, no antidote may be to hand for we lack the knowledge to overturn the simplifications. In the case of a living culture that we are part of, that we have been inducted into, that we have extended through use and seen change in our own lifetimes, it is easier to appreciate better the processes of change, adaptation of borrowings from other cultures and new influences, and yet at the same time to appreciate what is the *subject* of change. For change implies the continuation of something that has undergone change. It is the same in the case of a person: at the end of one's life one might reflect on how one's personality changed over time and through experience, and see how all the changes constitute a single person, without believing that there was an original, already formed, essential 'I' prior to the life experiences. As with a person, so with a culture. One does not have to believe that a culture, or for that matter an ethnic group as the agent of culture, has a primordial existence. A culture is made *through* change; it is not defined by an essence that exists apart from change, a noumenon hidden behind the altering configurations of phenomena. In individuating cultures and peoples, our most basic and helpful guide is not the idea of an essence, but the possibility of making historical connections, of being able to see change and resemblance. If we can trace a historical connection between the language of Shakespeare, the language of Charles Dickens and the language of Winston Churchill, we call that language by a single name. We say that it is the same language, though we may be aware of the differences between the three languages and of how the changes are due to various influences, including contact with and borrowings from other languages, and without having to make any claim about an 'essence'.

Caglar believes, however, that if in social science and politics we are to avoid reifying immigrants' practices and identities, we need to make a radical break with the idea of people or an ethnic group having any unified contemporary existence, let alone one maintained over long stretches of time. In her view notions of hybridity, of hyphenated identities (such as Black-British or Turkish-German) or of the plasticity of culture, all attempt to reform rather than reject a vision of cultural groups as reified and spacialised. They end up supporting a politics of multiculturalism that inevitably requires stable or frozen collective identities, for otherwise how are groups to be 'recognised', 'institutionalised' and so on. She suggests that a more radical project might take as its starting point person–object relations, and focus on commodities and consumption, bringing out how values and economic factors interact and how definitions are negotiated by collectivities. She recognises that this might simply mean a return of the banished cultural collectivities by the back door, but believes that because consumption is so patently located in material interests it will make transparent the constructed nature of communities and hold at bay the tendency to reify and mystify culture.

If Caglar's primary target is the use of 'culture' in anthropology, in Chapter 10 Wenonah Lyon's ethnographic study of a multi-ethnic community theatre group in Oldham, near Manchester, explores a level of identity not amenable to psychological study. Her interest is in the various ethnic labels people give to themselves and to other people, and how in turn they are labelled by others. Indeed, she argues that how people classify themselves is central to the issue of defining ethnicity. As ethnicity expresses relationships of both inclusion and exclusion, it follows that an ethnic group is partly formed by exclusion. Lyon, however, wants to define ethnicity not by reference to the content of a group (by reference, for example, to culture or physical appearance), or even by reference to the content of the exclusion or inclusion, but by reference to the *form* of the exclusion. She defines an ethnic group as a subset of a set. That is to say, an ethnic group is an excluded or differentiated part of a larger group. Ethnicity is defined as the exclusion of a group from the larger group with which it shares inclusion at another level. On this definition, Pakistanis in Britain are an ethnic group because (a) they are British *and* (b) they distinguish themselves and are distinguished by others as a group in Britain. Pakistanis in Pakistan, however, are not an ethnic group, because they are not a subgroup. (In Pakistan, Pathans may be an ethnic group but Pakistanis are not.) Similarly, Asians in Britain may be an ethnic group because of the relevant processes of inclusion and exclusion, even if 'Asian' is not an ethnic group anywhere else in the world.

This relational definition of ethnic identity applies particularly to the terms people use to refer to themselves and to others. The ethnic terms used in the Oldham theatre group, whose members are predominantly of

South Asian descent, are varied. People do not always use the same terms, for the choice of group labels is context-dependent, incorporating and excluding others as the situation requires. Lyon gives a fascinating account of these varied terms. She is quite clear that the use of labels such as 'Pakistani', 'Asian' and 'black' are ways of identifying oneself but they are not necessarily the kinds of things that psychologists seek for when they study personal identity. Lyon shows the misleading nature of some labels such as 'Asian', naïvely used by some white British people in ignorance of the cultural heterogeneity it encompasses, but also how they are tactically and politically used by some Asian people in some contexts. These 'labels-as-identities', however, are not necessarily superficial descriptions or lightly held. Far from it, they can be passionately held and disputed over, especially as to which is to have priority in public discourse, and are critical to community pride, ethnic mobilisation and anti-racist campaigning (Modood 1988; 1994). The discussions by Lewis (in Chapter 7) and Samad (in Chapter 13) of the politics of 'Asian', 'black', and 'Muslim' identities in Bradford and Birmingham show how these identities can be manipulated by local authorities for their own ends. Yet their chapters also show that while to date local authorities in Britain have had a tendency to reinforce exclusive identities in the way that worries Caglar, local authorities are far from in control of these public identities, which at least in Britain have been more shaped by grassroots campaigns and by political contestations within and amongst the ethnic minority groups themselves than by (pre-dominantly white) politicians and bureaucrats. The latter are themselves usually influenced by local discourses, partly shaped by the leading minority groups. Politicians and administrators have the power to throw their weight behind a favoured identity (such as 'black' in the 1980s), or to promote a particular kind of identity (say, identities based on national origins rather than religion), but the identities favoured by the authorities have so far not proved capable of maintaining anything more than a temporary hegemony.

The authorities, and this applies more widely than just in England, are less guided by an essentialist definition of who is the community than by strategies to avoid or minimise conflict, above all by the search for immigrant or minority interlocutors or representatives with whom they can create, implement and develop appropriate policies and institutions. The policy demands that particular minority groups make do vary from country to country, however, depending on the initial or current status of the group in question and on the local situation. The most pressing issue may be racial violence or harassment from the police – matters that have arisen in most countries and were at the forefront when the European Union (EU) declared 1997 as the Year of Anti-racism. Or the pressing issue may be electoral rights or rights of citizenship, as it is in most of the countries of western Europe. In Britain, where the majority of immigrants came from former colonies and were already subjects of the crown, for several decades they were granted effective citizenship from the very day of arrival, even where they did not take up naturalisation. In Britain, then, the policy focus for racial equality has been anti-discrimination and equal opportunities in fields such as employment, education and housing.

This is the context of Gideon Ben-Tovim's discussion in Chapter 11. Some of those who support anti-discrimination legislation and policies (who believe, for example, that jobs should be filled on merit and not on colour), object to 'positive action', the giving of targeted assistance to discriminated groups in order to redress the disadvantage that has held them back. They object to resources being targeted towards minority groups or special training being set aside for members of certain groups (this practice is not very extensive in Britain), arguing that everyone should have the same chances and that policy should be colour-blind. The debate in Britain is quite mild compared to the USA, mainly because policy is very limited in this field (for example, it is unlawful to fill a job on the basis of positive discrimination), but some of the terms of the debate, such as 'political correctness' are borrowed from the USA. Ben-Tovim offers a robust and eloquent defence of positive action as integral to racial equality and multiculturalism. He in fact wants to use the British experience to develop a common language of anti-racism for Europe. He argues that the principles of positive action are the same as those un-controversially used in the EU to integrate socially excluded groups. Indeed, he is in favour of social policy that targets needs rather than specific groups of people, and sees the obvious political advantages of integrating anti-racism within much broader programmes of economic development and welfare. He insists, however, that egalitarians and democrats must not overlook the specific dimension of racism, and how it disadvantages and excludes. He is mindful of the dangers of the exclusivist politics of ethnic identity, and does not recognise multiculturalism as an end in itself but as a component of the struggle for social justice, though he is clear that distinct oppressions cannot be reduced to a one-dimensional analysis of injustice.

Ben-Tovim's concern to build a broad European alliance for social justice that incorporates the complexities of anti-racism finds an echo in Chris Brewin's argument in Chapter 12. His concern is that social justice in one country is no longer possible. Some of the key functions of a state, such as the safeguarding of communities and the maintenance of the standard of living of the population, would be better discharged not by creating a new political order of individual states but only by a properly constructed continental polity comparable to the USA. In a wide-ranging argument he considers some North American political philosophy per-spectives on multiculturalism before examining the provision for EU citizenship in the Maastricht treaty. Brewin welcomes the innovation embodied in Maastricht that the European treaties apply to all citizens of member states, not just to workers, but believes that its voting provisions are less democratic than they might be. In particular he regrets that individuals from non-member states resident in a member state have no right to vote, observing that this contradicts the human rights philosophy which promotes the right to participation in the society in which one lives and works (he estimates that this provision discriminates against three-quarters of the 10–13 million Muslims legally resident in the EU). Moreover, he would make the whole of the EU a single constituency, and thus allow parties to compete in elections on an EU-wide basis. This would empower immigrant associations, but more fundamentally it would break the link with territory and weaken the link with nationality, and thus would be a major step forward in the making of a political Europe. From the point of view of multiculturalism, its advantage is to give some franchise, and therefore an impetus to political organisation, to minorities excluded from the politics of the member states in which they are resident.

It is worth noting, however, that those members of ethnic minorities that already have citizenship in a member state, especially in Britain, remain cool about the EU. The worry amongst anti-racists in Britain is of a harmonisation 'downwards'. In connection with British ethnic minorities, it has been contended that a:

> European path of minority status and rights within a framework of Euro-citizenship might offer better security in the long run, but the short term effect would be to deprive them of the special status they have enjoyed in the 25 years of British multiculturalism. Little wonder, then, that British ethnic minorities are so hostile to European proposals'. (Favell 1996: 20)

Favell believes that British ethnic minorities would only be likely to look to European solutions if a major jolt were to take place. For example, were the United Kingdom to break up, the ethnic minorities might then feel that their status was at risk, especially from an intolerant re-emergent English nationalism, and seek European protection (Favell 1996: 20). On the other hand, Favell believes that goverments that cannot, for domestic reasons, solve their problems may find it convenient to use European institutions. If, for example, Germany finds it too difficult to reform its blood-based idea of nationality, it may look for ways in which European citizenship can take off some of the pressure (Favell 1996: 19).

In Chapter 13, Yunas Samad offers some reflections on the nature of multiculturalism based on work undertaken with John Rex on two English cities (Rex and Samad 1996). There are many points of connection between his reflections and other chapters in the book. He emphasises, for example, that different kinds of multiculturalisms are coming into being in different cities, and especially in different countries. For multiculturalism builds on pre-existing institutions and political cultures, and especially on whatever arrangements exist to handle the kind of pluralism that the particular country is already familiar with. Like many of the contributors he is aware of the divisive nature of identity politics, but like Ben-Tovim he cautions against a return to ethnicity-blind social intervention even if the fundamental issue is not cultural pluralism but equality. Moreover, the politics of group labels and their dynamics, he argues, are led from the groups themselves rather than from the local state.

Samad also raises two new issues that are worth mentioning. For example, some have argued that the hope for multiculturalism lies in the development of new syncretic and hybrid youth cultures centred on black musical forms like rap and hiphop, and their Asian equivalents (Gilroy 1987). Samad notes that while such developments are real enough, other youth developments, no less hybridic, include the assertion of an Islamic identity generating a radicalisation of young Muslims in Bradford. Hybridity or youth cannot be assumed to produce just one kind of cultural formation. The current popularity of the new Islamic identities is also indicated by the many Muslim student societies found in British universities and colleges. The ultimate unreconcilability of the twin claims of transatlantic youth culture, based on music, and Islamic assertiveness for young British Asians has been well caught in a recent novel (Kureishi 1995).

A second issue that Samad points to is the need to reconsider our understanding of the private and the public. The interpretation of this distinction is indeed critical to a theory of multiculturalism. This is hardly a simple matter. There is a body of theoretical opinion that argues that the public–private distinction is essential to multiculturalism. Rex, for example, argues that the fundamental distinction between a pluralist society without equality and the multicultural ideal is that the latter restricts cultural diversity to a private sphere so that all enjoy equality of opportunity and uniform treatment in the public domain (Rex 1985; 1986). He readily recognises that this is a far from watertight distinction; education, for example, is an area in which both the claims of the public (the teaching of a civic culture) and the private (the teaching of minority religious and linguistic heritages) have to coexist, and Rex is open to the idea of state funding of schools that besides teaching a core curriculum are designed to meet the religious and cultural needs of minorities. He sees such state support for minorities as analogous to the many welfare and economic responsibilities assumed by the modern social democratic state. For him, therefore, the public–private distinction is not about a policy of *laissez-faire* in relation to culture, a state neutrality about conceptions of the good, but an insistence that while there may legitimately be a sphere of differential rights, it does not extend to law, politics, economics and welfare policy. Yet Rex believes that as a matter of historical fact, European societies have managed to extract a 'rational', 'abstract' morality and legal system out of the various 'folk' cultures, and that all citizens can share this without betraying their folk culture, for all folk cultures have been subordinated to this civic culture, which is the basis of the modern state and capitalist economy. 'Thus multi-culturalism in the modern world involves on the one hand the acceptance of a single culture and a single set of individual rights governing the public domain and a variety of folk cultures in the private domestic and communal domains' (Rex 1985: 6). On this view the multicultural state might be supportive of some or all folk cultures, but it effectively limits their scope and makes itself immune to folk criticism.

An important implication of this way of seeing the public–private distinction is found in a discussion by Habermas. To the question as to what extent a recipient society can require immigrants to assimilate, he answers that immigrants cannot be required to conform to the dominant way of life, but a democratic constitutional state must

> preserve the identity of the political community, which nothing, including immigration, can be permitted to encroach upon, since that identity is founded on the constitutional principles anchored in the political culture and not on the basic ethical orientations of the cultural form of life predominant in that country. (Habermas 1994: 139)

But surely there is not a valid distinction here: politics and law depend to some degree on shared ethical assumptions and inevitably reflect the norms and values of the society that they are part of. In this sense, no state stands outside culture, ethnicity or nationality, and changes in these will need to be reflected in the arrangements of the state. Indeed, Habermas goes on to recognise that, following immigration, 'as other forms of life become established the horizon within which citizens henceforth interpret their common constitutional principles may also expand' (Habermas 1994: 139–40). But then, what is the point of his initial distinction? It cannot simply be to state that the status of law is different from customs and lifestyles, that immigrants must obey the law and (like everybody else) use constitutional means to change it and the political system, because that neither requires nor implies that the preservation of a recipient society's political identity is more essential than other collective identities, say, the recipient society's linguistic or religious identity.

David Miller shows a much better appreciation of the fact that a political system is likely to be inseparable from a wider national culture (Miller 1995). In arguing for the existence and political importance of a British national identity, he too believes that a public–private distinction is essential in order to avoid a narrow, exclusivist, authoritarian nationalism. A form of the latter involves elevating 'cultural Englishness' – such things as drinking tea and patronising fish-and-chip shops – into public principles and institutions. He rightly wants to locate a national identity elsewhere, but there is an ambiguity in where that elsewhere is. On the one hand, '[t]o have a national identity is to take part in a continuing process of collective self-definition which is expressed in essentially public ways – in political institutions, in the policies of a government, and so forth' (Miller 1995: 161–2); on the other hand, it involves 'an essentially historical understanding' which recognises, for instance, the importance of a residual Protestantism in British political culture (Miller 1995: 163). The two descriptions are not incompatible with each other but point respectively to a narrow and broad view of political culture.

To participate in political institutions presupposes a great deal of commonality; language or languages, for instance, including an under-standing of the rhetorical and symbolic force of words, gestures and silences, the evocation of names and so on. Just as tea drinking and cricket must not be allowed to define membership of the national community, so too, perhaps, we ought to be wary of over-politicising national identity, of as it were putting all the burden of our commonality on the commonalty. The open and complex character of a rich and varied nationality must not be essentialised into a few quaint customs; but nor can it be reduced to a political system. People have a sense of constituting a society or a nationality or, as it were, a nest of communities by living and working and knowing each other in numerous and complex ways, from using the same local shops to reading the same newspapers; admittedly, none of these has the same formal status of membership as conferred by the rights of citizenship, and the points of trust and shared interests usually exist within a political and legal framework. My point is that even if some conditions are necessary to participation in a shared public culture, such as the rights of citizenship, a public culture or a national identity cannot be equated with the formally legal or institutional. A sense of society, of effective as opposed to nominal membership in a shared public culture over and above private and communal affiliations, may be dependent on many different points of contact and on sharing different things with different people. It may be like the philosophically proverbial cord, the strength of which does not depend upon a single thread.

Public and private, national and ethnic, then, may mark different spheres of activity, and different ways in which we relate to people, but they are not strict divisions. There are bound to be dialectical tensions and, as Rex recognises, points of inter-dependency; communities may look to the state to support their culture, for example through schools and other educational institutions, and the state may, reciprocally, look to communities to in-culcate virtues such as truth telling, respect for property, service to others and so on, without which a civic morality would have nothing to build on. If the public and private mutually shape each other in these ways, then however 'abstract' and 'rational' the principles of a public order may be, they will reflect the 'folk cultures' out of which the particular public order has grown, which provide its personnel and sustain it in all kinds of ways. There can then be no question of the public sphere being morally neutral; rather, it will appeal to points of privately shared values and senses of belonging, as well as to the superstructure of conventions, laws and principles. Those whose ethnic or community identities are most reflected in the national, those who are most comfortable in these complementary identities, will feel least the force of a public–private distinction; they may feel it more when they have to share the public domain with persons from other communities, persons who also wish the national to reflect something of their own community. The elaboration of a strict distinction between the public and private spheres at this point may act to buttress the privileged position of the historically 'integrated' folk cultures at the expense of the historically subordinated or the newly migrated folk. In this context the public–private division, far from underpinning multi-culturalism, will work to prevent its emergence.

If we recognise that the public order is not morally neutral, is not culture- or ethnic-blind, we can understand why oppressed, marginalised or immigrant groups may want that public order – in which they may, for the first time, have rights of participation – to 'recognise' them, to be user-friendly to the new folks. The logic of demanding that public institutions acknowledge the gender bias of their ways of doing things, and allow for female insights and perspectives, becomes readily intelligible, as does the whole phenomenon of minorities seeking increased visibility, of minorities contesting the boundaries of the public, of minorities not simply asking to be left alone and to be civilly tolerated.

It is important to recognise, therefore, that what is often claimed today in the name of equality is more than would have been recognised as such in the 1960s. Iris Young expresses well the new political climate when she describes the emergence of an ideal of equality not just based on allowing excluded groups to assimilate and live by the norms of dominant groups, but instead based on the view that 'a positive self-definition of group difference is in fact more liberatory' (Young 1990: 157). She cites the examples of the black power movement, the gay pride assertion that sexual identity is a matter of culture and politics, and a feminism that emphasises the positivity and specifity of female experience and values. These movements have not had the same impact in Europe as in parts of North America, but are certainly present here. In particular, there is an ethnic assertiveness in Britain that has parallels with North America, though it has been less evident amongst recent migrants and their descendants in other European Union countries, where, as contributors to this volume show, cultural assimilation has until recently been regarded as integral to citizenship and political equality (see also Baldwin-Edwards and Schain 1994).

The shift is from an understanding of equality in terms of individualism and cultural assimilation to a politics of recognition, to equality as encompassing public ethnicity: equality as not having to hide or apologise for one's origins, family or community but requiring others to show respect for them and adapt public attitudes and arrangements so that the heritage they represent is encouraged rather than contemptuously expected to wither away. There seems, then, to be two distinct conceptions of equal citizenship, each based on a different view of what is 'public' and 'private'. These two conceptions of equality may be stated as follows:

1. the right to assimilate to the majority/dominant culture in the public sphere; and toleration of 'difference' in the private sphere;
2. the right to have one's 'difference' (minority ethnicity, etcetera) recognised and supported in the public and the private spheres.

These are not, however, alternative conceptions in the sense that to hold one, the other has to be rejected. Multiculturalism requires, however, support for both conceptions. For the assumption behind the first conception is that participation in the public or national culture is necessary for the effective exercise of citizenship, the only obstacles to which are the exclusionary processes preventing gradual assimilation. The second conception, too, assumes that groups excluded from the national culture have their citizenship diminished as a result, offers to remedy this by accepting the right to assimilate, yet adds the right to widen and adapt the national culture and the public and media symbols of national membership to include the relevant minority ethnicities.

It may be thought that the second conception of equality involves something of a contradiction: it accepts that participation in national or shared culture(s) is necessary for effective equality, but encourages individuals to cultivate minority identities and practices. There is indeed a genuine tension here, and perhaps it can only be resolved in practice, through finding and cultivating points of common ground between dominant and subordinate cultures, as well as new syntheses and hybridities. The important thing is that the burden of change (or the costs of not changing) are not all dependent on one party to this encounter.

The multicultural state

The distinction between public and private, and the question of how it relates to issues of culture and ethnicity are, then, at the crux of the current debates about multiculturalism as a political project. For a better perspective about what is at issue and the sources of disagreement – not least amongst advocates of multiculturalism – it may, however, be better to step back a little. I suggest that how we conceptualise the public–private distinction will depend on the extent to which one believes that individuals, (ethnic) groups and the (nation-) state form coherent unities, are the bearers of ethical claims, and can be integrated with each other. I offer below five ideal types, marking five possible ways in which one could respond to the contemporary challenge of diversity consequent upon immigration in Europe.

1. *The decentred self* Some theorists describe the present condition as 'postmodern'. Amongst the many things meant by this term is that as a consequence of factors such as migration and the globalisation of economics, consumption and communications, societies can no longer be constituted by stable collective purposes and identities organised territorially by the nation-state. In its most radical version, it is not only politically constituted multiculturalism that becomes impossible, but the idea of a unified self becomes an unrealistic dream:

> If we feel we have a unified identity ... it is only because we construct a comforting story or 'narrative of the self' about ourselves. ... The fully unified, completed, secure and coherent identity is a fantasy. Instead, as the systems of meaning and cultural representation multiply, we are confronted by a bewildering, fleeting multiplicity of possible identities, any one of which we could identify with – at least temporarily. (Hall 1992: 277)[1]

The radical multiple self has a penchant for identities, but prefers surfing on the waves of deconstruction to seeking reconstruction in multiplicity. It is post-self rather than a multi-self. Even in less radical versions, the self is no more connected to one location/society/state than another, any more than the typical consumer is connected to one producer or the goods of one country. Reconciled to multiplicity as an end in itself, postmodernism's vision of multiculturalism is confined to personal lifestyles and cosmopolitan consumerism and does not extend to the state, which it confidently expects to wither away.

2. *The liberal state* The liberal expects individuals but not large-scale communities to survive the social changes that are in motion. Individuals may temporarily become disoriented, bewildered by the multiplicity of identities, temporarily de-centred, but they will soon re-centre themselves. Lifestyles in their neighbourhoods may change as persons of exotic appearance, with large families and pungent-smelling foods move in, and soon they or their children get office jobs and one day one of them becomes the local mayor. The old residents and the new have to adjust – perhaps gradually, certainly repeatedly – their sense of self, community and country as these changes occur, but no major political project other than the elimination of discrimination is required. The state exists to protect the rights of individuals, but the question of recognising new ethnic groups does not arise, for the state does not recognise any groups. Individuals relate to the state as individual citizens, not as members of

the group. The state is group-blind, it cannot 'see' colour, gender, ethnicity, religion or even nationality. In the parlance of North American political theorists (it is certainly easier to see the USA than any European state as approximating to this liberal ideal), the just state is neutral between rival conceptions of the good. It does not promote one or more national cultures, religions, ways of life and so on. These matters remain private to individuals in their voluntary associations with each other. Nor does it promote any syncretic vision of common living, of fellow feeling between the inhabitants of that territory, other than the legal entitlements and duties that define civic membership.

3. The republic   Like the liberal state, the ideal republic does not recognise groups amongst the citizenry. It relates to each citizen as an individual. But, unlike the liberal state it is amenable to one collective project; more precisely, it is itself a collective project, a project, that is to say, that is not reducible to the protection of the rights of individuals or the maximisation of the choices open to individuals. The republic seeks to enhance the lives of its members by making them a part of a way of living that individuals could not create for themselves; it seeks to make the individuals members of a civic community. This community may be based upon subscription to 'universal' principles such as liberty, equality, and fraternity; or to the promotion of a national culture; or, as in the case of France, to both. In a republic the formation of public ethnicity, by immigration or in other ways, would be discouraged, and there would be strong expectation, even pressure, for individuals to assimilate to the national identity. As we have seen, this is exactly what Melotti characterises as the dominant French policy response to date.

4. The federation of communities   In contrast to the first three responses to multicultural diversity, this option is built upon the assumption that the individual is not the unit, or at least not the only unit to which the state must relate. Rather, individuals belong to and are shaped by communities, which are the primary focus of their loyalty and which are the regulators of social life. Far from being confined to the private sphere, communities are the primary agents of the public sphere. Public life in fact consists of organised communities relating to each other, and the state is therefore a federation of communities and exists to protect the rights of communities.

As with all the ideal types listed here, one can think of a more radical or extreme version of the model, and a more moderate version which balances the rights of communities with the rights of individuals, including the right of exit from communities. The *millat* system of the Ottoman empire, in which some powers of the state were delegated to Christian and Jewish communities, who were granted the power to administer personal law within their communities in accordance with their own legal system, is an example of this model of the multicultural state, and has occasionally been invoked in Britain as an example to emulate. The *millat* system offered a significant autonomy to communities but of course did not offer equality between communities or any conception of democratic citizenship. As such it is unlikely to be attractive to many in contemporary Europe unless a democratic variant could be devised. The system of pillorisation in the Netherlands or Belgium might also be considered to be an example of this type of institutionalised communal diversity.

5. The plural state   On this model – again an ideal type of which there can be strong and weak forms – there is a recognition that social life consists of individuals and groups, and both need to be provided for in the formal and informal distribution of powers: not just in law, but in representation in the offices of the state, public committees, consultative exercises and access to public fora. There may be some rights for all individuals as in the liberal state, but mediating institutions such as trades unions, churches, neighbourhoods, immigrant associations and so on may also be encouraged to be active public players and forums for political discussion, and may even have a formal representative or administrative role to play in the state. The plural state allows for, indeed probably requires, however, an ethical conception of citizenship, and not just an instrumental one as in the liberal and federation-of-communities conceptions. The understanding that individuals are partly constituted by the lives of families and communities fits well with the recognition that the moral individul is partly shaped by the social order constituted by citizenship and the publics that amplify and qualify, that sustain, critique and reform citizenship.

If the state should come to have this kind of importance in people's lives, it is most likely that they will, as in a republic, emotionally and psychologically invest in the state and its projects. The most usual form of this emotional relationship is a sense of national identity. In an undiluted form national identity, like most group identifications, can be dangerous, and certainly incompatible with multiculturalism. On the other hand, assuming a plurality of identities and not a narrow nationalism, the plural state, unlike the liberal state, is able to offer an emotional identity with the whole to counterbalance the emotional loyalties to ethnic and religious communities, which should prevent the fragmentation of society into narrow, selfish communalisms. Yet the presence of these strong community identities will be an effective check against monocultural statism.

For the plural state the challenge of the new multiculturalism is about the integration of transplanted cultures, heritages and peoples into long-established, ongoing, historic, national cultures, heritages and peoples. It is about cultural synthesis in both private and public spaces, including in education and welfare provision. Above all, it is about extending, reforming and syncretising in new ways existing forms of public culture and citizenship. It is not about decentring society or deconstructing the nation-state, but about integrating difference by remaking the nation-state. In contrast to a common political rhetoric, 'integration' here is not synonymous with 'assimilation'. Assimilation is something immigrants or minorities must do or have done to them, whereas integration is interactive, a two-way process; both parties are an active ingredient and so something new is created. For the plural state, then, multiculturalism means re-forming national identity and citizenship.

As this book shows, there is indeed an emerging recognition that multiculturalism means a new way of being French, a new way of being German, a new way of being British – and perhaps also a new way of being European. National cultures and specific political histories and contexts will no doubt mean that multiculturalism in Europe will vary from country to country, region to region, and will not be confined to any one of the five possible responses sketched here, which are offered as ideal types. All these models (except perhaps the radically decentred self) are compatible with the development of transnational institutions and support structures through the EU – perhaps through a reconstituted European electorate as suggested by Brewin. What is clear is that multiculturalism will challenge and is already challenging our existing notions of culture, identity, nationality and citizenship across Europe, as peoples and states enter into political dialogues which may mark the crafting of new multicultural citizenships.

Note

1. Hall does not always argue as if the contemporary self was radically de-centered (Hall and Held 1989).

References

Akhtar, S. (1989) *Be Careful with Muhammad! The Salman Rushdie Affair*, Bellew Publishing, London.

Baldwin-Edwards, M. and M. A. Schain (eds) (1994) *The Politics of Immigration in Western Europe*. Special issue of *Western European Politics*, 17(2).

Dwyer, C. and A. Meyer (1995) 'The Institutionalisation of Islam in the Netherlands and in the UK: the Case of Islamic Schools', *New Community*, 21(1).

Favell, A. (1996) 'Multicultural Race Relations in Britain – an exceptional case? Problems of interpretation and explanation', paper given at European University Institute workshop on Immigration, Citizenship and Ethnic Conflict, Florence.

Gilroy, P. (1987) *There Ain't No Black in the Union Jack*, Hutchinson, London.

Habermas, J. (1994) 'Struggles for Recognition in the Democratic Constitutional State', in A. Gutmann (ed.) *Multiculturalism: Examining the Politics of Recognition*, Princeton University Press, Princeton.

Hall, S. (1992) 'The Question of Cultural Identity', in S. Hall and T. McGrew (eds) *Modernity and Its Futures*, Polity Press, Cambridge.

Hall, S. and D. Held (1989) 'Citizens and Citizenship' in S. Hall and M. Jacques (eds) *New Times: The Changing Face of Politics in the 1990s*, Lawrence and Wishart, London.

Hastings, A. (1992) 'Church and State in a Pluralist Society', *Theology*, xcv(765): 165–76.

Kabbani, R. (1989) *Letter to Christendom*, Virago, London.

Kirton, D. (1995) *'Race', Identity and the Politics of Adoption*, Working Paper 2, Centre for Adoption and Identity Studies, University of East London.

Kureishi, H. (1995) *The Black Album*, Faber and Faber, London.

Kymlicka, W. (1995) *Multicultural Citizenship*, Oxford University Press, Oxford.

Macedo, S. (1993) 'Toleration and Fundamentalism', in R. E. Goodin and P. Pettit (eds) *A Companion to Contemporary Political Philosophy*, Blackwell, Oxford.

Miller, D. (1995) 'Reflections on British National Identity', *New Community*, 21(2): 153–66.

Modood, T. (1988) '"Black", Racial Equality and Asian Identity', *New Community*, 14(3): 397–404.

— (1993) '"Kymlicka on British Muslims" and "Kymlicka on British Muslims: a rejoinder"', *Analyse & Kritik*, 15, 87–91 and 97–9.

— (1994) 'Political Blackness and British Asians', *Sociology*, 28(4): 859–76.

— (1996) '"Race" in Britain and the Politics of Difference', in D. Archard (ed.) *Philosophy and Pluralism*, Cambridge University Press, Cambridge.

— (ed.) (1997) *Church, State and Religious Minorities*, Policy Studies Institute, London.

Modood, T., R. Berthoud, J. Lakey, J. Nazroo, P. Smith, S. Virdee and S. Reishon (1997) *Ethnic Minorities in Britain: Diversity and Disadvantage*, Policy Studies Institute, London.

Muslim Parliament of Great Britain (1992) *Race Relations and Muslims in Great Britain: A Discussion Paper*, Muslim Parliament, London.

Rath, J., K. Groenendijk and R. Penninx (1991) 'The Recognition and Institutionalization of Islam in Belgium, Great Britain and the Netherlands', *New Community*, 18(1): 101–14.

Rex, J. (1985) *The Concept of a Multi-cultural Society*, Occasional Papers in Ethnic Relations No. 3, Centre for Research in Ethnic Relations, University of Warwick.

— (1986) *Race and Ethnicity*, Open University Press, Milton Keynes.

— (1996) *Ethnic Minorities in the Modern Nation State*, Macmillan, London.

Rex, J. and Y. Samad (1996) 'Multiculturalism and Political Integration in Birmingham and Bradford', *Innovation*, 9(1).

Slomp, J., G. Speelman and W. de Wit (1988) *Muslims in the Netherlands*, Muslims in Europe and Research Papers No. 37, Selly Oak Colleges, Birmingham.

Taylor, C. (1994) 'The Politics of Recognition', in A. Gutmann (ed.) *Multiculturalism: Examining the Politics of Recognition*, Princeton University Press, Princeton.

UKACIA (UK Action Committee on Islamic Affairs) (1993) *Muslims and the Law in Multi-faith Britain: Need for Reform*, UKACIA, London.

Weldon, F. (1989) *Sacred Cows*, Chatto, London.

Young, I. M. (1990) *Justice and the Politics of Difference*, Princeton University Press, Princeton.

PART ONE

Inclusion and Exclusion in the Making of the New Europe

CHAPTER 2

Globalisation and the Discourse of Otherness in the 'New' Eastern and Central Europe

László Kürti

'New nationalisms', 'ethnic', 'strife', 'anti-Semitic and anti-Gypsy feeling', 'ethnic cleansing' and 'tribalism' – these words have been with us since totalitarianism and communism were ousted in the countries of the former Soviet bloc. Contrary notions, such as 'returning to Europe', 'European-ness' and 'European unity', have also been in vogue among intellectuals of the East and West alike. Of the many utterances about 'return to Europe' which were so pervasive in 1989 and 1990 in the East, I cite the Polish historian Jerzy Jedlicki, whose views aptly characterise the times and at the same time have a healthy dosage of self-criticism:

> Return to Europe! Every day the Polish press brings new articles about the conditions of our return to Europe. We are returning to Europe because we just had our first free elections. We are returning to Europe because we expect Poland to become a member of the Council of Europe.
>   And yet we cannot return to Europe as long as our towns are dirty, our telephones dysfunctional, our political parties reactionary and parochial, and our mentalities sovietised. Europe is a measure, a purpose, a dream. (Jedlicki 1990: 6)

It was only natural that leaders and intellectuals of the West and East equally celebrated the collapse of communism (Cortona 1991; Fehér 1990) and at the same time noted that although the Iron Curtain was dismantled, a new, even more troublesome dividing wall separated the newly liberated east Europeans from the rest of the world. This was the moment at which, as E. P. Thompson noted sarcastically, 'The lumpenintelligentsia of Washington think-tanks [were] rabbiting on about "the end of history"' (1991: 7). Yet during 1989 and 1990, more and more euphoric utterances were to be heard about the former East bloc countries being part of the European Union (EU), and their willingness to return to Europe. France's President François Mitterrand said that Europe 'is returning in its history and geography like one who is returning home' (quoted in Derrida 1992: 8). Jacques Attali, adviser to President Mitterrand and president of the European Bank of Reconstruction and Development in London, wrote in similar euphoric tones: 'Dictatorships are collapsing throughout the world ... traditional notions of national sovereignty are increasingly irrelevant' (1991: 35). With the collapse of the East bloc, a new notion of Central Europe has emerged in the minds of many. As espoused by the former mayor of Vienna, 'Central Europe' literally means Europe – not the German idea of 'Mitteleuropa' – which, when the project is completed, would differ from the Eastern antecedent in that it will not have nationalist and nation-state ideologies (Busek 1992: 120–21).

Following 1989, which many felt was a true *annus mirabilis*, experts testified about the necessity of the historical collapse of totalitarianism and the building of a civil society and celebrated the moment for the implementation of a free market (Dahrendorf 1990). As the East disintegrated and the West was integrated, E. P. Thompson wrote whimsically:

> In the winter of 1989–90 much of the Western media was obsessed with the ludicrous notion that the whole of Eastern and Central Europe was intent upon hurling itself helter-skelter into a 'market economy', the institution of capitalism in a Thatcherite or Milton Friedmanite form. Certainly the absurdities and absolute failures of the Communist command economies made many heads turn in that direction, and these were often the heads that spoke English and could talk with Roger Scruton, Timothy Garton Ash and the endless flow of American, British and German funders, advisers, political and academic voyeurs, business agents, and others flooding through Prague, East Berlin, Warsaw and Budapest. (1991: 15)

Since 1990 when E. P. Thompson viewed the Western rush for capitalist investments, some states – the 'wayward children of Europe' to borrow a phrase of the writer-president Vaclav Havel – did in fact become members of the Council of Europe and have managed to shed their former Soviet heritage. During 1990, parties of both conservative and liberal leanings cheered the dismantling of the communist state and the creation of various democratic national parliaments.[1]

But that was not enough. Together with ethnic cleansing and tribal nationalisms, the new slogans since 1991 have been asking for even more of a 'return' to Europe. Membership in NATO and the EU, convertible currencies and credit cards, free travel and work all over Europe, and the creation of new national bourgeoisies are the new slogans in the East.[2] What is behind these movements? What do the terms 'European', 'Eastern' and 'Central European' really refer to? And what have been the reasons for constructing such seemingly opposite images of a region whose peoples so readily chiselled away at the Berlin Wall and in their millions demanded a democratic renewal and new constitutions? To answer these questions, I want to interrogate intertwined aspects of the same issue, the making of Central Europe, which will provide a key to an understanding of the present divide and misconceptions concerning various parts of Europe. I wish to argue that the making of a Central Europe and the discrediting of an Eastern Europe has been a curious blend of historical revision, fiction and intellectual contestations between national identities. It also provides a sense of wish-fulfilment for both elites of the former Soviet bloc and their western equivalents who want to abandon their 'backward' former selves to the annals of history by placing themselves in a terrain which, for many, is hallmarked by development, progress and modernisation.[3]

The backwardness project

Recently, scholars have begun referring to the mythologising of the European periphery as the 'orientalist variation' project for the Balkans (Bakic-Hayden and Hayden 1992; Todorova 1994). What I am conveniently proposing here is that we look at the remaking of European boundaries as an ideological separation of the backward East from the rest. In particular, I wish to argue that under the pressure of globalisation currently under way, many scholars continue to speak about eastern Europe as an area that lags behind the developed and democratic West. This, however, while it fosters the image of a politically and economically marginal region, also assists in a new bipolarisation and hierarchisation of Europe. The newly emerging anthropology of Europe can also be accused of such an ethnocentric bias; whereas western and Mediterranean cultures are over-represented, eastern European cultures are seriously under-represented with an underlying connotation that the East must remain East.[4] This sort of scholarly reconstruction of a new Europe solidifies the primacy of western European capitalism and, to some, it stands for western European democracy of the liberalist kind. For many, Europe continues to be what it once was: a developed north and west in opposition to the underdeveloped south. Sandwiched between the two are the undemocratic, unruly, and backward states of eastern Europe.

This project is akin to the orientalising project known from colonialism; whose totalising and hegemonic perspective was so important for exploitation of the colonies by the colonisers, and which was supported by a nationalist elite lending credence to this expansionism. In the orientalising myth, both foreign and native scholars participated extensively. It is my aim in this chapter to reveal how a similar perspective has been forged with reference to the new Eastern Europe. And, furthermore, to reveal how this image of backwardness engenders the current hierarchisation of the cultures of the East while it is intricately intertwined with another project, the remaking of Central Europe.

The scholarly discourse on the backwardness of the East is not novel.

Sixteenth- and seventeenth-century travellers from Hungary and Transylvania already noted the differences between their own cultures and those
of England, the Netherlands, Bavaria and France. Western travel literature
to the East, increasingly popular since the late eighteenth century, is filled
with similar descriptions. Not only the cultural uniqueness but also the
economic and housing conditions, neglected roads, unsafe mountain
passages, lack of sanitation, dirty clothing, and strange food habits are
standard elements of western travelogues.[5] Regions of the Habsburg,
Ottoman and Tsarist empires started to emerge as literary fiction, so much
so that by end of the nineteenth century, when these empires began to
fall, state education already spoke of national geographies, identifying and
endowing these regions with national symbols, pride and sentimental
histories. Local ethnographers have assisted in adding their own colour to
this self-conscious uniqueness by presenting obscure hay-threshing
methods, pastoral economies, spicy foods, and durable embroidered
clothing to this pot-pourri.

The incorporation of cultures in the Habsburg sphere of hegemony,
and their eventual separation from it, projected unbalanced images
discriminating between populations. Count Metternich was supposed to
have uttered the words that Asia begins at the *Landstrasse* of Vienna, and
such ethnocentric ideas are easily discernible in the everyday politics of
Habsburg's rule over its subjects. Similarly, others felt that the performance
in a town of the operetta *Die Fledermaus* was a good indication of
Europeanness, signalling the acceptance of Viennese cultural values by
the national elite. The influence of the Habsburgs, of the Viennese coffee
houses and the fashions of the turn-of-the-century elite on popular
cultures, was a yardstick by which spectators were able to view others, as
well as to distance themselves from those with whom they did not feel a
sense of shared identity. As a result, with more and more intellectuals
enjoying the benefits of state education and the ambience of
'Europeanness', certain parts of the East began to emerge not only as
distinct and separate from the economic and political centres but, equally
emphatically, as remote and backward as well.

Thus economic and cultural differences, aspects of which were none
the less punctuated and visible to both locals and foreigners alike, were
being translated more and more into an ideology of 'backwardness' and
provincialism. This conveniently masked the values of the central elites,
serving both to make them secure in their sense of superiority and to
convey to the 'lesser' elites of the nationalities how much they still had
to learn. At the same time, the backwardness project also educated the
populations about their rightful place in the hierarchy of nations: to respect
the emperor, the tsar, the bishop, or the landlord.

Recent scholarly discourse on backwardness in eastern Europe may be
dated from the elevation of the writings of Jenö Szücs to international

fame. In the influential article 'The Historical Regions of Europe' (1988), Szücs insists that between the democratic, Catholic/Protestant and economically advanced West and the backward, Orthodox and feudal East lies a central region of Europe (hence the re-emerging name 'Central Europe') which was always behind, and has (in vain) attempted to catch up with the West. At the same time, this central region exhibits several features that identify it with its easternmost neighbours. The intelligentsias of the region's various countries (which form a narrow corridor from the Baltics to Hungary) have continually tried to implement local change, to modernise and liberalise, but in their eagerness these intelligentsias were perennially caught by outside forces midway through their half-hearted attempts, and were thrown even further back into stagnation. One of the most important features of this backwardness was the absence of a strong middle class like that which existed in Germany or Austria. The missing bourgeoisie is a continual problem for the Eastern European elites trying to improve the image of their backward region.

In Szücs's writings, major characteristics of this backwardness also included an economy marginalised in the global market, an authoritarian state with a huge bureaucratic machinery, and increasing social atomism of the population at large. Religiosity and ethnicism were two more factors that contributed to the backward region theory; on the one hand, Catholicism and Protestantism in opposition to Orthodoxy, and the use of a Latin and not a Cyrillic alphabet, have been important departures; on the other hand, an ever-important ethnonational politics – infiltrating state policies into the everyday lives of citizens and nationalist inter-state relations, while helping the establishment of nineteenth-century nation-states – has been the hallmark of the specific Eastern European situation. Although this description hardly does justice to the intricacies of Szücs's writings, some of which deserve recognition beyond national boundaries (1992; 1993), it will suffice for my argument here to prove that the idea of a refashioning of Eastern and Central Europe has been a continual intellectual project before and after the collapse of communism.[6]

Szücs's scholarly erudition is supported by a number of historical and political studies. One of the most influential works has been Andrew Janos's historical study, *The Politics of Backwardness in Hungary, 1825–1945* (1982), which was followed by several others, in particular a collection edited by Daniel Chirot, *The Origins of Backwardness in Eastern Europe* (1989).

Janos, analysing Hungarian sentiments during the middle of the nineteenth century, makes some vitriolic statements on how the Hungarian elite realised, for instance, that the highest point of the Great Plains of Hungary was the 'horn of an ox', that 'dirty jackboots and stinking pipes' characterised country life, that the Spanish Madeira wine was better than the Tokay wines of Hungary, that the gondoliers of Venice 'sang better than the boatmen of the Danube'; and that, in all of this, Hungary was

in reality an 'oriental country' when compared to the West (Janos 1982:
48). True as it may have been, some Hungarian intellectuals indeed characterised their own country thus, seeing the peasantry as the *misera plebs
contribuens*. Yet this elite image of the peasantry and of rural Hungary in
general was far from a reflection of the truth. Such universalising tendencies notwithstanding, there were also among the intellectuals romantic
images, disenchanted outcries, as well as progressive and liberal voices.[7]

Like Szücs and Janos, the political scientist Daniel Chirot makes a
biased argument for the backwardness of Eastern Europe. For him Eastern
Europe has four subdivisions: Bohemia is the most developed, and in-
dustrially akin to Austria; western Poland and Hungary are less developed
than Bohemia but more advanced than the East; truly backward are the
Baltic states along with Russia, Ukraine, Wallachia and Moldavia; and,
finally, the region known as the Balkans is the most remote and un-
developed (Chirot 1989: 7). Such a typology serves even more to
homogenise these cultures and regions by glossing them into unitary
entities, a typology supported solely by historical 'facts' of backwardness.
What, for example, would be the case for a comparison between, say, the
smaller regions of Bukovina, Transylvania and Slovenia? Would they all fit
neatly into one of the regions discussed by Chirot? Or, allowing differences
and specificities to surface, would not a new typology have to be created
to cater to the needs of historians and political scientists?

Curiously, modernisation and development theory, as well as world
systems theory, also came in handy for the development of capitalism and
capitalist penetration into the eastern part of the Holy Roman Empire;
movements of commodities, consumerism and industrialisation in turn all
supported the uneven development and peripheralisation of eastern
Europe (Berend and Ránki 1985).[8] Historical studies of industrialisation
provided scholarly models with which to conceptualise the problems of
cultural and historical differences existing in various regions of the world
in general and in the East in particular. Such attempts at understanding –
I am thinking about the debates over the transition from feudalism to
capitalism or, to give a more recent example, the problem of state socialism
– all created an image of eastern Europe as even more backward and
exploited than previously had been argued (Chase-Dunn 1982). What is
clear is that the backwardness literature has been an ideologically constructed and elite-manipulated model based on a strong bias against the
East, and, more than that, on a strong intellectual conviction that in the
West everything is modernised, developed, and ethnically ordered, if not
outright superior.[9] Moreover, this literature was also based on the idea
that in the East, mostly because of ethnic heterogeneity as well as the
linguistic and religious internal diversity of polyethnic states, problems are
bound to arise from time to time.

A curious twist in this 'backwardness project' is that scholars continue to see the trajectory of a peripheral and a belated development in the East. The period between 1948 and 1989, known as 'state socialism', is no exception either. The whole socialist project is now being discredited and viewed in a negative light. The scholarly output of the early 1990s, or the 'transitological' enterprise, has concerned itself with clearing the path for a restructuring of the former East bloc countries' politics and economies (Bunce 1995). In fact, in the mind of many, Eastern Europe's backwardness has a lot to do with what happened after 1948. Endre Bojtár, a historian writing about the making of Central Europe, refers to the Hungarian István Bibó, who has called the Soviet occupation of Eastern Europe a 'dead-end street' which resulted in 'a distorted Hungarian structure' (Bojtár 1988: 254).[10]

This distorted Hungarian structure is easily discerned in the writings of intellectuals who base their assumptions on the reality of backwardness and its sociocultural repercussions. In a nutshell, backwardness in their eyes means that as a result of economic marginalisation, poverty increases, forcing people to become more intolerant, racist and ethnocentric. This is what contemporary intellectuals hold to be true in the case of 'Eastern European' ethnic intolerance, racist prejudice and xenophobia. How this manifests itself may be seen in the following statement of a Hungarian social psychologist who argues: 'Anti-Gypsy sentiment and prejudice must be seen as an inescapable defensive social-psychological response on behalf of non-Gypsy Hungarians who are becoming impoverished or have already joined the ranks of the poor' (Csepeli 1992: 160). While there is no denying that impoverishment *may* contribute to xenophobia and national-istic feelings, it must be stressed that in the backwardness project, definitive classism and ethnocentrism may play an integral part. It is only the poor and the exploited who are singled out for harbouring such feelings, a classic case of blaming-the-victim ideology transposed to ethnic strife and xenophobia in the East. Furthermore, the causes and effects of such behaviour are understood in terms of a simplistic, unidirectional model which has not been able to add anything new to what has been known in scholarship for many decades.

It is revealing, then, that the remaking of the new Central Europe involves political, economic and cultural factors. Interesting is the fact that countries that pride themselves on being Central European, namely Hungary, Poland, and the Slovak and Czech republics, in 1992 formed a Central European Free Trade Association (CFTA), obviously modelled on the North American Free Trade Agreement (NAFTA). The exclusivist nature of this project clearly aimed to divide eastern Europe as a region into more and less developed spheres; and only at the end of 1995 did the members of the association consider expanding its membership to include the Baltic states as well as Romania and Slovenia.[11] In the minds of the CFTA leaders, economic competition and performance are two components of being Central as opposed to Eastern European.[12] As was obvious from the beginning, such a 'separatist' tendency created strong resentment on the part of the former Soviet bloc states, especially those that were left out. Russia and Romania, in particular, have raised serious misgivings about their being excluded from the Central European project, and have even proposed some alternative organisations – both military and economic – which would naturally include them as well.[13] The states perceiving themselves to be Central European formed an exclusive five-member club (later expanded to six members), and since 1994, the group known as 'the Tens' has been assiduously engaged in creating an economic–political unity that would enable them to enter the European Union.[14]

What I am referring to as the 'backwardness literature' has been even more influential in certain political circles than the historical insights of Szücs. Regardless of current borders and allegiances, what characterises the development of the new Central European states and their leading elites is an obsessive wish to become full members of NATO and the EU. Western aid also relies on the 'backwardness' theory: for one, Western financial institutions often measure 'performance', 'output', and 'expenditures' of countries under their sphere of influence; moreover lending institutions – the EU, the IMF, the World Bank – seek through their loans to 'pressure' and, eventually, to eliminate the 'indebtedness' of countries they are supporting.[15]

Since 1989, more and more countries of the former Soviet bloc have been turning to banks and investment firms for their economic restructuring plans, for the privatisation of industry and agriculture, and for the implementation of government policies at local levels. One of the most important funding possibilities is provided by the European Commission's Phare Programme, mainly through its European Investment Bank. 'European integration', that is, joining the EU, is thus a process that involves economic shock treatments in the form of industrial restructuring according to the standards set up by the European Commission. In the race to restructure, Eastern and Central European states compete for funding by Western governments and private institutions on the basis of their performance in fulfilling their plans.[16]

Yet, curious as it may sound, more investment and loans may further the indebtedness and financial burdens of the countries involved. Thus, the image of the East as 'backward' will continually be reconstituted and the East will be seen as a place in need of more and more financial assistance since the failure to secure such aid will inevitably precipitate escalating poverty and social malaise.[17]

In fact, historians, political scientists and government officials have listed several doomsday scenarios of what could happen to the new democracies if the Europeanisation processes do not take place.[18] Some scholars have felt that in the worst scenario Hungary, and in fact the entire newly created Central Europe, could be 'Balkanised' – another ethnocentric reference to the region – or 'Latin Americanised' (Ágh 1993: 249; Przeworski 1991). The political scientist Attila Ágh envisions that Hungary's future lies somewhere between the Latin American road and the Spanish road, the former referring to increasing poverty and free elections only in theory, and the latter involving genuine progress and substantial stability in democracy (1993). Ágh even believes that the only way for Central Europe to become 'European' is through Western economic assistance similar to that received earlier by southern Europe (specifically, Greece, Italy and Spain) (1993: 240).

In similar vein, economists were fast to reflect that the West must pay attention to the East's economic and political 'failures', for such events may have deleterious consequences not only for the East but equally for the West as well. The American economist Paul Marer argues this point very specifically: 'The interest of the West lies in seeing that Hungary moves, with all deliberate speed, toward becoming a democratic and market-oriented country in which human rights are respected and international obligations observed' (1991: 238).

The making of a new Central Europe

As we have seen above, the backwardness project has placed a wedge between Europe's two halves since the middle of the nineteenth century. However, since boundaries are never stable and impenetrable, the borders of the two halves were never clearly identified. Thus, the exact line between 'East' and 'West' was always contested and politically sensitivised. Defining this fine line has always been a Janus-faced experience, and statesmen and writers have argued that between East and West there is a 'central' region which must be separated from both the developed capitalist West and the Orthodox, semi-feudalist East. Erazim Kohák, a Czech writer, summarises this point as follows:

> The cultural boundary between Europe's East and Europe's West has always been quite clear. It is demarcated by orthography. Wherever the Latin alphabet is used, the cultural identity is distinctively Western, shaped by Latin Christianity, scholasticism, the Renaissance, the struggles of the Reformation and the Counter-reformation, the Enlightenment, industrialisation, and social democracy. (Kohák 1990: 17)

Just like the writings of Szücs, Kohák's historical assessment privileges certain states at the expense of others. This kind of Central Europe is envisioned as a 'bridge' between East and West. The bridge (though some writers used the metaphor of a 'gate') unites three separate historical regions. This bridge region – often cloaked with the mantle of the Germanic notion of Mitteleuropa – is not Eastern and not Western

Europe, but has a stronger footing in Western 'civilisation' than in that of the East. (Authors who use the phrase 'East Central Europe' are refining this notion even further.) This is how the standard ideology of the remaking of Central Europe may be summed up in a few words. A new twist in all of this is that this 'central(ised)' positioning of Hungary has become a recent issue of post-1990 national as well as international politics, following the collapse of the Soviet bloc. Hungary's first post-communist president, Árpád Göncz, for instance, who is a writer and dramatist, summarised this new location: 'Hungary may be a springboard for the West toward the East; for the Eastern countries [it may be a springboard] toward the West.'[19] This belief has a history in the period between the First and Second World Wars, an era of equally serious debates about international allegiances for eastern European nation-states.

Such notions, filled with pride as they are, assert the geophysical situation of the nation: neither in the East nor in the West, but a belonging to a *central* region. This had also been the wish of the populist or Third Road intellectual school of the 1930s.[20] Many attempted to envision an *embourgeoisement* of the peasantry that would lay the foundation for a 'Garden Hungary', a unique nation-state copying neither the capitalist Western model nor the nationalised agriculture of the Soviet Union.[21] That this did not happen was not only the fault of the idealist thinkers of the 1930s and 1940s. According to some scholars this process was forcefully stopped by the invasion of Hungary by the Soviet Union. The sociologist Ivan Szelenyi, for example, writes: 'For a while it appeared that the sovietisation of Eastern Europe in 1949 and the forced collectivisation of agriculture had irreversibly closed off the possibility of a Third Road' (1988: 17). For him, and for his Hungarian colleagues, while the Third (or Central) Road has more 'ironic overtones', they seem to continue this development which is not 'just a theoretical fantasy, but a stubborn trend in history' (Szelenyi 1988: 17). It might not be the 'stubborn trend in history', however, but the stubborn trend of the sociologists that underlies the notion that the peasantry in this region is 'uniquely East European', which means that it can be 'distinguishable from both Western capitalism and Soviet-style socialism' (Szelenyi 1988: 17). Here is another, carefully moulded 'middle road' solution to regional backwardness.

The making of Central Europe was, and continues to be, a literary and scholarly project, envisioned in large part by national elites and émigré scholars. Timothy Garton Ash, for example, names those few leading intellectuals participating in this project: György Konrád, Vaclav Havel, Czeslaw Milosz, Danilo Kis, Mihály Vajda and Milan Simecka (1990b: 1–2). Since literature in eastern Europe has always been fundamentally intertwined with politics – the Czech president Havel and his Hungarian opposite number Göncz are two contemporary examples – this myth-making is also a political act *sui generis*.

The number one champion of Central Europe, and perhaps the strongest and most influential voice, has been that of the Czech writer, Milan Kundera, who has always believed that Central Europe was never outside the West, only separated from it by the force of Soviet tanks and the implementation of Soviet rule throughout the whole region.[22] Kundera's ideas were influential beyond European intellectual circles. In 1982, a new annual was launched, *Cross Currents: A Yearbook of Central European Culture*, published by Yale University Press and edited by Ladislav Matejka, a professor of Slavic languages and literature at the University of Michigan. It is not without coincidence that the annual got off the ground with the help of Kundera and the Polish-American Nobel Prize laureate Czeslaw Milosz. In an editorial, this region is characterised as follows:

> Central Europe was defined as a cultural unit tied together by historical awareness of a common past and maintaining its own identity even while placed in the eastern orbit by force of arms and by pacts between superpowers. (Matejka 1991: vii)

In this context it is interesting to note that there are now countries – namely Poland, the Czech Republic, Hungary, Croatia and Slovenia – which proudly boast the most distance from their communist past and identify themselves as Central, or East-Central European, while in contrast, they view other states – Slovakia, Bulgaria, Romania, Serbia, Albania, Ukraine and Russia – as East Europeans proper, whose national heritage includes a much more serious dosage of communism and, thus, backwardness. Besides this war of labels, this distinction is also an important aspect of the Europeanist intellectual discourse – the 'return to Europe' of Vaclav Havel – adding to the already antagonistic geopolitical relationships in the region. Vaclav Havel's 'velvet revolution' seemed to provide food for thought to Western analysts such as Samuel P. Huntington who, borrowing from Havel, writes that the 'velvet curtain' has replaced the 'iron curtain' and seems to be the most significant dividing line in Europe.[23]

Contrary to these views, the historian Maria Todorova argues that a skewed debate on a Central European identity versus an Eastern or Balkan one is currently being manufactured:

> Ideologists seeking to rationalise and legitimise emancipatory breaks from the tutelage of the Soviet Union have viewed the region in terms of opposites, e.g. between Catholic and Orthodox, Byzantium and the West. East Central Europe has been relegated to the nebulous realm of 'Western values' while the Balkans with Russia are, if not strictly Asian, then semi-Asian, 'Halb-Asian', 'Savage Europe', 'The Other Europe' or the newly coined and ostensibly neutral 'Eurasia'. (Todorova 1994: 478)

Another historian and long-time observer of nationalistic fervour in Eastern Europe, Alexander J. Motyl, puts it sarcastically as follows:

Ukrainians, Slovaks, Serbs, and Belarusians are too primitive to aspire to be truly Western; instead, the status of 'Little Russians' may be the most they can hope for. Naturally, Romanians, Bulgarians, Macedonians, Montenegrins, Albanians, Moldovans, Georgians, Armenians, Azerbaijanis, and Central Asians are too exotic, too swarthy, too prone to squabble, too inclined to sport thick black mustachios to be Western. (Motyl 1994: 268)

Such a division of cultures is nothing new, of course. One could cite examples from the mid-nineteenth century from the writings of Marx and Gobineu, and from the twentieth century by many others. While many of these aspiring populations present themselves as enlightened 'Europeans', they themselves fare no better when it comes down to their internal relations with their own minorities. In a perceptive insight, Misha Glenny describes the relationship between the Serbs and Albanians of Kosovo as follows:

> Serbs insist that if Kosovo became a Yugoslav republic, this would be the prelude to secession, which they cannot countenance, as they consider Kosovo to be the cradle of Serbian civilisation. Despite this historical bond, it is striking that few Serbs from outside Kosovo have ever visited the province. They will, of course, spend many hours denouncing Albanians as terrorists, separatists, Shiptars (a derogatory term in Serbian), rapists, primitives and bandits despite never having spoken to an Albanian from Kosovo. Above all, they consider them stupid and uncivilised. (Glenny 1990: 135)

Bogdan Denitch, a long-time observer of the Yugoslav scene, provides a fascinating glimpse into the fashioning of nationalistic hatred that characterised the Yugoslav state since its inception:

> A genuine disservice to scholarship and intra-ethnic peace has been done by generations of national historians and ethnographers who laboured mightily in trying to prove the special role of their own ethnic groups. Thus the best known Serbian ethnographer, Jovan Cvijic, argued that mountain *Dinaric* types (oddly enough they just happen to be mostly Serbs and Montenegrins) are the people with hardy state-building virtues, while the mild *Panonian* types (who happen to be mostly Croat) have a more gentle and servile mentality. The Croat ethnographer Dinko Tomasic accepted this division of typologies but argued that the Panonians were the natural democrats and builders, while the Dinarics were suited for war and violence, and therefore turned to police, the military and authoritarian rule. (Denitch 1990: 141)

Such semi-paranoid styles of nationalistic indoctrination – which may explain some of the vicious hostilities in the Balkan war to a certain degree – are rampant throughout eastern Europe, just as they are common in states (in Western Europe, Asia, and Africa) with multiethnic populations. One only has to think of the Basque–Spanish, or the Northern Irish–English contestations of political realities. Numerous other examples of similar intellectual 'contests' could be provided which attest to the various rages of nationalisms, ranging from the Hungarian and Romanian to the Slovak and Hungarian, from Ukrainian and Russian, Bulgarian and Romanian, to Greek and Turkish historical enmities.[24] These culturally fashioned enmities sadly attest to the fact that multiculturalism and inter-ethnic alliances in this part of the world will be extremely difficult to inaugurate, if not outright impossible.

Clearly, while different minorities sometimes manage to work out some kind of acceptable *modus vivendi* in their everyday interactions, the national elites have been indulging in a perverse form of indoctrination. In this new literary representation, which has dominated the eastern European, and for that matter the Balkan intellectual scene, the principal culprits continue to be national 'others'. For each nation-state emerging out of the Soviet empire, the 'neighbouring other' assumes the characteristics of the externalised evil; at the same time, in their quest to prove their own 'Europeanness' and 'modernity', the intellectuals look at the internal and neighbouring 'others' in disgust (Held 1993; Kürti 1993; Poulton 1993). As long as the mythological Western 'other' continues to persist (not only in the personifications of Goethe, Fichte, and Herder of the eighteenth century but, more and more, in the embodiments of the late-capitalist West of Michael Jackson, Ted Turner and Bill Gates of Windows '95 fame), there will always be images of the mythological 'Eastern' or 'Balkan' 'others'. Naturally, this implies a refashioning of negative stereotypes of the brutish, unclean, and inferior ethnic minorities, and of unpleasant or quarrelsome neighbourly relations. In this sense, each of the nationalistic fervours also upholds a racial and cultural superiority of the national majority – the *Herrenvolk* of Herder – when compared to minorities or neighbouring populations. The elite always manages to pose this problem as a competition between the 'Easterners', the nationally minded intellectuals, versus the 'Westerners,' the modernisers (Pesonen 1991; Verdery 1990). This duality, however, continues to mask the real problems for both sides who tend to swing to the extremes of categorisations and homogenisations in their projections of ethnic and cultural minorities and the superiority of majority cultures.

In the remaking of Eastern and Central Europe, just as in the nine-teenth century, the representation of 'otherness' has become a political issue once again. The new pluralistic states foster an image of unity and ethnonationalism (majority ethnic group identification with the state), often supported as an official ideology. Indispensable in this new nationalistic discourse is the figure of the stigmatised 'other', 'the enemy', reoriented to include not only the competitive neighbouring nation-states but the minorities *inside* the territory. For every major nationality group there are several 'others' – often described as less literate, less European, and less democratic than their antagonists – against whom they can measure and identify themselves. The negative stereotypes and the positive images coalesce to form a heretofore unknown nationalistic mentality that supports and at the same time subverts its own agenda. For the Bulgarians the image of the unintelligent, barbarous, and cruel Turk may be counter-balanced by that of the pious but dangerous Greek; for Poles and Czechs the ruthless, overzealous Germans stand against the idle Slovaks; for the Slovaks and the Romanians the eager and dominating Magyars continue to present a threat; at the same time Magyars feel suffocated by the Pan-Slavic Russians and Pan-Germanic groups surrounding them.

All the while, the majority groups feel ambivalently towards the figure of the 'nationalised' yet 'foreign' Jew, an image recalling the dualities between the 'local' and the 'stranger' introduced by the German sociologist Georg Simmel decades ago. This form of hegemonic ethnocentric thinking not only fosters the creation of distorted national-level politics, party formations, religious associations and majority-manipulated media, but inadvertently leads groups themselves to relearn the symbolic images of 'us' versus 'them' through the nationalised and uniformalised educational systems. This leads me to the argument that not only in the nineteenth century but increasingly at this post-communist moment, the small nationalities and neighbouring states of eastern Europe exist within the confinement of what Worsley calls 'hegemonic nationalism'. He character-ises this as the recognition of only one ethnic identity as legitimate: 'The national culture is the culture of the dominant class and its region' (1984: 188). In the post-Soviet space, this has resulted in a forceful conversion of local ethnic identities and boundary mechanisms to the existing mode of nationalistic discourse propagated by the national, and increasingly a dominant transnational, elite.

Thus, the current remaking of the new Central Europe has its origin in the post-Cold War climate when the Soviet Union and the United States, together with its Western allies, accelerated arms developments and hostilities *vis-à-vis* each other. However, with Kundera and Milosz in the background, the new Central Europe is understood as:

> No longer a mere conglomerate of small nations passively accepting their destiny in an imposed political environment, but an invigorated meeting ground of cultures stretching from the Baltic to the Mediterranean and encompassing Slavic, Baltic, Germanic, Jewish, Hungarian, Romanian, and Balkan components. (Matejka 1991: viii)[25]

What would this multicultural 'meeting ground' achieve? Some, such as a Hungarian-born Viennese lawyer and champion of human rights, have provided their sympathetic answers: 'Will there be a new Central Europe? I believe there will be and if not, the consequences will be tragic. ... I am convinced that only a healthy Central Europe can save the entire continent' (Barki 1989: 9).

However, that this Central Europe project is far from being crystallised is easily ascertained from a few recent publications in which certain countries are privileged to be more European than others. Many historians refer to East-Central Europe as including Poland, the Czech and Slovak republics, and Hungary. One of these is Piotr S. Wandycz who argues, similarly to Szücs, Kohák, and Kundera, that East-Central Europe was part of European events such as the Renaissance and the Reformation, the French and industrial revolutions, as well as having social and economic connections to these (1992).

Yet, other historians are not so limiting in their definitions. By analysing Eastern European and French connections between the two world wars, the historian Nicole Jordan, for example, uses the term 'Central Europe' to discuss the complex interrelationships between Paris, Warsaw, Prague, Bucharest and Belgrade (1992). Yet, how Bucharest and Belgrade figure in Central Europe is never elaborated by the author.

In his recently published, highly acclaimed historical atlas, the Canadian historian Paul Magocsi discusses 'East-Central Europe' from the perspective of both history and geography. Perhaps this is the most inclusive designation of the region: for him this terrain is exactly at the centre of the European continent; that is, between the western coasts of Ireland and Portugal and the Ural Mountains (1993: xi). When discussing this large geographical area, Magocsi separates the region into a northern, an Alpine-Carpathian, and a Balkan zone (1993: 2). For him Italy, Greece and 'European Turkey' are justifiably part of 'East-Central Europe' just as much as the Baltic states, Ukraine and Moldova.[26] It is worth mentioning, however, that such an extensive geography for the region is hardly acceptable to European geographers and cartographers who, perhaps still under the influence of the colonial Germanic Mitteleuropa, do not regard the Baltic states, the former Yugoslavia and Greece as members of this region.[27]

At this point we need to ask, do these new borders and regional alliances only reveal the fancies of a few historians and literary minds, or, if seen more critically, is a new totalising hierarchy being created? To be sure, in the 'Central Europe' project, post-1989 Hungary, the Czech Republic and Poland – and possibly Slovenia or some of the Baltic states – are earmarked for progress, for democracy and for the planting of (western) European institutions on their native soil. The rest (Russia, Romania, Ukraine, Bulgaria, Yugoslavia, Albania, Macedonia, Slovakia), must remain what they always have been, East European. While the former states are closer to the West, the latter will have the responsibility, the arduous task, of coming to terms with their Stalinist legacies and their troubled multiethnic milieus. An important duality of states has emerged out of the former East bloc in the minds of many, as figure 2.1 suggests. What is clear from all this is that attendant upon the revolutions of

Central Europe	Eastern Europe
multi-party system	ethnically divided multi-party system
democratic developments	only half-hearted reforms
market economy	state intervention in economy
close ties to the pan-European institutions	lack of ties to pan-European institutions
liberalisation of social life	social tension
consumerism	shabby goods
limited ethnic tension	ethnic hostilities
no anti-Semitism	anti-Semitism
free media	state-controlled media

Figure 2.1 Images of Central and Eastern Europe

1989 and 1990 was the establishment of multi-party systems throughout the region, a characteristic feature of which has been intensified conflict between ethnic minorities and majority political parties: in Bulgaria, for example, the Turkish party; in Moldova the Russian; in Poland and the Czech Republic the German; in Slovakia and Romania the Hungarian and Gypsy parties are illustrative of this fissure. That inter-ethnic and national identities are now emerging with greater vehemence is discernible in the rhetoric of these political parties. In this, Central Europe and Eastern Europe do seem divergent: Poland, the Czech Republic and Hungary do not have profound ethnic-based party cleavages. Yet that does not mean that these countries do not have ethnic problems or that nationalism does not plague them as well. The 'true' East European states, on the other hand, are stranded in a quagmire of ethnopolitical strife and warfare.

However, despite the creation of this new duality, it would be senseless to deny the specificities of the common East European experiences, in view of the globalisation of capital and the appearance of a nearly seamless transitory period. E. P. Thompson has warned of the 'Cola–vodka drive', presenting a bleak vision of new states becoming 'a dumping ground and a cheap labour resource for West German and Japanese capitalists' (1991: 16). Timothy Garton Ash sees a similar tendency when he writes about the coming of the 'second Ostpolitik' of German dependency (1990b: 17). All over the former Soviet bloc, western consumerist products have appeared: for example, while most Hungarians only looked at Volkswagens and Suzukis with desire in the 1970s and 1980s, now both cars are manufactured in the country.[28] All the major drug companies (CIBA-GEIGY), food processing multinationals (Coca-Cola, Pepsi, Nestlé), videos and computer makers (Sony, IBM), designer fashion houses (Estée Lauder, Chanel, Ungaro) together with western mass-produced goods (Adidas, Levi Strauss jeans) and fast-food chains (McDonalds, Kentucky Fried Chicken and Pizza Hut) are setting up operations all over the region.[29]

With such feverish consumerist drives and patterns of westernisation, local ethnic conflicts and nationalist outbreaks are hard to fathom. For enduring anti-Semitism and xenophobia, as well as peasant-based populist movements and revived, nativist fascist symbols, are as much a part of east Europe's contemporary landscape as are the legacies of its heroic partisan myths, gigantic Stalinist factories, and collective farms. Memories of smoky East German cars spewing forth leaded gasoline fumes, of apparatchiks and of the subservient intelligentsia of the 1960s and 1970s will undoubtedly exist in the east European consciousness as a terrible nightmare for years to come. These phenomena must, however, be interpreted in particular cultural and historical contexts – the ways in which they were constructed and subsequently deconstructed. This slanted remembering, too, is an essential part of the ways in which the east European states (dis)claim their histories.

The momentous political and economic changes in the former East bloc – the breakup of the Soviet empire, Yugoslavia, and Czechoslovakia, the construction of fledgling nation-states, and civil war in Bosnia–Serbia–Croatia, the anti-Gypsy mood in Hungary and anti-Hungarian outbreaks in Romania – may be viewed as results both of the international re-alignments of the globalised European terrain and of the chaotic state of affairs following the collapse of communist hegemony and centralised economic systems. These alterations must be taken into account when we want to reconceptualise theories of identities, nationalism and interethnic conflict in this post-communist moment. Only then can we fully comprehend the message of Erazim Kohák:

> The East is disintegrating. Years of Communist rule have destroyed habits of responsibility and reality and have left the lands of the former Soviet empire without a legitimate vision. The only available alternative, the Central European version of the American dream, led to frustration and anger when liberation did not bring instant affluence. Now ambitious demagogues are using that anger to subvert patriotism into the service of nationalist passions as the newly freed peoples prepare to use their freedom to blow each other to kingdom come. (1992: 214)

Conclusions

In conclusion, we may ask the question: What does all this intellectual gerrymandering really entail and why the seeming identification of some states as still 'backward' and 'eastern', and the contrary positioning of others on a pedestal as progressive and 'central' European? For one, as scholarly output in the East comes to be increasingly under the influence of the 'globalism' that is taking place everywhere, releasing enormous political and economic forces in these countries for many years, elites are focusing on the transitional nature of developments within the former East bloc. Many blame the current problems on the moment of transition.

In post-1990 eastern Europe, states of the former Soviet bloc are left on their own to fill the vacuum created by the disbanded political, economic and cultural institutions. Some are more successful than others in overcoming their internal difficulties; the cultural differences between them are enormous in the ways in which they go about reconstructing their economies, social networks, education and artistic life. Another reason, perhaps, has to do with the rush to devise international alliances and solidarities in the wake of the collapse of the Soviet bloc. Many of the intellectuals who have deeply entrenched ideas on progress, homogenisation, and westernisation do not realise that the fashioning of Central Europe is, at the same time, a remaking of Eastern Europe. The existence of the Central European Time Zone is taken perhaps too literally by the ideologues of the 'Central European' scheme. Such myths die hard, and the expenditure of enormous intellectual energies may be anchored in notions that cultures are still under the same, age-old influences as they were before, and that change arrives slowly in certain parts of the world.

Thus the remaking of Europe, with large parts of the former Soviet bloc now claiming allegiance with the non-communist West, arises as a wishful thinking on the part of a selected few. While the integrationists' dream of the United States of Europe of 1992 is yet to be realised, a new nationalist geopolitical typology is being created in its place. A contemporary hierarchy of order is of those who were 'really' communists and those who 'never' really accepted communism wholeheartedly. Some of the newly liberated states claim that since the 'year of truth', as Timothy Garton Ash phrases the events of 1989, they now truly belong to Europe, an act that parallels their distaste for their former communist allies. As Zygmunt Bauman suggests, 'Friends are reproduced by the pragmatics of co-operation, enemies by the pragmatics of struggle' (1990: 144). The early 1990s may be described as a struggle with the formation of friendships and enemies among the former East bloc nations.

Yet, it must be realised that the orientalising project cuts like a double-edged sword: states and their elites involved with this newly manufactured hierarchy may be creating their own sense of distorted identities, as well as histories. At the same time, as the West keeps assisting in this, and, as it pushes some of these states more and more backwards into the realms of myths by relegating them to either the feudal past or the communist era, so too does the West also keep deluding itself that it is a perfect, harmonious, homogeneous, and powerful entity whose sole mission is to champion free democratic polities.

While it may just be that the triangle of France–Britain–Germany is the political and economic engine of Europe, it is far from universally accepted that these states must be the richest, the best, and the most democratic among all.[30] The new hierarchisation of various parts of Europe may be one of the most enduring myths of our *fin de siècle*. Like most myths, however, this too is fraught with difficulties and a stubborn refusal to give up and die. This delusion just may be what is at the heart of the current problems plaguing the northern, western and southern parts of Europe: cultural differences in economic development, increasing population movements, and an uneasiness about the coming of the United States of Europe. If the West sees the East as living in the past and mortgaged to its ethnonationalisms, then the West should also see itself as having plenty of the same in different disguises, including racism, expansionism, and xenophobia (see Bjørgo 1993 and Chapter 3 in this volume). Is it realistic to contemplate that only the East may be disintegrating, as Kohák seems to suggest (1992), while the West continues to consolidate? Could it be that Europe, and in fact the globe, is integrating into a world culture and community, of the kind suggested by Arjun Appadurai, Ulf Hannerz and, earlier, Immanuel Wallerstein?[31] Or could it be that integration in one part of the globe engenders disintegration and chaos elsewhere, but not necessarily in a unidirectional fashion; rather, in ways that ultimately cause repercussions in the integrating part as well? As far as the remaking of Eastern and Central Europe is concerned, Bruno Bauer's statement may well be as pertinent today as it was in 1854: that Central Europe is 'a great territory of unanswered questions and unresolved contradictions, a region of half-demands which until now have enjoyed as little realisation as proposals counter to them, and which seem to be products of visionary caprice because they aim at something whole, something new and enormous' (quoted in Ash 1990b: 1).

Notes

1. See the analysis of Ferenc Miszlivetz in which he cites the liberal János Kis, from the Free Democratic party, and János Lovász of the Democratic Forum, both arguing for a Central European identity (1991: 2–3).
2. The Hungarian daily *Magyar Nemzet* inaugurated a series titled 'The Bourgeois' (*A Polgár*), illustrating the existence of middle-class values and lifestyles in Hungary both before and after World War Two; see, for example, 'A Polgár', *Magyar Nemzet*, 18 September 1995, p. 8.
3. A useful introduction to this subject is Schöpflin and Wood (1989).
4. The newly emerging subdiscipline the anthropology of Europe continually marginalises eastern Europe by producing ethnographies of 'Western Europe' and of a separate 'Eastern Europe'. Of the three recent collections I have, for example, only one has a chapter on the former Yugoslavia; basically they do not include eastern European cultures; see Goddard et al. (1994); Macdonald (1993); and Wilson and Smith (1993). For the emergence of the specific 'new' Eastern European ethnography see Kideckel (1995), and, perhaps for a more balanced view, the volume edited by DeSoto and Anderson (1993). See also Kürti and Langman (1997).
5. The travel literature written by western visitors to the eastern and southern regions of the Holy Roman Empire and the Habsburg crown lands is vast. I have only selected one glaring example for illustration. The nineteenth-century Hungarian

poet, writer, and newspaper editor János Arany notes in one of his editorials that a newspaper article published in Leipzig in 1864 claimed that highway robbery in Hungary was an everyday occurrence and seemed to be a 'historical legacy and right of the Hungarians' (Keresztury 1963: 151). In all fairness, however, it must be mentioned that not all travellers looked with disdain at the conditions of the East. Ethnocentric insights and shocking revelations, however, are a standard trope of travel fiction and diaries (Boon 1982; Porter 1991).

6. Jenö Szücs (1928–88) was an excellent student of medieval Hungarian history who published extensively on the foundation of the Hungarian kingdom, its state formation and its early centuries. It was, however, his 1981 article 'A Sketch on the Three Historic Regions of Europe', published originally in Hungarian in the historical periodical *Történelmi Szemle*, which despite his description of it as a 'sketch' elevated Szücs from being a medievalist into a 'theoretician' of European development. This article later appeared in English ('The Three Historical Regions of Europe: An Outline', *Acta Historica*, 29 (1983)2/4: 131–84), and as a Hungarian-language book in the same year.

7. See, for example, Czigany's analysis of Hungarian literature with its various images of the peasantry and of the beginning of the populist literary project (1984). For the intricacies of the Transylvanian differences between Hungarians, Romanians and German-Saxons see Verdery (1983).

8. In all fairness to Szücs, I have to mention that while world systems theory advocated the different capitalist development of the West and East from the sixteenth century onwards, Jenö Szücs was convinced that, especially in the case of Hungary, this backwardness originated back in the Tatar invasion in the thirteenth century and even before, during the mismanaged state of affairs in the period of Conquest and the solidification of the rule of the Árpád dynasty in the ninth and tenth centuries (Szücs 1992; 1993).

9. See, for example, Daniel Segal's convincing argument, against Verdery, that in France pluralism and heterogeneity were also important factors in making the French nation-state (1988: 309–10)

10. Bojtár goes on to claim that this 'distortion' can be extended back to the 'end of the 18th century with the unfolding of capitalism that should have established bourgeois society' (1988: 254).

11. See the press release in *Népszabadság*, 12 September 1995, pp. 1–3.

12. In the same issue of the Hungarian daily *Népszabadság* (p. 3), the per capita GDP for 1994 is listed: Slovenia ($9,000), Czech Republic ($8,100), Slovakia ($6,900), Hungary ($6,500), and Poland ($5,500).

13. See the following articles in Hungarian dailies: 'Bukarest hasznositaná a VSZ hagyományait', in *Magyar Hirlap*, 22 September 1995, p. 3; and 'Varsó elzárkózik a KGST felélesztésétöl', in *Népszabadság*, 6 September 1995, p. 3.

14. Only at the end of 1995 did the 'Tens' consider allowing Romania, Albania, Belarus, Bulgaria and the Ukraine to apply for full membership. Yugoslavia, however, has remained outside of this elitist group formation for the moment.

15. The various papers collected for the Joint Economic Committee of the United States Congress (Joint Economic Committee 1989) are revealing of the ways in which socialist economies were perceived.

16. See, 'The Phare Countries – Towards the Internal Market', *Info Phare* No. 8 (July 1995), pp. 1–2. In a special section on Hungary the justification is spelled out as follows: 'It will not be easy to implement these vital reforms. In Hungary, like anywhere else, there is always resistance to change. But the government's determina-

tion to proceed is buttressed by the average Hungarian's desire to join the western "club". He knows deep down that he will have to tolerate a few more lean years before he can take a well-deserved break from austerity' (p. 5).

17. Hungary's external debt, for instance, has increased from 1994 to 1995 from $24 billion to $28 billion as a result of more and more borrowing. This debt increased slightly after Hungary's prime minister, Gyula Horn, and Germany's Helmut Kohl signed another $1 billion loan to Hungary in the autumn of 1995. Only at the beginning of 1997 was Hungary's external debt decreased slightly.

18. From the Hungarian economic historian Ivan T. Berend to economist János Kornai the list is impressive. All see a possibility of chaos, recentralisation, totalitarianism, and even enduring economic crises amounting to civil unrest as one possible outcome if the market economy fails; see Kornai's concern for 'freedom' under government-controlled economy (Kornai 1990: 214–40).

19. See his speech in the daily *Magyar Hirlap*, 22 June 1993, p. 1.

20. The writer László Németh was perhaps the most vocal and respected ideologue of this movement. In his influential study *Hungarians and Europe*, he argued that Hungarians are the 'chosen' people with the mission to create the idea of Central Europe. He wrote: 'Central Europe expects the chosen people to work on two enormous tasks: (1) to create Central Europe in spirit and science; and (2) to bring Good News (*euangelion*) to this region which will make the connections between interest and culture into a morality. ... The chosen people must convince these countries that they can be melted into one unit. ... Central Europe is not something that exists yet, it must be created. And in this there is nothing unnatural and against the flow of history'; see László Németh, *A magyarság és Európa*, Franklin Társulat, Budapest, 1935, pp. 127–8.

21. Francis Fejtö, an expatriate Hungarian living in France, summarises this dichotomy as follows: 'However heterogeneous the group that called itself Populist was, most of its intellectual representatives agreed that Hungary must find its road to progress somewhere between East and West, between Communism and Capitalism; that the peasants should be given land and the opportunity to advance socially and that the country must be led by intellectuals of peasant origin because the peasantry had most meticulously preserved Hungary's pure national traditions. In contrast, the Urbanists – liberals, democrats, and social democrats – held that a 'Hungarian third way' was utopian; that the Hungarian people, committed to Western civilization for a millennium, should, after a revolution and a counter-revolution, return to Western-style democracy; and that in this struggle, the leading role must be played by a liberal bourgeoisie and the working class – organized in the Social Democratic Party and in labour unions – without, of course, losing sight of the interests of the peasantry' (Fejtö 1990: 29).

22. Kundera's influential article 'The Tragedy of Central Europe' (*New York Review of Books*, 26 April 1984) was widely circulated and read by East European intellectuals during the 1980s. For a good discussion of Kundera's ideas and writings concerning central Europeans see Timothy Garton Ash's essay 'Does Central Europe Exist?' (1990).

23. Huntington's article, 'The Clash of Civilizations' (*Foreign Affairs*, Summer 1993) has prompted the editors of *Slavic Review* to print an excerpt from Huntington's piece as well as to print the map which shows East and West Europe separated by a thick black line. The editor of *Slavic Review* ends by asking: 'What's wrong with this picture?' (Mossman 1995: x).

24. I have dealt with the specificities of Hungarian–Romanian nationalistic controversy elsewhere (Kürti 1989, 1995).

25. The American-Hungarian historian Stephen Borsody understands Central Europe similarly. He also used this term systematically to refer to the Soviet-dominated European states in his *The Tragedy of Central Europe*, published in 1980, and in his latest updated version of it, *The New Central Europe* (1993). Interestingly, the titles of Borsody's 1980 book and Milan Kundera's 1984 influential essay are both: 'The Tragedy of Central Europe'.

26. It is clear that Magocsi's political and geographical definitions notwithstanding, historical definitions are equally important (1993: xi).

27. See, for example, the recent (i.e. post-1989) edition of the German *Euroatlas* for ZentralEuropa (Gütersloh: Mohndruck, 1992/93), which includes only Denmark, the Netherlands, France, the Benelux states, Austria, Switzerland, Germany, Czechoslovakia, Hungary and Italy in this region. Interestingly, it still shows no Czech and Slovak republics proper and there is no mention of the Baltic states, Poland, and Slovenia as being part of Central Europe.

28. Hungarians, for example, have been especially keen since 1989 to import used German cars – the Great Mercedes Migration as some have referred to it; at the same time, used Russian, Romanian, and Polish-made cars are being dumped back to Russia and Romania. Dacias (cars made in Romania) have been taken out of Hungary by the thousands since 1990, while at the same time, Trabants and Wartburgs made in the former East Germany have been taken off the road with government help.

29. What is interesting in this unbridled consumerism is the fact that products of multinational companies are marketed as home-grown; in Hungary Suzukis are marketed as Hungarian cars and German beer is advertised to thirsty consumers as the 'best the country has to offer'.

30. We may, of course, recall that for Derrida Europe – 'Old Europe' – may be analogous to the body, with France at its 'head' (1992: 48–65).

31. It is not without reason that I mention these three names together. They all contributed to the 1990 study *Global Culture* edited by M. Featherstone in which they seem to agree, though with different approaches, that the end of modernity, post-communism, and postmodernism coalesce under the sway of globalisation.

References

Ágh, Attila (1993) 'The "Comparative Revolution" and the Transition in Central and Southern Europe', *Journal of Theoretical Politics*, 5(2): 231–52.

Ash, Timothy Garton (1990a) *The Uses of Adversity: Essays on the Fate of Central Europe*, Vintage Books, New York.

— (1990b) 'Mitteleuropa?' *Daedalus* (Winter): 1–21.

Attali, Jacques (1991) *Millennium: Winners and Losers in the Coming World Order*, Random House, New York.

Bakic-Hayden, Milica and Robert Hayden (1992) 'Orientalist Variations on the Theme "Balkans": Symbolic Geography in Yugoslav Politics 1987–1990', *Slavic Review*, 51: 1–15.

Barki, Eva Maria (1989) 'Lesz-e ujra Közép Európa' (Will There Be a New Central Europe?), *Magyar Fórum*, 3 November: 9.

Bauman, Zygmunt (1990) 'Modernity and Ambivalence', in M. Featherstone (ed.) *Global Culture: Nationalism, Globalisation and Modernity*, Sage, London, pp. 143–70.

Berend, Ivan, T. and Gyorgy Ránki (1985) *The Hungarian Economy in the Twentieth Century*, Croom Helm, London.

Bjørgo, Tore (ed.) (1993) *Racist Violence in Europe*, St Martin's Press, New York.

Bojtár, Endre (1988) 'Eastern or Central Europe?', *Cross Currents*, 7: 253–64.

Boon, James A. (1982) *Other Tribes, Other Scribes: Symbolic Anthropology in the Comparative Study of Cultures, Histories, Religions and Texts*, Cambridge University Press, Cambridge.

Borsody, Stephen (1993) *The New Central Europe*, East European Monographs No. 366, East European Monographs, Boulder.

Bunce, Valerie (1995) 'Should Transitologists Be Grounded?' *Slavic Review*, 54(1): 111–27.

Busek, Erhard (1992) *Az elképzelt Közép-Európa* (The Imagined Central Europe), Századvég, Budapest.

Chase-Dunn, Christopher K. (ed.) (1982) *Socialist States in the World System*, Sage, Beverly Hills.

Chirot, Daniel (ed.) (1989) *The Origins of Backwardness in Eastern Europe*, University of California Press, Berkeley.

Cortona, Pietro Grilli di (1991) 'From Communism to Democracy: Rethinking Regime Change in Hungary and Czechoslovakia', *International Social Science Journal*, 28: 315–30.

Csepeli, György (1992) 'Coping with the Conflict Between Backwardness and Modernity in Eastern Europe: Fascism, Communism, What's Next?', in *Proceedings Workshop Transformation Processes in Eastern Europe*. SRO/SSCW, The Hague, pp. 155–62.

Czigany, Lorant (1984) *The Oxford History of Hungarian Literature from the Earliest Time to the Present*, Clarendon Press, Oxford.

Dahrendorf, Ralf (1990) *Reflections on the Revolution in Europe*, Random House, New York.

Denitch, Bogdan (1990) *Limits and Possibilities: The Crisis of Yugoslav Socialism and the State Socialist Systems*, University of Minnesota Press, Minneapolis.

Derrida, Jacques (1992) *The Other Heading: Reflections on Today's Europe*, Indiana University Press, Bloomington.

De Soto, Hermine and David G. Anderson (1993) *The Curtain Rises: Rethinking Culture, Ideology and the State in Eastern Europe*, Humanities Press, Atlantic Highlands, NJ.

Featherstone, Mike (ed.) (1990) *Global Culture*, Sage, London.

Fehér, Ferenc (1990) 'The End of Communism', *Thesis Eleven*, 27: 5–19.

Fejtö, Ferenc (1990) 'Once More About Populists and Urbanists', *Uncaptive Minds*, 3(2): 28–9.

Glenny, Misha (1990) *The Rebirth of History: Eastern Europe in the Age of Democracy*, Penguin, London.

Goddard, Victoria A., Josep R. Llobera and C. Shore (eds) (1994) *The Anthropology of Europe: Identities and Boundaries in Conflict*, Berg, Oxford.

Held, Joseph (ed.) (1993) *Democracy and Right-wing Politics in Eastern Europe in the 1990s*, East European Monographs, Columbia University Press, New York.

Janos, Andrew (1982) *The Politics of Backwardness in Hungary, 1825–1945*, Princeton University Press, Princeton.

Jedlicki, Jerzy (1990) *The Revolution of 1989: The Unbearable Burden of History*, Occasional Papers No. 29, the Wilson Center, Washington DC.

Joint Economic Committee (1989) *Pressures for Reform in the East European Economies*.

Study Papers Submitted to the Joint Economic Committee, Congress of the United States: Volume 1. 101st Congress 1st Session. US Government Printing Office, Washington DC.

Jordan, Nicole (1992) *The Popular Front and Central Europe: The Dilemmas of French Impotence, 1918–1940*, Cambridge University Press, New York.

Keresztury, Dezsö (ed.) (1963) *Arany János Müvei: Prózai Müvek 3* (Collected Works of János Arany: Prose Vol. 3), Akadémiai Kiadó, Budapest.

Kideckel, David A. (ed.) (1995) *East European Communities: The Struggle for Balance in Turbulent Times*, Westview, Boulder.

Kohák, Erazim (1990) 'What's Central to Central Europe?' *Harper's Magazine*, 17–24 June.

— (1992) 'Ashes ... Ashes ... Central Europe after Forty Years', *Daedalus*, 121 (2): 197–216.

Kornai, János (1990) *Vision and Reality, Market and State*, Routledge, New York.

Kürti, László (1989) 'Transylvania, The Land Beyond Reason: Toward an Anthropological Analysis of a Contested Terrain', *Dialectical Anthropology*, 14: 21–52.

— (1993) *Culture of Enmity: Hungary, Romania, and the Transylvanian Question*, Working Papers 23, Centre for Peace and Conflict Research, Copenhagen.

Kürti, Lászlo and Juliet Langman (eds) (1997) *Beyond Borders: Remaking Cultural Identities in the New East and Central Europe*, Westview, Boulder, CO.

Macdonald, Sharon (ed.) (1993) *Inside European Identities: Ethnography in Western Europe*, Berg, Oxford.

Magocsi, Paul R. (1993) *Historical Atlas of East Central Europe*, University of Washington Press, Seattle.

Marer, Paul (1991) 'Hungary: Reform and Transition', in I. J. Kim and J. S. Zacek (eds) *Reform and Transformation in Communist Systems*, Paragon House, New York, pp. 219–40.

Matejka, Ladislav (1991) 'Editor's Preface', *Cross Currents*, 10: vii–viii.

Miszlivetz, Ferenc (1991) 'Central Europe – The Way to Europe'. Unpublished manuscript.

Mossman, Elliot D. (1994) 'From the Editor', *Slavic Review*, 53(2): x.

Motyl, Alexander J. (1994) 'Negating the Negation: Russia, Not-Russia, and the West', *Nationalities Papers*, 22(1): 263–73.

Pesonen, Pekka (1991) 'The Image of Europe in Russian Literature and Culture', *History of European Ideas*, 13(4): 399–409.

Porter, Dennis (1991) *Haunted Journeys: Desire and Transgression in European Travel Writing*, Princeton University Press, Princeton.

Poulton, Hugh (1993) *The Balkans: Minorities and States in Conflict*, Minority Rights Publications, London.

Przeworski, Adam (1991) *Democracy and the Market*, Cambridge University Press, Cambridge.

Schöpflin, George and Nancy Wood (eds) (1989) *In Search of Central Europe*, Polity Press, London.

Segal, Daniel A. (1988) 'Nationalism, Comparatively Speaking', *Journal of Historical Sociology*, 1(3): 301–21.

Szelenyi, Ivan (1988) *Socialist Entrepreneurs: Embourgeoisement in Rural Hungary*, University of Wisconsin Press, Madison.

Szücs, Jenö (1988) 'The Historical Regions of Europe', in J. Keane (ed.) *Civil Society and the State*, Verso, London, pp. 291–332.

— (1992) *A magyar nemzeti tudat kialakulása* (Formation of the Hungarian National Consciousness), Szegedi Nyomda, Szeged.

— (1993) *Az utolsó Árpádok* (The Last of the Árpád House), Magyar Történet-tudományi Intézet, Budapest.

Thompson, E. P. (1991) 'Ends and Histories', in M. Kaldor (ed.) *Europe from Below: An East–West Dialogue*, Verso, London, pp. 7–26.

Todorova, Maria (1994) 'The Balkans: From Discovery to Invention', *Slavic Review*, 53(2): 453–82.

Verdery, Katherine (1983) *Transylvanian Villagers: Three Centuries of Political, Economic, and Ethnic Change*, University of California Press, Berkeley.

— (1990) 'The Production and Defense of "the Romanian Nation", 1900 to World War II', in R. Fox (ed.) *Nationalist Ideologies and the Production of National Cultures*, American Anthropological Association, Washington DC, pp. 81–111.

Wandycz, Piotr S. (1992) *The Price of Freedom: A History of East Central Europe from the Middle Ages to the Present*, Routledge, New York.

Wilson, Thomas M. and Estellie M. Smith (eds) (1993) *Cultural Change and the New Europe: Perspectives on the European Community*, Westview, Boulder.

Worsley, Peter (1984) *The Three Worlds: Culture and Development*, Weidenfeld and Nicolson, London.

CHAPTER 3

'The Invaders', 'the Traitors' and 'the Resistance Movement': The Extreme Right's Conceptualisation of Opponents and Self in Scandinavia[1]

Tore Bjørgo

A key issue in this book is the conceptualisation by anti-racist activists and researchers of the groups victimised by racism and the extent to which racism may be opposed through multiculturalist politics. In this chapter, I shift the perspective and focus on how racist and xenophobic groups conceptualise their various 'enemies'. These include both social categories they consider to be alien to their ethnic in-group, such as immigrants, asylum seekers or ethnic minorities, and their political opponents within their own ethnic group, such as anti-racists and – some-times – the media and the authorities. I analyse these conceptualisations as they are embedded in both the political world-views and the rhetorical strategies of these extremists.

By analysing the statements, verbal exchanges, texts, and other forms of communicative interaction deployed by such groups and movements, we may gain insight into how they construct their social realities (Berger and Luckman 1985) – and, further, into how they try to influence social realities through these discursive practices. It is mainly through their *discourses* that we are able to study the ideologies, political cultures and key symbolic practices of extremist groups or movements.

If discourse implies a form of cultural practice (see, for example, Lutz and Abu-Lughod 1990; Kårhus 1992), I use the term here to refer to the process of communicative interaction: the speeches, texts and other social practices through which people codify and reflect upon their experiences. In the process of developing specific ways of speaking about certain topics, these discursive practices 'systematically form the objects of which they speak', as Michel Foucault puts it (Foucault 1972: 49; Lutz and Abu-Lughod 1990: 9–10). Discourses may be products of our experiences but they are also constitutive of the social realities in which we live, and the truths with which we work. When ideas and arguments are exchanged within a group or a moral community, these notions may gradually become common property. In the course of this process of communicative inter-action, sets of conventionally linked concepts are established, determining premises for interpreting situations and making decisions. Such conclusions and choices may appear logical and justified within the context of the relevant discourse and the moral community sharing it. To outsiders who do not reason in terms of this discourse, however, the cultural practices arising from the discourse may seem irrational or even reprehensible. To bring out the reasoning of racist groups and activists and to provide glimpses of their particular constructions of reality, I include in the chapter statements and texts by them, cited at some length.

The concept of 'rhetoric' as used here refers to a special form of discursive practice that has as its specific purpose communicative per-suasion.[2] Successful rhetoric organises the experiences of an audience by evoking a context which endows these experiences with meaning. This requires the rhetorician to capture and tune in to the concerns and experiences of his audiences. Political rhetoric normally seeks to promote certain interpretations of current events by presenting them in the light of specific constructions of reality, and to influence the audiences to act in accordance with these conceptions and values. In other words, it is a call for action.

Yet there is no necessary or direct causal link between ideology or rhetoric and action. Most rhetoric leads to little or no real action. Neither do ideology and rhetoric always come prior to action. In many cases, action comes first; subsequently, the actor tries to work out a convenient justification for transgressive acts, a *post hoc* legitimation of what is known to be officially illegal. Most acts of racist violence, at least in Scandinavia, are perpetrated by individuals and small groups – often juvenile petty criminals in loosely organised youth gangs – which initially neither hold an explicit racist ideology nor have any direct relations to racist political organisations. Frequently, perpetrators of racist actions are approached by anti-immigrant or racist organisations only *after* they have carried out an arson attack or similar spectacular action. At that stage they may suddenly find themselves hailed as patriots or 'white resistance fighters' – an image they often eagerly embrace as their own.[3]

Varieties of Scandinavian nationalisms

There are two main types of extreme right-wing movement in Scandinavia: anti-immigration groups with a radical nationalist or ethnocentric outlook, and groups with a neo-Nazi or explicit racist ideology. Historical analogies and traditions play an important role for both, but they link themselves to two extremely different – even opposed – historical and ideological traditions: the anti-German resistance movement of the Second World

War, on the one hand, and traditions and discourse of anti-Semitism and National Socialism, on the other. In spite of the contrasting idiomatic content of their rhetoric, however, the fundamental structure of these discourses is almost identical. The anti-immigration movement claims to be the 'new resistance movement', fighting against the Muslim invasion and the national traitors who support it. Neo-Nazis claim to be the white/ Aryan resistance movement, fighting the Zionist occupation government (ZOG) and the racial traitors. The political establishment's embracing and promotion of notions like 'multicultural society' and 'variegated community' are considered by both types of activists as treacherous participation in malicious plots to destroy indigenous culture and race by mixing them with alien elements.[4] Regarding violence, the first type of activist claims that a civil war will break out unless its warnings are heeded, while the ZOG ideologues claim that the racial war has already started. Both groups justify the use of violence through their rhetoric, although to a different degree.

Because of their different historical experiences, most Norwegians and Danes relate to their national symbols and feelings quite differently from the way in which their Swedish neighbours relate to national symbols and sentiments. This difference has important consequences for the way in which extreme nationalists are able to exploit or appropriate national symbols.

Sweden's past as an expansionary great power in northern Europe, particularly during the seventeenth and eighteenth centuries, and the extent to which it was influenced by the political culture of Prussia/Germany have shaped present-day Swedish nationalism. The notion of a 'Greater Sweden' was alive in influential circles way into the twentieth century – at least until the middle of the Second World War. Because of the strength of their state, Swedes could generally take their national identity and independence for granted. By contrast, the Norwegian national identity that emerged during the nineteenth century was predominantly a liberation nationalism, linked to the process of winning independence first from Denmark and then from Sweden. After Denmark's status as a regional great power was shattered during the seventeenth century, Danish national identity came to be characterised by the realisation that 'Denmark is a small country' – and a country that at times is threatened by an aggressive neighbour in the south.

During the twentieth century, the Second World War was the single critical event that had the most significant impact on the development of nationalism in Scandinavia. The wartime experiences of occupation and resistance in Norway and Denmark made national feelings a legitimate and uniting force in ways that have no parallels in recent Swedish history, as Sweden remained unoccupied throughout the war. The Swedish people have never undergone a national crisis in which patriotism and national feelings have played a similarly positive and uniting role in the struggle for freedom and democracy. To many Swedes today, nationalist feelings and symbols appear problematic, even dubious. In this Sweden resembles the UK, where 'nationalism' is routinely equated with racism and xenophobia as a predominantly negative ideology (see, for example, Gilroy 1987).

Compared to most other countries occupied in the Second World War, Norway had a relatively large number of persons who collaborated actively with the German occupation forces. The leader of the Norwegian fascists, Vidkun Quisling, literally gave national treason a name. But Norway also had a strong civilian and military resistance movement, and from exile the Norwegian government actively continued the struggle against Nazi occupation. Denmark had less active collaboration, but also a weaker resistance movement and a government that, at least until 1943, followed a policy of accommodation in relation to the occupation forces. After 1942, popular resistance increased in Denmark. The king of Denmark openly identified with Jews by wearing a yellow Star of David in public, and the Danes organised a major operation which succeeded in smuggling Danish Jews across the North Sea to Sweden. Sweden was able to avoid German occupation by practising an accommodating form of neutrality during the first years of the Second World War. However, there were also strong pro-German and even pro-Nazi elements within leading circles of Swedish society and its political establishment. Although these forces lost influence when it became evident that Germany was losing the war, there was never a purge of Nazis in Sweden after the war ended. Unlike in occupied Denmark and Norway, Swedish Nazis never became traitors to their country, and were not considered as such.

The divergent historical experiences in these three Scandinavian countries determine to a large extent which types of nationalism and national symbols the extreme nationalist groups play on – and which symbols they may have prospects of appropriating. Swedish history, strongly characterised by Great Power traditions and ambitions, lends itself to a more aggressive and chauvinist version of nationalism than does the history of Denmark and – in particular – Norway. Present-day extreme nationalists in Sweden attach themselves to this established Greater Sweden tradition. Notions of a brotherhood of arms and of war heroes, together with 'martyr' worship, are central values among groups like the neo-Nazi Vitt Ariskt Motstånd (VAM, White Aryan Resistance), the folk-socialist Riksfronten (National Front) and the nationalist-xenophobic Sverigedemokraterna. Since the political mainstream in Sweden does not embrace the main symbols of the nation such as the flag and the national anthem with much enthusiasm, extreme nationalists have seen their chance to appropriate these symbols. Furthermore, National Socialist and anti-Semitic symbols and notions have not in principle been incompatible with Swedish patriotism. In Norway and Denmark, such a conjunction would be almost impossible in consequence of the historic legacy of Nazi occupation and the abhorrence felt towards local Nazi traitors during the war – especially among the older generation which still has vivid memories of the occupation. In these two countries, extreme nationalists have also faced many more obstacles in their attempts to take over central national symbols such as the flag, the national anthem, the national independence day and royal traditions. These symbols are embraced as positive embodiments of the collectivity by almost the entire population as well as by the political establishment, and are firmly linked to anti-Nazi and democratic traditions. Nevertheless, anti-immigrant nationalists in Denmark and Norway have launched a strong offensive aimed at capturing a very central set of national symbols as their own: the resistance movement against the Nazi occupiers and local traitors during the Second World War.

The anti-immigration discourse: 'resistance' against 'invaders' and 'national traitors'

A central element in the rhetorical strategies of organised anti-immigrant activists in Norway and Denmark is the desire to establish themselves as the new 'resistance movement', fighting 'foreign invaders' and present-day 'national traitors'. They try to achieve this desire by relating themselves to a set of symbols and values that in their original version are held in high esteem by the great majority of the population – symbols that represent true patriotism.

The discourse concerning 'the new resistance movement' and 'the national traitors' draws its symbolic material from a movement that was anti-Nazi (and therefore presumably anti-racist) and which – at least in Norway – saw itself as defending the legally elected institutions of democracy.[5] Today's anti-immigration activists have transformed this symbolic material into a discourse in which 'the resistance movement' embodies nationalism and patriotism directed against all foreigners (and particularly Muslims), and threatens violence and other forms of reprisal against elected institutions and civil servants involved in determining and administering current immigration policy. Most people consider this analogy is far-fetched – it is even highly offensive to many of those who had personal experience of Nazism during the war. Even so, a tiny minority of the population can be said to have accepted the analogy and have consequently lent their support to the transposition and appropriation of the notion of 'the resistance movement' to the fight against immigrants and the 'traitors' who support them.[6]

Arne Myrdal, the former head of Folkebevegelsen Mot Innvandring (FMI, the People's Movement Against Immigration)[7] who split off to establish the more militant Norge Mot Innvandring (NMI, Norway Against

Immigration), has been the leading proponent of a violent rhetoric that evokes civil war and violent reprisals against mainstream politicians and anti-racists defined as 'traitors' because of their immigration policies. He himself has a considerable record of violent behaviour.[8] Myrdal is certainly not the only one among the leaders of anti-immigrant organisations in Scandinavia to harbour such views. Other central leaders of the FMI and other nationalist organisations have expressed similar ideas publicly – although rarely as bluntly as does Arne Myrdal's civil war romanticism. The common denominator in all these discourses is a metaphor or trope that draws an analogy between the alleged mass immigration of Third World refugees, portrayed as an 'invasion', and Nazi Germany's invasion of Norway (and Denmark) in 1940. In this analogy, anti-immigration activists depict themselves as heroic resistance fighters, while anti-racist activists and proponents of a culturally plural Norway (often branded as 'red Nazis') along with politicians and civil servants, are redefined by analogy as the 'national traitors', the new quislings. These people will have to answer for their treason – just as Vidkun Quisling and his party, Nasjonal Samling, (NS, National Unity) had to.

FMI spokesman Jan Høeg, who uses every opportunity to stress his active participation in the Resistance during the Second World War, has played an important role in developing a common discourse among Norwegian and Danish anti-immigrant activists.[9] He writes thus in the periodical of the FMI's sister organisation Den Danske Forening (DDF, The Danish Association) about the Norwegian immigration policy:

> Twenty to thirty years from now, Quisling's treason will probably appear relatively insignificant compared with what [Prime Minister] Gro Harlem Brundtland has initiated in Norway. [...] Gro Harlem Brundtland's name [will also] be remembered as the name of the traitor who removed Norway's border posts and opened the gates for a free invasion of asylum parasites, deserters, and drug mafiosi by the thousands. ... Unless the course is altered very soon, we must unfortunately conclude that Norway has got its second traitor government within the span of a few years. (*Danskeren*, No. 5, December 1989)

The analogy with the resistance movement serves two important rhetorical purposes. First, it is an attempt to give the nationalism of anti-immigrant activists an aura of legitimacy as positive patriotism. If this is accepted, it may counter the claim that anti-immigrant activists are racists colluding with neo-Nazis. The second purpose by the analogy – sometimes expressed explicitly, at other times implicitly – is to legitimate the use of violence and other forms of reprisal against 'foreign invaders' and 'national traitors' (*landssvikerne*) – just as the resistance movement used violence against collaborators during the Second World War. Arne Myrdal, the FMI/NMI leader, has declared the legitimacy of violence in very unambiguous terms in an interview:

'The Norwegian population will no longer accept this national treason. When the politicians provoke the people, then the youth will resort to violence. First against the immigrants, then against those who promote immigration, and finally against the politicians and the System. Then the civil war will break out. It is too bad that the immigrants will be targeted – it is not their fault. [The young militants] should rather go for the politicians.'

'How?'

'By beating or killing them. The people will rise against them with violence. The Government and the Storting [the parliament] are out of touch with the people. When they do not govern the way we want, things will escalate to a civil war. There are many resistance groups, and the boys are armed. I know everything about this, I direct the resistance all over the country. There have been many weapon thefts [from military depots] during the last few years. These weapons end up with the resistance groups. It is not our intention to use the weapons against the immigrants. It is our own national traitors we have to fight against.'[10]

In apparent contradiction to this argument, Myrdal also describes immigrants and asylum seekers as 'pioneers' in a Muslim army of conquest. According to this theory, the 'so-called refugees' have come to establish 'bridgeheads' for Islam in Norway. This is part of an evil Muslim conspiracy to establish global Islamic rule.

> ... all those foreign intruders who have come here ... have not come to save their lives, as they have tried to make us believe. They have come for nothing less than taking over our country, in order to become so numerous as to make the Norwegians a minority in their own country. The Pakistanis in particular are highly determined in this respect. The FMI is a very unpleasant obstacle to their attempt to achieve this goal. It is therefore no wonder that they try to fight us with all possible means. (Myrdal 1990: 3–4)[11]

Thus, the argument goes, the resistance struggle must also involve 'resistance' against the Muslim intruders:

> The Muslims have come to conquer Europe. I believe there will be civil war in three years' time. We can either surrender and let them take over our country – rape our country! – or we may prepare ourselves for resistance, and that is what we are doing right now.[12]

Several of the central personalities in the anti-immigrant organisations did in fact take an active part in the wartime resistance movement. This historical link to the Resistance constitutes an important rhetorical resource for both Danish and Norwegian anti-immigration activists, exploited for all it is worth – and even more. The secretary of FMI, Gunnar Øi, mailed a series of harassing letters to the female secretary of a local anti-racist organisation in Norway, Brumunddal på nye veier (Brumunddal on New Paths). In one of these letters, he wrote: 'Hello, Judas! ... The writer of this letter took an active part in the resistance struggle through the war and consequently has had long experience in dealing with small national traitors of your calibre.' Arne Myrdal has also tried – though with some credibility problems – to exploit the legitimacy of the resistance movement: 'In my family, a cousin of my mother was a member of Milorg [the military resistance] – and they still dare to call me a Nazi! Such libels make me worry that we will have to take recourse to weapons in the future.'[13] In 1992, Arne Myrdal and the so-called Landsforeningen mot landssvikere (the National Association Against Traitors), with links to neo-Nazi activists, intensified their work of building up what they called a Traitor Register (Landssvikerregister). Myrdal even applied to the Data Protection Registrar (Datatilsynet) for a licence but – not surprisingly – was turned down. All the same, he and his partners continued to register enemies. During the autumn of 1992, his organisation NMI sent a form to a large number of individuals whom they wanted to have registered in their Traitor Register. Recipients were asked to fill in the form themselves 'to save us the work', as was stated in the accompanying note. This could perhaps be interpreted as a joke, but many of the recipients undoubtedly felt it threatening to be registered by extremists. This was probably also the purpose of informing them that they were under surveillance. The note also explained who the 'traitors' are:

> When foreign troops invaded and occupied our country in 1940–45, Norwegian traitors who assisted and cooperated with the foreigners were registered in a traitor register by good Norwegians and patriots. This register came to be used later during the treason trials.
>
>   Today it is again necessary to register new traitors who provide service for the enemy. … It is useful to assign and register such traitors in three categories:
>
>   1) *Governmental officials*: Major state/regional/municipal officials who by their acts or statements aid the foreigners and make possible further occupation – also by aggravating the situation of Norwegian patriots (ministers of state, government employees, civil servants, etc.).
>
>   2) *Political traitors*: Politicians and extremists in parties/groups/organisations who actively work against Norwegian patriots and assist the foreigners in their occupation of Norway (left-wing extremists, activists of Blitz [an 'autonomous' group], organised 'anti-racists', etc.).
>
>   3) *Other traitors*: Individuals who by *clear* acts and statements serve the enemy (for example, 'pro forma' wives of foreign immigrants,[14] dishonest journalists, frequent contributors to newspaper letter-columns, etc.).[15]

These registration and harassment activities bear clear parallels to the so-called Anti-Antifa lists circulating among German neo-Nazis, who have close connections to similar groups in several other countries – including Denmark, Norway and Sweden, Germany, Austria and Britain.[16]

The ZOG discourse: the 'white resistance movement' against the 'Zionist occupation government'

Whereas Norwegian and Danish anti-immigrant activists compare their struggle against immigrants and their helpers with the anti-Nazi resistance, neo-Nazi groups like the Vitt Ariskt Motstånd (VAM, White Aryan Resistance) take rather the opposite point of departure in their rhetoric. They see their fight as a direct extension of Nazi Germany's struggle against the 'insidious influence' of the Jews. Swedish neo-Nazis (and their Norwegian and Danish counterparts) base their ideas of the 'great race war' against the 'Zionist occupation government' and their lackeys on the old notions of a Jewish world conspiracy aimed at destroying the white race and subjugating the entire world to Jewish domination. More specifically, it is the further development of these ideas into a highly violent, revolutionary and terrorist doctrine by North American racist movements during the 1970s and 1980s that was adopted by Swedish neo-Nazis during the late 1980s. The ideological novel *The Turner Diaries* (see note 25) and the US terrorist group The Order, are important sources of inspiration for European racists.

Within the framework of the ZOG ideology, immigration is presented as a strategic weapon in the hands of 'the Jews' in their ongoing race war against 'the Aryans'. Through their 'malicious scheme of racial mixing' – and with the help of their liberal lackeys the Zionist occupation government – 'the Jews' disseminate perverting humanistic ideas of 'a common human race', such as tolerance and multiculturalism. This ZOG ideology has strong apocalyptic resonances. And since its adherents are the only ones who have seen the 'truth' of what is about to take place, they have no other choice but to resort to drastic, violent methods to impede the catastrophe. The pervasive feeling of fear that the social world they know – and the race they belong to – is threatened with annihilation, is apparent in the following extract from an editorial in the VAM magazine *Storm* (1992, No. 7–8):

> Our wonderful race is on the brink of *total* extermination. It is *our* assignment to save the *remnants* out of the decadence and misery of the present situation and restore [our race] to its former honour and greatness. This can *only* take place in *one* way, by struggle!

The idea that it is really 'the Jews' who are behind the immigration problem and the wave of refugees is fundamental to the way most neo-Nazis perceive the issue of immigration. This view is also shared by the less militant Norwegian organisation Zorn 88:

> As National Socialists we are more concerned with exposing the worldwide Zionist activities of deceit and banditry, and attacking the actual *cause* of the immigration problem, rather than turning against the individual *immigrant*.[17]

Moreover, the militant activists of the VAM network will often claim that in the race war it is more important to fight 'the Jews' and their obedient servants within politics, the bureaucracy and the media, than to go after the individual immigrant, who is merely a small pawn in a large game. The terrorist-oriented VAM cell Werwolf makes the following declaration in its magazine:

> Let us once and for all state clearly that the primary targets of the national revolution are not refugee camps or individual niggers. Attacks on these are generally a waste of our resources. Attacks must be aimed at newspapers, politicians, journalists and the police/prosecuting authorities. They are the ones who constitute a great but not insurmountable obstacle in our fight for freedom. For too long these traitors have escaped unpunished, despite their maladministration of Sweden, with mass immigration, increasing homosexuality, assaults on minors, the giving of Sweden away to the EC, etc.
>
> After every article harassing national movements, heavy attacks must be aimed at the newspapers and journalists who are responsible. Everything from bomb threats to grievous bodily harm and murder [is permissible]. For every national soldier who is sentenced to imprisonment we shall extract bitter revenge. We shall attack judges, jurors, prosecutors, witnesses and policemen.[18]

The virulent racism and anti-Semitism of the ZOG discourse has the potential to attract support from only a very marginal part of the population. For most anti-immigrant activists and 'moderate' nationalists this discourse is far too extreme.[19] Thus the movement's symbolic 'capital' is unsuitable for creating a rhetoric with any chance of winning support from larger segments of the population. On the other hand, this is hardly the objective of VAM activists. Within Nazi groupings and among young people who are attracted by their kind of rebellion against society, this extreme discourse serves as a test to cull out the 'soft' from the 'hard'.[20] These groups aspire to be an elite, not a mass movement. As a banner of rebellion and a boundary marker against the rest of society this extreme discourse is highly functional. The reactions of disgust and dissociation received from the group's surroundings merely serve to strengthen group identity and solidarity. But as a basis for more extensive political mobilisation aimed at winning political influence in the public arena, the ZOG discourse is totally unsuitable, as it lacks any links to values and symbols widely shared by the general public. However, the movement's rhetoric is not directed at society at large but at a small segment of the populace who are alienated from society and its hegemonic values.[21]

Although a marginal phenomenon, the Nazi-affiliated ZOG discourse has won somewhat larger support among racist and nationalist youth groups in Sweden than in Norway and Denmark.[22] This may be explained by the fact that, because of its wartime history, as discussed above, in Sweden there is no contradiction in terms between being both a patriot and a National Socialist.

In comparison, the rhetorical discourse that attempts to establish an analogy between the present-day resistance to immigration and the resistance movement against Nazi occupation has a much larger potential for mass mobilisation – even if this discourse is too much for most people to swallow.

Similarities and differences

Although the ideological points of departure of nationalist anti-immigration activists and of racist revolutionary neo-Nazi groups are different, the contents of their rhetoric and their agendas for action are strikingly similar.

Today's situation is defined as an *invasion/occupation* where the *foreign occupants* are supported by local *traitors*. These traitors are identified as the political establishment which by its immigration policy has laid the country open to foreigners who want to take it away from the indigenous population. The media, anti-racists and anyone who in one way or another takes a stand against racism or in support of immigrants and refugees, as well as local women who have intimate relations with foreign men, are all included among the traitors who are leading the nation/race towards annihilation. The only force standing up against this coalition – a *conspiracy* of evil forces – is a *resistance movement* of true patriots. To save the nation/ race from total disaster, this resistance movement will – if necessary – wage a *civil/race war*; it will wage this war partly against the 'foreign invaders', but primarily against the national 'traitors'.

The content and the structure of this rhetoric are almost identical whether used by nationalist anti-immigrant activists or by racist revolutionaries such as the neo-Nazis. The main difference relates to the sources and the bases of legitimacy, and to the subject identified as the foreign enemy. Nationalist anti-immigration activists in Norway and Denmark, who take the anti-Nazi resistance during the Second World War as their model and basis of legitimacy, stress the nation; racist revolutionary groups all over Scandinavia, on the other hand, who take their ideological material and symbols from National Socialism and related racist movements, put more emphasis on the notion of race. Although nation and race tend to intermingle in the rhetoric, the new generation of racists tends to be internationally oriented – these activists proclaim their solidarity with the 'white' or 'Aryan' race. Nationalist anti-immigration activists identify the primary threat as that of cultural mixing, while neo-Nazi and racist ideologists see racial mixing as the great threat.

There is, in fact, a fundamental dilemma built into all nationalisms with racist elements in their ideologies: the question of whether loyalty to 'race' or to 'nation' should take precedence in situations of conflict.[23] The tension between these two contradictory ideological principles has been a cause of discord and division within the National Socialist movement since its early days. Collaboration and treason have been common solutions to this ideological and political dilemma, illustrated by the behaviour of Nasjonal Samling and Danmarks Nationalsocialistiske Arbejderparti during the Nazi occupation, and by praise expressed by many British nationalists for Britain's arch enemy, Adolf Hitler.

When it comes to the question of who the main foreign enemy is, National Socialists and some other racist ideologists claim that we are facing a *Jewish* conspiracy to annihilate the white race and gain world domination. The nationalist anti-immigrant activists, on the other hand, claim that there is a *Muslim* conspiracy to conquer Europe and subjugate it under the rule of Islam.

Neo-Nazis and other radical racist ideologists share with the nationalist anti-immigration activists the idea that immigrants and refugees are merely instruments in a larger malicious scheme, but they may differ as to whether these immigrant groups are seen as independent actors or as relatively passive agents for the actual schemers. Accordingly, there is also some variation in the extent to which immigrant groups are seen as a main enemy in the allegedly approaching race/civil war – although there is no dispute that they will be expelled from the country, if necessary by violence. There is also full agreement that, on the day of retribution, true patriots will direct their wrath at the national/race traitors – those who have laid the country open to the foreign invaders.

Although some elements in the discourses described above are shaped by the particular national histories of the Scandinavian countries, the underlying patterns are certainly not unique to the Scandinavian scene. I will argue that these discursive patterns are typical of right-wing extremism in general.

The ZOG discourse and varieties of a Jewish world conspiracy theory appear in many parts of the world, and at times such ideas have not been limited to typical right-wing extremist circles. These notions have been spread through cultural diffusion and various forms of communication. Books and pamphlets such as *The Protocols of the Elders of Zion* and *The Turner Diaries* have played an important role in disseminating and popularising these anti-Semitic ideas. Certain religious traditions, represented in Christianity as well as in Islam, have also sometimes been instrumental in spreading anti-Jewish ideas to the more general public.

Conspiracy theories are recurring themes in right-wing extremism – although they also appear in the ideas of groups occupying other parts of the political spectrum and in different cultural and political contexts.[24] The most common form of conspiracy theory in right-wing extremist circles is undoubtedly the anti-Semitic variety. However, some observers, such as Michael Billig (1989), argue that these anti-Semitic conspiracy theories are essential and non-substitutable traits of right-wing extremism.

He claims that although fascist groups may have found new targets for their anti-immigrant rhetoric (now directed at Muslim rather than Jewish immigrants), they have not adjusted correspondingly the targets of their conspiracy theories. The anti-Islamic theme has not supplanted the themes of a Jewish or Zionist conspiracy, he argues.

Billig uses Jean-Marie Le Pen's Front National and the magazine of its anti-Islamic faction, *Vanguard*, as his main example. In order to distance itself from FN's pro-Islamic faction, *Vanguard* (November/December 1987) attacks Islam as 'the third deadly enemy of the white race, apart from communism and capitalism'. According to Billig, the ideology of Front National – as expressed in its publications – conceives of communism and capitalism as outward forms of a single enemy: Zionism (this view is probably not shared by everyone within the FN). The anti-Islamic theme that was added was not really integrated into this conspiracy theory, either as controlling the other two enemies (communism and capitalism), or as being controlled by them. On the question of why an anti-Islamic conspiracy theory was not slotted conveniently into an ideological space previously occupied by an anti-Semitic conspiracy theory, Billig's answer is that it is easier to adapt old arguments than to invent new ones. His argument and example are not quite convincing, however. One cannot expect an Islamic conspiracy theory to be an exact carbon copy of the Jewish conspiracy theory. Even the most inventive conspiracy theorist would not dream up the idea that capitalism and communism were invented and controlled by Muslims. Conspiracy theories need a grain of truth to work – they need isolated facts to which grand theories can be attached ('Karl Marx was a Jew'; 'many of the world's wealthiest capitalists are Jewish', etcetera).

In fact, Norwegian and Danish anti-immigrant activists (and some of their counterparts elsewhere) have actually done some inventive ideological work by integrating a theory of an Islamic conspiracy to conquer and dominate the world with their own notion of resistance against foreign invaders and local traitors. It should be noted that the idea of an Islamic conspiracy plays a relatively minor role in the overall discourse, particularly when compared with the more grandiose theories of Jewish conspiracies current in many right-wing extremist circles. It is also significant that Jewish conspiracy theories are almost completely absent from the discourse of leading Norwegian and Danish anti-immigration activists of the older generation. This is the case partly because in Norway and Denmark anti-Semitism is too closely associated with Nazism, and partly because these activists feel threatened by Islam and Muslims, not by Jews, Judaism or Zionism. Thus, contrary to Billig's view, an anti-Islamic conspiracy theory does indeed serve as a substitute for – and not as a supplement to – anti-Semitic conspiracy theories, at least in this particular brand of right-wing extremist discourse. The image of the Islamic threat parallels some aspects of the Jewish conspiracy theory, but is far from a carbon copy. Whereas anti-Semites hold that communism, capitalism and even liberalism were created as parts of a Great Zionist Conspiracy, the Islamic conspiracy theorists are more modest in their claims. They hold that the 'waves' of Muslim immigrants and asylum seekers are parts of a coordinated plan to conquer Europe for Islam, serving as vanguards to establish bridgeheads in preparation for the final *jihad*. This relatively simple conspiracy theory offers few clues to explain why local 'traitors' are assisting the Muslim conquerors – other than their 'internationalist', 'communist' and 'unpatriotic' orientation. Anti-Semitic conspiracy theorists are able to present elaborated explanations of why liberalism was created by 'the Jews' in order to destroy 'the white race' by poisoning the minds of naïve Christian whites with destructive ideas of 'multiculturalism' and 'racial equality'.[25] No anti-immigrant activist has yet to my knowledge come up with similar theories, or claimed that liberalism was an Islamic invention. Theories of Islamic conspiracies are so far not nearly as elaborated, sophisticated and pervasive as the corresponding Jewish conspiracy theories.

Islamic conspiracy theories may appear more credible to larger segments of the public, however, due to the fact that even among political elites, Islam is more and more replacing communism as the perceived main threat to Western civilisation. One expression of this trend was Samuel P. Huntington's controversial but highly influential article 'The Clash of Civilizations?', in which he asserted that 'the fault lines between civilizations will be the battle lines of the future' (Huntington 1993).[26] In particular, the notion that Islam is the West's new main opponent has been expressed in several statements by the former General Secretary of NATO, Willy Claes. In the post-Cold War political climate, Islamic conspiracy theories are likely to become more and more elaborated and appealing.

The 'Clash of Civilizations' theory, with its emphasis on cultural conflicts, combines well with the forms of nationalism promoted by such far-right politicians as Jean-Marie Le Pen and his Front National in France, the New Right in England, and the Scandinavian anti-immigration activists. The conception of a 'Muslim invasion' is widely held and promoted. In addition to displaying a taste for Islamic conspiracy theories, these movements focus on cultural rather than racial purity. They insist that cultural assimilation is inconceivable, and that mixing within a society will inevitably cause severe conflicts.

These versions of nationalist ideology are based upon the assumption that the 'natural order' of the world before history, modernity or imperialism started to mix things up was that ethnic or cultural groups were living apart in neatly separate territories. Ethnic conflict, racism, war and instability are seen as necessary outcomes when these 'natural' boundaries are overstepped and different cultural groups become mixed. Stability and peace can only be re-established when the various national (or cultural) groups find a way back to their natural, separate and homogeneous societies.[27] Some proponents of this form of nationalism hold that all cultures are, at least in principle, of the same value, although the same activists may (privately or even publicly) characterise these 'others' in strongly negative terms, indicating that some cultures should be held to be 'better' than others. This version of nationalist ideology may thus be seen as a form of cultural apartheid, closely resembling the theory of 'separate development' of different races expressed in the South African apartheid ideology.[28] Critical observers such as M. Barker and Etienne Balibar have respectively described this ideology as 'the new racism' or as 'differentialist racism'. More sceptically, Robert Miles argues that although the discourse of the New Right must be distinguished from traditional biological racism, politicians who use this discourse are merely making a disguised appeal to a broad constituency of voters – many of whom they know to be racists in the biological sense.

My comparative study of the two main discourses of the extreme right in Scandinavia brings out both the differences and the striking similarities between the anti-Jewish and openly racist discourse on the one hand and the anti-Muslim 'cultural clash' discourse on the other. Whether those promoting the latter are merely racists in disguise, using a discourse that is more acceptable to the general public for tactical reasons only, cannot be answered once and for all. Many of these activists do occasionally reveal that they hide 'real' racist attitudes behind the facade of cultural nationalism (anti-racists gleefully collect and publish such revealing statements), but other nationalist activists painstakingly steer clear of any deployment of an anti-Semitic or racist vocabulary, and may not even hold such beliefs. As Miles points out (Miles 1993: 73), however, what is clear is that the discourse they use is sufficiently ambiguous to appeal to both racist and non-racist constituencies. Seemingly incompatible discourses and conspiracy theories are fully able to coexist, and even to feed on each other. Many individuals seem to be able to shift between these discourses without being troubled much by logical inconsistencies and ideological contradictions.

Considered in the perspective of the discussion above, anti-Jewish conspiracy theories are not likely to have any kind of mass appeal in Scandinavia during the coming years; rather, they remain the preoccupation of a relatively small fringe. Some groups of youthful rebels may be inclined to embrace the ZOG discourse though, not least for its provocative effect. On the other hand, images of the Muslim enemy and Islamic conspiracy theories are likely to appeal to much larger sections of the population. Such notions may even gain some foothold within segments of the political and military establishment as part of a search for new enemy images following the end of the Cold War.

Notes

1. This chapter is a shortened version of a larger study presented in full as 'Extreme Nationalism and Violent Discourses in Scandinavia: "The Resistance", "Traitors", and "Foreign Invaders"', in Tore Bjørgo (ed.), *Terror from the Extreme Right*, Frank Cass, London, pp. 182–220.

2. Whereas the notion of 'discourse' focuses on communicative interaction, 'rhetoric' is often seen as involving a one-way communication – speeches rather than conversations. There are various definitions and approaches to the concepts of 'rhetoric' and 'rhetorical analysis'. For further discussion, see Heradstveit and Bjørgo (1992).

3. For more detailed analysis of these processes, see Bjørgo 1993a; 1993b.

4. Immigrants and refugees from non-European countries and their children born in the country of destination constitute only about 2 per cent of the total population in Norway and Denmark, but about 8 to 10 per cent in Sweden, which has had a longer and more generous history of immigration. Different definitions used in official statistics make it hard to come up with exact and comparable figures.

5. In Denmark, however, these institutions were to some extent discredited by their compliance with the German forces of occupation.

6. The nationalist, anti-immigrant parties that make use of this discourse have never been able to muster as much as 1 per cent of the vote on a national level in elections in Norway. They have nevertheless won single seats in a few municipal councils and regional assemblies. In Denmark, Stop Indvandringen (Stop Immigration) lists attracted up to 2.4 per cent of the votes in some localities in the 1989 local elections. Nationalist and racist parties are too small to qualify for parliamentary elections in Denmark.

7. Arne Myrdal was squeezed out of the FMI leadership in April 1991; he had become an embarrassment to the organisation on account of his not-so-subtle inciting to violence and his record of violence (see next note).

8. Myrdal was sentenced to one year in prison for preparing to blow up an asylum centre in 1989 (*Agder Lagmannsrett*, 12 September 1989; *Norges Høyesterett*, 24 May 1990); he was later sentenced to seven months in prison (reduced to four months on appeal) for inciting and leading a band of followers to attack a group of anti-racist demonstrators with sticks and clubs in 1990 (*Sand Herredsrett*, 24 November 1992; *Høyesterett*, 8 October 1993). Born in 1935, Myrdal has had a varied career, although limited formal education. He has been a low-ranking military officer, an unsuccessful businessman (convicted several times of financial offences), and the author of a highly controversial book on local history. He was also a rebellious local councillor of the Labour Party – from which he split to establish a competing local party which failed to win any seats in the subsequent election. Myrdal retired from political activism in 1994–95 due to failing health.

9. One example of the development of a common discourse among Danish and Norwegian anti-immigration activists is the notion of 'red Nazis', used to denote leftist and militant anti-racists. Whether this notion was coined in Denmark or in Norway originally is not clear, but it is much used by activists in both countries.

10. Quoted from this researcher's interview with Arne Myrdal, 23 June 1989.

11. This 'theory' is a recurrent theme in Myrdal's book (see pages 12, 17, 25 and 31).

12. Quoted from my own interview with Arne Myrdal (12 August 1989).

13. Arne Myrdal, quoted in *Verdens Gang*, 10 November 1991, after his un-successful 'popular meeting' in Oslo at which 10,000 people literally turned their backs on him in a massive demonstration of disgust.

14. Women having relations with male foreigners have also in many cases been subject to systematic harassment. This is a main topic in a 'school edition' of Myrdal's FMI periodical *Norge Er Vårt* (Norway Is Ours): 'Women who had affairs with Germans [during the Second World War], we used to refer to as "German whores" and "German mattresses". Today, women who have relations with asylum immigrants should be spoken of as *asylum mattresses*. Remember that!' Such relations appear to be extremely provocative to some white men, evoking primitive feelings of 'our women' being stolen and defiled by strangers. Many cases of racist street violence have taken the form of assaults on 'foreign men' who have taken local white girls out for a night on the town. In such situations, the racial dimension tends to come to the surface much more strongly than in other types of conflict between locals and immigrants. Violence may be directed both at the foreign man and the local woman.

15. Quoted verbatim from the note dispatched with a Traitor Register form mailed to this researcher, with a request that it be filled in 'to save us the work'.

16. Antifa is the name of the main militant anti-fascist movement in Germany, and Anti-Antifa was a campaign started by a number of neo-Nazi groups during the early 1990s to register, harass and attack these and other political opponents.

17. Erik Rune Hansen, editor of the Zorn 88 periodical *Gjallarhorn*, writing in No. 1/1, Autumn 1989. The name *Zorn* means 'holy wrath' in German, *88* is a common Nazi code for two of the eighth letter of the alphabet, 'HH', meaning 'Heil Hitler'.

18. Cited from *Werwolf*, No. 9 (undated, 1992). This internal VAM magazine is probably edited by Göran Gullvang, one of the most notorious neo-Nazis in Sweden, who has been convicted of several violent offences, including participation in the killing of a homosexual. Part of his reputation stems from the allegation that both his grandfathers were Norwegian quislings (one of them a guard in a German prison camp, Grini) who fled to Sweden after the Second World War (Swedish police source).

19. Norwegian and Danish anti-immigrant parties and organisations such as the FMI, DDF, Fedrelandspartiet and Stopp Innvandringen painstakingly avoid using concepts like 'Jews', 'Zionism' and 'race' in order not to be linked to the discredited Nazi tradition. There is no trace of anti-Semitism in the public statements of these organisations.

20. See *Storm*, No. 5–6, 1991, p. 16.

21. This is evident from the fact that these extremist groups conduct very active and organised recruiting activities among prison inmates (see *Storm* No. 7–8, 1992, p. 17).

22. Lööw (1993: 62) estimated the number of activists, members and sym-pathisers of the Swedish racist counterculture to be five to six hundred, growing slowly (seven to eight hundred is a realistic assessment for early 1994). In Norway, I estimate the number of young racists who subscribe to the ZOG and Nazi discourse at less than one hundred, based on available knowledge of the size of the relevant groups (the wartime generation of old Nazis is not included). More general racist and nationalist notions have a much wider appeal, and several new groups have been established and have grown during 1994–95. Many of these groups include both nationalists and National Socialists, however, and distinctions

are not clear. At the first skinhead concert in Norway in July 1995, about two hundred Norwegians and more than one hundred visiting skinheads from Sweden, Denmark and Germany were present. The Danish situation is much like the Norwegian one in terms of numbers.

23. The Norwegian historian Øystein Sørensen has discussed this dilemma in *Hitler eller Quisling?* (1989) and in his comment on a longer, Norwegian-language version of the present article 'Nasjonalisme og rasisme – et historisk apropos' (1994).

24. The Moscow Trials during Stalin's reign of terror exemplify an extreme case of a 'left-wing' conspiracy theory, whereas my study of agent and conspiracy accusations in Palestinian politics represents a completely different context (Bjørgo 1987). For a more general approach to conspiracy theories, see Graumann and Moscovici (1987).

25. See, for example, Andrew Macdonald (pseudonym for William L. Pierce) *The Turner Diaries*, The National Vanguard Books, Hillsboro, 1978/1980 (p. 42) and *Hunter*, The National Vanguard Books, Hillsboro, 1989 (chapters XII to XVI).

26. Huntington's article provoked a lively debate, but his views did receive support from many former cold warriors and others. In military circles, Huntington's views have been widely embraced.

27. Modern anthropology has shattered this myth. A large body of literature has shown that in all parts of the world, ethnic (and cultural) boundaries were overlapping geographically long before any corrupting Western influence had a chance to destroy the natural order of things. The articulation of ethnic or cultural differences has been a way of handling complex social situations arising out of such contexts. Ethnicity, it is argued, is primarily a political rather than a cultural phenomenon. See, for example, Moerman (1965); Barth (1969); Coon (1976).

28. The leading international proponent of this form of nationalist thinking is Jean-Marie Le Pen's Front National in France: according to it, each race or nation should stay in its place. In Scandinavia, several organisations and leading activists are strongly influenced by Le Pen, such as Sverigedemokraterna and the Norwegian nationalist magazine *Fritt Forum/Norsk Blad* along with its editor Michael Knutsen (see Knutsen 1993).

References

Balibar, Etienne and Immanuel Wallerstein (1991) *Race, Nation and Class: Ambiguous Identities*, Verso, London.

Barker, M. (1981) *The New Racism*, Junction Books, London.

Barth, Fredrik (ed.) (1969) *Ethnic Groups and Boundaries*, Universitetsforlaget, Oslo.

Berger, P. and T. Luckman (1985) *The Social Construction of Reality*, Penguin Books, London.

Billig, Michael (1989) 'The Extreme Right: Continuities in Anti-Semitic Conspiracy Theory in Post-War Europe', in Roger Eatwell and Noël O'Sullivan (eds) *The Nature of the Right: American and European Policies and Political Thought Since 1789*, Pinter Publishers, London, pp. 162–4.

Bjørgo, Tore (1987) *Conspiracy Rhetoric in Arab Politics: The Palestinian Case*, NUPI Report No. 111, Oslo, October.

— (1993a) 'Terrorist Violence Against Immigrants and Refugees in Scandinavia: Patterns and Motives', in Bjørgo and Witte (eds).

— (1993b) 'Role of the Media in Racist Violence', in Bjørgo and Witte (eds).

Bjørgo, Tore and Rob Witte (eds) (1993) *Racist Violence in Europe*, Macmillan, Basingstoke; also published in Norwegian by Tiden Norsk Forlag.

Coon, Carlton (1976) *Caravan: The Story of the Middle East*, Robert E. Krieger Publishing Company, New York.

Foucault, Michel (1972) *The Archeology of Knowledge and the Discourse on Language*, Pantheon, New York.

Gilroy, Paul (1987) *There Ain't No Black in the Union Jack*, Hutchinson, London.

Graumann, C. F. and S. Moscovici (eds) (1987) *Changing Conceptions of Conspiracy*, Springer Verlag, New York.

Heradstveit and Tore Bjørgo (1992) *Politisk kommunikasjon: Introduksjon til semiotikk of retorikk*, TANO, Oslo.

Huntington, Samuel P. (1993) 'The Clash of Civilizations?' *Foreign Affairs*, Summer.

Kårhus, Randi (1992) 'Diskurs som analytisk begrep', *Norsk antropologisk tidsskrift*, 2(3).

Knutsen, Michael (1993) 'Hva er egentlig nasjonalisme', *Norsk Blad*, 2–3: 9–12.

Lööw, Hélène (1993) 'The Cult of Violence – The Swedish Racist Counter-Culture' in Bjørgo and Witte (eds).

Lutz, C. A. and L. Abu-Lughod (eds) (1990) 'Introduction', in *Language and the Politics of Emotion*, Cambridge University Press, Cambridge.

Miles, Robert (1993) *Racism After Race Relations*, Routledge, London.

Moerman, Michael (1965) 'Ethnic Identification in a Complex Civilization: Who are the Lue?' *American Anthropologist*, 67: 1215–30.

Myrdal, Arne (1990) *Sannheten skal fram* (The Truth Must Be Told), Lunderød Forlag, Oslo, pp. 3–4.

Paine, Robert (ed.) (1981) *Politically Speaking: Cross-cultural Studies of Rhetoric*, Institute for the Study of Human Issues, Philadelphia.

Sørensen, Øystein (1989) *Hitler eller Quisling?* Cappelen, Oslo.

— (1994) 'Nasjonalisme og rasisme – et historik apropos', *Internasjonal Politikk*, 52(1).

CHAPTER 4

International Migration in Europe: Social Projects and Political Cultures

Umberto Melotti

International migration in Europe

International migration from the South to the North and, more recently, from the former communist Europe to the West poses an immense challenge for west European countries. Almost everywhere, immigration policies are intensely debated. Yet the policies adopted in response to this population movement show striking differences at both national and local levels. A comparison between European countries might thus be useful, especially because the differences between them have persisted even though in the last few years they have encountered the same dynamic factors, and have had to orient their policies towards the same general principles as a result of the increasing influence of the European Union (EU).

This chapter focuses on the peculiar situation in Italy, and on southern Europe more generally. It opens, however, by sketching an overview of international migration to and within Europe (see Figure 4.1). In western Europe non-citizen immigrants from both continental and extra-continental countries, total about twenty million, one sixth of all aliens worldwide. Of these, nearly seventeen million (more than four fifths) live on a regular basis in the fifteen EU countries, in very high concentrations in some of them. In fact, about 12.5 million (more than two thirds) live in just three countries with long traditions of in-migration: Germany, France and the UK. Italy, a new country of immigration, comes fourth.

In so far as EU countries are concerned, a distinction needs to be made between immigrants originating from other countries of the EU (5.5 million, less than one third) whose legal status in many respects equals that of local citizens, and those coming from countries outside the Union (11.5 million, more than two thirds). The latter nowadays constitute the core of the immigration issue, all the more so since only a small percentage come from developed countries, with the large majority (90 per cent) coming from underdeveloped countries, and in many cases

Figure 4.1 Non-naturalised immigrants in the EU and Switzerland (based on Eurostat data on 1 January 1993, published in 1995)

Country	Immigrants	Immigrants as % of all EU immigrants
Germany	6,496,000	38.5
France	3,597,000	21.3
UK	2,020,000	12.0
Italy	924,000	5.5
Belgium	909,000	5.4
Netherlands	757,000	4.5
Austria	518,000	3.1
Sweden	496,000	2.9
Spain	385,000	2.3
Greece	200,000	1.2
Denmark	180,000	1.1
Luxembourg	129,000	0.8
Portugal	122,000	0.7
Ireland	90,000	0.5
Finland	41,000	0.2
Total EU	17,000,000	100.0
Switzerland	1,260,000	–

experiencing severe social problems. The same three countries with the highest absolute number of immigrants rank highest for non-European immigrants.

These data, although referring to legal immigrants only, give a rough picture of the present situation. In some countries such as Italy, however, the number of undocumented immigrants is extremely high. If these are taken into account, the total number of foreigners in Italy triples to almost 1.5 million according to the latest – and very cautious – estimates, from the significantly lower official figure of around half a million (230,000 resident and 270,000 non-resident) provided by the 1991 census; this census completely missed the goal of measuring the actual size of the immigrant presence. Italy probably wins a less-than-desirable first place in Europe: for the highest number of irregular immigrants, both in absolute and in relative terms.

It is important to stress that these statistics do not include naturalised citizens, whether those obtaining citizenship prior to immigration (frequent in the past in countries with longstanding colonial traditions such as Britain, France, the Netherlands and Portugal) or after immigration, through naturalisation, which in some cases (France, the Netherlands and Sweden, especially) still is, or at least was until recently, a fairly easy practice. In

France, citizens born in other European countries such as Italy, Spain, Portugal, Greece, Poland, Yugoslavia and Russia, or descended from people born in these countries, comprise more than six million, and those of African origin almost match this figure. The Federal Republic of Germany has always regarded Germans coming from the former German Democratic Republic and other East European countries as its own citizens. As for Italy, the descendants of Italian emigrants, although born abroad, can easily obtain or recover Italian citizenship. Thus, many Argentinians or Brazilians of Italian origin do not appear in the Italian immigrants statistics.

Immigration policies in Europe

Explicitly or implicitly, the policies of the traditional European immigration countries are all inspired by a global social project: a set of ideas with an overall coherence that orients their choices, both on the control of incoming flows of migrants and on how to handle the stocks of immigrants already present on their territories. These projects are subject to substantial criticisms, however, and, moreover, they have already reached crisis point as a result of remarkable changes that have recently occurred in migration patterns. This point is highlighted by the three paradigmatic cases of France, the UK and Germany, to which I now turn.

The French project: ethnocentric assimilationism The French project is characterised by its ethnocentric assimilationism. This constitutes an answer to the specific function performed historically by immigration in France, the only European country that has used it from as far back as the nineteenth century to cope not only with temporary labour shortages, but with a chronic demographic crisis.

Indeed France, which at the time of its revolution in 1789 had the largest population in Europe, at the beginning of the nineteenth century experienced the demographic effects of the revolution and the Napoleonic wars and also experienced a sharp fall in its birth rate. So when, after 1820, the industrialisation of the country began, the demand for labour could not be met by the internal supply. The demographic crisis has continued, with peaks and lows, to this day; among the various reasons can be counted the continuous toll in lives taken by the wars fought both in Europe and in the colonies (notably, in the twentieth century, the two great world wars and the wars in Vietnam and Algeria).

This situation has favoured continual in-migration, both temporary and permanent. French society has tried to integrate migrants in the only way conceivable in a country that pictures itself as a great homogeneous nation and is deeply identified with a strong centralised state – a state that acknowledges no national minorities or local ethnic groups and vigorously contests any claim for particularist mediations between its institutions and its citizens. The latter, on the other hand, are entitled, on a egalitarian basis, to the formal rights solemnly proclaimed by the Declaration of 1789, of which the French Republic considers itself to be heir.

Integration, in this context, calls for assimilation to French culture as shaped by the ideology of the *État-Nation*. In effect, according to this project, immigrants, far from using their ethnic and cultural identities as strategic resources, must drop them completely in order to become 'good Frenchmen', a process that rests upon assimilation in the fields of language, culture and, if possible, mentality and character itself (for further discussions, see Chapters 5 and 6 of this volume). In return, the French state grants immigrants the same rights enjoyed by native citizens, thanks to so-called 'naturalisation' (as the grant of citizenship is significantly termed). The beginning of assimilation is thus rewarded and further social integration is encouraged. Indeed, even those immigrants who do not obtain French citizenship do at least give birth to French children (*ils feront des bons français*, as proclaims the title of a recent book on immigration in France). In accord with its assimilationist approach, since the middle of the nineteenth century (1851) France has privileged the *jus loci* (right of place) as concerns citizenship, in contrast with countries of emigration, which usually privilege the *jus sanguinis* (right of blood) in order to allow their emigrants' children to retain their citizenship (this was specifically the case in Italy, which, as a country of emigration until a few years ago, has continued to privilege the *jus sanguinis* and only recently, after becoming a country of net immigration, has partially reviewed its norms to give more weight to the *jus loci*).

This French national assimilationist project has long found a specular image in French colonial policy. Indeed, the ethnocentric universalism that was a prominent feature of that policy rested upon the principle that the *évolués* of all races and cultures could acquire the same rights as native French citizens thanks to their assimilation (though in practice only a small percentage of them achieved this). But just as the colonial policy, after significant results, ultimately failed to counter the desire for independence of the colonised, so too the national immigration policy, after remarkable successes, has entered a deep crisis and seems now to be unable to cope with the problems of the new immigration.

Because it favoured assimilation, France preferred for as long as possible to draw its immigrants from other Latin and Roman Catholic countries: in the nineteenth century from Belgium, which in its Walloon area was, moreover, a French-speaking country; then, from the beginnings of the twentieth century up to the 1970s, from Italy, Spain and Portugal. But the labour reserves of these countries have become exhausted and now most immigrants come from areas both geographically and culturally far more remote: the Maghreb countries, which speak Arabic and observe Islam; West Africa, another region where Islam prevails, and Southeast Asia, where Buddhist or Confucian traditions prevail. Although immigrants from some of these ex-colonies speak French as a vehicular (that is, practical) first foreign language, the assimilationist project has collapsed in the face of the greater cultural distance of these immigrants, their much more obvious ethnic distinctiveness, their significant numbers and their organisation in family groups and ethnic communities that claim their own cultural identity and promote the preservation of links with their countries of origin. At the same time, the assimilationist project has begun to appear inherently less and less legitimate, as the old idea of France's civilising mission fades away and the value of respect for cultural differences increases, together with awareness of the moral unfairness of making the granting of many important rights conditional on the acquisition of citizenship – all the more so in a context where this implies renouncing one's own cultural identity, the preservation of which is more and more regarded as an inalienable personal human right.

For these very reasons, sensitive circles have begun to debate the need to promote a more 'secularised' view of the relationship between citizenship and nationality which in France, with its powerful republican tradition, are unduly conflated even more than in other countries.

Against this trend, the growing Arab and Muslim presence, which is the most sizeable element in today's immigration and perceived to be the hardest to assimilate (see Chapter 6), has generated a real 'invasion syndrome' which feeds xenophobic sentiments and reactions. In this context, a radical reform of the code of citizenship has been demanded by some in order to reinstate the ancient *jus sanguinis*. This reform, initially proposed by the extreme right (namely, the Front National), but later advocated also by the former President of the Republic, Valéry Giscard d'Estaing (1991) who is generally respected for his liberal ideas, was finally approved at least in part by the new political majority (1993). But this has stirred up the harsh reactions from the French left, faithful to the old assimilationist project, which it refers to as 'the republican model of integration'. Sami Naïr (1993: 2), for instance, a French sociologist of Algerian origin who was very close to the former leftist president Mitterrand, defined this reform as 'ill-fated not only for the immigrants, but for French citizens too, as well as for the French Republic itself'.

The theoretical efforts of certain 'progressive' intellectual circles seem no more satisfactory, however. These, in accord with the old ethnocentric universalist values (in France traditionally championed by the left), have stigmatised the defence of cultural differences as a new kind of 'differentialist racism' based upon culture instead of biology. Among the people blamed in this way has been Claude Lévi-Strauss himself, in spite of his seminal critique of any kind of racism and ethnocentrism. The French left, indeed, seems to be affected by a strong defiance of all attempts to confront the problems of immigration from outside the traditional assimilationist approach. Of course, this is partly a reaction to the New Right, which, using Lévi-Strauss's ideas in its own way, has theorised the 'right to difference' as the right to ethnic and racial segregation, completely ignoring Lévi-Strauss's complementary invitation to implement a dialogue between cultures.

At any rate, in France the problem of immigration is still discussed in terms of 'integration': an expression often hardly more than a euphemism for the old notion of 'assimilation' (though with a stress on its social, rather than cultural, dimensions), which continues to reduce new settlers to France into raw materials, without history or culture, ready to enter the great assimilating machine of French society.

In fact, in the last few years, this machine has shown signs of grinding to a halt. Besides the increased resistance of the new immigrants themselves to assimilation, there is the crisis affecting the old socialising agencies (schools, army, factories, trade unions, political parties), as well as the difficulty for the Roman Catholic Church (which, however, plays a much lesser role than in Italy or Spain) of speaking to the immigrants, who are now mostly Muslims. In addition, French culture itself is changing as a result of processes of globalisation, European integration and the adoption of foreign habits, especially by French youth.

Despite the evident ideological crisis, many institutions linger on by inertia, driven by old ideas. Suffice it to recall here that schools, which should play a crucial revitalising role, in France still fail to grant any room for diversity, as we have been reminded in all too grotesque a fashion by the severe measures repeatedly taken against Muslim girls 'guilty' of wearing their headscarves in state schools.

Nevertheless, the evident inadequacies and contradictions of the traditional model of integration have generated an important debate regarding the possibility of introducing a new 'intercultural' approach to social life, and particularly in education. Its aim, almost revolutionary in France, is not only to defend cultural pluralism, but to use the new cultural presence as an important opportunity for mutual enrichment.

Despite this debate, however, what still prevails in practice is the old policy, so deeply rooted in French political culture. This policy turns out to contain increasing contradictions in the aims and purposes it officially proclaims (Touraine 1991).

The British project: uneven pluralism The British project is substantially different from the French, as substantially different as is the political culture that inspires and supports it; that political culture is a pragmatic one, which underlines the role of intermediate social formations, autonomy, decentralisation and particularism. Social regulation, for example, is marked by a mistrust of abstract principles and a reliance upon the decisions of local administrations, with reason termed 'local government' owing to their significant power. In France, by contrast, despite the recent attempt at regional decentralisation, almost everything goes through the central organs of the state or its peripheral extensions.

A common feature of the British and French projects is a strong ethnocentrism. This, however, assumes quite different, if not opposing, forms in the two countries. In France, as we have seen, it manifests itself in a universalist way, with the claim that all immigrants, regardless of their race and culture, can and must become 'good Frenchmen'. In the UK it manifests itself in a particularist way: there is no expectation that immigrants should ever become good Englishmen, Scotsmen or Welshmen, although they are expected to be loyal and law-abiding British citizens. The differences of immigrants are therefore taken for granted, and the main concern is to make sure that immigrants cause as little damage as possible to the 'British way of life' (since it is implicitly assumed that control must remain in the hands of native Britons, who democratically term themselves not 'whites' or 'Anglo-Saxons', but 'the majority').

Such a project, as in the French case, is in part a counterpoint to and in part an extension of the old colonial policy. This policy, which in the French case was characterised by direct rule and an assimilationist approach, in the British case was distinguished by indirect rule and a differentialist approach. In other words, Britain generally allowed the colonised people to preserve their own traditions and social and political organisations if they would, provided that above them they recognised the authority of its representatives: the viceroy or the British governor. This tolerance of difference has subsequently been the basis for the Commonwealth, which has outlived decolonisation, whereas the Communauté Française, its untimely imitator, was soon obliged to declare its own failure.

In the UK, immigration from distant regions started soon after the second world war, typically from countries of the New Commonwealth – former British colonies in Asia, Africa and the West Indies whose natives could, until the Commonwealth Immigration Control Act of 1962, freely enter the UK as 'British subjects'. The racially, ethnically and culturally distinct groups created by this population movement soon formed their own communities, whereas in France, until 1981, any kind of association between immigrants was practically forbidden. As a result in Britain 'ethnic communities' are very important reference points for public authorities, while in France, partly by choice and partly by necessity, the authorities tend to address immigrants individually and directly (see also Chapters 5 and 6 of this volume).

In the UK juridical status itself, rather than drawing a clearcut line between citizens and non-citizens, envisages a range of intermediate positions linked to the prior existence of a special category, citizens of the Commonwealth, and the present differentiation between citizens according to their place of birth and British ancestry (so-called 'patriality'). But this barely affects the status of ex-Commonwealth immigrants domiciled in Britain who have been granted full citizenship rights, including the right to vote and stand for Parliament, as well as in local elections. Since immigrants are often concentrated in certain electoral districts this affords them considerable political influence.

Thus we are dealing with a highly flexible system which has long proved to have an enviable capability to cope with social change. Yet even this system is revealing its own inadequacies and deficiencies.

The most important ethnic community push has been for a shift to a true multiculturalism, which would involve the abandonment of cultural hegemony by the native Britons. In particular, the second generation of immigrants has harshly criticised a system that recognises communities but confines their members to a subordinate position, unduly emphasising their ethnic and racial 'difference'.

At this point, we must recall that the debate on the presence of immigrants, which in France is mainly centred on the 'integration of immigrants', in the UK is focused upon 'race and ethnic relations'. The problems most passionately discussed are those of the rights of 'racial and ethnic minorities'; the very words themselves indicate the contentious nature of the debate. John Rex (1990) has defined this situation as a 'segregated form of inequality', arguing that the UK has yet satisfactorily to 'integrate' its immigrants.

To counter the development of racism, the UK has taken special legislative and administrative measures aiming not only to prevent social and economic discrimination, but also to promote equal opportunities for racial and ethnic groups (see Chapter 11). At the same time immigrants are expected to master the English language fully and to participate on an equal footing in most national civic and political institutions, rather than as culturally defined 'groups'.

Thus the future of immigrants and their descendants in the UK remains open. As Mike O'Donnell has written, 'Britain could either become a successful multi-racial and multi-ethnic society or very much the opposite' (1991: 139).

The German project: the institutionalisation of precariousness The German social project is very different. Indeed, Germany, which is the European country with the highest absolute number of immigrants and the highest absolute and relative number of immigrants from outside the EU, tends to deny its well-established status as an immigrant host country. This is why many official documents, as well as many politicians, continue to repeat the old saying, surely much more ideological than descriptive, according to which 'Deutschland is kein Einwanderungsland' ('Germany is not a country of immigration').

In fact, Germany, which for a long period was an important country of emigration, became an immigrant country as far back as the end of the nineteenth century. After the Second World War it even recruited foreign labour abroad to meet the needs created first by post-war reconstruction and then by the long period of economic expansion that reached its peak in the so-called German 'economic miracle'. Immigrants, however, have always been considered 'guest workers' (*Gastarbeiter*), that is, workers present in the country only temporarily.

Nevertheless, the kind of temporary migration that configured them as such vanished long ago, in 1973, when Germany closed its border to further labour immigration. This measure indirectly favoured the settlement of a large proportion of the workers already present in the country, who, together with their families which soon joined them, have eventually generated what demographers call a 'population issued from migration'. But refusal to acknowledge this dramatic change has prevented the politicians from working out a clear project for that population. Indeed, the policy followed can more easily be defined in negative than positive terms: 'Neither integration nor segregation', to quote an anthropologist highly familiar with that situation (Giordano 1987).

In Germany, in fact, immigrants fundamentally remain 'foreigners' (*Ausländer*). Their economic contribution may be appreciated, but their permanent settlement is in no way encouraged. They are allowed to live in the country for lengthy periods, even generations, but this fact, at least in principle, does not entail any change in their status. Indeed, the acquisition of citizenship by immigrants is not envisaged at all: naturalisation is very difficult to obtain and even an immigrant's children born in Germany remain foreigners – foreigners in their own land – since *jus sanguinis* prevails over *jus loci*, if they are not in the position to become naturalised. Far from favouring the 'nationalisation' of immigrants, Germans expect them to be ready to leave the country at any time, not only out of free choice, but also in consequence of an economic or political crisis or even a government decision. Social policies do not aim at assimilating immigrants, therefore, but rather at safeguarding their language and culture in anticipation of their return, which has for long been the object of several incentives, though with limited results.

Like the immigration projects of France and the UK, Germany's is deeply rooted in a local, historically evolved, political culture. Germany was the last of the great European countries to be constituted into a nation-state and this was formed far later than the German nation. On the other hand, in Germany 'belonging' to the nation – far from being conceived in subjective and ideological terms as in France, where in Renan's words it constitutes a 'daily plebiscite' – was always conceived of in objective, ethnocultural terms as a fact linked to blood and land (*Blut und Boden*) and founded on the putatively irreducible specificity of the German people (*Deutsches Volk*). Even after the Second World War, as a result of the humiliating division of Germany by the Allied powers, this notion of belonging continued to have priority over membership in a state. German refugees coming from Eastern Germany (the so-called *Übersiedler*) and even descendants of the Germans who established themselves many generations ago in East European countries (the so-called *Aussiedler*) have always been regarded by the Fundamental Law of the Federal Republic of Germany as potential citizens in their own right (as such they have never been considered 'foreign' immigrants). Similarly, the central idea of the nation has favoured a tendency to preserve the alleged ethnocultural homogeneity of the German people and to resist its dissolution (albeit implicitly more than explicitly, since the Nazi regime thrived upon that myth of homogeneity with well-known results).

The influence of this idea on immigration policy could not be clearer. Its 'crucial care' is to distinguish between Germans and foreigners, as a well-known German specialist has pointed out (Blaschke 1993). In fact, all the existing norms encourage only a temporary presence of immigrants, and aim to prevent their rooting in German soil. With this negative goal, priority is given to measures emphasising presence for reasons of work, such as the establishment of hostels paid for by the employers and therefore only open to workers (in Italy, by comparison, hostels are paid for by the state or the municipalities and are open also to the unemployed and to any kind of marginalised person).

Moreover, this policy has the effect of discouraging families from joining workers, a choice allowed for the sake of human rights, but not embraced with any enthusiasm. In the same way, social and cultural activities both for workers and their children tend to favour the preservation of links with their country of origin. In particular (as both Schiffauer and Yalçin-Heckmann show in this volume) with regard to primary education, efforts are made to allow foreign children, both those born in Germany and those born abroad, to acquire or preserve the knowledge of their parents' country and language, while in France by contrast (see Chapter 6) education favours socialisation into the culture of the host country: it is given only in French, in the name of an absolute equality of treatment which is often interpreted in an all too chauvinistic way, and attempts to induce young people into forgetting the very existence of their country of origin, according to the approach already experimented with in the former French colonies, where the textbooks began with the now proverbial words 'Nos ancêtres les Gaulois'.

In the past few years, despite the well-known German efficiency and the laudable care of many local administrators, the situation of immigrants in Germany has manifestly worsened. Forty years of this ostrich policy (the only possible definition for this stubborn denial of the immigratory character of the country) has generated a piling up of so many problems that any optimism about their eventual likely resolution would seem quite misplaced.

Indeed, the government's programme of 1973 (after stating, once more, that Germany is not an immigrant country) set as an objective the so-called 'temporary integration' (*Integration auf Zeit*) of foreigners which, although a contradiction in terms, implied a serious effort 'to make the situation of immigrants more human'. But the transformation in the nature of immigration caused by the closing of borders the same year made the measures then foreseen totally inadequate. In fact, the complexity of immigration increased during the years that followed. On the one hand, there was a consolidation of the presence of immigrants already there, who sent for their wives and children. On the other hand, the arrival rate of clandestine and undocumented immigrants rose, the rate of unemployment increased even among the legal immigrants, and masses of 'refugees' (both genuine and fake) began to arrive from the Third World. Last, but not least, at the end of the 1980s the crisis of the Eastern European countries precipitated a flood of refugees which poured into the Federal Republic of Germany in successive waves, unprecedented in peacetime: more than 1.5 million refugees – a net total of around one million – arrived between 1989 and 1990, before Germany's reunification, counting both the *Übersiedler* and the *Aussiedler*. The absorption of the German Democratic Republic into the German Federal Republic in 1990 further complicated the situation by raising quite a number of new problems, arising from internal migration from the new *Länder* to the old ones and from the tensions that emerged between the Germans of both the new and the old *Länder* and foreign immigrants. In subsequent years the arrivals of *Aussiedler* did not stop (222,000 in 1991 and 230,000 in 1992) and arrivals of other refugees continued to increase (from 193,000 in 1990 to 256,000 in 1991 and 438,000 in 1992) until new restrictive measures were introduced in 1993. In this context, perhaps it is not surprising that racism and xenophobia have become a very serious threat – all the more so since the isolation of immigrants in hostels breeds prejudices and discords.

Nevertheless, the words pronounced by Richard von Weizsäcker, the president of the German Federal Republic, in front of the biers of five Turkish immigrants killed in 1993 in a cruel racist riot, give grounds for hope:

Do the extremists claiming 'Germany for Germans' want to change our Constitution? For it does not say *Germans'* dignity is inviolable; it says *human beings'* dignity is inviolable. ... As to the Turks, would it not be much better to begin to call them German citizens of Turkish origin?

What these experiences can teach

Some claim that history teaches life, others answer that it is only an idiot's tale, replete with sound and fury, signifying nothing. In the case of Italy, I think that by paying attention to the experiences of the three main European countries of immigration many mistakes in immigration policy could have been avoided, and other mistakes could still be avoided. But what do these experiences really teach?

France and Germany each had its own project for the post-1945 flow of immigrants: while France envisaged the permanent settlement of at least a share of them, and their assimilation, Germany envisaged only their temporary stay, and that there would be a turnover of immigrants to prevent their rooting. Both these aims were satisfactorily attained up to a point; but they were relatively easy to achieve in the context of economic expansion and so long as immigrants came from areas that were both culturally (with regard to the French project) and geographically (with regard to the German one) close. In Britain too immigrants experienced a relatively easy initial social insertion, thanks to a fairly steady demand for labour and the demographic decrease of the native population.

In the 1970s, when economic crisis severed the previous links between immigration and the demand for labour, migration spiralled out of control and all these countries were forced to close their borders. But, whereas it had been fairly easy to elicit immigration through recruiting policies, it turned out to be very difficult to stop it, and almost impossible to reduce the number of immigrants already present in a country. Immigrants, though unwelcome, kept on coming in through the channels of family reunification and political refuge whenever possible, or otherwise through clandestine channels. In the meantime, the nature of immigration changed even more profoundly, for the workers from southern European countries were progressively replaced by people originating from more distant areas. So immigration, which once could appear as the simplest and cheapest solution to a limited problem, labour shortage, became a major social problem.

'We have been looking for working hands, men have arrived', wrote the Swiss storyteller Max Frisch. His comment was not merely a populist criticism of the scant attention paid by the labour-importing countries to the human aspects of the process. This statement pointed out that immigration is a 'total social fact', to use Marcel Mauss's phrase. Even when it begins in response to an actual demand for labour, for a mutual economic interest (as in the three countries discussed above and in many others, such as Switzerland, Belgium and the Netherlands, but not Italy, Spain, Portugal and Greece), migration can never be a bare economic fact. It is a very complex social process, which usually creates far more problems than it solves.

During two decades of official closing of the borders in France, Germany and the UK, three countries with a long-standing and well-established immigration experience and, moreover, a remarkable capacity to manage social phenomena, the immigration process has undermined all the policies meant to contain it. Instead, each of these countries has been reduced to reacting to 'emergencies' after they surface, while the very tensions and conflicts their projects were supposed to avoid have become endemic. Moreover, the tensions and conflicts produced by the new containment policies all too often contain menacing ethnic and cultural undertones.

The holistic nature of labour immigration has always been underestimated by capitalist societies. In Europe it was believed that immigration could continue to be managed by assimilation (France), subordination (the UK) or separation (Germany), or a mix of these strategies (Switzerland). Yet all these policies have failed. Assimilation through loss of cultural identity, in France, hierarchisation disguised as pluralism, in the UK, and the perpetuation of mutual estrangement, in Germany, have all proved to be wholly inadequate, when not a remedy worse than the illness. In particular, in the context of these policies the cultures of immigrants, rather than becoming a factor in a process of mutual enrichment, have become perhaps the most explosive elements in a scenario already characterised by a strong propensity towards conflict.

The case of Italy

In this context, the envisaging of an idyllic passage to a peaceful multicultural society can only be an expression of cultural lag or ideological bias. But this is the picture indulged in by so many people of good will, engaged in an effort to describe the situation while avoiding any mention of its problematic features.

As a typical example, we may quote the first book on the 'multicultural society' in Italy, published by the Department of Information of the Italian government. Its author, a well-known TV journalist, portrays a smiling world made up of

> oriental rhythms and lambadas, couscous and Eritrean *zighinis*, African textiles and Arab-style trousers, kink hair plaits and gorgeous carpets in the underground stations, Muslim prayers and Ramadans, Brazilians *viados* and Nigerian prostitutes, Egyptian bakers and Polish and Bengali windscreen washers, Cape Verdian maids and Filipina nurses, Andean flutes and greetings with joined hands. (Ghirelli 1991: 78)

None of this can hide the fact that in Italy, immigration entails problems even harsher than in other European countries, that a unitary social project for dealing with it is still lacking and, in any case, its implementation would inevitably be entrusted to a crumbling administration incapable of performing even the most mundane duties of a modern state: defeating the Mafia and all the other forms of gangsterism, fighting the spread of drugs and Aids, keeping petty crime under control, uprooting the practice of bribery, or making retailers, professionals and self-employed workers pay their taxes.

In such a situation realism and concreteness are needed. Good will alone will not suffice; indeed, it might cause more harm than good. The shift to a multicultural society in these circumstances is an extremely difficult challenge. It calls for new relationships between state and civil society, between citizenship and nationality, between culture and social organisation. It is a process affecting the history not only of events, but also of institutions. Indeed, it is an epoch-making change which is inscribed in a conflictual and contradictory way in the *longue durée* of history.

As mentioned above, Italy has recently become one of the most important countries of immigration in Europe; it is now the major immigrant host country in the Mediterranean area. For Italy this was an major transformation. For more than a century Italy was a country of emigration, and even after the Second World War for two decades it continued to make the largest contribution to European migration (there are still 5 million Italian emigrants worldwide and 1.2 million in Europe, where they represent the second-largest national immigrant group after the Turks).

The change occurred at the beginning of the 1970s, but for a long time it remained almost unnoticed. In the 1960s, Italian emigration had gradually declined and foreign immigration had begun, together with a substantial return immigration of Italian emigrants back to Italy. In the following decade, foreign immigration to Italy increased, and in particular illegal immigration, in spite of the deep economic crisis of that period. This was mainly as a result of the persistent absence of any immigration controls in Italy, whereas at the beginning of that crisis all the traditional countries of destination in Western Europe had closed their borders to further labour immigration. In the 1980s, with the rapid recovery of the Western economies, immigration to Italy grew steadily and soon became numerically significant, in consequence both of pull factors (the considerable economic expansion of the country in the so-called 'golden eighties', 1982–1990) and of push factors (the increasing economic and political crisis of the Third World first, and Eastern Europe subsequently).

According to the Italian home ministry, the number of foreigners legally present in Italy doubled in the 1970s, rising from about 150,000 in 1970 to about 300,000 in 1980, and increased even more rapidly in the 1980s, reaching 781,000 in 1990 (these data reflect only the 'permits of stay' issued by the police). In subsequent years the number of immigrants continued to increase, in spite of restrictive measures approved in 1990,

and by August, 1996 it exceeded 1.2 million. The actual foreign presence
in Italy has always been far greater than these figures suggest, however,
because of the large number of undocumented immigrants. Even after
the three generous amnesties of 1987, 1990 and 1995 (which together
allowed almost 600,000 people to regularise their status), the number of
undocumented immigrants is estimated at between 300,000 and 500,000.
Of course, not all these 'foreigners' are 'immigrants', but most of them
are since the great majority do not regard their stay as only temporary.

Most immigrants, both legal and illegal, come from outside the EU,
the majority from Africa and East Asia; many others come from Eastern
Europe, the Middle East, Central and South America. Indeed, Italy is the
EU country with the highest proportion of non-EU immigrants to total
immigrants. Immigration in Italy began with the development of mass
emigration from the Third World (it is not by chance that foreign immigrants were long referred to as *terzomondiali*, 'people from the Third
World', a term which was later replaced by *extracomunitari*, 'people from
outside the EU', to include the immigrants from Eastern Europe). The
growth of powerful push factors in many African, Asian and Latin
American countries during the last decades has forced considerable
elements of their populations to move to Europe, including to those
southern peripheral countries (such as Italy, Spain, Portugal and Greece)
where immigration presents a rather paradoxical aspect since it coexists
with emigration (which is persistent, though modest) and unemployment
(which is very high: in Italy more than 12 per cent, with a remarkable
concentration in southern regions – where it reaches 20 per cent – and
among women and young people – 16 per cent and 25 per cent respectively).

This paradox is partly explained by the tendency of immigrants to
establish themselves in segments of the labour market that are relatively
uncontested by local nationals. In Italy the remarkable growth in household
incomes, largely based on precarious work and the shadow economy
especially in southern regions, cushions even long periods of youth unemployment. Social security schemes fulfil a similar function. Despite the
expansion of higher education, curricula hardly relate to actual labour
market demands, causing qualitative mismatches in demand and supply.
Nevertheless, in Italy, as in Spain, Portugal and Greece, many immigrants
remain unemployed or find insertion only in the informal economy; this
is the fate not only of undocumented immigrants. According to the
Ministry of Labour, two thirds of legal immigrants are themselves unemployed or only irregularly employed. It comes as no surprise, therefore,
if many immigrants eventually become involved in petty crime and, to a
lesser extent, in the illegal activities of the famous Italian criminal organisations – Sicily's Mafia, Campania's Camorra and Calabria's N'drangheta –
which now operate even outside their original territories. Many immigrants

create new 'jobs' for themselves, such as hawking and car window washing. These are extremely precarious, however, often verging on begging.

Immigrants are mainly present in the tertiary sector of the economy: domestic work, hotels and restaurants, catering, cleaning enterprises. However, they are also present in the primary sector, in seasonal agriculture and fishing, especially in southern regions, and to a more limited extent in the secondary sector, especially quarries and mines, building and foundries. After the amnesties for illegal immigrants of 1987 and 1990, more regular insertion into petty industry did begin, especially in northern Italy, but the renewed economic crisis soon stopped this process.

Particular nationalities tend to concentrate in a particular sector of the labour market. Most immigrants from the Philippines, Sri Lanka, Somalia, Eritrea, the Dominican Republic, Mauritius, Cape Verde and Salvador – in their great majority women – take up domestic work; the Chinese favour the catering sector; many Tunisians work on fishing boats; and many Moroccans and Senegalese become street vendors. This ethnic segmentation of the labour market was more evident in the earlier stages of immigration, however, and is now decreasing.

Immigrants once were concentrated in the regions containing the main ports of entry and the largest urban centres, and in some farming areas in the south, but nowadays are spread all over the country. However, they still congregate in the regions, provinces and towns where they are more likely to find work or at least living opportunities.

The first foreign immigrants to Italy were Chinese. Some small groups of them arrived between the two world wars, mainly from France. Their arrival did not remain unnoticed, but it was not regarded as a migratory event, though many of them established themselves in a part of Milan that later became the first little Chinatown in Italy. In the beginning, the Chinese worked mainly as street vendors; then they developed leather goods workshops, and in the mid-1960s they opened the first Chinese restaurants in Italy, which have now become very numerous and are distributed all over the country.

The start of the 1960s witnessed the first arrival of foreign women intending to work in Italy as maids. Most of them came from the former Italian colonies of Somalia and Eritrea in East Africa, accompanying Italian families returning from those countries when the Italian trusteeship of Somalia came to an end (1960) and when Eritrea was annexed by Ethiopia (1962). These women soon called for their sisters, cousins and friends, and many of these came willingly, all the more so as the economic and political conditions in the ex-colonies rapidly worsened.

Between the end of the 1960s and the mid-1970s, other women arrived with the same project from other countries: Cape Verde, the Seychelles, Mauritius, El Salvador, the Dominican Republic, Peru, the Philippines and India (specifically from Kerala). Most of these women were Roman

Catholics and were helped to immigrate by Catholic organisations, first in their countries and then in Italy. Because of the high demand for maids, these flows rapidly increased and women soon came to make up 50 per cent of all foreigners in Italy. This proportion – mainly a result of the scarce demand for male labour – remained almost unchanged until the second half of the 1980s, when male mass migration from North and West Africa considerably changed this situation. The high percentage of women, quite unusual in initial phases of immigration, was for many years one of the most remarkable traits of immigration to Italy.

During the 1970s, two other important groups arrived in Italy: the Tunisians in Sicily, called to work in agriculture, quarries and fishing, and the Yugoslavs in Frioul, called to work in the building industry after the earthquake of 1976, which caused considerable damage in this border region. The same period also saw the arrival of the first Egyptians. They established themselves in the main towns, particularly Milan, where they could find jobs in the tertiary sector, and to a lesser extent in some other areas (namely the provinces of Modena and Reggio Emilia, in Emilia-Romagna) where they were inserted into industrial activities, mainly foundries and pottery workshops. But employment in industry remained quite exceptional for all immigrants until the end of the 1980s.

In fact, throughout the 1970s the most important flow was that of political refugees, coming from a great number of Third World countries: Chile, Argentina, Uruguay, Brazil, Libya, Palestine, Turkey (Kurds), Iran, Ethiopia (Eritreans), Somalia, Sri Lanka (Tamils), and Vietnam (so-called 'boat-people'). Italy did not grant them the refugee status foreseen by the Geneva Convention of 1951, since like some other countries it had signed that convention with a 'geographical clause' that limited its application to people originating from other European countries. Nevertheless, all refugees could remain in Italy, even if not officially recognised as such, with substantial Italian financial support and under the protection of the United Nations High Commissioner for Refugees (UNHCR) with which the Italian government had signed a special agreement.

Another trait of immigration to Italy has thus been the presence of a very large variety of national and ethnic groups since the very early phases of immigration, while for a long period in France, the United Kingdom and Germany, the large majority of non-European immigrants came from a much more limited number of countries: Algeria and Tunisia in the case of France; India, Pakistan and the West Indies in the case of the United Kingdom; and Turkey in the case of Germany.

The 1980s in Italy saw the arrival of masses of North Africans, mainly from Morocco and Tunisia, West Africans, mainly from Senegal, Nigeria and Ghana, and South and East Asians, mainly from the Philippines, Sri Lanka and Pakistan. The same period also witnessed the arrival of many East Europeans – first Poles, attracted among other things by the presence of a Polish pope in Rome; then Romanians, Russians and Bulgarians. In the next decade there was the shock arrival of two unprecedented waves of Albanians (thirteen thousand in March and twenty thousand in August 1991) followed by refugees from Somalia and the former Yugoslavia, fleeing violent civil wars. From Eastern Europe came many thousands of Gypsies. In the first months of 1997 there was a new wave of Albanians, over twenty thousand in a few weeks.

As a result of this rapid but very complex process, the migratory panorama in Italy is characterised by a great number of national groups, none of which (at least so far as legal immigrants are concerned) comprises more than 100,000 people.[1] This extreme variety of national and ethnic groups in part favours and in part impedes immigrant integration.

For many years (1970–87) the political response to immigration was a sort of *laissez-faire*, that is, no response at all. Later, for a brief period (1987–90), there was a policy of unconditional regularisation, inspired by Christian and leftist feelings of solidarity. Later again (1990–97), when owing in part to such policies the presence of unemployed immigrants (both legal and illegal) reached a worrying level, there was a shift to a policy of control and restrictions, though poorly implemented and scarcely effective. This obliged the government to adopt a new extraordinary regularisation measure in 1995.

Italian legislation concerning immigration is very recent, though immigration began more than twenty years ago. This legislation mainly consists of two laws: the n. 943 of 1986 and the n. 39 of 1990 (known as Martelli's Law after the young socialist vice-president of the Council Ministries who proposed and imposed it). Some subsequent laws concern the introduction of visas for citizens of countries considered an 'emigration risk' and some 'humanitarian exceptions' for people coming from countries at war or in deep crisis, such as Somalia and the former Yugoslavia, and now Albania.

The two laws mentioned above mainly deal with the regularisation of non-EU immigrants already in Italy (as in the decree law of the technical government of Signor Dini in 1996). They also outline the immigrants' rights and define some measures for their integration. Between them the two laws guarantee all non-EU workers legally resident in Italy and their families complete equality of rights and treatment with Italian workers. At the same time, they recognise their right to obtain houses, attend schools, organise associations and maintain their cultural identities. They have also instituted a national consultative body composed of representatives of immigrant 'communities'.

Included in the laws is a programme of social and economic measures aiming to integrate immigrants socially and culturally, with considerable funds allowed to implement their rights to education and housing. In addition, the laws guarantee free registration for health and welfare care for one year (later extended to three) after regularisation. They also abolish the geographical clause that had prevented the Italian administration from granting refugee status to people coming from non-European countries, and provide particular forms of aid for political refugees.

The regional and local authorities have been entrusted with many of these tasks. Despite the notorious differences between Italian regions, local consultative bodies and monitoring systems have been set up almost everywhere; policies of social and health assistance have been defined, together with some measures dealing with the initial reception of immigrants; literacy and vocational courses have been introduced and the constitution of associations has been promoted.

This legislation tends to endow non-EU immigrants with all the civil, social and economic rights enjoyed by Italians. However, the right to vote was not granted until 1997, and then only at a local level. By contrast, the immigrants' right to sustain their national and religious identities is strongly affirmed. On the other hand, the new citizenship law (1992) has introduced a new discrimination. The period of regular stay in Italy required for the acquisition of Italian citizenship, which was previously five years for all residents, has been reduced to four years for EU citizens and prolonged to ten years for others.

Conclusion

Italy seems to be moving, though with some contradictions, along the same lines as European countries with longer experiences of immigration. In effect, all of them are now moving from their old, reductive policies of 'assimilation', 'separation' or 'uneven pluralism' to a new multicultural model of integration, which should favour equality and respect for cultural differences. However, a substantial discrepancy still exists between the formal definition of rights and their implementation. In most cases the rights to housing, work and health care remain theoretical (as is true also for many Italians). A good deal of assistance, especially in central and southern regions, is still provided only by voluntary associations, often depending on the Roman Catholic Church, which in this field still performs a considerable role of substitution for public authorities.

Moreover, in the last few years the situation has greatly deteriorated and remarkable social tensions have emerged. Italy has not historically been a racist country, but intolerant attitudes towards immigrants have increased. To a large extent, this seems to be the result of a long-standing underestimation of the magnitude of the changes and thus poor policy implementation for a lengthy period, in spite of the best intentions officially proclaimed.

Note

1. The numbers of legal immigrants originating from different countries are as follows: Morocco 93,000; Former Yugoslavia 89,000; Tunisia and the Philippines 41,000 each; Albania 32,000; Senegal 25,000; Egypt 21,000; Brazil, Romania and China 20,000 each; Poland and Sri Lanka 19,000 each; Somalia 16,000; India, Ghana and the Former Soviet Union 13,000 each; Argentine 11,000; Ethiopia 10,000; Peru, Colombia, Iran, Dominican Republic, Mauritius, Nigeria, Pakistan, Bulgaria, former Czechoslovakia, Bangladesh, Turkey, Hungary, Lebanon, Mexico, Cape Verde and South Korea – between 4,000 and 10,000. There are, moreover, many alien residents in Italy originating from developed countries, both inside and outside the European Union: the United States (57,000), Germany (37,000), the United Kingdom (26,000), France (26,000), Switzerland (18,000), Spain (16,000) and Greece (14,000).

References

Blaschke, Jochen (1993) 'Tendenze delle migrazioni e relazioni etniche nella Repubblica Federale Tedesca', in M. Delle Donne, U. Melotti and S. Petilli (eds) *Immigrazione in Europa: solidarietà e conflitto*, Dipartimento di Sociologia, Università di Roma 'La Sapienza', Rome, pp. 143–56.

Ghirelli, Massimo (1991) *La società multiculturale in Italia*, Presidenza del Consiglio dei ministri, Dipartimento per l'informazione e l'editoria, Rome.

Giordano, Christian (1987) 'Né integrazione, né segregazione. Il contesto migratorio nella Repubblica Federale Tedesca', in G. Giordano (ed.) *L'immigrazione dal Terzo Mondo verso l'Europa: un fatto umano e un problema sociale destinato a crescere*, La Quercia, Genoa, pp. 61–71.

Giscard d'Estaing, Valéry (1991) 'Immigration ou invasion?', *Le Figaro*, Paris, 21 September, pp. 7–15.

Jelen, Christian (1991) *Ils feront des bons français*, Laffont, Paris.

Melotti, Umberto (1989) 'Migrazioni, divisione del lavoro, cultura', in D. Demetrio, G. Favaro, U. Melotti and L. Ziglio (eds) *Lontano da dove. La nuova immigrazione e le sue culture*, Angeli, Milan, pp. 15–65.

— (1991) 'Specificità e tendenze dell'immigrazione straniera in Italia', in M. I. Macioti (ed.) *Per una società multiculturale*, Liguori, Naples, pp. 71–88.

— (1992) *L'immigrazione: una sfida per l'Europa*, Edizioni Associate, Rome.

— (1993) 'Xenofobia e razzismo: concetti, dati, analisi', in S. Gindro (ed.) *La xenofobia*, Guida, Naples, pp. 99–139.

Naïr, Sami (1993) 'Où va la France?', *Le Monde*, Paris, 18 June.

O'Donnell, Mike (1991) *Race and Ethnicity*, Longman, New York.

Renan, Ernest (1882) 'Qu'est-ce qu'une nation?' in *Oeuvres complètes*, Calmann-Lévy, Paris, 1947, pp. 887–906.

Rex, John (1990) 'L'atteggiamento verso gli immigrati in Gran Bretagna', in A. Bastenier et al. (eds) *Italia, Europa e nuove immigrazioni*, Edizioni della Fondazione Agnelli, Turin, pp. 67–85.

Touraine, Alain (1991) 'Face à l'exclusion', *Esprit*, Paris, (169): 7–13.

PART TWO

From Immigrants to Citizens: The Politics of Inclusion

The Perils of Ethnic Associational Life in Europe: Turkish Migrants in Germany and France

Lale Yalçın-Heckmann

An implicit premise of multicultural policies is the existence of ethnic spokespersons able to assume a legitimate representative role in the public sphere; to 'speak' for their 'community' and its concerns. Yet as Anne Phillips has pointed out in her analysis of the politics of presence, ethnic differences are intrinsically contested: 'ethnic minorities lend themselves to a process of ever more precise sub-division', she argues, so that 'ethnic quotas will always fail to capture the diversity of ethnic identities' (Phillips 1995: 168). As this chapter too highlights, ethnic groups are divided not only by subnational and transnational affiliations but by age, gender and political or religious tendencies cutting across them, all of which generate a tendency towards splits and cleavages. It is this tendency of ethnic groups to fragment that makes the case for what Soysal has called a 'corporatist' multiculturalism (Soysal 1994: 37) so hard to defend.

Members of a single ethnic group may be engaged, Yuval-Davis argues, in intense competitive struggles for hegemonic positions. Indeed, some of the projects they promote 'can involve different constructions of the actual boundaries of the collectivity' (Yuval-Davis 1997: 194). This chapter explores the challenge that ethnic organisational conflicts pose for any multiculturalist politics of presence. I begin with a cultural encounter.

The visit

In February 1994, a report appeared in the daily newspaper of Bamberg about a visit to one of the city's local mosques by a class of pupils from a gymnasium. The ninth-graders who contributed this news item to the paper began their report as follows:

'*Allahu akbar!*' (God is great!) is heard in the prayer room. About sixty men are sitting on their knees on the floor. Their look is directed towards Mecca. It is

Friday prayers of the Muslims. But it is not at some mosque on the Arabian Peninsula: we are, in fact, in the prayer room of the Islamic community of Bamberg. (*Fränkischer Tag*, 24 February 1994: 8)

The report continues with a factual description of the mosque association, of how the Muslims pray, of the objects in the prayer room and of the assistant *imam*,[1] and of the Qur'an in German which he gave the children as a present. The report ends with the following passage:

> As we go out to the main avenue … we return back to everyday life again. Here is a Turkish snack bar. Some of us share the opinion that we should definitely complete this experience [*Erlebnis* also means adventure – L.Y.] with a *Döner Kebap*.

This is a very mild and friendly report, written by pupils who share an interest in getting to know the Turkish Muslim community and its Islamic practice in Bamberg. I had attended the visit of these pupils with their teacher to the mosque. These teenagers have no direct experience of Turkish contemporaries in the classroom as there are very few Turkish pupils in their school. They are open towards the Turkish community, but have distant and mistrustful feelings towards their 'alien' religion. Nevertheless, for them religion is part of Turkish identity in Bamberg. The other marker of this 'alien' identity is, fortunately, *döner kebap*, which even non-Turkish youngsters like, and which helps them to escape from the solemn mood that the visit to the mosque has induced.

Mosques and mosque organisations in Germany are of interest to pupils and youngsters as part of their involvement in anti-racist and multiculturalist discussions and activities. Nevertheless, the task of understanding the practitioners of another religion is a difficult one. Later in class, pupils raised questions of the kind an anthropologist might ask: How is religiosity experienced by praying Muslims? Are Friday prayers compulsory? Are Turkish youth equally motivated to attend? Is the mosque organisation solely voluntary? What are membership fees? Are religious services open to all?

From the migrants' point of view, joining an ethnic or religious migrant association in Germany may be seen as a process with sometimes unpredictable results. The men attend the mosque prayers for different reasons: to fulfil their religious obligation, to 'live their religion', to comply with their elders' commands or expectations, to meet others and enjoy a conversation with them.[2] But by attending the mosque they risk small or large perils too: the individual takes part in a self-conscious act of living/ practising and being seen as living/practising a religion, as this was perceived by the German pupils above. The sense of attending the mosque and becoming a member of a mosque organisation may reflect a private religiosity but it also functions at the same time as a way of expressing a public identity and with it a set of values and attitudes.

The identity expressed is also indexical to the group of reference: older men are more often identified with the mosque than young ones; only Sunni Turks and not Alevis are usually (or stereotypically) associated with it; religious 'puritans', 'extremists', or 'radicals' (depending on whose definition one accepts) are associated with the Süleymancı, rather than the Diyanet.[3] The categories Turks themselves use echo those used by non-Muslims. Above all, the meaning and explanation of mosque attendance are always contested and, as such, are critical points of struggle in the drawing of boundaries between self and others.

The perils of ethnic leadership have been explored by Werbner and Anwar (1991). Werbner argues that in Britain 'ethnic communities suspect their ethnic leaders, because they act within the parameters defined by the state' (Werbner 1991a: 17). This is equally true in Germany and France. Indeed, the mistrust extends not only to leaders but to associational life in general, partly reflecting the negative experiences of political associations in Turkey's recent history. Although associational activities of Turks in Germany and France show some variations, they share an oft-expressed Turkish sentiment that 'Turks can never unite' and 'bring five Turks together and you'll have five opinions on any issue'. These self-debasing views are, of course, uttered in specific contexts which reflect the generational and migrational experiences of individuals and groups. The point is, however, that associational participation is perilous because of such public perceptions which impute to activists ulterior motives and non-civic world-views or affiliations.

These aporias are revealed in the history of associational formation over a period of thirty years in two Turkish communities: in Bamberg, Germany, and in Colmar, France. The associations' rise and decline reveals the dilemmas of incorporative multiculturalism as played out in practice, and throws critical light on Werbner's (1991a) argument that ethnic social movements go through predictable stages of (a) efflorescence and (b) ideological convergence. Paradoxically, the life histories of migrants evoke a nostalgic picture of their early life in Germany and France as one of solidarity and unity despite individual hardship and an almost complete absence of self-help organisations. By contrast, the present is seen as marked by disintegration and disunity, despite the sizeable growth of the community and the consolidation of its internal services and resources, and notwithstanding increased public recognition and respect for ethnic identity and difference.

Of the two towns studied,[4] Bamberg lies in the northern Franconian part of Bavaria, and has about 70,000 inhabitants, of whom some 1,400 have Turkish nationality, a relatively low proportion compared to the German average.[5] It is a picturesque small town, deeply Catholic and fairly prosperous, characterised by its rich art and history reaching as far back as the Middle Ages.

The French counterpart in the research, the town of Colmar in Alsace, resembles Bamberg in being a tourist attraction, historically and economically rich, Catholic and conservative. There are about 2,000 Turks in Colmar in a population of about 65,000, in which alien residents (*étrangers*) make up some 9.9 per cent of the urban population, a proportion far higher than that in the rest of France (6.3 per cent).[6] In 1990, some 20 per cent of the foreign residents of Alsace were Turks as against a national average of 5 per cent.

Associational efflorescence

Turkish labour migration to Bamberg began in the mid-1960s; the rate of movement reached its peak around 1973. The Turks who arrived after this year were almost all family members of the firstcomers, and this led not only to a substantial increase of the Turkish migrant population but also to its increasing youthfulness.

Currently, there are five Turkish formal associations in Bamberg, including two mosque organisations, one soccer club, a recently founded Turkish academic association, and a newly founded Alevi cultural association (the Alevis are a religious denomination close to Shi'ism). In addition, there are three or four informal associations functioning mainly as pubs and card-playing saloons, and a few informal circles.

In Colmar too there are five Turkish formal associations: two with conservative, right-wing nationalist orientations, one politically left-oriented and 'multiculturalist' association, another a women's group whose members sew and attend various courses together, and an Islamic association encompassing Turkish, North African and French Muslims. Apart from these formal associations there are numerous ethnic businesses, such as construction firms and snack bars, as well as cafés, clubs and card game saloons.

Formal associations are by no means restricted to one specific activity. Associations bring together a surprising range of activities, including card games for men, tea parties and language courses for women, soccer for youth, childcare, and even the ritual purification of corpses and their transport back to Turkey. These activities are initiated by the participants themselves and not only by community workers or by the federated European–Turkish migrants' associations such as the National View (Milli Görüş).[7]

The histories of the Turkish associations, both in Bamberg and Colmar, can only be understood with reference to the differing development of the two migrant communities. The initial phase of migration in Bamberg was characterised by the recruitment of *Gastarbeiter* Turkish men and women in Turkey and their arrival, often directly to Bamberg, on a contractual basis. In the 1970s, the Workers' Association was founded.

The oldest labour migrants described its establishment as a response to the perceived need to break the monopolistic power abuses of early ethnic brokers.

The second phase of community development was one of population expansion through family unification. During this stage, ethnic associations increased in number and diversified ideologically. The first mosque organisation was formed in the 1970s by the Süleymancı group; by 1977, a power struggle had emerged between it and Turks close to Turkish state Islamic politics, the so-called Diyanet followers. The latter managed to take over the first mosque organisation and established it anew as the Diyanet mosque. In response, the Süleymancı group set up its own mosque association; both these mosques coexist today in Bamberg as inimical rivals. Being the voice of 'official Islam' (see note 3), the Diyanet encompasses far more than one political view or party affiliation. Yet although the association and its soccer club are formally apolitical, their members are drawn mainly from Turkish conservative circles. The political left among the Turkish migrants appears to channel its associational activities into the newly founded Alevi cultural association. Finally, except for the Alevis, all the associations are male-dominated, delimiting a male space.

Despite these underlying affiliations to Turkey, however, associations in Bamberg are less overtly political than those in Colmar. During the second stage of associational growth, the Workers' Association seems to have expanded into a multi-functional and populist movement, mobilising gatherings of up to three hundred people and holding a wide range of activities. In the late 1970s, however, like the mosque, it too became politicised, responding to political developments in Turkey, allegedly as a result of the activities of politicised teachers and *imams*. The emergent social differentiation of the ethnic community by occupation and age was reflected in the takeover of the management committee by younger and more educated members, following their stronger presence and attendance. The educated 'new ones' were interested in conducting political discussions and open debate, not an easy challenge in those times of extreme political violence in Turkey. But this populist character of the Workers' Association was lost at the beginning of the 1980s and it was effectively dissolved towards the end of the decade, leaving a lacuna. Ethnic politics seems to have given way to individual activities and representations.

As in Bamberg, in Colmar too the first Turkish Workers' Association was registered in the 1970s (in 1977). The activities of this association, Amicale des Travailleurs Turcs, included public articulation of the problems of labour migrants and their families and the demanding of various services from local and central authorities. The association was, it seems, close to the republicanist and laicised views of the centre and centre-left parties in Turkey at the time. In 1980 a section of the leadership split off, founding the Association Culturelle Islamique Turque which has an openly

Islamist agenda; the new organisation announced plans to open a new 'Turkish' mosque in Colmar, which it did in 1984, and to provide Qur'an courses for Turkish migrant children. Amicale, for its part, opened a second mosque in the same building as the first in 1986, despite the protests of the Association Culturelle that two 'Turkish' mosques, supported by two politically separate groups, would divide the community. These two associations renamed themselves around 1990. The Association Culturelle has adopted a name that clearly proclaims its political affiliation: it is now a formal branch of the federal organisation of Milli Görüş (see note 7). Amicale has also renamed itself, and although the new name seems to imply that it has become depoliticised, it is nevertheless led by a radical nationalist cadre with explicit party affiliations.

The third association in the town is a 'mixed' association which encompasses Turks, Moroccans and other North Africans. A politically left-oriented association was founded in 1990 and declared its aims specifically as anti-racist in the struggle against the town's housing policies. Soon afterwards, another association arose, apparently with a multiculturalist programme. This latter has French members as well, but the activists are all Turks and Kurds from Turkey. Finally, there is a women's association, founded in the last few years, of which more below.

The politicisation of community

It is evident that in both towns local associational politics are intertwined with Turkish national and transnational politics, and that these affect local mobilisation. There are also differences. In France associations display their political symbols openly in their rooms. The French authorities are concerned and keen – even if in a restrained manner – to control the groups, checking their finances and speculating about their political inclinations and intentions. The associations compete with one another for resources and rooms provided by the municipal administration. French and Turkish social and community workers are involved in these associations as mediators with the authorities, while having the power to determine their future through their monitoring and evaluations. While the French political system retains its centralised hold, it allows at the same time for a *multiplicity* of policy-forming and decision-making state institutions. It seems that the Turks in Colmar are able to access this complex institutional framework and manipulate it for their own interests, as long as they stick to the ground rules imposed on them by the state.

The Turkish community in Colmar nevertheless seems to be politically fragmented and marked by extreme ideological oppositions: Islamist, left and nationalist. This creates an aura of impenetrable closure, especially in the eyes of outsiders. French bureaucrats talk about their hesitation to get directly involved in Turkish associational affairs and internal conflicts;

Arab activists involved in anti-racist campaigns and organisations claim that Turks do not report any incidents of racial discrimination. Finally, Turkish migrants themselves talk about the dubiousness of some organisations, about their alleged involvement in drug trafficking, their Kurdish extremist affiliations, or their Islamic radicalism. This distanced attitude towards associational life is also historically reconstructed. The fragmentation of the unity of Turkish migrants in Colmar is attributed to political developments in Turkey, and the arrival of political ideas and people from Turkey. Despite all this, individuals continue to be involved in organisations and contribute to the complexity of ethnic identity articulations, as I discuss in the case of the women's organisation below.

The imagination of the ethnic community (Werbner 1991a: 21) in Bamberg has followed a rather different path. On the one hand, the Bavarian system favours only limited cultural and social integration into German society, so that ethnic minority groups are perceived as, and remain, culturally different and, in effect, politically excluded, as *Ausländer*. This contrasts with the 'integration' promoted by the republican French model, which allows for political inclusion at the cost of cultural assimilation (Schnapper 1991; see also Chapters 4, 6 and 8 of this volume). Turkish associational life in Bamberg seems to have started out of a communal need to cope with the German political and administrative system. The first gatherings were in private homes or in German bars. In meeting their associational expenses, the settlers did not have the option of applying for funds from the municipal authorities, so this may explain the relatively few associational facilities they possess. The associations initially helped with translation and bureaucratic problems, services also offered by individual official translators. There was no state-managed 'ethnic' infrastructure available, such as existed in Colmar.

Yet significantly it is only the two mosque organisations, branches of European Turkish Islamic federations, that have managed to survive from the early days. The populist Workers' Association, initiated by local migrants with grassroots, all-embracing goals and representation has collapsed, in consequence partly of intergenerational conflicts and partly of political divisions carried into Germany from Turkey.

Internal differentiation was also associated with the emergence of 'peripheral' ethnic leaders, quite unlike earlier organic leaders rooted in the ethnic core (see Werbner 1991a; 1991b). The first Turkish university students came to Bamberg around the beginning of 1980 and became involved in ethnic or left-wing politics. The students and other left-oriented young Turks have formed an informal circle of activists, naming themselves 'the intellectuals'. They first took part in public discussions on the status of foreign residents. Later they linked up with German social workers and assumed the role of mediators (*Multiplikatoren* in German) between Turkish migrant families and the German authorities.

Clearly, then, despite differences in German and French state policies, the process of Turkish communal politicisation and internal differentiation in both Bamberg and Colmar may be characterised as a process of political *visibilisation*. Over time the multiple and potentially conflictual identities fracturing diasporic Turkish migrant communities have come to be visibilised in response to the need to mobilise for joint action. The emerging divisions highlight the problematic nature of corporate multiculturalism in Germany, and the pitfalls of both French and German state interference in communal affairs, as the following case studies, one taken from Bamberg and the other from Colmar, illustrate.

Bamberg: the case of the Foreigners' Council

The intense politicisation of the Turkish community in Bamberg became apparent in the recent case of the Foreigners' Council (*Ausländerbeirat*) elections. Foreigners' councils exist in many cities in Germany, having an advisory role. Despite their very restricted power, they are politically and symbolically significant in being the central representative bodies for so-called 'foreigners'. The Bamberg Foreigners' Council was elected in July 1994, on a turnout of 48.5 per cent of the total of 5,300 foreigners in the city. Yet nearly 78 per cent of Turks turned up for the election. There were rumours that even the sick were taken by cars to the election polls. Occupying four seats on the council, the Turks were the largest nationality group on it, and they ran two lists of candidates. Election turnout rates in other major German cities have tended to be very low indeed. So why did Turkish migrants take the elections to the council so seriously, and what did people expect from it?

In 1991, a group of foreigners in Bamberg established an Initiative for a Foreigners' Council. The group could, in fact, be seen as a continuation of an earlier anti-racist initiative. As part of the initiative, the local trade unions sent an invitation to many alien residents and institutions. These included church organisations as well as university professors, social workers and students. The Turkish participants included students and representatives from the Diyanet mosque organisation, and various state employees. The Initiative group met regularly and eventually became a lobby group, collecting signatures and putting pressure on the municipal administration to establish a local foreigners' council. Although numbers fluctuated, by the end the Initiative had a core of activists who had accumulated some experience in mobilising both the press and politicians.

Despite the public recognition they received and their success in convincing the municipal administration to set up a foreigners' council, the group could not sustain the support of all its Turkish participants. As a result, allegedly, of political differences, but probably also of intergenerational, class, ethnic/religious, and personal differences, the younger group of mainly students remained in the group and the first-generation labour migrants withdrew from it.

The conflict among the Turks politicised the Initiative and some of its non-Turkish members as well. Prior to the elections to the Foreigners' Council, a series of political meetings was held in the Turkish community. Nesrin, a German-language teacher who had attended the first Initiative meetings and later withdrew from the group, and Selami, who joined the Initiative at an early phase and became a key actor in it, emerged as the main protagonists in the ensuing political drama, which dominated the election period. Selami was a Kurdish student from Turkey, married to a German woman who works for the municipal administration. From Selami's point of view, his conflict with Nesrin arose partly from his success in the Initiative, and from his interest in becoming a candidate for the elections. He believes that Nesrin was simply jealous of him and wanted to secure a safe position for herself on the Foreigners' Council. Other participants in the Initiative and members of the Turkish community emphasise the personal aspect of the conflict between the two protagonists as a major factor leading to the breakdown of relations within the founding group.

But such personal antagonisms revealed deeper schisms as the Turkish diplomatic representatives in Nürnberg and the Bamberg municipal administration were called in to intervene and mediate. Selami was allegedly accused of being a pro-Kurdish nationalist/separatist. He publicly disclaimed these accusations. Nesrin, on her part, claimed to have been threatened by Selami and his Kurdish friends, a claim supported implicitly by the Turkish authorities. In a meeting in the Diyanet mosque, the Turks of Bamberg were invited by the Turkish diplomatic authorities to come and discuss the elections and the candidates. This invitation was interpreted as partisanship on the part of the authorities; furthermore, it brought about a *de facto* exclusion of the Alevi Turks and Kurds, who were said to reject any meeting in a mosque. If there really were any Alevis at this meeting, we do not know. The authorities claim to have made an effort to reconcile Nesrin with Selami. They expressed their doubt, however, about the suitability of Selami as a popular candidate. Nesrin, interestingly enough, received the support of the Diyanet association, probably because of the language courses she gave for Turkish women there. Other than this teaching activity, she has no affiliation with the mosque, is not evidently religious and, in fact, was known to work with the Green Party in Bamberg!

The conflict between the two protagonists and their supporters resulted in the splitting of the list of candidates to the Foreigners' Council into two separate lists, one of which was made up of Turks and Kurds who were closer to the Initiative. The candidates on this list included three members of the second generation. Two of the four were Alevi, the third candidate was Selami (a Kurd), and the fourth was one of the earliest student residents of Bamberg, who later became an ethnic businessman. They named this list the Democratic List, but it was referred to by everyone else as the 'Alevi' list, the 'Kurdish' list and, later, the 'Arab' list. The second list, which included Nesrin and three other men, called itself Turkish Unity (*Türk Birliği*). Two of the men were second-generation Turks, both involved with the soccer club. One was supported by the Süleymancıs and the other – the son of a former chairman of the Diyanet association – was supported by that organisation. The third male candidate was the husband of a pioneer labour migrant. He too was active in the Diyanet association.

Turkish Unity won the elections with a clear majority. The younger generation of students and workers who had carried out the preparations for the elections with the Initiative group experienced a bitter defeat. The irony was that the non-Turkish members of the elected Foreigners' Council had all participated in the Initiative and some of them were directly, if not deeply, involved in the conflict between the two Turkish sides. They are now trying to find a way of cooperating with the four 'new' Turks in the council without damaging the old alliances and friendships they had forged with the members of the Democratic List.

Will the Turks on the council develop a 'multicultural' attitude and cooperate with the other foreigners on issues of mutual interest? On which issues will they be able to form a united front? Was the segmentation of the Turkish community as 'Kurds' versus 'Turks', 'Alevis' versus 'Sunnis', 'the left' versus 'the right' only temporary and tactical? Or will the sedimented remnants of this line of segmentation come to be permanently reified? To what degree will the Turkish members of the council be able to pursue their representative role? These are all questions that only time will answer. The interesting point here is that through the establishment of a formal body in the shape of the Foreigners' Council, members of the Turkish community were motivated to think of themselves as forming a corporate 'community', to 'imagine themselves a community' at the very moment of their fragmentation. Moreover, even though the elected Turkish members of the council come from the 'ethnic core' of the local community, they still risk being alienated from it through their very activities within the council, since these demand cooperation across communities; their politics may be construed as self-interested or they may be accused of collaborating with the municipal administration's policies.

The process of conflict escalation described here can be put in broader theoretical terms. In *Schism and Continuity*, Victor Turner argued that as a social drama develops and reaches a point of crisis:

> there is a tendency for the breach to widen and extend until it becomes co-extensive with some dominant cleavage in the widest set of relevant social relations ... the phase of crisis exposes the pattern of current factional struggle

... and beneath it there becomes visible the less plastic, more durable, but nevertheless gradually changing basic social structure, made up of relations which are constant and consistent. (Turner 1957: 91)

By examining microprocessual developments in a small community of Turkish settlers, living in a remote German town, we can uncover some of the internal dynamics that fracture the Turkish diaspora and thus open it up to external manipulation and influence – in this case, from the Turkish and German states and local states and from other diasporic settler communities. At the height of the crisis that the conflict between Nesrin and Selami generated, the scale of involvement increased dramatically, with both Turkish state representatives and German municipal authorities drawn into the dispute and placing their own political constructions upon it. What was represented locally as a factional struggle between two strong personalities exposed some fundamental and relatively enduring divisions among Turks, between Turks and other ethnic groups, and between Turks and the German authorities. These structural cleavages were also reflected in the rise and fall of Turkish associations in Bamberg during the formative period of the community. At the same time, the events highlighted the possibilities of alliance and dialogue, at least for some Turkish settlers, across the boundaries that surfaced during the social drama. Similar processes were also evident in the Colmar case study.

Colmar: the case of the women's associations

The case of the women's associations in Colmar is illustrative of (a) the perils of political labelling that an involvement in associational activities carries; (b) the effects of the 'global' on the 'local', in this case the effects of the political debate in France on Islam, the French Republic and the 'headscarves' affair; (c) the struggle for recognition and resources between different ethnic groups within the French context. Colmar's women's associations are offshoots of a multiethnic women's organisation that was founded around 1992 and was financed by the French authorities. This multiethnic organisation was frequented by Moroccan, Arab and Turkish women and had as its chief aim the organising of sewing and language courses for immigrant women. Although the Turkish women came to the first multiethnic organisation more or less as customers and job seekers, they founded their own organisation after a short period of associational experience.

The chairwoman of the Turkish Women's Association, Feride, is a self-made woman who has been a resident of Colmar for many years. Through her skills in running the affairs of the association, she managed to increase the attendance as well as representing the association in multicultural events. She is enterprising and willing to take on further responsibilities and chores, and seeks to find further resources and rooms for new activities. What is significant about her role is the public image she has generated, its ambivalence and contested nature. Because of the headscarf she wears, she is immediately classified as primarily 'Muslim', 'Islamic' or even 'Islamist', depending on the speaker's political view. If she manages to attract new women to the association, some of whom wear headscarves, then both the French social workers and 'progressive' Turks suspect that Feride is trying to organise an Islamist women's organisation. In fact, Feride does have contacts with the women belonging to the mosque organisation of Milli Görüş, but she never discusses her contacts with the organisation in public. Her contacts with it are apparently primarily personal, since she has relatives associated with Milli Görüş. But her kinship ties and networks cause Feride to be suspected of having hidden political agendas and motives.

What is striking here are the lines of demarcation that have emerged between the Turkish Women's Association and the former multiethnic centre which has become for all practical purposes an Arab women's association. Feride explains the need she perceived for her own organisation in pragmatic terms: the rooms were too small, there were too many women crowded into them together, and it was difficult to handle the management of finances between two chairwomen. In her view, these problems of cohabitation were reasons enough to call another association into life. It is difficult to read too much into what appears to have been a competition for resources, but nevertheless our impression is that the Moroccan women have stronger and more differentiated contacts with French administrators and social workers, especially because the second- or third-generation Arab migrants are better integrated into the social work services dealing with migrant women, and all of them speak good French. A younger generation of French-speaking Turkish women in Colmar has begun to emerge only recently. In the French context the image of the 'traditional' and 'non-emancipated' Muslim woman seems to stick primarily to Turkish women, even if this image is strongly contested by some of the educated and religiously nondogmatic sections of the Turkish migrant society.

Once again, then, we find an apparent dispute between two personalities revealing more fundamental divisions based on partial identities and identifications. Despite the fact that Muslim women would seem to have a good deal in common, other identities – Islamic tendency, national affiliation, length of residence in western Europe, local networks, external stereotypes, linguistic capacities – all impinged on the personal relationship between the women to create the potential grounds for an organisational split. In this case, unlike the previous one, the split followed national–regional lines, but it was nevertheless interpreted in some sections of the French and Turkish contexts as being about Islamic radicalism versus moderation. Whereas in Bamberg Turks were numerically the largest group and the emergent dispute revealed the cleavages *within* the Turkish community, in Colmar Turks were a less established minority even within the immigrant community and thus the cleavage that surfaced was a national-cum-linguistic one, between Turks and Maghrebis.

Conclusion: multiculturalism, transnationalism and ideological convergence

Despite their recent emergence, Turkish migrant associational activities are only partly shaped by local factors. Both in France and in Germany, powerful transnational organisations act upon Turkish migrants as sources of both information and political motivation. As a result, associational activities have expanded across national boundaries, be it from Turkey to Germany or France, or from Germany to France, often despite legal and organisational barriers and borders. Some of these associational activities, such as those of the Alevi association in Bamberg or of the Mosque Association affiliated with Milli Görüş in Colmar, have come over time to link the local immigrant associations to federated single-interest associations beyond the local community, in a process typical of ethnic associational expansion (see Werbner 1991a; 1991b).

However, if we regard these associations as opening up new spaces for potential emancipatory social movements, the associations are still apparently caught up in an 'initial stage of [a] social movement [in which] associations remain relatively discrete and often compete with one another, both for state allocations, and on ideological grounds' (Werbner 1991a: 16). The Milli Görüş Mosque Association, for instance, competes with its counterpart (formerly Amicale) in the same building, although the points of conflict and accommodation between them often remain obscure to the French authorities, despite some attempted surveillance.

Yet along with these conflicts there are also signs of the gradual emergence of what Werbner identifies as the second stage of a social movement, that of '*ideological convergence*, [which] involves the formulation of a common discourse and set of objectives in relation to the state or local state, and with regard to the contemporary condition of the groups within the larger society' (Werbner 1991a: 16). The common stand of these associations against the 'second-class citizen' status of aliens in Germany and France exemplifies this ideological convergence. The multicultural association in Colmar and the Ausländerbeirat in Bamberg articulate this ideological convergence publicly.

Nevertheless, associational conflicts and disputes continue to plague the two communities. I suggest, then, that the model of stages in a social movement identified by Werbner (1991a) and their correspondence to different forms of associational formations need to be partly modified in the light of the examples analysed here. The two stages seem to reflect differences between associations which are, in fact, co-present. Not all associations at a local level participate in broader social movements or do so at the same time. The coexistence of differing forms of associational types is partly explained by the continuation of migration and by the processual character of migratory experiences. These affect political dispositions and knowledge about the problems of living as a settler–stranger in Western Europe, and are differentially acquired by different groups at different phases of migration.

Although the synchronous quality of associational stages (from local to federal, from efflorescence and fragmentation to ideological convergence) is found both in Bamberg and Colmar, the organisational trajectories in the two communities show some differences. The Turkish migrant community in Colmar seems to be even more fragmented than in Bamberg because of its complex history of migration, which is still continuing, and which produces significantly different types of migrants ('illegals', first-comers, asylum seekers, marriage migrants, and so forth). Second, the attitude of French local authorities towards the Turkish associations, allowing them more political autonomy – even if with financial dependence – than in the Bamberg case, and enabling different interest groups to coexist side by side (in an extreme case, approving two 'Turkish' mosques in the same building), has effectively strengthened the particularist trends of these French-Turkish associations. But strikingly, in both communities the direct influence of Turkish and European Turkish politics has meant that political parties and organisations in Turkey and Europe often set the agenda for local associational activities.

Associational splits both affect and emerge from the type of multiculturalisms the towns foster. In Bamberg, multiculturalism is 'corporative', a semi-official policy, coordinated through the Foreigners' Council; the Turkish members of the council have to be chosen by the Turkish 'community' in order, on the one hand, to represent the whole community vis-à-vis other national communities in the town, but also, on the other hand, to find a common language in which to cooperate with them as a collective body of non-Germans. Hence, multiculturalism of the German type reifies community while revealing its cleavages.

By contrast, Colmar represents a case of hybrid multiculturalism where grassroots movements are granted state backing at the cost of some control; associations, however, can hardly be said to be representative of whole ethnic communities since self-proclaimed multiculturalists in Colmar act on their own initiative, disguising internal differences based on age, class, religion and ethnicity.

Finally, the community could be said to be 'imagined' differently in the two places: in Bamberg, the expectation is of sustaining intimate, face-to-face relations among community members, which underpins the definition of 'we Turks, in Bamberg'. In Colmar, on the other hand, the complex migratory history and experiences of Turkish settlers prevent any such expectations of solidarity and lead to a multiplicity of fragmented self-images for Turkish settlers in the town.

Notes

1. An *imam* is a Muslim leader in public worship.

2. See Sunier (1995), for an insightful discussion of the motivations and perspectives of two young Turkish Muslims in joining the youth organisations of two 'Turkish' mosques in Holland.

3. Süleymancı, literally followers of Süleyman Tunahan, a religious leader who lived in the 1940s in Turkey and gathered radical Muslims around him through his Qur'an courses and preaching. His opposition to the control of religious affairs by the Turkish state has been adopted by his followers, who have been organised among Turkish labour migrants since 1970. Diyanet, or in full Diyanet İşleri Türk İslam Birliği, is the European federation of mosque associations under the Turkish Directorate of Religious Affairs. As it is controlled by the Turkish state it is politicised, but on the whole it represents official Islam in Turkey and seeks to control other mosque organisations and Qur'an courses in Europe.

4. Together with Gaby Strassburger and Horst Unbehaun I carried out a research project on social networks and the history of the communities of Turkish migrants in the cities of Bamberg (Germany) and Colmar (France). The project, which lasted from April 1994 to May 1996, was financed by the German Volkswagen Foundation and was based at the University of Bamberg, the Chair of Turkish Language, History and Culture. I thank Gaby Strassburger for the data on Colmar and for allowing me to interpret her findings; both Gaby Strassburger and Horst Unbehaun have read and discussed various versions of this chapter. Special thanks are due to Pnina Werbner who helped me sharpen some of the theoretical points in it. I alone, of course, am responsible for any shortcomings.

5. Foreigners make up 7.5 per cent of the urban dwellers of Bamberg; the average in Germany was around 9 per cent in 1994. Some major metropolitan centres have much larger proportions of foreigners; Frankfurt, for instance, has around 29 per cent foreigners, a figure similar to that in some French cities, for example Marseille.

6. This figure for the population of foreigners in France has to be interpreted with caution as it does not include French citizens with foreign ethnic origins, such as the ethnic North Africans or Turks with French citizenship. Furthermore, there is the problem of large numbers of estimated but unverified 'illegal' residents: people who came with a tourist visa and have overstayed.

7. Milli Görüş is political federation of Turkish migrants which is organised across Europe and affiliated to the conservative–religious Welfare Party in Turkey.

References

Phillips, Anne (1995) *The Politics of Presence*, Clarendon, Oxford.
Schnapper, Dominique (1991) *La France de l'intégration, sociologie de la nation en 1990*, Gallimard, Paris.

Soysal, Yasemin N. (1994) *The Limits of Citizenship: Migrants and Postnational Membership in Europe*, University of Chicago Press, Chicago.

Sunier, Thijl (1995) 'Disconnecting Religion and Ethnicity: Young Turkish Muslims in the Netherlands', in G. Baumann and T. Sunier (eds) *Post-migration Ethnicity*, Martinus Nijhoff Int., The Hague.

Turner, Victor (1957) *Schism and Continuity in an African Community*, Manchester University Press, Manchester.

Werbner, Pnina (1991a) 'Black and Ethnic Leaderships in Britain: A Theoretical Overview', in Werbner and Anwar (eds).

— (1991b) 'The Fiction of Unity in Ethnic Politics: Aspects of Representation among British Pakistanis', in Werbner and Anwar (eds).

Werbner, P. and M. Anwar (eds) (1991) *Black and Ethnic Leaderships in Britain: The Cultural Dimensions of Political Action*, Routledge, London.

Yuval-Davis, Nira (1997) 'Ethnicity, Gender Relations and Multiculturalism', in P. Werbner and T. Modood (eds) *Debating Cultural Hybridity: Multi-Cultural Identities and the Politics of Anti-Racism*, Zed Books, London.

CHAPTER 6

Negotiating Religious Difference: The Opinions and Attitudes of Islamic Associations in France

A. Moustapha Diop

Islam in France

Islam is today the second religion of France, as is often pointed out in a tone of fear and foreboding. This exogenous religion, expressed through both faith and ritual practice, is sometimes grasped as a cultural identity both by its adherents and by the French population at large. At different times it has been variously regarded as a *Weltanschauung* (world-view), a totalitarian system ('frozen in its contemplation of a society which was real seven centuries ago' – Levi-Strauss 1955: 468), a refuge for the 'voices from the South', or an ideological instrument open to manipulation by Islamist activists. Depending on the frame of reference chosen, Islam raises new questions, generates vague feelings of unease, or inspires doubts and fantasies (Diop 1991: 83).

The non-European immigrant population in France lives a double adventure. The majority come from countries that are Islamic either in theory or in practice, but their lives in France are the very opposite to that of *dhimmis* ('protected ones') in Muslim lands; they are no longer the People of the Book, but citizens of a secular state, albeit one impregnated by Judeo-Christian culture. In this context they are judged by the yardstick of secularism as people who belong to a religion that is perceived as a 'total order'. Although divided between various institutionalised nationalities, ethnic categories and regional groupings, they find themselves lumped together into one homogeneous entity: the 'immigrant Muslim community'.

In reality this so-called community remains for the moment a multi-national mosaic, split by different ways of life and customs, crisscrossed by varied, if not contradictory, currents. It includes within it some numerically preponderant groups and minorities (Etienne 1987: Chapter IX), and a range of nationalities: Algerians, Moroccans and Tunisians; Pakistanis, Malians, Comorians, Turks and Senegalese. And within these last two nationalities there are some Christians.

Among the range of regional groupings are to be found Berbers, Kurds, Soninke and Toucouleurs, all cultivating strong ethnic identities. Although the vast majority of Muslim immigrants (that is, the Maghrebis and West Africans) are followers of the Sunnite faith in its Malekite version, there are other Muslims, such as Turks or Comorians, who, although Sunnis, adhere to either Hanafism or Shafism. Alongside this Sunni world exist groups that follow the Shi'ite teachings, for example, the Ismailis.

Despite this patchwork, the French state's approach to the religious question is most often oriented principally towards the Arab–Berber sector of the Muslim population. Allegedly incontrovertible reasons are put forward to justify this bias, such as the demographic factor, which militates in favour of privileging the Maghrebi group. But on top of this might be added the traumatic legacy of the Franco-Algerian war and the wounds it has left, the impact of world events, and the presence of Islamic activist movements originating in the Near or Middle East. This combination of factors tends to mean that Islam is heard through a Maghrebi voice, so that the Arabo–Berber tree seems to hide the Islamic forest (Diop 1988: 77).

In these circumstances the Muslim population of France, which represents a truly kaleidoscopic cross-section of the *umma islamiyya* ('community of the believers'), is at present attempting, despite false preconceptions and stereotyping, to create certain experimental 'trailblazers' with a view to the eventual construction of a genuinely unified Islamic identity. The manufacturing (to borrow an expression used by George Balandier) of this reviewed and reinterpreted *umma* uses many materials: chains of solidarity and friendship, investment in a structure of associations, and the creation of federations of these associations at regional and national level.

After sketching the history of Islamic associations in France as a whole, this chapter reports on the different types of discourse emanating from those Islamic associations located in the region around Paris (Île-de-France), a region that has a high concentration of aliens who are Muslim by faith and in culture. These discourses, as voiced by the leaders of the associations and federations, revolve around the perception of Islam by French society, around Muslims' own view of themselves, and around the recurrent theme of integration. Cutting across this theoretical output are certain expectations, if not demands, and in consequence, certain types of attitudes, concerning strategies intended either to defend the 'Islamic banner' – that is to say, to enable Muslims in France to live within a hermetically sealed order – or, conversely, to propose an eventual meeting ground between two different visions of the world.

Islamic associations: a long-standing presence in France

At the dawn of the twentieth century, during a period of earth-shaking and violent confrontations centred around the problem of the separation of church and state, a foreign organisation was founded that had as its objectives 'the establishment of bonds of solidarity and fraternity between Muslims living in Paris'. It aimed to 'lend a hand and give help to sick and needy students who had displayed a serious attitude to their studies', and to 'look after their funeral and burial arrangements in the case of death'. This association, the Fraternité Musulmane (Muslim Brotherhood) founded in 1907, recruited exclusively amongst intellectuals and students of Arab origin (Diop 1990: 15–16).

Controlled during the 1930s by Egyptians, the Fraternité Musulmane actively participated in the preparations for the European Muslim Congress which was held in September 1935 in Geneva, under the leadership of a Lebanese émigré, Shakib Arslan (Kramer 1986: 142–3). In the course of the First World War, the religious dignitaries of French West Africa responded to the 'Appel à l'Afrique' (Call to Africans) issued from metro-politan France, and this despite *fatwas* (judicial decisions) supporting the holy war launched by the Ottoman Sultan-Caliph. In 1915 the French camps of Senegalese riflemen, such as at Frejus, were said to have resonated with the voices of the followers of the Murid brotherhood who 'assemble, pray or sing hymns accompanied by tom-toms, make their reverences and indulge in frenetic dances' (cited by Michel 1982: 380–81).

During the 1920s and 1930s it was reported that the North African members of the Sufi orders in France – Tijaniyya for the Moroccans, Qadiryya and Alawiyya for the Algerians – 'maintain their religious fervour … every week … joining together to recite holy texts, to sing the mystical verses of Ibn-al Faridh or Hallaj, and to give themselves over to ecstatic dances' (Dermenghem, cited in Sellam 1987: 272–3). Confronted with the administrative control of the Paris Mosque and determined nevertheless to practise their religion, Muslim immigrants took the initiative by opening 'places of worship and koranic schools near to their homes' (Sellam 1987: 273). This movement for the building of pulpits was at the same time accompanied by the creation of *nadis* (religious circles) run by the Associ-ation of Algerian Ulema, which offered 'language courses in both Arabic and French, discussion groups, and moral or religious lectures' to North African immigrant workers (Stibe, cited in Sellam 1987: 443). Moreover, the religious circles claimed a role as social arbiters, since 'games of chance and alcoholic beverages' were forbidden there; they were also innovative once they had given themselves 'as a goal the pursuit of the intellectual, moral and social education of Muslim residents of the Paris area' (Stibe, cited in Sellam 1987: 443).

In the 1950s, the action of the Association Algerian Ulema received rather hesitant support among French Muslim settlers, who in 1958 numbered some 15,000 adults and 45,000 children under the age of fourteen. These settlers, it seems, turned away from their religion and their culture, and ended up 'forgetting Islam and Colloquial Arabic, without [in its place] speaking Classical Arabic'. If, according to the upholders of the faith, the mothers of these families were 'deserving of praise, intelligent in their handling of life, and in not refusing a place for religious training in the education of their children, provided somebody is available to carry it out' (*Al Bacair* 20 March 1951, cited in Sellam 1987: 444), then the fathers were regarded completely differently, as 'themselves being in need of this sort of education' (ibid.). Hence already in 1951 the question of the inculcation of religion to children was seriously posed in relation to the need to provide the necessary education, first of all for parents and only then for the children. In the absence of this process of transmission, it was argued, the sociocultural gap between parents and children was likely to widen.

The arrival of Algerian students on the scene during this period contributed, at least in the provinces, to a slight change of direction. Some students chose to occupy religious space by creating the association Union Générale des Étudiants Musulmans Algériens (UGEMA – General Union of Muslim Algerian Students), which took over from the Muslim Brotherhood. Active in both the religious and political spheres, this student avant-garde also tried to enhance public awareness of the oppressiveness of colonial rule in their country of origin by opting for spectacular actions, such as a hunger strike carried out by one of the leaders of the association.

Taking over the torch from UGEMA, in 1963 a teacher of Pakistani origin by the name of Hamidullah founded an organisation having as its objective to 'take care of Muslim intellectuals coming for short periods to continue their studies in France'. However, the new structure – the Association des Étudiants Islamiques en France (AEIF – Association of Islamic Students in France) – unlike UGEMA aspired to 'group together students of Muslim origin of *different* nationalities'. One is forced, all the same, to note that until the mid-1970s the AEIF recruited its members almost exclusively from among the Maghrebi students. The real impact of the AEIF until the 1980s, whether among students or immigrant workers, still remains to be determined (Kepel 1987: 246).

From that period onwards, not only did the association infiltrate university towns where it had founded branches, but it also started to take into consideration the preoccupations of migrant workers. According to a national-level leader of the association:

> People who don't know whom to turn to come to see us, those who want to write letters and those who have family problems. There is the problem of bereavement, and of helping youngsters with their schooling, and generally responding to the needs of parents and children.

At the same time as opening up the association to other nationals – Senegalese, Ivoirians, etcetera – the AEIF began to weave a transnational solidarity network, 'addressing invitations to Muslim associations in

Germany and Holland', and participating globally in the affairs of the *umma* through the World Union of Islamic Student Organisations.

The second half of the 1960s witnessed the flowering, admittedly timid, of associations with a religious character directed not by intellectuals or students but by migrant workers themselves. This movement, the Jamaat Tabligh (known as Foi et Pratique [Faith and Practice] in France) which was initiated by a French citizen of Algerian origin and consolidated by the members of an organisation originating in India, was still expanding at the beginning of the 1980s.

During the period from 1978 to 1984, Islamic enthusiasm was reflected in an efflorescence of formal organisations. Among the reasons suggested for this Islamic revival are the following:

- the impact of the Iranian revolution – the so-called Iranian Moment;
- the unstable, stagnant situation of Muslims in France;
- the generous funding by the Gulf States, motivated by a desire to propagate a certain form of Islam (Kepel 1987: passim);
- the perceived need for a religious education, aimed as much at adults as at children, in order to achieve a better integration into the host society;
- the impact of national events (the 'Le Pen effect'), or international events (the Soviet invasion of Afghanistan);
- the awakening of an international Islamic movement;
- the Appeal to Muslim Immigrant Children launched by the World Islamic League (Paris) on the occasion of the International Year of the Child in 1979, which invited children to ask their parents to form Islamic associations which would arrange to teach children their religion, their culture and 'the civilisation of the host country';
- the arrival of a new era for Muslims, the fifteenth century of the Hegira (November 1979 to January 1980), considered as that of renaissance and the propagation of knowledge;
- control exerted by the countries of origin and battles for hegemony between foreign states;
- the new French law of 9 October 1981 which facilitated the constitution of foreign associations (Diop 1990: passim).

By 1994, the Islamic organisations had imprinted their mark on the whole field of associative activity in France. With their numbers estimated at between 1,050 and 1,100, these organisations can be defined according to a variety of criteria:

- natio nality;
- profession (doctors, marabouts);
- gender, following the emergence of feminist groups;
- age or generation;

- Sufi brotherhood allegiance (Diop 1990: 54–6; Diop and Kastoryano 1991: 97–8).

In tandem with this efflorescence, movements towards federation and unification have also increased at regional and national levels (see also Chapter 5). At the moment, three federations exist and are in competition with each other for the mantle of 'representative of French Muslims':

1. the Union des Organisations Islamiques de France (UOIF – Union of Islamic Organisations of France), registered in 1983, with 150 member associations;
2. the Federation Nationale des Musulmans de France (FNMF – National Federation of French Muslims), founded in October 1985 as a reaction to the ambitions of the Paris Mosque, grouping together 141 associations;
3. the Federation des Associations Islamiques d'Afrique des Comores et des Antilles (FAIACA – Federation of Islamic Associations of Africa, the Comores and the Antilles) with thirty or so registered associations and about twenty informal associations, created in December 1989 with the aim of emphasising the black African contribution to Islam in France.

The policies of these federated organisations are situated in general within a French framework, even though one of them, the UOIF, has sometimes shown an affinity with certain currents of political thinking emanating from the Near or Middle East. One grouping stands out as distinct from these federations in its community-wide nature, aiming to bring together the different members of the *umma islamiyya*. This is the Jamaat Tabligh which, whilst tackling the problems of religious recognition and of the practice of the faith, opts for the principle of *dawa* (the call to Islam). Such an approach implies an opening up not only towards the Muslims in France, but also (and above all) towards Muslims living in other European countries, and even those in Africa.

The Islamic associations in the Paris region: Muslims speak about Muslims and about Islam

In *Tristes Tropiques* (1955: 466), Claude Levi-Strauss defined Islam (by contrast to other religions) as a 'great religion which is based less on the evidence of a revelation and more on the impossibility of forming external ties'. Placed in a minority situation within a secular society, the various Muslim immigrant populations in France seem, in their relationships with the exterior, to test the second of Levi-Strauss's propositions, either by confirming its validity or by denying it. Differing views on how Muslims can or should relate to non-Muslims were expressed by activists, very much depending on the association to which they were connected (Diop: 1990).

At first glance, the associations that were surveyed – seventy-four in number, of which three were federations and one was a grouping of a particular community (Jamaat Tabligh) – sketch a stereotypical portrait of 'the Muslim'. This portrait emphasises 'his' submission 'to God's wishes', his sense of respect towards others, his tolerance and his capacity for adaptation. As far as this last feature is concerned, the example of the Prophet as a point of reference is seen to be continually present and rich in meaning. Given that in the beginning the Prophet had lived 'amongst a tribe of unbelievers', the Muslim can live, strengthened by this example, in a 'non-Muslim country, even one ready to lead you away from the path of God'. For those who experience it, this sort of conduct takes on an educational character, as long as one's life is lived modestly, according to the requirements of the law, avoiding ostentatious attitudes and responsive to the demands raised by any contingency. However, this low-key approach to living among strangers is not shared by the Jamaat Tabligh, which opts for a more direct approach, if need be engaging in a sort of provocation, and this in the name of *dawa*. According to one of its members, a leader of Moroccan origin, who teaches in a private school and is an *imam*:

> When I go to see the deputy mayor I talk to him about religion, and I invite him to come to prayer. Another example; when I'm in the metro I engage a nearby passenger in conversation and talk to him about religion. But generally it's my fellow passenger who asks me questions about the way I dress; and then I can explain to him the meaning of Islam and invite him to come to pray with us. ... You've got to be daring, to dare to approach the other person. There are no barriers, since God created us to love him. For us religion comes before everything.

Divided since time immemorial into nations and ethnic groups (Qur'an, XLIV, 13: The Apartments), the various Muslim populations in France engage in the struggle by emphasising their differences, by playing upon their particularities, and by perpetuating byzantine quarrels: 'We are divided on the essentials.' What might be termed this 'narcissism of little differences' provokes continuing mutual criticism between certain associations who query the practices of their supposed fellow believers and their professed faith. The gap between the ideal Islamic prescribed way of living and reality creates perverse effects. And, in consequence of the provocative actions of those with little sense of collective responsibility, the image of Islam comes to be sullied in the public domain. That is why the Catholic Church, which gave such encouragement to Muslim expectations in the 1970s, felt obliged to effect a tactical retreat in the face of the attitude it encountered on the part of certain Muslim organisations. According to the chairperson of one association, who is of French extraction, 'The great help from the Catholic side was perceived as an invasion of Islam, but often it was the Muslims themselves who did not have the necessary tact to cut short this sort of thinking.'

This lack of tact emanates, in fact, from men who reduce Islam to their own vision of the world. Poorly equipped in their religious education, these men imprison themselves in their ignorance by following narrow-minded *imams*. By contrast, the interpretation of Islam that is given by the women's associations is at the other end of the spectrum from that of the men, who are described by the women as 'narrow-minded and illiterate'. For the Muslim women leaders, 'According to the Qur'an, women are born free and have the same social rights as men.' This liberty is personified by the two wives of the Prophet: 'Khadija [the first wife of the Prophet] was a merchant, whilst Aysha [his beloved youngest wife] went out to nurse the injured on the battlefield'. Masculine misunderstandings some-times lead to 'absurd' situations, as one woman leader who is a medical doctor noted: 'When a husband accompanies his wife and he sees that I also treat male patients, he sometimes gets up and goes; this is, indeed, absurd.' Fortified by the saying that 'the Muslim does not expect his punishment to be from men but only from God', the Muslim women leaders recommend an emphasis on religious studies in order 'to show the true face of Islam to children and to society at large'.

Islam and French society

The topics raised by the associations invariably turn around the question of the 'non-recognition' of Islam, despite its being the second religion of France. Although the practice of religion is permitted – and there exist no constraints as far as this is concerned – it is nevertheless a fact that 'the Islamic presence has never been accepted by the majority of French people'. The discretion shown by Muslims, and their political non-intervention, instead of being factors winning them high marks for good conduct seem, on the contrary, to have marginalised them. According to a leading member of the Conseil de Reflexion sur l'Islam en France (CORIF – the Council for Reflection on Islam in France – which has been suspended since the arrival of Charles Pasqua at the Ministry of the Interior and Religion in 1993), 'At no time has the Muslim community shown any signs of disagreement with the Elysée or the Matignon (the prime minister's office) when there were international conflicts with Muslim countries; whereas there are other communities who have caused problems and troubled the public order.' Islam merely serves as a scapegoat: 'When there is any sort of problem, it's Islam and some fanatics or fundamental-ists' that are accused of causing it. This stereotypical image of fanaticism and of terrorism stigmatises the non-European immigrant, which in itself creates a state of inferiority before the law: 'Practising Muslims or not,

our surnames or our first names advertise the fact that we are Muslims,'
says a Turkish leader of CORIF.

The policy of segregation and discrimination is confirmed at different
institutional levels, as much at the level of administrative practices (for
example, in relation to Eid-el-Kabir, the celebration of which is a source
of clashes with the authorities who object to animal sacrifice outside
abattoirs), as in relation to the law on the right to a first option of buying
land (which is abused by municipalities), as at the state level, in the
application of the basic law of the land. According to a convert to Islam,
who is a former chairman of the FNMF and chairman of an association
for the protection of Muslim food products:

> The constitution guarantees the liberty of worship to every citizen; but when it
> comes to the construction of a church or cathedral at Evry, it's the government
> which finances it on the pretext that it is the intention to create a museum in
> it. Whilst, when one wants to build a mosque, there are a whole series of
> objections raised, and means are always found to avoid anything being done
> about it.

Being constituted as a religious scapegoat can produce radical reactions.
In the case of a minority of associations, mainly composed of young
people and in particular women, the birth of the Republic of Iran, the
privileges given to associations of a secular type such as SOS Racisme
and France Plus, as well as political/media incitement surrounding the
chador (headscarves) affair, have all pushed their leading elements towards
a radical reaffirmation of their Islamic identity. For the great majority of
organisations, however, these events have served, rather, as a test and
crucible, challenging them to show a sense of proportion and to prove
the maturity and spirit of tolerance of the Muslims of France. According
to a leader of Moroccan origin, 'We have received a whole succession of
slaps in the face: Rushdie, headscarves, refusals to install places of worship,
... so that those who accuse us of being fundamentalists, of not being
very tolerant, they might like to modify their understanding of the situation
a bit.'

In response to the stereotypes and prejudices attached to Islam, the
associations project a parallel image of a religion that is 'a factor of
stability and social peace'. Through its teachings, Islam preaches a distancing
from gross materialistic concerns, and brings to the youth of the suburbs,
those suffering from the poor quality of life in their neighbourhoods, a
'philosophy which allows them to express themselves'. The example of
the youth of Lyon's suburbs encourages an association such as the Jamaat
Tabligh in its socialising mission. According to one leader:

> In a neighbourhood such as Les Minguettes which hit the headlines [because
> of its vandalism], all the youths of the neighbourhood have joined the Jamaat

and now the area is calm. It is a triumph for Islam and for peace. We play a social role, since these youngsters were abandoned, and we went out to them and they have been saved thanks to our actions.

Integration as perceived by the Islamic associations

The idea of 'integration' elicits powerful responses from the leaders of the associations. Reactions revolve around four types of attitude, in decreasing order of vehemence

The first, which has made the most public impression on the basis of comparison with the 'beurs', as the generation of French-born Arabs are commonly called, sees integration as a means of turning oneself away from religion. As the leader of a student association states: 'Integration is distancing oneself from Islam, that's the impression that I have – I've seen youngsters born in France who have never had any religious education whatsoever'.

A second reaction is to reject the term 'integration' totally and to see in it a disguised way of erecting barriers. A Turkish leader says: 'If I live in a free country, the word "integration" should not appear – as far as I am concerned, I can dress as I like and think as I like – they've got to tell us whether this is a free country or whether it's not.'

Then there are those associations for whom the very word 'integration' derives from a 'false problem', from a 'debate invalid from the start'. A Franco-Senegalese leader points out: 'Integration of whom? The people are there, they live their own way of life, and they feel good.' A Franco-Madagascan Ismailian agrees: 'It's a false problem, because the people who live in France work there, speak French at work, dress like the French, and travel in a car or on the metro like the French.'

Finally, the majority of the associations, who stress the basic ambiguity of the concept, react against the slippage that occurs from 'integration' towards the notion of 'assimilation'. For them, integration must be grasped as a means of 'participating in French life, while at the same time keeping each group's specificities, both cultural and religious'. Once the line of demarcation has been drawn, each side will have to respect the rules. On the Muslim side, practitioners bear a responsibility to demonstrate the perfect compatability of 'being a Muslim and living in a society which is not'. On the side of the host nation, the transaction concerns the move between generations. What must be politically avoided is saying, 'The first generation is yours, but the second is ours.'

Whatever response is given, the notion of mutual respect is a repeatedly recurring refrain in the discourses emanating from the associations. The same is true of the statements on the educational effects of participation in the associations concerned, which tend to favour the inculcation of personal social responsibility and education towards the discovery of the 'other'.

The Islamic associations: types of attitude

The different opinions held on integration by the organisations reveal the types of attitude and behaviour practised by the associations. These attitudes revolve around four typical categories, with some overlap between one category and another, depending on the context.

1. *Religious beliefs in the private sphere* The most important group from a numerical point of view is one that exists within its own 'internal citadel', in the words of Gilles Kepel. This group can be subdivided into three subgroups. First, the Sufi orders or brotherhoods, whose members participate in weekly prayer meetings, readings of the Qur'an, and singing. Whether they are Turkish, Algerian or Senegalese, the brotherhoods invite their disciples to favour an *interior* religious life. All the same, some of these groupings, the Alawiyya and the Muridiyya, for example, open themselves up to the outside world, partly through the widespread dissemination of their teachings, and partly by inviting non-Muslims to their song and prayer meetings. Some associations are of the informal type, for whom a certain secretive discretion surrounding their acts of worship constitutes the fundamental rule of Islam. Second, there are the associations of minority groups, such as the Indo-French Shi'ites, who initiate an opening out in the direction of their fellow co-religionists from Madagascar or Pakistan, at the same time turning inwards on themselves in order to preserve their cultural identity through the use of the Gujarati language. Finally, it is important not to forget those associations which, by the nature of their living conditions in the *foyers* (residential centres for single men) – and also as a result of their perception that they are a subordinate, dominated minority – seek shelter and comfort in religious observance, and this in a hermetically closed environment.

2. *Away from inward-turning and towards an opening out* Hinging around the principle of 'a truly constructive dialogue between Islam and the West', some associations propose fighting against the 'muezzin syndrome' of Muslim confrontational politics. This policy chooses various avenues: for example, symbolic representation by a neutral colour (in fact, blue) so as not to encourage fantasies of 'the green peril'; an opening up of the activities of the associations to outside persons; a policy of visits and open days on religious holidays. The associates take part in discussions on general social questions (moral principles, organ donation, *in vitro* fertilisation, and so forth), and participate in an Islamic–Christian dialogue.

3. *From an opening out to a militant strategy* One association stands out from the rest, led by a French convert to Islam. In the words of its president, Intégrité (Integrity), as the association is called, seeks to be the

spokesman and defender of all Muslims. Using a soap-box style of politics (to paraphrase Lavau), the organisation, through an 'Islamic publication of general information' called *Index*, takes on itself the role of attracting the attention of Muslims as well as French society to 'events which touch upon the community'. It does so 'each time a principle of Islam is endangered'. Whilst deploring, in common with many associations, the disunity of Muslims in France and in the world, Intégrité suggests that in the case of France, 'We should only busy ourselves with things we have in common.' Foremost among these are religious activities because, according to this association, 'Better a mosque than an oriental bar or delinquency.'

4. *Between a militant strategy and the call to Islam*   Working on people's affiliations remains the keystone of Jamaat Tabligh's approach. Created with the goal of bringing sinners back to the 'straight and narrow' path of Islam, the French organisation remains faithful to the teachings of its founder. According to the latter, the materially and spiritually impoverished Muslim is the beginning and the end of any missionary action. Favouring socialisation directed at the social base of society, the Maghrebi and West African followers, under the influence of the *markaz* (central office), go into places of everyday living: cafés, hospitals, immigrants' homes, residential areas afflicted by social problems, the metro, etc. This work on the streets allows direct contact, and defines the frontiers of Islamic identity.

The quest for the holy grail of representative status

Despite this vast efflorescence of Muslim associations, which represents the full spectrum of attitudes towards integration in the competition to represent Islam in France, the Paris Mosque (built in honour of Muslim servicemen and opened in 1926) was until the 1980s considered to be its central point of reference by the Muslim population; and as the sole body representative of Muslims by the various French governments, despite numerous expressions of opposition and disagreement (Sellam 1987; Etienne 1989; Kepel 1987). Three years after an attempt was made by the rector of the Muslim Institute of the Paris Mosque to set up a 'Conseil Supérieur des Affaires Islamiques' (Higher Council for Islamic Affairs), a Consistoire Islamique de France (French Islamic Consistory) was created in 1984 by a former French non-commissioned officer of Algerian origin. Its aim was to undermine the hegemony of the Paris Mosque, managed under the iron rule of Si Hamza Boubakeur. During the same period, a grouping of associations appeared under the name of Tayyibat ('excellent things'), which set its objective as the organisation of a 'commission for the inspection of meat and *halal* products'. Confronted with the opposition of the French Ministry of the Interior and Religious Affairs, the leaders of Tayyibat, on the advice of an official from the Ministry of Social Affairs and with the benefit of financial help from the World Islamic League, in October 1985 founded the FNMF, which presents itself as one of the principal rivals to the Paris Mosque. Between 1985 and 1989 (the year of the death of Sheik Abbas, who was nominated by Algeria to replace Si Hamza Boubakeur) what took place via the media was a fight over the control of *halal* meat between the Paris Mosque and the president of the FNMF.

Occupied with the two 'affairs' (Rushdie and the headscarves), on 6 November 1989 the French government, under the umbrella of the Ministry of the Interior and Religious Affairs and after a 'long period of consultation', created a study group to investigate the organisation of Islam in France; the group comprised six members. Following successive meetings in Paris, in the provinces and in the suburbs of Paris, the Group of Six decided to 'enlarge itself by co-opting other members'. On 9 March 1990, the ministry created the Conseil de Reflexion sur l'Islam en France, which consists of fifteen members (of whom eleven are of French nationality) chosen *intuiti personae*. The Minister of the Interior set the council two objectives, the first being 'to give the Minister of the Interior (in charge of religious affairs) its opinions and points of view on the practical problems encountered in the practice of the Muslim faith in France'. The second objective was 'to encourage Muslims living in France to create for themselves a representative organisation like that of the other religious groups': the Jewish Consistory [*consistoire* – 'religious council'], the Bishops' Conference [Conference Episcopale] and the Federation of Protestant Churches.

The idea of an official representative organisation, perceived as the logical conclusion of a search for an identity, received the near-unanimous approval of the associations, but with some nuanced differences. For some, the institutionalising of Islam in France prevents takeover attempts by certain foreign Islamic states. For others, this process will allow Islam to be legitimised, and thus to be recognised by the French state and French society.

Conclusion

It is around the idea of constructing a common Muslim identity – 'all Muslims are brothers' – that the social partners to this enterprise are trying to sketch intra- and inter-national regroupings. As Muslims in France confront the temptations generated by an urban, capitalist, consumer, society, it is apparent to many responsible members of the community that the strategy of turning in on oneself is highly unsatisfactory. Rather, the need is for a more dynamic approach. What I want to call the 'sponge' strategy consists, after taking stock of the differences between Muslims

and non-Muslims and between Muslims themselves, of selectively squeez-
ing these differences out, or of absorbing them in the name of the 'umma'
ideology, the ideology that Muslims form a single transnational, global
community. Such an approach depends upon the strengthening of the
bonds of solidarity between Muslims. To become operative, it has to be
based on something concrete. Hence, the recent creation of a 'solidarity
fund', which had a double objective: to resolve the problems of the here-
and-now, and to settle those of the afterlife (namely, the repatriation of
corpses to a Muslim land or, failing this, verifying that local burials take
place according to religious requirements).

According to the leaders of this movement towards solidarity, the degree
of internal integration within the remodelled 'community' is based on
religious knowledge and the practice of the faith, factors that are a fertile
soil for promoting and validating Islamic civilisation. Caught between the
images and stereotypes circulating about their religion and the 'muezzin
syndrome' of a confrontational Islam, the associations are marking out a
new pitch: the 'open door' policy, which favours dialogue with Christians;
the advocacy of Islam as a factor of social peace in the suburbs; and, yet
again, the policy of religious education for the children. But against this
movement other organisations, in their race to achieve representative status,
resort to powerful rhetorical language in their dealings with public bodies
and civil society in general, usurping for themselves the role of guardians
of the image and traditions of the Muslim population.

Inasmuch as they are the keepers of ethnic origins, these organisations
constitute the 'dangerous other half' of Islam in France, introducing
trouble and sedition, the origins of which are foreign and external, into
the field of action of the Muslim associative movement in France.

In short, then, if we consider multiculturalism as a negotiated order
and examine it from the perspective of religious minorities themselves, it
is evident that several important factors are essentially required if the
negotiation of an agreed cultural order is to succeed. First, the immigrant
community must draw on its own internal resources to address the social
problems of the community in its reproduction over generations; second,
it must try to reach out and cooperate with other organisations and people
of good will in the wider society; third, its representatives must work to
bury the differences between them so as to be able to speak with a single
voice on matters of general concern or in times of crisis. Finally, and this
is the fourth crucial point, all this is achievable only if the minority
religious community of believers refuses to be drawn into international
ideological matters which inevitably fragment local unities. Hence, in the
French case, the religious community can only act effectively to address
the very difficult problems facing the Muslims of France if its religious
commitments are enframed within an encompassing ideology of citizenship

which places as its priority the harmonious establishment of a respected French Islamic civilisation.

References

Diop, A. M. (1988) 'Stéréotypes et stratégies dans la communauté musulmane de France', in Rémy Leveau et Gilles Kepel (eds) *Les Musulmans dans la société française*, PFNSP, Paris, pp. 77–87.

— (1990) *Le Mouvement associatif islamique en Île-de-France*, Rapport, CERI/FNSP–Ministère des Affaires Sociales.

— (1991) 'L'Islam confrérique des immigrés africains', *Panoramiques*, 1: 83–7.

Diop, A. M. and R. Kastoryano (1991) 'Le Mouvement associatif islamique en Île-de-France', *Revue Européene des Migrations Internationales*, 17(3): 91–117.

Etienne, B. (1987) *L'Islamisme radical*, Hachette, Paris.

— (1989) *La France et l'Islam*, Hachette, Paris.

Kepel, G. (ed.) (1987) *Les Banlieues de l'Islam. Naissance d'une nouvelle religion en France*, Seuil, Paris.

Kramer, M. (1986) *Islam Assembled: The Advent of the Muslim Congresses*, Columbia University Press, New York.

Lévi-Strauss, C. (1955) *Tristes Tropiques*, Plon, Paris.

Michel, M. 1982 *L'Appel à l'Afrique*, Publications de la Sorbonne, Paris.

Sellam, S. (ed.) (1987) *L'Islam et les Musulmans en France: Perceptions, craintes et réalités*, Tougui, Paris.

CHAPTER 7

Arenas of Ethnic Negotiation: Cooperation and Conflict in Bradford

Philip Lewis

In seeking to accommodate religious and ethnic diversity, Britain has three assets: the pioneer migrants from Pakistan and the Commonwealth enjoy rights of citizenship; since 1965, some legislative protection against racial discrimination;[1] and the existence of an established church.[2] My inclusion of a Christian component – the Church of England– in the political establishment as an asset rather than a liability in the struggle for racial justice is, perhaps, controversial and might well be contested (for example by Sahgal and Yuval-Davis 1992, but see Modood 1997 for how the minorities view the question).

My argument responds, however, to a growing acknowledgement of the increased salience of religion worldwide, not least as a vital component in ethnic identity (Juergensmeyer 1993; Kepel 1994). Further, developments in communications technology, transport and information, mean that contextualised local versions of Hinduism, Islam or Sikhism will have to be located within such a global perspective (for Islam, see Ahmed and Donnan 1994; Lewis 1994). This means that Britain is not immune to the impact of inter-religious tensions in South Asia or the Middle East, and this renders any homogenising discourse about black or Asian identity increasingly problematic. The reason is not simply that minority communities have different cultural capital, enabling them to circumvent racial exclusion, but also because they see each other in some British contexts as rivals, rehearsing ancient antagonisms, fuelled by the recrudescence of what has been called 'religious nationalism' (Juergensmeyer 1993; Van der Veer 1994).

Using the northern industrial city of Bradford as a case study, I wish to identify and illustrate five crucial arenas in which members of different ethnic minority communities interact with the ethnic majority and with each other: local politics, race relations, education, business and religion. This will illustrate the impact on interethnic relations of the 'civic culture which prescribes the terms in which culturally differentiated groups interact' (Rex 1995: 246). It will also indicate why I believe that an acknowledged role for religion in the public domain has often facilitated a constructive dialogue across the religious traditions.

Bradford: worsted textile capital of the world

Religious and ethnic diversity has long characterised Bradford. The city has been synonymous with textiles for 150 years and has attracted migrants, rich and poor, throughout this period. In the 1820s, the Irish began to come to work as hand weavers and combers. An area of the city is still known to this day as Little Germany. This is a memorial to the German merchants, many Jewish, who began to come at the same time. In 1864 the city had its first Jewish lord mayor and in 1881 its first synagogue (in the Reform rather than the Orthodox tradition). The distinguished Bradford writer J. B. Priestley, looking back on his youth in Bradford before the First World War, remembered it as 'one of the most provincial and yet one of the most cosmopolitan of English provincial cities ... determinedly Yorkshire ... yet some of its suburbs reached as far as Frankfurt or Leipzig' (1934: 153). These suburbs now reach to Warsaw, Dominica, Lahore and Dacca.[3] Today there are some 52,000 Muslims in the city, the majority Pakistanis, and about 9,000 Indians, both Hindus and Sikhs, as well as 5,336 Africans and Afro-Caribbeans.

Irish Catholics in Bradford: an awkward minority[4]

Before focusing on this last phase of migration, which saw the creation of substantial Muslim, Hindu and Sikh communities, it is worth pausing to reflect on the Irish Catholic experience in Bradford. The Irish Catholics anticipate, in several important particulars, the South Asian, especially Muslim, experience, not least their involvement in Labour politics and their concern for their own schools. By 1851, about 10 per cent of Bradfordians were Irish-born.

Most of the Irish migrants were from rural Ireland, had no formal education and spoke a foreign language. They were often blamed by the indigenous working class for depreciating wages, and they were seen as a threat to jobs in times of recession. In 1822, the first recorded Mass in Bradford since the Reformation was celebrated in a room in a local pub: popular anger at this 'popish Mass' led to threats that the licence would be withdrawn if such an event happened again. There is evidence of a campaign in the city in the mid-nineteenth century to repatriate these recent immigrants. Such antagonism was legitimised by an anti-Catholic sentiment reaching back to the Reformation, with Roman Catholicism considered a synonym for superstition, moral corruption, intolerance and potential treason, linked to the assumption that the Pope rather than the Crown was for Catholics the active centre of loyalty and affection. A recent history mapping the emergence of a sense of British nationality between 1707 and 1837 argues that the anti-Catholicism of a pan-Protestant majority was one of three major factors in its creation (Colley 1992).[5]

The liberal prime minister, William Gladstone, who had opposed anti-Catholic bigotry and intolerance, also eventually succumbed to anti-Catholic sentiment in the wake of the First Vatican Council of 1869–70. 'Liberal principles were no bar when an adversary was believed to be essentially illiberal' (Norman 1968: 21–2). Such prejudices were not confined to liberal politicians; one has simply to read Engels's *The Condition of the Working Class in England*, written in 1845 and set across the Pennines in Manchester, to realise that there was a shared pool of insidious stereotypes about Irish Catholics, who were obvious candidates for control and even suppression. For the Protestant and liberal imagination they were the significant 'other' in contrast to whom identity was defined.

As with much South Asian migration, Irish Catholic migration to Britain after the Second World War was concentrated in regions associated with traditional working classes: southeast Lancashire, west Yorkshire, Tyneside and London's East End. Progressive thinkers assumed in the first four decades of the twentieth century that these immigrants' class solidarity, involvement in the trade unions and in labour politics would dissolve the national and religious components of their Irish Catholic identity. They did not. The Irish 'neither wanted full assimilation nor separation from English society' (Fielding 1993: 12). The key factors in the maintenance of their identity were attendance at a Roman Catholic school and marriage within the community. Socialisation was more important than theology in their identity. A seminal study of Irish Catholics in Manchester makes clear that notwithstanding their loyalty to the labour movement, between the two world wars they were mistrusted for entering the Labour Party simply to pursue their own ends. They were viewed with suspicion by labour activists on three accounts: they favoured denominational schooling rather than secular education; they were opposed to birth control, and they viewed the communists in the Spanish Civil War with hostility, given the alleged atrocities committed by them against the Catholic clergy (Fielding 1993).

Among the multiple factors that led to a reassessment of attitudes and antagonisms to Irish Catholics – whether the need to recruit Catholics into the army from Ireland and Scotland, the desire to placate the many Catholics in the British empire, their involvement in the emerging trade unions and Labour Party, or the Established Church's reaffirmation of its own Catholic roots with the Oxford Movement – one development was particularly important in allowing Catholics eventually to feel accepted and part of British society. This was a measure of state funding for their schools, a step that was only possible because there existed already in Britain an established church. Indeed:

Catholic schools would never have begun to be subsidised by the Education

Act of 1902 were Church of England schools not needing subsidy too. The whole structure of Anglicanism from Archbishop to curate prepared English-men, high church, low church or agnostic, for an essentially similar structure in Catholicism. The British state was in some way committed to Christianity and bound at least to be respectful of its representatives, as France was not, and this in practice provided a useful starting point for Catholic relations with government. (Hastings 1990: 49)

A unitary Asian identity: a fragile invention

The Irish Catholic experience in Britain is significant in that it highlights a continuing failure of progressive thought to anticipate the importance and tenacity of religion as a component in ethnic identity, and the pos-sibility of maintaining multiple identities, or what the Americans would call 'hyphenated' identities. The supposed unitary identity generated by class solidarity did not obliterate other loyalties and commitments.

It is instructive, in this regard, to reflect on the fate of the Asian Youth Movement (AYM) in Bradford. AYM was founded in 1978 as a pan-Asian, anti-racist Asian youth movement transcending Hindu, Sikh and Muslim communal identities. AYM was built on the assumption that racial discrimination ran parallel to and thus reinforced 'the better-known structures of class inequality ... [with Blacks/Asians] the victims of exclusion' (Ballard 1992: 484). This tradition of anti-racist discourse was congenial to many on the left and underwrote social policy. Thus AYM enjoyed financial support from the local authority: in 1985, Urban Pro-gramme money went into the creation of a youth centre – the Saathi centre – hospitable to the movement's ethos and direction. Many of its members were given jobs in the local authority (poachers turned game-keepers!). Yet even in its heyday, as one of its founder members makes clear in his novel reflecting its history, it had to contend with the powerful centrifugal pull of Hindu, Sikh and Muslim identities, and the tension between 'Asian' and Afro-Caribbean communities (Mehmood 1983). AYM did not survive the return, in the late 1980s, to community consolidation around separate Hindu, Sikh and Muslim identities.

This process of community formation around distinct religious and ethnic identities was already evident in a report the local authority produced in 1981: *Turning Point: A Review of Race Relations in Bradford*. The report characterised the previous twenty years of migration into Bradford as 'settlement by tiptoe', whereby jobs, housing and schools were vacated in the inner-city areas and filled by the South Asian settlers, who had de-veloped a network of goods and services. A parallel economic infrastructure and self-sufficient religious and cultural world had been created; there had emerged a dual society, physically separate, looking outward to mainstream British society in certain respects (jobs, welfare services and education) and inward to preserve its religious and cultural values.

Ten years later, the consolidation of distinct communities is even more evident. Three umbrella organisations exist to represent the religious interests of Hindus, Muslims and Sikhs: the Bradford Council for Mosques (1981), the Federation for Sikh Organisations (1984) and the Vishwa Hindu Parishad (1984); discrete business forums also exist: the Institute of Asian Businesses, largely Hindu and Sikh (1987), the Hindu Economic Development Forum (1989) and the Asian Business and Professional Club – Muslim – (1991). These distinctions were also evident in the community and youth centres established in the 1980s, such as the Pakistan Community Centre, Bangladesh Porishad and al Falah.[6] While in the early phase of pioneer migration Hindu, Sikh and Muslim males often lived together or in close proximity, with the emergence of family units and consolidation of communities Sikhs and Hindus tended to move away from the large Muslim concentrations.

AYM did not only fall apart because of its failure to manage the ancestral tensions between Hindu, Sikh and Muslim. An imagined unitary 'Asian' community was not sufficiently alert to specific issues that troubled different communities. There was little enthusiasm amongst non-Muslim 'Asians' for the campaign Muslims launched against Salman Rushdie's novel *The Satanic Verses*. Too often 'Asians' were presented as 'victims' rather than active subjects able to resist and circumvent racism; religion and culture were often ignored as providing resources in this struggle (see Werbner and Anwar 1991). Finally, those operating with a class analysis and assuming that the ethnic minorities are to be found exclusively within the working-class or underclass end of the spectrum, could find no space for the fact of economic success enjoyed by certain communities (Werbner 1990; Modood 1991; Ballard 1992).

In Bradford, racial exclusion clearly exists and all South Asian communities have borne the brunt of radical changes in the local economy away from manufacturing to service industries. Textiles, the very niche for which South Asian labour was sought, was devastated locally and nationally. Bradford lost over 80 per cent of textile jobs between 1961 and 1991, more than sixty thousand jobs. However, unemployment levels within the South Asian communities are markedly different: for Indians in Bradford – largely Hindu and Sikhs – in 1991 the rate was running at 15.4 per cent, for Pakistanis and Bangladeshis in excess of 36 per cent. Muslim businesses were smaller than their Indian competitors (Rafiq 1992: 43), perhaps for cultural reasons (Ballard 1990: 228).

Politics as an arena of ethnic negotiation

When discussing Bradford politics, commentators seem confused as to which label to use: 'black', 'Asian' or 'Muslim'.[7] Recent studies have shown that 'Asian' voters have higher turnout rates in parliamentary and local elections than the ethnic majority (Anwar 1994), this notwithstanding the persistence of racism amongst many Labour voters. Whilst Asian Labour candidates have been crucial in Bradford in winning three key marginal wards, Asian candidates have not been supported in wards where the large majority of voters are white (Le Lohe 1990).

Bradford exemplifies how a shared Muslim identity can cut across regional and linguistic particularities. By 1992, although the city had twelve 'Asian' councillors, with the exception of one Sikh all were Muslims and all were Labour members. Eight were from Azad Kashmir, the numerically dominant Muslim community, the others included a Bangladeshi, elected in 1991, and a Gujarati woman, elected in 1992. These last two indicate that a new generation of younger politicians was beginning to develop tactical alliances across regional and linguistic divisions on the basis of a common Muslim background, since both were selected in wards with a Pakistani majority amongst the 'Asian' electors. The concentration of Muslim communities in certain inner-city wards has thus provided a useful launch pad for their entry into local politics. The Muslim group includes the deputy leader of the ruling Labour group, Muhammad Ajeeb, the city's first 'Asian' lord mayor in 1985 and elder statesman of the community, who was just pipped in the parliamentary selection battle for Bradford North in 1992.

Muslims throughout Britain have long looked to Bradford or Birmingham to return them their first MP. While six 'black' MPs were returned in 1992, none was Muslim. In 1993 Max Madden, the Labour MP for Bradford West, a safe Labour seat, declared his intention to retire. Some 34 per cent of Bradford West's population are members of ethnic minorities, and, more particularly, 26 per cent are Pakistani. Therefore, it should have been relatively straightforward that a Muslim could be returned. In fact a Sikh candidate was selected by the Labour Party and duly became an MP.

The waters were muddied by three factors, however. First, Max Madden has used his influence to declare that Bradford should return a woman, in line with the positive action programme of the National Executive Committee (NEC) of the Labour Party. Thus, just at a time when the local Muslim communities have strong male candidates they were potentially thwarted by NEC policy. In the absence of positive action for ethnic minority candidates, women-only seats will work to their disadvantage, since at present only about 6 per cent of all 'Asian' and 'Afro-Caribbean' councillors are women (Geddes 1993). In the event, the all-woman shortlist for Bradford West was overturned 'amidst rumours of intimidation' – 'some unpleasantness' was the preferred phrase of the local party chair. The article that rehearsed these developments pointedly quoted the words of Faz Hakim, Labour's development officer for ethnic minorities: 'We must get to a situation where "black" doesn't only mean black men and "women" doesn't only mean white women' (*New Statesman and Society*, 7 October 1994).

Second, given the importance of the prize, two leading Muslim contenders, both from Azad Kashmir, were competing with each other. Thus the Muslim vote was split, enabling a non-Muslim to take the seat. What dismayed many Labour activists was that one Muslim contender was playing his high 'caste' card against his Muslim opponent, who belonged to an artisan caste. The latter in his turn challenged the former's political credentials by insisting that while *he* supported the left-wing party in Pakistan – the Pakistan People's Party – his opponent supported the 'ultra-conservative Muslim conference in Pakistan': 'You can't support Labour in Britain and Le Pen in France' (*Yorkshire Post*, 15 April 1994).

A third feature of this selection process was the accusation that Labour local ward parties have been packed by members of the respective 'clans' (kindred groups or *biradari*). Certainly one ward's membership has jumped from fifty to five hundred in a short time. Such accusations are damaging relations between these 'Asian' councillors and some of their white colleagues. Recently a highly respected white woman, with an acknowledged expertise in education matters, was deselected from Toller ward in favour of a relative of a leader of one of the powerful 'Asian' factions (on such factions see Werbner and Anwar 1991). This caused considerable resentment among many Labour councillors for a number of reasons: the Labour group has very few women councillors; if the factional ticket increasingly becomes the criterion for selection in certain wards this will freeze out able 'Asians' outside the clan network – Muslim and non-Muslim alike – and will enable candidates to bypass the usual nursery for such candidates – whether trade union activity or involvement in organisations such as the Racial Equality Council.

Many accusations similar to those levelled at Irish Catholic involvement in Labour politics between the world wars can now be heard in Bradford. The irony is that a seat that could have returned one of the country's first Muslim MPs did not, because of internal rivalries shaped by Pakistani politics.[8] If this happened it would probably be misinterpreted by Muslims outside the city as part of an 'establishment' conspiracy to exclude Muslims from the corridors of power. It could also strengthen the hand of those within the Muslim community who argue that separate organisations are the way forward, whether the Islamic Party of Britain or the Muslim Parliament – both of which remain marginal to the interests of most Muslims in Bradford.[9]

Race relations in the city

There is no need here to rehearse the history of race relations legislation culminating in the Race Relations Act of 1976 and the variety of policy initiatives that stemmed from it (Hiro 1992; Scarman 1983). In Bradford, little priority was given by policy makers to meeting the needs of all sections of the community and fostering good race relations – as mandated by the 1976 legislation – until 1981. Stung by a damning report of the Commission for Racial Equality in 1979, and reminded of the potential seriousness of such issues by the explosion of urban violence across the country, in November 1981 the local authority committed itself to a twelve-point race relations plan. Along with initiating positive action to encourage equal opportunities and to fight racial disadvantage, it recognised that Bradford was a multiracial, multicultural city, and that every section of the community had 'an equal right to maintain its own identity, culture, language, religion and customs'.

A powerful Race Relations Advisory Group was established to make sure that all local authority directorates implemented this policy (see also Chapter 13). The next section will consider the important initiatives taken in education – an arena of concern for all 'Asian' communities in the city. The local authority sought to honour its commitments and within ten years its workforce began to reflect the ethnic diversity of the city: from less than 1 per cent it had reached 7 per cent! The lead taken by the local authority in this regard has been crucial since it is the biggest local employer, with a workforce of some 27,000. It also recruited race aware-ness trainers to review with managers their recruitment and training procedures, as well as the ethos informing the various directorates and institutions for which the local authority is responsible. This policy has not been without its difficulties: an outside consultant produced a report in 1993 entitled *Alibis for Inaction*, seeking to understand why there was a continuous stream of industrial tribunal cases against the authority for failure to honour its equal opportunities policy.

The role of the local Community Relations Council (CRC) – renamed the Racial Equality Council (REC) in 1991 – has been of great importance. The CRC was the earliest institutional acknowledgement of religious and ethnic diversity in Bradford. Created in 1966, it was one of a network spawned across the country, a product of partnership between central government, local authorities and local communities. Race relations legisla-tion provided for the funding through the Commission for Racial Equality (CRE) – and its predecessor bodies – of paid, professional staff who then worked with the many voluntary bodies in the city. From being a predominantly white organisation at its inception, concerned with the welfare needs of the black and South Asian settlers, and the removal of friction points between the emerging minority communities and the ethnic majority, it became a vehicle for racial equality, with a majority of its membership drawn from South Asian communities.

The importance of the CRC was enhanced with the authority's 1981 race relations plan. In the words of one of its most distinguished chairs, Ramindar Singh, later a deputy chair of the CRE:

[The CRC] was given representation on various committees, policy review bodies and working parties ... its growing influence on local decisions, particularly in the allocation of resources and funds under community programmes, was quickly grasped by Asian community leaders ... the demand for REC membership increased, and competition for its leadership became much more intense. ... Currently, the staff employed in the REC is of predominantly Asian origin [that is] almost eighty per cent of its membership. ... So it is virtually controlled by Asians. (Singh 1994: 19)

Its first Asian chairman was Mohammed Ajeeb in 1975. He was the first of five Muslims and three Sikhs to hold this position, including a Muslim woman – the only woman to date – in 1992–3. The CRC was possibly the central forum for interethnic meeting and active collaboration in the 1980s. It functioned as a nursery for at least six 'Asian' politicians – five Muslim and one Sikh – who belonged to it in the 1980s. I have written elsewhere of the importance of the CRC – especially with regard to the Muslim communities – in creating a forum where members who also belonged to the Council for Mosques or who were councillors could test opinion across communities on a range of issues, whether the controversies around the provision of halal meat in schools, multicultural education (in Bradford associated with the name of a local headmaster, Ray Honeyford), the *Satanic Verses* affair or the Gulf crisis (Lewis 1994). In the debate between supporters of the CRCs (Ben-Tovim et al. 1986) and their critics, who expect little from such 'paternalistic' institutions (Rex and Tomlinson 1979: 88), my research adds weight to the arguments of the former (see also Chapter 11 in this volume).

As long as issues could be construed as falling within an anti-racist framework, the Muslim communities could generally count on broad-based support within the CRC. But this broke down with the Rushdie affair. Many anti-racist activists, white and Asian alike, had earlier enthusiastically used Rushdie's anti-racist writings and media appearances in the struggle for racial justice. While Sikhs and Hindus were careful not to criticise the Muslims publicly on this issue, the Bradford CRC – to the chagrin of many Muslim members – refused to take a position on it, preferring to leave it to the Bradford Council for Mosques. In reality, Hindus and Sikhs were worried about a possible white backlash against Muslims in which they, as 'Asians', would be caught up. Further, as one prominent Sikh commentator noted: 'The feelings of a growing dominance of Muslim influence on local politics [was] likely to continue hindering the development of "Asian" unity in the city' (Singh 1994: 21).

The 1980s also saw the emergence of large umbrella organisations – the Council for Mosques, the Federation of Bradford Sikh Organisations and the Hindu Vishwa Parishad – intent on fighting for 'direct representation in the future to defend their particular interests, rather than through the REC' (Singh 1994: 19). It is clear that interreligious and intercommunal conflicts in South Asia are rendering cooperation between Hindu, Sikh and Muslim communities in Britain more difficult. This is particularly evident in relations between Muslims and Hindus. As a local response to the destruction in India of the Babri mosque at Ayodhya, in December 1992, at the hands of militant Hindus, Hindu temples and properties were firebombed in Bradford (Burlet and Reid 1995). The reactivating of ancient suspicions and antagonisms can override the desire to cooperate in the area of racial justice. In this environment the existence of other arenas for active cooperation become very important. One such is local education.

Education: multiculturalism as an answer to underachievement?

Educational provision in the city has long been a field of contention between the local education authority (LEA) and the different religious and ethnic minorities. In 1979, Hindu, Muslim and Sikh parents' opposition to the policy of bussing was successful. This policy of dispersing some (15 per cent of) 'Asian' children from the inner city to suburban schools was intended to assist their acquisition of English by avoiding monolingual 'Asian' schools, and ensuring some mutual contact between them and indigenous children. However, it denied young children the security of neighbourhood schools, affected their involvement in extracurricular activities, and was seen as little more than a policy of social engineering directed at their assimilation (Bowen 1981; Halstead 1988).

The 1980s saw the LEA attempting with a measure of success to honour the pledge given in its twelve-point race relations initiative that any community had 'an equal right to maintain its own identity, culture, language, religion and customs'. LEA memoranda, under the new educational banner of 'multiculturalism', sought to accommodate the special needs of religious minorities within the framework of a common curriculum. The goad to action was furnished by the Muslim Parents Association which pressed for five LEA schools to become Muslim voluntary-aided schools on the pattern of many Christian and Jewish schools. The LEA hoped that such Muslim demands for voluntary-aided schools would be neutralised by responding to their specific needs. An influential Muslim councillor lent his weight to LEA policy by opposing separate Muslim schools: 'I don't want separatism in any form ... what we want is the accommodation of our cultural needs, especially in the educational system' (Halstead 1988: 52). A series of measures was taken that won widespread support within all the 'Asian' communities: flexibility was to be shown in relation to Muslim dress codes for girls, single-sex swimming, physical education, and extended visits to South Asia. Halal meat would be introduced in key schools. The LEA was able to capitalise on generous government subventions from the Home Office, under section

11 of the Local Government Act 1966, established to meet 'special needs' of Commonwealth children; in 1989, the LEA had some 280 language support staff, 97 nursery nurse posts, 40 home–school liaison staff, 18 bilingual assistants, and 34 community language teachers.

Of particular value to all the religious minority communities was a renegotiated religious education syllabus in 1983, involving the city's five main religions – Christianity, Islam, Hinduism, Judaism and Sikhism. In 1986, a pioneer Inter-faith Education Centre was founded to implement the syllabus with staff from all the faith communities. Since religious education has long been a sensitive issue in British society, it is the one subject of the curriculum that is exempt from central direction under the Education Reform Act of 1988 – a local Standing Advisory Council for Religious Education (SACRE), including members of all religious communities, draws up the local syllabus. A recent innovation is 'model syllabuses' developed nationally in 1994, whereby members of each tradition draw up their own suggested syllabus as a resource for use locally. This attempt to accommodate religious and cultural sensitivities of minority communities within the curriculum and ethos of the state educational system stands in marked contrast to the French system's model of individual integration and hostility to any assertion of community identity in the secular space of state schools (Kepel 1995: xix–xxii; Nielsen 1995: 20–22; on religious education in Germany, see Chapter 8 of this volume).

It would be idle to pretend that the Bradford LEA's attempts to respond to the religious and cultural needs of minority communities have been free of controversy. The provision of halal meat was vigorously opposed in 1983 by animal rights activists and many others, including the National Front, whose advocacy of 'animal rights' met with some incredulity. Multiculturalism was challenged by an inner-city headmaster, Ray Honeyford, who argued that concessions by the LEA to accommodate the special needs of Muslim parents indicated a value judgement that gave priority to the preservation of cultural identity over the promotion of social integration. Foolishly, he chose to publish one of his many articles on such sensitive and complex educational issues in a small-circulation right-wing journal, the *Salisbury Review*, committed to the repatriation of ethnic minorities.

The protracted controversy his articles triggered dragged on for 18 months, until December 1985, when the headmaster was persuaded to take early retirement with a generous financial settlement. The Honeyford saga did considerable damage to community relations in the city. The headmaster's opinions on three important interrelated issues – racism, free speech and accountability, the nature and limits of multiculturalism – were never properly debated, with Honeyford demonised by the left as a 'racist' and lionised by the right as a doughty defender of freedom of speech. Since Honeyford made disparaging remarks about Indians and

Afro-Caribbeans, as well as Pakistanis/Muslims, the campaign to oppose him enjoyed support from all ethnic minorities and the CRC (Halstead 1988; Lewis 1994; Murphy 1987). In the 1980s, then, 'Asian' was still a viable category around which ethnic minorities could be mobilised on certain issues.

While the LEA has sought to meet the special needs of the minority communities there has long been 'support from all Asian parents for the establishment of more single-sex [girls'] schools in the city' (Singh 1994: 17). As early as 1973, Riaz Shahid stood as an independent candidate in a local election pressing the local authority to provide more single-sex, girls' schools. He defeated the Labour candidate in the ward election, and just failed to pip the Conservative candidate (Le Lohe 1979). Although in 1983 the Council for Mosques did not support Shahid's Muslim Parents' Association (MPA) scheme for five Muslim voluntary-aided schools, this was because they had no confidence in the ability of the association to finance, organise and administer such schools. They were not opposing the principle of a Muslim state-funded school. Finally, in 1984 one section of the Muslim community represented in the Council for Mosques established a small private Muslims girls' community school.

By the early 1990s, there was evidence of a shift in priorities amongst Bradford Muslims. The LEA had worked hard on the back of 'multi-culturalism' to meet the linguistic, religious and cultural needs of the minority communities. In 1992, however, when educational performance tables were published for the whole of England, Bradford languished almost at the bottom. It was evident that in Bradford, as elsewhere in the country, children from Pakistani and Bangladeshi backgrounds were underachieving in schools compared to white, Afro-Caribbean and Indian children (Jones 1993).[10] In 1993, Bangladeshi and Pakistani parents in one area of the city concluded that their children were being excluded – whether intentionally or unintentionally – from the best schools in the city.

The parents sought a judicial review of the LEA's allocation policy, claiming that it contravened the Education Act of 1980 and the Race Relations Act of 1976. The former had emphasised parental choice, but the parents claimed this was negated in their case since some 31.5 per cent of Asian applicants in Manningham, the inner-city ward with the highest Asian population, were not admitted to any of the three schools of their choice – as against only 5.3 per cent of non-Asians. Second, while in many suburban areas there were two or three 'good' schools within the catchment areas, this was not true of Manningham. Thus, with regard to allocation of places to oversubscribed schools, 'Asian' parents lost out with regard to the two criteria normally used, sibling preference and catchment area.

The parents lost the judicial review and subsequent appeal.[11] However, the LEA acknowledged the *prima facie* case of the parents and went to considerable pains to reallocate the children to different schools. The important point here is that these Bangladeshi and Pakistani parents made it quite clear that they do not wish to remain encapsulated within local, all-Muslim inner-city schools.

Because of the considerable demographic pressure on inner-city schools, the LEA also came round to supporting a Muslim voluntary-aided school. The school in question is the Muslim Girls' Community School. The school has benefited from the conjunction of a number of factors: first, there is a perceived national injustice to correct: the Islamic Schools Trust in Brent – despite Yusuf Islam's vigorous advocacy and a High Court judgment declaring the Department for Education's behaviour towards the school 'manifestly unfair' – has still, after ten years, failed in its bid to get voluntary-aided status. The reason given is the existence in the Brent authority of surplus school places. This argument cannot be used in Bradford. Further, state support for at least one Muslim school is fast becoming 'a political symbol ... for Muslims, who consider that their needs ... have been systematically ignored and their status undermined' (CRE 1990: 11).

As a sign of its support, the Bradford education authority has recently given the Muslim Girls' Community School a large, middle-school building at a peppercorn rent. It now enjoys widespread local support, including that of all the political parties and all the faith communities, while Yusuf Islam has promised financial support. In endorsing the school's bid the Roman Catholic Bishop of Leeds made this pointed remark:

> The experience of my own community, which had been a persecuted minority, is that having our own schools within the state system helped us to move out of our initial isolation, so as to become more confident and self-assured. The effect of separate schools for us has been integration, not divisiveness. (*Telegraph and Argus*, 3 January 1991)

The wheel has turned full circle. Roman Catholics, who were able to press for government subsidy of their schools on the back of the existence of Anglican schools, now support the Muslim community as they press for voluntary-aided status. Education remains the one arena where cooperation across religious and ethnic minority communities has continued to be relatively unproblematic.

The business community: a cautious welcome for ethnic minorities

Since 1983, all the Asian communities have generated a growing professional and business sector, largely institutionalised around religious groupings. One of these, mainly Hindu, is supported by the Conservative

Party; another, the Eid Committee, was established by a group of Muslim businessmen and professionals to fundraise and, through conspicuous philanthropy, to challenge the negative images of Muslims generated in the post-Rushdie, post-Gulf crisis. Two further Muslim and Hindu organisations were established, one by a Hindu businessman known for his unapologetic support for anti-Muslim, right-wing Hindu parties in India.

The creation of organisations where members of distinct Hindu, Sikh and Muslim religious and political persuasions can meet in business forums has been the task of various government and local authority initiatives, funded by the state and the European Union (*The Journal*, October 1994: 42).

In all, the local authority, central government and the business community have generated initiatives that aim to incorporate ethnic minorities and breathe life into an inclusive definition of 'Asian'. Such centripetal forces act as a brake on powerful centrifugal forces. The latter are evident from the controversy that has surrounded the control of the local ethnic minority radio station. In 1989 the Independent Radio Authority granted Bradford City Radio (BCR) a franchise to set up a commercial radio station providing services for the ethnic minorities in the city. BCR had directors from all the Asian communities and its executive director was a Muslim. Because of economic difficulties BCR changed hands in 1991 with the controlling share going to a Hindu media moghul, Avtar Lit, who controlled the London-based Sunrise Radio. BCR was renamed Sunrise Radio Yorkshire (SRY). A new executive director was brought in from London. She too was from a Hindu background.

The change in control led to press complaints that SRY was little more than a satellite of the London station, that it emphasised Hindi rather than Urdu, and that it was at times biased against Muslims.[12] Muslim pirate radio stations in Bradford became more active. In 1992, Muslims were given a licence for a pioneer radio station to broadcast during the whole month of fasting, Radio Fast FM. Some of those involved then put in a competing bid, under the name of Rainbow FM, to vie with SRY for the franchise in 1994. The directors of Sunrise were largely Hindu, although there was some Muslim investment in the company. The directors of Rainbow were largely Muslim, although one-third of its investors were Sikh.

In the event, SRY won the bid. Protagonists of Rainbow FM felt they lost because of a fear of 'fundamentalist Islam' – a fear that SRY exploited in its bid. This was expressed in a recent article in the British Muslim weekly, *Q News*:

Muslims are still excluded from representation on the airwaves. ... 'in Bradford, the Muslims were asked questions like, "What do you think of Rushdie?" ... the implication is clear: in the minds of Lord Chalfont and his pals, Muslims are equated with extremism and must be denied access to the radio media at all costs.' (14–21 October 1994)

Along with the absence of a Muslim MP and a Muslim state-funded school, this absence of a Muslim-run minority station can fuel fears that there is a sustained 'establishment' attempt to marginalise British Muslims.

Forums for interreligious meeting

Churches in Britain have generated or contributed to that dense network of associations and voluntary organisations that comprise civil society. In a stimulating work, the late Ernest Gellner insisted that civil society was a crucial condition of Western liberty and, in part, a fruit of Western Christianity (Gellner 1994). In Britain, civil society includes civic religion with chaplaincies to Parliament, to lord mayors, to the armed forces and wherever people are vulnerable, whether in hospital or in prison. Public service broadcasting continues to include religion, with audience figures for 'Songs of Praise' exceeding those of 'Match of the Day' (Davie 1994). Taxpayers fund students to study theology as a university subject, which means that the discipline is not ghettoised in confessional colleges and maintains a conversation with academic life in all its diversity. As part of general culture, such religious studies can act as a brake on irrational and intolerant expressions of Christianity.

The peculiarity of English Christianity is that the Anglican establishment has been pluralised to make space for other Christian denominations without in the process being privatised:

> Today Christian Aid, the Catholic Institute of International Relations, and ever-so-many bodies and individuals from Frank Field [the MP] to the Bishop of Oxford, all represent differing faces of the Church vis-à-vis the state and public political life … [with] the establishment still there to assert constitutionally, publicly and symbolically the church's relevance both to public policy and to the care of the most needy. (Hastings 1995: 117)

In the context of this chapter, the public role of Christianity is important for three reasons. First, churches are themselves multiethnic in composition and part of transnational communities. Thus they act as an antidote to Little Englander sentiment which favours narrow and exclusive definitions of national identity.[13] The first chairman of the National Committee for Commonwealth Immigrants (NCCI), appointed by the Labour government in 1966, was the Archbishop of Canterbury, who consistently opposed restrictive immigration policies (Chadwick 1991: 165–76). The bishops, who sit in the House of Lords, continue this tradition today with their current rearguard action against the Asylum and Immigration Bill (April 1996).

Second, because public and civic life is permeated with Christian influence it is proving increasingly hospitable to the religious concerns of minorities – as the minorities increasingly recognise (Modood 1997). Many departments of theology have been extended to include religious studies. My discussion of education above made it clear that religious education in schools is no longer confined to Christianity, and also, that Muslims enjoy active Christian support when pressing for state funding for Muslim schools, on a par with Christian and Jewish schools. In Bradford, the Anglican hospital chaplain – himself a Nigerian – has been active in making space for the religious and pastoral needs of all patients and staff. In 1995 he brought to fruition a bold project to provide, in a new hospital complex, a worship area that all faiths can use. In the last ten years, a Jewish and a Muslim lord mayor have had civic services held in a synagogue and a mosque respectively.

Third, churches are active in the creation and support of many institutions where members of different communities work together on issues of common concern. In Bradford, the Anglican bishop was in 1966 the first chair of the city's Community Relations Council, an organisation that continues to be supported by all the mainstream Christian denominations in the city. He also persuaded a retired local policeman – well respected in all the communities and an active churchman – to become its first community relations officer.

Two other initiatives supported by the churches are worth mentioning in this respect. The charitable trust Common Purpose, set up in 1988, brings together people from all the city's communities who have been identified as future leaders in the public, private and voluntary sectors. Through a programme of monthly seminars they explore together how they can make a greater contribution to the public life of the city. It is no coincidence that the prime movers behind the Eid committee had gone through this programme. Second, the Inner Cities Religious Council (1992), which operates within the context of the government's Action for Cities programme, has actively sought to work in partnership with all faith communities, at local *and* national level, on the regeneration of inner cities and deprived urban areas. Bradford has its own ICRC. The initiative has been given a cautious welcome by religious minority communities since it affords recognition of the commitment and resources all have invested in religious and community developments in these areas.

The Anglican bishops of Bradford have long used their influence to involve the leaders of the city's religious minorities in major civic occasions. A striking example of this was the visit to Bradford in 1988 of the South African Archbishop Desmond Tutu as guest of the bishop. He preached on racial justice before a crowd of ten thousand people at the local football ground. At this service, members of all the city's religious communities were present, and contributed readings on this theme from their own traditions. In the same year a radical conservative administration came to power in Bradford under the leadership of Councillor Eric Pickles, and introduced a range of dramatic financial cuts which seemed to threaten many of the most vulnerable people in the city. The bishop's advocacy of the most disadvantaged won him additional respect among the religious minorities.

Regular meetings with religious and community leaders meant that the bishop was well placed to maintain a dialogue in the midst of the Rushdie affair, when communities were threatening to polarise into mutual in-comprehension. He arranged a series of meetings to review the impact and implications for the city of the affair: first, between Muslims and leaders of all the other religious traditions; then, between Muslims, civic leaders, politicians and the police. All spent a day at the diocesan retreat centre in the Dales, far from the clamour of the city. Finally, a dialogue was opened nationally, between Muslim leaders and church leaders at Lambeth Palace, including representation from the Bradford Council for Mosques, the Bishop of Bradford and the two archbishops. This was important in that it meant that at least one component of the Establish-ment was prepared to continue a dialogue with Muslims (see Lee and Stanford 1990: 85–96; Lewis 1993).

Such crosscutting links between members of different religious com-munities, in a variety of forums across the city, have been valuable at other times of crisis. As early as 1986, religious and community leaders showed considerable wisdom in creating the Joint Committee of South Asian Organisations (JCSAO) as a forum for the three Hindu, Sikh and Muslim umbrella groups in the city. The JCSAO seeks to manage inter-communal tensions and to prevent conflict in South Asia from spilling over on to the streets of Bradford. After the demolition of the Babri mosque in 1992, a committee was set up comprising civic and religious leaders of all traditions to monitor the situation and to identify, expose and isolate extremist elements in both Muslim and Hindu communities (Burlet and Reid 1995).

Conclusion

It is not the purpose of this chapter to dismantle one invented category 'Asian' in favour of supposedly primordial religious categories, whether Christian, Hindu, Muslim or Sikh. From the perspective of the ethnic majority, the term 'Asian' will continue to be serviceable to identify shared relations with Hindu, Sikh and Muslim communities with regard to racial, educational or religious exclusions. However, it is clear that if different religious and ethnic minorities are to collaborate in a range of forums it will not do to be beguiled by such labels as 'black' or 'Asian' into supposing that there exist ready-made solidarities. This study has under-scored the findings of the Policy Studies Institute which noted that 'the divergence between specific ethnic groups has been increasing' (Jones 1993: 151).

Much more work needs to be done in understanding the relationship between ethnicity and religion. Further, if Gilles Kepel is right, commentators will need to be increasingly alert to the growing salience of religion in public life (Kepel 1994). It is clear that, as recent critics have argued, too many social scientists grounded their theories of modernity in a secularisation thesis and thus find it hard to comprehend the persistence of religion and its increased importance in the public domain (Sacks 1991; Davie 1994; Van der Veer 1995). The downside of the increased significance of religion in community identity is that it can render cooperation across religious minorities more precarious. Hindu–Muslim and Muslim–Jewish relations in Britain are inevitably coloured by Islamophobia in India and Israel (Halliday 1995; Burlet and Reid 1995). The director of the Jewish Council for Racial Equality, Eddie Friedman, recently remarked on this tension and called for a 'more relaxed and generous attitude' between the two communities (*Jewish Chronicle*, 7 July 1995).

It is clear from this local study that minority communities are increasingly engaging with and acting upon British public and civic life at many points. But equally important, 'as a result of their struggles for equality the civic culture becomes part of their minority culture[s]' (Rex 1995: 249). This can be illustrated with regard to Muslim involvement in local politics and education. For Muslims from Pakistani and Bangladeshi backgrounds, learning to share power as minorities within political parties whose 'priorities, ethos and culture owe nothing to Islam' is a totally new experience (Lewis 1994: 175). Similarly, unlike the new model Islamic syllabus referred to earlier – the fruit of collaboration involving all Muslim traditions – in Pakistan there are still separate religious syllabuses for Sunni and Shi'a Muslims. In short, an inclusivist ethos of civic society, supported by central and local government funding for selective projects, acts as a brake on the disaggregation of 'Asian' into separate religious communities locked into a dangerous spiral of suspicion and increasing social separation. At the same time, religious identity as a vital component of ethnicity is also given considerable public and civic recognition, not least by the churches.

As with the Irish Catholic and Jewish communities, Hindus, Sikhs and Muslims are finding it possible both to work through the political mainstream and to mobilise on a religio-communal basis. National and religious identities of the new minorities are no more likely to dissolve than those of older communities. In such a situation, the specificity of British civic culture with its strong Christian colouring needs to be acknowledged as a major asset. Leading members of religious minorities are now challenging a secularist argument that favours disestablishment. They contend that this would further disadvantage them (Davie 1994: 141–9). If multicultural society is to cohere there will need to be an honest encounter between the religious and the secular imaginations.[14]

Notes

1. The legal situation is somewhat different in Northern Ireland, where, given the prevalence of Catholic–Protestant antagonism, law against incitement to religious hatred was put in place before race relations legislation.

2. In England the Church of England is the established church; in Scotland the established church is the (Presbyterian) Church of Scotland.

3. Until the civil war of 1971, Pakistan comprised both West Pakistan and East Pakistan (now Bangladesh).

4. I have borrowed the phrase 'awkward minority' from Steven Fielding's book *Class and Ethnicity: Irish Catholics in England, 1880–1939*.

5. The other two factors Colley identifies are continental wars and imperial expansion.

6. *Al falah* is a Qur'anic word, meaning 'success'. It is used in the call to prayer.

7. This confusion is evident in the article in the *New Statesman and Society* (7 October 1994), 'Equal Fights', which reviewed the disputes in Bradford West.

8. The first Muslim MP, Mohammed Sarwar, was elected in May 1997 in Glasgow Central – a constituency with a much smaller proportion of Muslims and Muslim political activity than Bradford West or several other English constituencies.

9. In the 1992 general election, the Islamic Party of Britain put up three candidates for Bradford constituencies. All lost their deposits. In Bradford West, with an estimated 16,000 Muslim votes, they picked up a derisory 471 votes – they did worse in the other two constituencies. None of the five handpicked members of the Muslim Parliament for Bradford is an influential member of local Muslim communities.

10. The statistics Jones presents are deeply disturbing, and are, perhaps, explained by the fact that most Pakistanis and Bangladeshis come from some of the least developed rural areas in both countries, whether Azad Kashmir or Sylhet; trans-continental arranged marriages from these areas still account for well over 50 per cent of all marriages and this institutionalises linguistic disadvantage; too many monolingual staff entertain unreasonably *low* expectations of such pupils; curriculum and teaching methods are not adequately addressing such complex realities; funds from central government have been squeezed, while the growing privatisation of local government has reduced the resources available to the LEA to meet the special needs of inner-city schools.

11. The judge argued that while 34.4 per cent of 'Asian' children did not get their choice of schools, the figure for non-Asians in the same area was even higher, 37.5 per cent.

12. Spoken Hindi and Urdu are very similar: only with literary Hindi and Urdu do the differences become apparent, with the former drawing on Sanskritic and the latter on Arabic and Persian alphabets.

13. The appointment in 1994 of the first Asian to an English bishopric – the Reverend Dr Michael Nazir Ali as Bishop of Rochester – created considerable interest in both the mainstream and the ethnic minority media.

14. A recent review in the *Jewish Chronicle* (10 May 1986) – of *Yitzhak Rabin: Soldier of Peace* – indicated that the book was valuable in illuminating the 'religious–secular cleavage in Israel, the dominant cleavage in the current political system. ...

There was virtually no one in the Labour leadership who knew how to speak to members of the religious camp in their language ... [still less able] to challenge them in their language.' This cleavage is clearly dangerous and is not confined to Israel and Judaism.

References

Ahmad, Akbar S., and Hastings Donnan (eds) (1994) *Islam, Globalization and Postmodernity*, Routledge, London.

Anwar, Muhammad (1994) *Race and Elections: The Participation of Ethnic Minorities in Politics*, Monographs in Ethnic Relations No. 9, Centre for Research in Ethnic Relations, University of Warwick, Coventry.

Ballard, Roger (1990) 'Migration and Kinship: The Differential Effect of Marriage Rules on the Processes of Punjabi Migration to Britain', in C. Clarke et al. (eds) *South Asians Overseas*, Cambridge University Press, Cambridge.

— (1992) 'New Clothes for the Emperor?' *New Community*, 18(4): 481–92.

Ballard, Roger and V. S. Kalra (1994) *The Ethnic Dimensions of the 1991 Census: a Preliminary Report*, Department of Religions and Theology, Manchester.

Ben-Tovim, Gideon et al. (1986) *The Local Politics of Race*, Macmillan, London.

Bowen, D. (ed.) (1981) *Hinduism in England*, Bradford College, Bradford.

Burlet, Stacy and Helen Reid (1995) 'Cooperation and Conflict: The South Asian Diaspora after Ayodhya', *New Community*, 21(4): 587–97.

Chadwick, O. (1991) *Michael Ramsey: A Life*, Oxford University Press, Oxford.

Colley, L. (1992) *Britons: Forging the Nation 1707–1837*, Yale University Press, New Haven and London.

CRE (1990) *Schools of Faith: Religious Schools in a Multicultural Society*, Commission for Racial Equality, London.

Davie, Grace (1994) *Religion in Britain since 1945: Believing without Belonging*, Blackwell, Oxford.

Fielding, Steven (1993) *Class and Ethnicity: Irish Catholics in England, 1880–1939*, Open University Press, Buckingham.

Geddes, A. (1993) 'Asian and Afro-Caribbean Representation in Elected Local Government in England and Wales', *New Community*, 20(1): 43–58.

Gellner, Ernest (1994) *Conditions of Liberty: Civil Society and Its Rivals*, Hamish Hamilton, London.

Halliday, Fred (1995) *Islam and the Myth of Confrontation*, I.B.Tauris, London.

Halstead, Mark (1988) *Education, Justice and Cultural Diversity: An Examination of the Honeyford Affair, 1984–85*, Falmer Press, Sussex.

Hastings, Adrian (1990) *Church and State: The English Experience*, The Prideaux Lectures, University of Exeter, Exeter.

— (1995) 'Church and State in a Pluralist Society', in *The Shaping of Prophecy: Passion, Perception and Practicality*, Geoffrey Chapman, London.

Hiro, Dillip (1992) *Black British White British: A History of Race Relations in Britain*, Paladin, London.

Jones, Trevor (1993) *Britain's Ethnic Minorities*, PSI, London.

Juergensmeyer, M. (1993) *The New Cold War? Religious Nationalism Confronts the Secular State*, University of California Press, Berkeley.

Kepel, Gilles (1994) *The Revenge of God: The Resurgence of Islam, Christianity and Judaism in the Modern World*, Polity Press, Cambridge.

— (1995) 'Between Society and Community: Muslims in Britain and France Today', foreword to Daniele Joly, *Britannia's Crescent: Making a Place for Muslims in British Society*, Avebury, Aldershot, pp. IX–XXIII.

Lee, S. and P. Stanford (eds) (1990) *Believing Bishops*, Faber and Faber, London.

Le Lohe, M. (1979) 'The Effects of the Presence of Immigrants Upon the Local Political System in Bradford, 1945–77', in Robert Miles and Annie Phizachlea (eds) *Racism and Political Action*, Routledge, Kegan and Paul, London.

— (1990) 'The Asian Vote in a Northern City', in Harry Gouldbourne (ed.) *Black Politics in Britain*, Avebury, Aldershot.

Lewis, Philip (1993) 'Beyond Babel: An Anglican Perspective on Bradford', *Islam and Christian–Muslim Relations*, 4(1): 118–38.

— (1994) *Islamic Britain: Religion, Politics and Identity among British Muslims*, I.B.Tauris, London.

Mehmood, T. (1983) *Hand on the Sun*, Penguin Books, Harmondsworth.

Modood, T. (1991) 'The Indian Economic Success: A Challenge to Some Race Relations Assumptions', *Policy and Politics*, 19(3): 177–89.

Modood, T. (ed.) (1997) *Church, State and Religious Minorities*, Policy Studies Institute, London.

Murphy, D. (1987) *Tales from Two Cities, Travels of Another Sort*, John Murray, London.

Nielsen, Jorgen (1995) *Muslims in Western Europe*, Edinburgh University Press, Edinburgh.

Norman, E. R. (1968) *Anti-Catholicism in Victorian England*, Allen and Unwin, London.

Rafiq, M. (1992) 'Ethnicity and Enterprise: A Comparison of Muslim and Non-Muslim Owned Asian Businesses in Britain', *New Community*, 19(1): 43–60.

Rex, John (1995) 'Multiculturalism in Europe and America', *Nations and Nationalism*, 1(2): 243–59.

Rex, John and Sally Tomlinson (1979) *Colonial Immigrants in a British City: A Class Analysis*, Routledge and Kegan Paul, London.

Sacks, J. (1991) *The Persistence of Faith: Religion, Morality and Society in a Secular Age*, The Reith Lectures (1990), Weidenfeld and Nicolson, London.

Sahgal, Gita and Nira Yuval-Davis (eds) (1992) *Refusing Holy Orders: Women and Fundamentalism in Britain*, Virago Press, London.

Scarman (Lord), (1983) *The Scarman Report: The Brixton Disorders 10–12 April 1981*, Penguin Books, London.

Singh, R. (1994) 'Introduction to Pictorial History', in *Here to Stay, Bradford's South Asian Communities*, City of Bradford Metropolitan Council, Bradford, pp. 9–23.

Van der Veer, Peter (1994) *Religious Nationalism: Hindus and Muslims in India*, University of California Press, Berkeley.

Werbner, Pnina (1990) *The Migration Process: Capital, Gifts and Offerings Among British Pakistanis*, Berg, Oxford.

Werbner, Pnina and Muhammad Anwar (eds) (1991) *Black and Ethnic Leaderships in Britain: The Cultural Dimensions of Political Action*, Routledge, London.

CHAPTER 8

Islam as a Civil Religion: Political Culture and the Organisation of Diversity in Germany[1]

Werner Schiffauer

Within the political cultures of Europe, a variety of different models have been developed for the organisation of cultural and ethnic diversity. These models reflect the specific shape of the respective civil societies that have evolved in different European states – and, in particular, the solutions they have developed to the problem of national solidarity. A brief sketch of the French and the British solutions to this problem constitutes a backdrop against which we can begin to understand the specificity of the German model (for a comparison also to the Italian model see Chapter 4).[2]

In France's political culture, critical emphasis is placed on 'individual' integration. Related to this is the idea that social solidarity is based on equality of opportunity, and is guaranteed by a powerful central state operating according to rational criteria. Ethnic and religious ties (which are defined as intrinsically antithetical to individual equality) should, according to this model, play no role in public exchange – they are defined very strictly as private matters. The principle of the general good, of the nation, is built precisely in opposition to all cultural particularisms. The nation is, as it were, a framework for individual emancipation (Dumont 1991: 142).[3] Given these assumptions, it is only logical that French policy is based on strict laws protecting individuals from discrimination and that the recognition of group rights is carefully avoided (Costa Lascoux 1991: 285). This explains the nervousness with which the French public reacts to Islamist demands that girls be granted the right to wear headscarves in schools: schools are, after all, institutions in which the foundational principles of citizenship are taught (see Bourdieu and Passeron 1977; Gellner 1983; Harker 1984; Anderson 1991).

In the UK a very different solution to the organisation of cultural and ethnic difference is to be found. Emphasis is placed, in general, on processes of collective bargaining and collective integration. By this I mean that it is not merely the state but a range of social institutions that develop mechanisms for the constitution of national solidarity. This emphasis comes along with a civil ethic dictating mutual respect and fairness in public. It corresponds to a general British scepticism regarding systematic and centralised solutions that can only be guaranteed by a strong state. Instead, pragmatic solutions are sought that take account of the specific circumstances of each case (for examples of this tendency, see Chapters 7 and 13). The result, however, is a greater acceptance of cultural inequality and difference at the national level than in France. The debate on the Rushdie affair before the passing of Khomeni's *fatwa* is a telling instance of this tendency: Muslims felt unfairly treated by the British press and media – while the British press and media expressed the opinion that whatever the verbal offence caused, burning books was a severe violation of the basic principles of civil debate. In other words, virtually the whole Rushdie affair was constructed by political actors outside the formal sphere of centralised state politics.

I want now to approach the German case through a case study – the German state project to develop an Islamic school curriculum. This is a story that I feel illustrates the key elements that constitute the German version of organising cultural and ethnic diversity. Not that it is typical (what, after all, is typical?) but it was developed in the context of a particular political culture and therefore bears the stamp of that culture.

The project

In 1978, three Islamic Turkish groups submitted a petition to the Ministry of Culture, Education and Church Affairs in North Rhine-Westphalia (Nordrhein-Westfalen) demanding the establishment of Islamic religious education in schools. The ministry's response was a positive one and it appointed an assistant of the then newly founded Landesinstitut für Schule und Weiterbildung to devise a primary school curriculum. Klaus Gebauer, an agnostic with a Jesuit Catholic family background, set up a commission composed initially of interested Turkish teachers (selected on the basis of their teaching qualifications), an Islamic theologian, an academic specialising in Islam, and Protestant and Catholic religious education teachers. Later on, additional Islamic theologians were co-opted. Over a period of several years, this body has devised a curriculum for the first eight years of school education and developed a series of school textbooks. The curriculum and the textbooks were presented to various Islamic institutions for assessment: the Divinity Faculty of the Al Azhar University, the Divinity Faculty of the University of Istanbul, and various Islamic Turkish organisations in the Federal Republic of Germany. The remarks of the universities and ministries were by and large positive. The assessments from the Islamic organisations were of a more critical nature. There are good chances that the curriculum and the schoolbooks are going to be introduced in all the other German *Bundesländer* as well.

Integration and control

The state's unusual plan to develop a curriculum for a religious minority was at first justified by a structural problem. In contrast to the Christian Churches, the Islamic religion is not organised along corporate lines and so does not speak with one voice. As far as Islamic Turkish groups in Germany were concerned, this meant that at the time the petition was being considered there were five sizeable Islamic organisations vying with one another. Three Turkish Islamic groups, the Milli Görüş, the Nurcu and the Süleymancı, had approached the Ministry of Culture, Education and Church Affairs and they had forged an action coalition for that very purpose. Apart from the fact that these three groups acted on behalf of only a section of Turkish Muslims, it became apparent during the second meeting that the alliance was showing signs of crumbling when it came to spelling out actual objectives. According to Ferdi Zimmermann, who is in charge of training teachers for the project, 'It all started with a meeting which Gebauer had arranged for anybody who was interested. All hell broke loose. ... The ministry could only say, "Everybody out, we'll do it ourselves," and after this he got a group together.' Here we should note that the reaction of the ministry's representative can primarily be read as a Social Democratic profession of faith in integration. The internal divisions in Islam were used by the other German *Länder* (that is, federal states), as an excuse to do absolutely nothing. Politically, the project is supported by liberals and others on the left.

The ministry could now have taken the easy route of contacting the Office for Religious Matters in Turkey as a possible partner. Officially, this body represents a 'modern', laical Islam.[4] A complex mixture of partly heterogeneous factors seems to have played a role in the ministry's decision not to commission the Turkish Office for Religious Matters to conduct the required curriculum development, but rather to take the matter into its own hands. On the one hand, there was a conspicuous lack of information on the part of ministry officials – Klaus Gebauer maintains that they had no idea what they were letting themselves in for. On the other hand Gebauer himself, an ambitious young man who recognised the opportunity of a lifetime in the project, had been commissioned with its successful completion and evidently did all he could to prevent it being taken out of his hands.

Perhaps more important in this decision was the need for control. There was a general feeling that the schools should be opened for Islamic religious education, but also that certain limits ought to be imposed. More exactly, there was concern that if responsibility was delegated, it would mean giving *carte blanche* to an unmanageable, nondemocratic, political influence.

Behind this need for control there was a twofold estimation of the importance of religion. It was considered both dangerous and necessary. On the one hand, people can be manipulated through religion. According to Gebauer, religion is in principle a dangerous weapon, and that is as true of Christianity as it is of Islam. At the same time, however, religion is also necessary. Although he considers 'every kind of monotheism' to be misanthropical because of its claim to absolute truth, it is a fallacy to believe that religion can be abolished because, as he puts it, 'by and large people construct meaning for themselves by means of religion'. Gebauer maintains that from a sociological point of view, the function of religion is simply to reduce people's fear, when confronted with the infinite complexity of reality, by drawing simple conclusions. Religion is a fact of life which has to be lived with and therefore the need is to make the best of it: 'It should be civilised, not abolished.' For this reason, Gebauer finds the French solution, excluding religion from the state domain in the name of laicism, highly problematic. Since religion quite obviously fulfils a basic need, he argues, ignoring it only leads to the abandonment of an open field to Islamist groups. He poses the question whether it is wise that

> Fundamentalist groups can band together in the suburbs of Paris and the French police then has to move in to clamp down on them. ... Wouldn't it be better to give them their own religious space, something which would also be supported by society at large?

Gebauer believes that the French solution merely leads to the development of religious ghettos and, at the end of the day, to a situation whereby fundamentalism and a discourse of exclusion only serve to strengthen each other and eventually lead to the development of national conflicts. In contrast, he sees his project as a way of working towards an open society, as an attempt to reduce the force inherent in the dynamics of immigrant 'resentment, alienation, exclusion and self-exclusion'. While the French solution strikes him as being problematic because it imprudently overlooks the *persistence* of religion, the British solution, which grants considerable influence to local groups in the development of Islamic religious education, also appears problematic because it fails to take account of the *danger* of religion.

This line of reasoning makes clear German political culture's suspicion, if not fear, of religious difference in the face of the problem of collective solidarity. The German solution to the problem of religious diversity lacks the kind of faith reflected in the British solution: namely, a faith in a culture of religious tolerance arising from the interaction of different religious groups; a faith in the likelihood of fair play governing their mutual dealings with one another; and therefore also a faith in a common ground that allows for solidarity. Though it may be asked whether the Rushdie affair did not show the limits of this model. The German solution also lacks the faith that is reflected in the French republican solution:

namely, faith in the existence of a secular sphere in which every *citoyen* has the right to participate, regardless of origins, culture or creed, a participation that establishes the ground for a collective solidarity. It may be argued against this solution, however, that the banishment of particularities into the private sphere makes it far more difficult to maintain a check on the political agendas arising out of diverse sentiments.[5]

The individual and the general

Be that as it may, the wish to control religion cannot fully explain the ministry's project. It would of course have been possible for the state to retain an element of control if the project had been entrusted to the Turkish Office for Religious Matters or to German Muslims. Indeed, the existence of a positive motive seems to have been a decisive factor in the way the project was managed. One of the main aims of the project was to appropriate the influential power of religion for the process of social integration. In brief, it may be argued that the project wanted to make a *civil religion* out of Islam.

The solution to the 'problem of solidarity', as widely perceived in German society, can be reduced to Schiller's formula of the individual and the general.[6] Unprompted solidarity is possible, in Schiller's view, when the individual and the particular are fully realised in the general, and vice versa; that is, when the general and the individual are not related mechanically to one another, but dialectically. With reference to the curriculum project, this means that in and through the observance of their particularity (that is, Islam) Muslim children can be integrated into the general (namely, the civil society of the Federal Republic of Germany). Unprompted solidarity is only possible, then, when the particular is not uncoupled from the broader social consensus. Admittedly, this presumes that the general is also contained in the particular and furthermore that the particular, Islam in this case, is depicted in such a way that the general can be perceived through the particular. This notion was now expressly taken as a central platform of the curriculum project. It was a matter of showing 'that Article 1 of the Constitution ("the dignity of man shall be inviolable") can be corroborated fully by Islam' (Gebauer). Since mutual respect for human dignity is an essential condition for the establishment of a humane, multiracial society, religious education that espouses such respect also serves the common good.

Contributions are thus made towards collective solidarity: via an education that teaches an Islam that enables children to learn the basic values upon which the society of the Federal Republic of Germany is based. Or, in Gebauer's words:

> A kind of moral cement is turned out, a kind of unspoken and unquestioned common consent about the rules of living together. I say cement because if

there is not a minimal level of agreement within a society then it will fall apart, there can be no security in it.

In Gebauer's opinion, the integration of Muslim children into German society is assisted in yet another way by the project. The reference to the compatibility of Islam and the Constitution is a potent argument against those who base a discourse of exclusion on the irreconcilability of 'basic Christian values' and Islam.

> If I can thoroughly prove Article 1 of the Constitution from the Qur'an, then I have created a great deal of acceptance for Muslims here. ... If I can demonstrate that in terms of the actual words used, the attitude of Islam towards women is in no way different to that of Christianity, and if at the same time I can show that Islam is a tolerant religion, more tolerant than Christianity towards transgressions, then what I have said is that Muslims understand Article 1 better than the Christians who formulated it. (Gebauer)

The reproach that this might be a paternalistic takeover, albeit with the best intentions, suggests itself here. The project workers counter this argument with a reference to the religious division of labour. The task of state religious education is not the imparting of religious faith – this is best taken care of by Qur'an schools, confirmation and communion classes – but rather, the creation of solidarity. In turn, such a division of tasks gives Gebauer the freedom to interpret:

> The Qur'an does not get worse in any way because of all my interpreting. ... And no Muslim will believe such interpretations if they do not appear self-evident to them. In this respect, I'm doing Muslims no harm, but rather compelling my own society to give up its foolish arguments against Islam.

If we use the terminology developed by Mary Douglas (Douglas 1970; 1978; see also Thompson, Ellis and Wildavsky 1990), we may say that the German solution to the organisation of diversity corresponds to that of a hierarchical social order, while the English solution would be egalitarian, and the French individualist (see Chapter 4 of this volume, however, for a different view of the English solution). The end in view, in the German case, is the 'integration' of the Muslim minority, and that means first of all giving it a place in school. Diversity is taken account of, but it is incorporated into an overall scheme; particularities are acceptable even in the public domain, but they must not lead to the separation of various Islamic factions or sectarian groups. The attention of the political culture is directed towards the structure and forms of delimitations: these may and should exist, but should not harden and ossify. Concern in this culture is directed less towards the suppression of the diversity of voices than towards a well-regulated togetherness.[7] The main anxiety that such a political culture exhibits concerns the creation of enclaves and ghettos that become separate, beyond the reach of the state. On the other hand, it may be argued that a hierarchical solution to the problem of diversity implies an even greater pressure to assimilate than an individualistic or egalitarian one. In France, differences can thrive more freely because they are not tied into the public sphere; in England, they can contribute more to the general good because they are given expression within the context of a political structure that places more emphasis on pragmatic, *ad hoc* solutions than on systematic regulation.

Hierarchy and the experts

It would be an oversimplification to create the impression that the German Islamic education project was simply an ingenious attempt at assimilation into German society. In fact, integration into German society as it really exists is not so important to the initiators of the project; rather, what concerns them is the integration of Muslims into a civil society *still to be developed* in Germany. They see their undertaking as a contribution to the development of a heterogeneous yet nevertheless still German culture.

Despite this, it was symptomatic of the hierarchical political culture of the Federal Republic that civil servants and experts took responsibility for the task. This was consistent with a deep-seated belief underlying German political culture that the common good is most effectively served by those who are best-informed about a discourse, free of domination (Schiffauer 1993a: 196). In this view, it is necessary for such best-informed people to be taken away from what is often termed 'the pressure of the street'. An important condition for this is that experts be made financially independent and be granted tenure – both of which enable them, in principle, to be neutral. In brief, the belief is that it is civil servants/experts drawing a salary from the state who can be most trusted with discovering what is best for everybody.

The confidence felt by the expert that s/he stands above the petty politics of everyday life is expressed without a hint of embarrassment. The project workers claimed that they were best able to interpret religion, in this case Islam, in accordance with the common good. Their neutrality allowed them, they believed, to take up the stance of a religion researcher or an ethnologist who does not share the beliefs of those he is investigating, but who can explain and deduce on the basis of textual evidence, and who is, moreover, in a position to grasp the rational dimensions of the religion in question. Such a method rules out the securalist tendency to run around the world 'preaching that there is no God'; as Gebauer points out: 'In so doing, I would only create more insecurity, if I had any effect at all. Anyhow, this would only achieve the opposite of my real aim: namely a sensible, rationally functioning democratic society.'

The truth is that it is easy for the ethnographer to believe that Klaus

Gebauer is doing his utmost to establish a sympathetic understanding between religious groups – indeed, the spirit of the project is marked by the seriousness with which an attempt is being made to do justice to Islam. However, paradoxical situations arise with the management of the project again and again. Gebauer has enough distance from the project to recognise the irony implied by the fact that he, a German liberal, has taken on the task of imagining how a Muslim father would treat his daughter.

> Sometimes I feel rather odd when I write texts and commentaries for educational purposes. I often notice that I act as if I were a Muslim. I almost certainly still make mistakes, but through my own feelings and self-awareness I have learnt in the meantime to feel like a *hodja*.
>
> The feelings of superiority of the religious traditionalists are self-evident: I believe that my interpretations are just as valuable as Mr Kaplan's ... since mine foster Islam in Germany more widely than do the interpretations of Mr Kaplan, and I believe mine to be in accordance with Islam – because Islam calls on the faithful to further the cause of Islam.[8]

The obligation of the middleman to stand above groups and collectives in society becomes most apparent when the project workers speak about German institutions which, in their opinion, are opposed to their vision of a civil society. It expresses itself in the pride with which they report, for example, how the churches – which initially gave notice of their hostility to the project – were misled by the fact that the Islamic lessons were not classified as religious classes but as lessons in the native language. This is also manifest when, in the higher interest of the establishment of an open, multicultural society, Klaus Gebauer attempts to show that Islam is even in compliance with the German Basic Law, even though this is not the case in his opinion – in private he recognises, for example, that Islam's negative treatment of those religions not in possession of holy writings does not accord with the Basic Law. ('In this respect I am not being quite loyal towards German society when I reinterpret the Qur'an to such an extent.')

Democracy and education

The mediation between the general and the particular in German society is made by means of education (Schiffauer 1993; Norman 1991: 19ff). By attending classes in Islamic religious education, Muslim children internalise the basic values of the Federal Republic of Germany. Furthermore, they are brought up to be citizens with the capacity to act responsibly, that is, in accordance with the common good. This notion determines not only the context of the mediation but also its methods. The way this knowledge is imparted has even greater consequences for the teaching and dogma of religion than its interpretation along the lines of the Basic Law which, even if it is occasionally farfetched, only refers to specific dimensions of the Islamic corpus.

The aim of the lessons in Islamic religion, which at the same time determines their inner structure, is as follows: first, to provide the children with an Islamic identity ('the formation of identity through the use of tradition'); second, to enable the children to apply their knowledge of Islam to their particular experiences in the Federal Republic; and third, to enable them to acquire the ability to enter into a dialogue with Christians in Germany. In other words, the ability to present their own beliefs and defend them – 'to know enough about their own religion so that they don't portray themselves as a minority of little worth' as Gebauer put it – is a critical element in the lessons. The aim is, therefore, to achieve a fusion of religious knowledge and everyday life. The objective, as Zimmermann explains, is:

> to give the children the opportunity to decide for themselves, to find their own way. Not to say: 'Now you must do this', but to open everything to the child and show him or her what is possible and the children can say for themselves when they grow up – 'and that's why I want that'.

In other words, what is at stake is a matter not only of knowledge, but also of the ability to apply this knowledge to the special context of the Federal Republic, and to defend it discursively.

In practical terms, this is translated into action by the development of a pupil-centred education. The fundamental educational consideration is to 'pick up' the children where they already are:

> It is not a question of trying to put something into the children's heads – you can't put anything in anyway, you have to bring it *out* of them. But what is in doesn't come out and something happens in this process which I can gauge because I am there at the time.

It is generally presumed that experiences in early childhood are stored in the form of pictures: 'If you want to recall the child's basic experiences, early socialisation in childhood, then you have to show the typical experience pictorially.' This was the background to the development of picture-based lessons. The children are shown pictures and they then begin to interpret them. The teacher picks up on the children's interpretations, draws general conclusions from them and then associates them with one another. The picture sequence 'Cleanliness is part of faith' serves as an example (see pictures 1–5).[9] In the pictures, connections are made to situations the children already know (Landesinstitut 1986: 76): personal hygiene, cleaning teeth, washing clothes, ritual cleansing, the park, and so forth. The children's interpretations can then be taken up and related to surahs (chapters) in the Qur'an (surahs 4: 43, 5: 6, 8: 11 and 74: 4 and 5 are quoted). By means of these pictures, a connection to the situation in Germany is made and, incidentally, socially responsible actions, in the form of ecological values, are imparted. Finally, it is intended that the children should be put in the position of being able to speak for their religion – in other words, they should be able to stand up to offensive expressions of racism that characterise Muslims as dirty. In the concept of the lesson unit, the curriculum outline states:

> This series of lessons is concerned with preparing the pupils for the Islamic understanding of cleanliness in everyday life and ritual purity by means of concrete questions and problems of cleanliness. They should be made aware that everyday cleanliness and purity are obligations which, through their grounding in the Islamic tradition, represent more than just hygienic or aesthetic demands. It should also be made clear to the pupils that keeping the body clean is necessary to the maintenance of good health and that in this way they can and should act for their own good. They should learn that cleanliness is a command of Allah. (Landesinstitut 1986: 77)

In effect, through this way of teaching the subject matter a certain reading of Islam is taught. Inasmuch as society is presumed, it is set as something of primary importance. The question asked of religion is then as expected: how can religion teach us to deal with the contemporary situation in society? Almost automatically, thereby, a historical way of reading is adopted by posing the question: 'What kind of position did Muhammad take up in another social situation?' to issues of cleanliness, and 'How can this position be applied to today's society?'[10] Simultaneously, a discursive, argumentative handling of religious tradition is instilled in the pupils.

A model for this explanation in relation to the emotive subject of the 'position of women in Islam' looks something like this: Islam took up a progressive position in relation to women during Muhammad's time and therefore it should today too take up a progressive position. When this historical way of reading is employed, according to Gebauer:

> You can make out of Islam a very peaceful, very morally stable frame of mind which is even more humane than the Christian and Jewish religions, because, strictly speaking, Islam does not punish people for their transgressions. What it says is this – 'Mankind is basically good. Of course, it sometimes has problems staying good and that is why it has to be guided by the Qur'an and the sayings of the Prophet.'

Accordingly, the main adversary to be reinterpreted is a scriptural reading of the holy texts. 'What I'm saying is that I cannot accept [literally] a law which people claim comes from God. In doing so, they close the door to the possibility of getting to know the origins of this law.'

This way of teaching is not only practised in relation to Islam – a similar position is taken towards Christianity. The state defines the teaching method, and by defining the 'how' of religious learning, it has effect on the spirit of the religion taught:

> We forced a Bible-orientated method on the Catholic Church. They didn't want it. So the Catholic curriculum for secondary schools was developed in 1985 under my guidance. The Protestant curriculum was ready two years earlier and consisted mainly of us saying – on the one hand, there is this basic experience [that we all share]; on the other, the biblical tradition and the story of its effect [must be juxtaposed]. So then we selected certain biblical quotations for certain situations in daily life and said: 'This has to be connected'. Because of the requirement that religious education be a school subject, we cannot allow that the basic elements that go into making the decision are not made publicly.

In other words, the German hermeneutic tradition is applied with the same rigour to Islamic texts as it is to Christian texts. A text is read by systematically posing the question of which problem it may be able to answer (in this case, the position and circumstances of women at the time of the Prophet); it is read by identifying a central message, a key issue to which all other issues are related (the basic humanity of the Qur'anic message); and it is postulated that an adequate understanding can only be reached if the context in which a text is read is systematically taken into account (in this case, the situation of Turkish children in Germany).

This last point bears witness to the close relation of hermeneutics to existentialism, as it takes up the point raised by Kierkegaard, that thinking can only be taught when it is systematically related to individual existence. This is true also with regard to the insistence that the children should discover the meaning of the texts themselves. Truth, according to Kierkegaard, cannot be taught by another, but has to be developed and discovered by each individual him/herself. The recipient thus plays an active role which implies that the boundaries between text and interpretation are blurred.

The question arises, of course: is it Islam or some imaginative construction of what Islam might be that is reconstructed in this way? The question is all the more pertinent when one considers that the roots of the hermeneutical tradition date back to the school of Bible reading developed during the Reformation. It was initially the Protestants' emphasis on direct access to the holy scripture which led to the development of interpretative techniques aiming at an adequate 'understanding' of a text.[11] The tradition was rationalised and secularised during the Enlightenment, systematised during the nineteenth century in the context of the development of historicism (Dilthey), and philosophically grounded in the twentieth century (Gadamer, Heidegger). Although hermeneutics thus has a long history, it is undeniable that its principles were formulated within a Christian tradition.

The question of an adequate understanding of Islam is all the more difficult to answer when one refutes the notion that there is one authentic interpretation of Islam. Rather than attempting to answer this question in a definitive way, it may be sensible to point out some differences and commonalities that arise when comparing Christian hermeneutics to various Islamic hermeneutical traditions. Even in the classical Islamic exegetic tradition, a historical reading of the Qur'an always played an important role. The historical circumstances of the revelation were particularly important with regard to the problem of abrogation – that is, with regard to outdated commands which continue to be part of the Qur'an although they have been replaced by other, later *hukms* (Fischer and Abedi 1990: 115ff). Examples are the different commands with regard to drinking alcohol. In these cases one had to know the historical circumstances of the revelation in order to know which command had been replaced. But then, it is clear that history in this case is secondary to scripture as it helps to clarify the scripture but not to review it in a critical tradition. It is the scripture that is primary and history that is secondary; on the other hand a radical hermeneutical tradition would reverse that sentence and so finally arrive at the position that historical knowledge allows the discovery of a truth in an obviously wrong sentence.[12]

This difference between the German hermeneutics school and Islam also exists with regard to modernisers like Muhammad Abdu or Rasid Rida who give more weight to historical reasoning. These two scholars tried to reconcile historicity (and temporality) with the absolute character of the Qur'an by pointing out that the course of history was already anticipated in the Qur'an. So they arrive, for example, at the conclusion that monogamy is in fact the marital ideal in the Qur'an and that polygamy was only justified in the historical conditions of a tribal society (Gätje 1971: 64ff/ 324ff). Klaus Gebauer would certainly stress his closeness to this position (and certainly the positive reactions from Al Azhar and the Divinity Faculty of the University of Istanbul bear witness to these affinities between the two hermeneutical traditions). But then, of course, one might point out that the modernisers feel much more bound to the exact literal meaning of the text, whereas Gebauer tends quite easily to refer to a certain 'spirit' of Islam.

Parallels and differences can be seen too with regard to the technique of identifying a key issue in a text and taking it as a point of reference for interpretation. Important voices exist in Islamist circles that would subscribe to such a reading: Cemalettin Kaplan, for example, took the position that it is necessary today to concentrate on the political messages of Islam rather than on ritual duties, as the former were suppressed in laicist Turkey whereas the latter are taught everywhere.[13] It is in this perspective that he reads and interprets the Qur'an. This reading in perspective, on the other hand, is controlled and bounded by a strict application of reasoning by analogy (*kiyas*), that is, a reasoning that decides a problem by referring to a rule created for a case that is analogous. This way of reasoning is decisively ahistorical, as the historical circumstances at the time the ruling was passed are deliberately left out of consideration, thus stressing the absolute character of the revelation. A look at one of Kaplan's *fetvas* (legal edicts) illustrates this type of argument. In the 52nd issue of his journal *Teblig* (1988: 10) he argues that football is prohibited in Islam as the Qur'an recognises only horseriding and archery as legitimate forms of physical training, and condemns all other sports as a waste of time. The argument is that football is not an analogue to horseriding and archery because (first) it does not serve the purpose of military training, and (second) it does not serve the purpose of inner peace within the community but rather leads to conflicts which (third) may be abused as a weapon in the hands of the powerful. This example is less interesting with regard to the conclusions Kaplan arrives at than in relation to the structure of the argument it reveals, which stresses the timeless character of the Islamic revelation.

Last, but not least, there are parallels and differences with regard to the third hermeneutical principle mentioned above. The insistence that reading is not a passive but an active undertaking, and that it has to relate to a person's existential condition, is stressed also in mystical Islam. Verbal truth is meaningless unless it is experienced and thus related to one's existential situation. But here again, stress is laid in Islam on the fact that this experience can only be made with the help of a spiritual guide.

What results from this discussion is that none of the hermeneutical principles translated into pedagogics by Klaus Gebauer and his team is alien to Islam. To my knowledge, they have not, however, hitherto been combined before in the likes of this project. In the final run what will be decisive is whether these ideas are received or rejected by German Muslims themselves; only they can decide whether it is Islam that is being taught to their children or some imaginative reconstruction of what Islam might be.

Conclusion

What, then, is the German vision of the organisation of diversity that emerges from this case study? In a way one might say that in Germany the catchword is taken more literally than in France or in Britain: more diversity is admitted in the public sphere than in France and more organisation is considered to be necessary than in Britain. On the one hand, there is the strong idea that a group that is part of German society should have the right to be represented in the public domain – the idea being that a stable identification with society as a whole is only possible if the particular (in this case, Muslim religion) is a recognised part of the whole. This, by the way, is one of the reasons for the very hesitant attitude of the German public to the admission of new groups into the nation: integration into German society usually takes one to two generations longer than in other European cultures.

On the other hand, there is an emphasis on the fact that this process should take place more systematically (and therefore that it should be more centralised) than in Britain, in order to avoid too much heterogeneity and therefore inequality, or – worse still – incommensurability. There is a strong concern about how to control the process of integration – the central fear being of the development of cultural ghettos (that is, environments that, by definition, escape control). In fact, German politics have been relatively successful in this respect (and the critique of the French and the British solutions refers to the fact that both, although for opposite reasons, lead to the establishment and perpetuation of ghettos, both cultural and residential). The price for this integrative arm is, however, a tendency towards paternalistic resolutions of apparent cultural incommensurables and, correspondingly, a higher expectation of conformity demanded of all residents in Germany than in the other two political cultures.

Appendix

'Sauberkeit gehört zum Glauben' (Cleanliness is part of faith)
Source: **Dinimizi Öğreniyoruz,** *The didactical unit*, **pp. 30–37.**

1. God loves the clean ones.

2. Ayşe is a clean child.

3. Our clothes also must be clean.

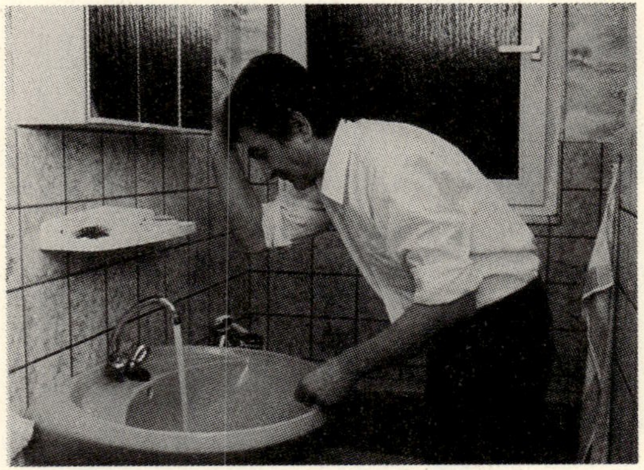

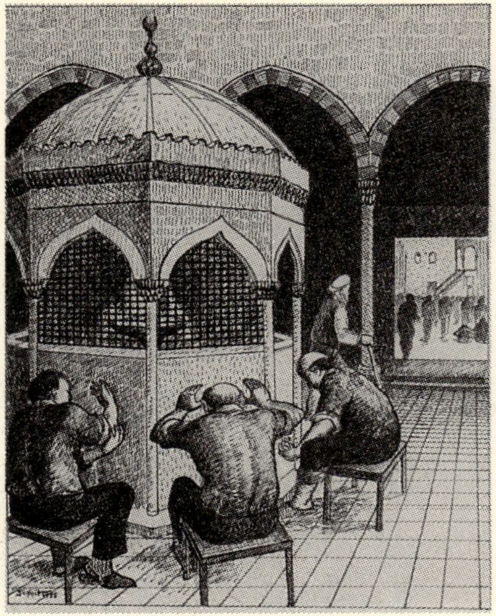

4. Without *abdest* one cannot pray the *namaz*.

5. Let us not pollute our environment.

Notes

1. This chapter is primarily based on interviews with Klaus Gebauer, the Spiritus Rector of the project described in this article and with Ferdi Zimmermann, who is in charge of the training of teachers in the context of this project. I would like to thank them for their kindness and willingness to help.

2. The French and the British models have been frequently compared. See, among others, Kepel (1993), Neveu (1993), Nielsen (1992), Schiffauer (1993a), Melotti in Chapter 4 of this volume. Still recommendable also is Troeltsch (1925).

3. The institution which, in my opinion, expresses this idea most clearly is the omnipresent *concours* (competitions and selection tests): it is an absolutely rational, universal and egalitarian procedure for the distribution of social positions.

4. Due to its very nature, the Office for Religious Matters is in fact a contested field between the various Islamic factions in Turkey.

5. The German fears can probably only be explained by the 'histoire des mentalités', namely, as emanating from the development of the German idea of the state as an answer to the problem of religious wars. It was, in fact, an historical experience, namely the inability of any of the religious groups to create solidarity on the basis of absolute truths, which found its echo in the German idea of the state and found its way into the architecture of the state. 'I said to myself that if I can prevent one single bloody, religion-based conflict in Germany, then I will die a happy man' (Gebauer).

6. Schiffauer (1993a: 195). Schiller formulates this concept in his 'Über die ästhetische Erziehung des Menschen in einer Reihe von Briefen' (1966: 193–286). See also Dumont (1991: 128–59).

7. In order to prevent misunderstanding, it should be pointed out that this type of organisation of diversity seems to me to be characteristic of German political culture in general. The same conviction of an ordered plurality underlies German federalism. The right-wing position would doubtless object that the integration of Muslims is going too far – Muslims being too different to be integrated. On the other hand, the social-liberal position would claim that the migrants could enrich society without any problems necessarily arising for the existing order.

8. On Cemalettin Kaplan see note 13.

9. I picked this particular sequence because it shows the imparting of a value – cleanliness – which is highly regarded in German culture, and which also represents a negative racist code for clichés about immigrants.

10. Gebauer: 'My Turkish families can't understand anything by Islamic truth in its literal sense as far as their lives here are concerned; even in the most simple things; unless they abstract from concrete things and then look for general ideas and principles. If I have an admonishment from the Prophet to the people of Mecca – to respect the property of orphans, for example – then it is a statement which a Turkish child from Cologne cannot identify with at all. First of all, I have to see what the word "orphan" means in our context. What does embezzlement mean in its general substantive meanings and then I get to a moral code which is usable.'

11. With the development of the hermeneutical tradition the Protestants tried to counter the argument of the Catholic Church that the Bible is principally incomprehensible without the ecclesiastical tradition.

12. Consider, for example, the problem of miracles. By taking the position that whereas miracles cannot be understood, the belief in miracles can very well be

understood, Spinoza was in a position to identify the truth in a (for him) wrong sentence. Historical reading thus served to reconcile reason with revelation (see Gadamer 1986b: 96–7).

13. Cemalettin Kaplan, who died in 1995, headed the opposition within the Milli Görüş, the European branch of the Refah Partisi if Erbaken. In 1983, he broke with the party and set up his own community, which was working for an Islamic revolution in Turkey according to the Iranian model. Kaplan declared himself representative of the Caliph in 1992 and 1994.

References

Anderson, Benedict (1991) *Imagined Communities: Reflections on the Origin and Spread of Nationalism*, Verso, London.

Baumann, G. (1993) 'Syncretism, Delineation and Convergence: Religious and Civic Dynamics in a Suburb of London', paper delivered at the conference 'The Anthropology of Existence', Amsterdam, December 1993.

Bourdieu, Pierre (1982) *Die feinen Unterschiede: Kritik der gesellschaftlichen Urteilskraft*, Suhrkamp, Frankfurt/Main.

Bourdieu, Pierre and Jean Claude Passeron (1977) *Reproduction in Education, Society and Culture*, Sage, London.

Costa-Lascoux, J. (1991) 'Gesetze gegen den Rassismus', in U. Bielefeld (ed.) *Das Eigene und das Fremde – Neuer Rassismus in der Alten Welt*, Junius, Hamburg, pp. 283–310.

Dinimizi Ögreniyoruz (Learning About Our Faith) (1988) Textbook for Primary 1 pupils, Ferdinand Kamp, Bochum.

Douglas, Mary (1970) *Natural Symbols: Explorations in Cosmology*, Barry and Rockliff, London.

— (1978) *Cultural Bias*, Royal Anthropological Institute Occasional Paper, No. 35, London.

Dumont, Louis (1991) *Individualismus – zur Ideologie der Moderne*, Campus 1991, Frankfurt/Main and New York.

Fischer, Michael M. J. and Mehdi Abedi (1990) *Debating Muslims: Cultural Dialogues in Postmodernity and Tradition*, University of Wisconsin Press, Madison.

Gadamer, Hans-Georg (1986a) 'Rhetorik und Hermeneutik', in H. G. Gadamer (ed.) *Wahrheit und Methode*, Mohr und Siebeck, Tübingen.

— (1986b) 'Klassische und Philosophische Hermeneutik', in H. G. Gadamer (ed.) *Wahrheit und Methode*, Mohr und Siebeck, Tübingen.

Gätje, Helmut (1971) *Koran und Koranexegese*, Artemis Verlag, Zurich and Stuttgart.

Gellner, Ernest (1983) *Nations and Nationalism*, Basil Blackwell, Oxford.

Harker, R. K. (1984) 'On Reproduction, Habitus and Education', *British Journal of Sociology of Education*, 5: 118–27.

Kepel, G. (1993) 'Zwischen Gesellschaft und Gemeinschaft: zur gegenwärtigen Lage der Muslime in Grossbritannien und Frankreich', in F. Balke (ed.) *Schwierige Fremdheit*, Fischer, Frankfurt/Main, pp. 81–102.

Landesinstitut für Schule und Weiterbildung (1986) *Religiöse Unterweisung für Schüler islamischen Glaubens. 24 Unterrichtseinheiten für die Grundschule – Entwurf Soest*, Landesinstitut für Schule und Weiterbildung.

Neveu, Catherine (1993) 'National Identity and Minority Formation: France and

Britain', paper presented at the seminar for 'Ethnicity, Nationalism and Culture in Western Europe' organised by the Amsterdam Centre for Comparative European Studies.

Nielsen, Jorgen S. (1992) 'Islam, Muslims, and British Local and Central Government: Structural Fluidity', paper given at the conference 'Islam in Europe', organised by the Fondazione Agnelli, Turin, May 1992.

Norman, K. (1991) *A Sound Family Makes a Sound State: Ideology and Upbringing in a German Village*, Stockholm Studies in Social Anthropology 24, Stockholm.

Schiffauer, Werner (1993a) 'Die *civil society* und der Fremde -Grenzmarkierungen in vier politischen Kulturen', in Balke (ed.) *Schwierige Fremdheit*, Fischer, Frankfurt/Main pp. 185–200.

— (1993b) 'Auf dem Weg zum Gottesstaat. Die fundamentalistischen Gemeinden Türkischer Arbeitsmigranten in der Bundesrepublik', *Historische Anthropologie*, 1(3).

Schiller, F. (1966) 'Über die ästhetische Erziehung des Menschen in einer Reihe von Briefen', in *Werke*, IV, Insel, Frankfurt/Main, pp. 193–286.

Thompson, M., R. Ellis and A. Wildavsky (1990) *Cultural Theory*, Westview, Boulder.

Troeltsch, E. (1925) *Deutscher Geist und Westeuropa – Gesammelte Kulturpolitsche Aufsätze und Reden*, Mohr, Tübingen.

Verband der Islamischen Kulturzentren (1988) 'Stellungnahme zum Curriculumentwurf "Religiöse Unterweisung für Schüler islamischen Glaubens" aus der Sicht praktizierender Muslime', unpublished typescript, Köln.

PART THREE

Situating Plural Identities

CHAPTER 9

Hyphenated Identities and the Limits of 'Culture'

Ayse S. Caglar

A massive critique has been raging in anthropology since the mid-1980s, challenging earlier theoretical constructions of 'culture' as homogenised and bounded, and of 'identity' as something fixed and stable, allegedly anchored in such discrete cultures.[1] Today, in the face of unprecedented translocal flows of capital, labour, people, goods, technology and media images, national borders have become increasingly permeable. To confront the resultant proliferation of boundary-crossing lifestyles, cultural practices and institutional forms, it is no longer possible to confine our scholarly discourses about legal rights or cultural affiliations to nation-states. A growing number of people define themselves in terms of multiple national attachments and feel at ease with subjectivities that encompass plural and fluid cultural identities.

Attempts to theorise the lifestyles pursued by such people, bearers of hyphenated identities, highlight the inadequacy of commonsense assumptions about culture as a self-contained, bounded and unified construct. This concept of culture, it must be stressed, is not restricted to anthropology. On the contrary, it is widely enunciated by national or minority intellectuals in their claims to articulate or recover an authentic 'culture'; by ordinary people who stereotype strangers and outsiders as culturally alien; by administrators and politicians wishing to govern ethnic collectivities or to mobilise their votes; and by sociologists who contrast modernity and postmodernity with the passing of 'tradition'.

The evident inadequacy of closed concepts of culture for analyses of multilocale cultural formations has inspired more general critiques that attack the static nature of earlier anthropological conceptualisations (Abu-Lughod 1993; Clifford 1994; Keesing 1994; Stolcke 1995). Ironically, such critical deconstructions themselves construct an essentialist notion of anthropology as the study of the 'little community', ignoring a wealth of accumulated anthropological writing on labour migration, urbanism, pilgrimage, nomadism, religious movements, syncretism, translocal gift economies, and nationalism. Nevertheless, the current critical discourse is useful in that it reiterates the need for a fresh look at what exactly we mean by 'culture'.

According to Lila Abu-Lughod (1993), despite its anti-essentialist intentions the notion of 'culture' deployed in anthropological discourses retains earlier tendencies of 'race' to 'freeze' difference. It thus acts as an essentialising tool, constructing a radical alterity – the 'Other'. We encounter here too a tendency to essentialise the anthropological project as fixed and unchanging: to ignore the fact that modernist social anthropology always regarded as its main priority the disclosure of current social configurations and present cultural diversity, rather than the recovery of lost authenticities. Nevertheless, the stress on synchrony and integration in the modernist project did tend to appeal to metaphors of continuity and cultural repro- duction.

But to call for a new theorising of culture that stresses its fluidity remains an empty programmatic statement unless we can evolve effective methodologies that will enable ethnographic research, not only on stable communities engaged in subsistence agriculture, but on postmodern cultural nomads. How to study the complex cultures and identities of transnationals in a globalising world? For such persons there are no self-evident cultural truths or subjectivities. Often, they no longer even imagine themselves as belonging to spatially bounded, culturally separate social entities or 'communities'. In her call to contest essentialising concepts of culture, Abu-Lughod urges anthropologists to develop strategies for 'writing against culture' (from a position within it). This requires, she suggests, a radical reconfiguration of what we mean by culture and a vigilant reflexivity about our ethnographic research and writing. The call for 'writing against culture' – which echoes Spivak's claim to write 'against the grain' of (post)colonial discourse – fails to reflect critically, however, on what anthropological research *practice* might be like for those adopting such a theoretical position. Indeed, Abu-Lughod's own research has been quite conventionally bounded: her main ethnographic study was of a single Bedouin family, and particularly of the women's world which she herself perforce inhabited. The growing impact of external economic and media forces which she describes makes little advance beyond the usual acknowledgement of 'external' influences characteristic of most 'village studies'. The question is, to what extent do our anthropological research designs – even those that claim to take a critical stand against essentialism – reveal a break with essentialist concepts of culture in anthropological discourse?

In refocusing on the social formations and 'disjunct' subjectivities of persons with multilocale and translocal attachments, a number of concepts have come to be celebrated: 'hybrid', 'creolised', 'hyphenated' and 'diasporic' identities are the most prominent among them. These concepts aim to capture the complexity of the practices, cultural configurations, and identity formations of translocal and culturally nomadic groups and individuals. The 'disjunct' identities implied by the concepts are understood as 'products of cultures and histories in collision and dialogue' (Clifford 1994: 319). Designations of settlers in European societies now mark their identities as hyphenated: German-Turks, British-Pakistanis, French-Algerians. Such hyphenations, familiar from the US context, have gained prominence in European minority discourses as much as in the scholarly discourses of European anthropologists and sociologists. The discussions of hybridisation or creolisation that are currently deployed thus reframe the discourse on European immigrants and 'minority' identities in terms of complex cultural configurations.

This shift in the terms of debate is important for deconstructing what Strathern calls 'our cultural fiction of the integrated and bounded individual who is presumed to be a member of a "culture" and who lives his or her life as a continuous directed person' (1992, quoted in Eriksen 1993: 148). Of course, Strathern's reference to a collective 'we' raises the spectre of another kind of essentialism: that of 'Europe' and its modernist notions of the individual. Whether 'we' (that is, Europeans or Westerners) necessarily always work with the kind of stereotyped notions of individualism that Strathern conjures up is highly debatable. Since, however, European nationalism in the past has tended to reify language communities and their cultural products as 'natural', it seems reasonable to use her deconstructive question as a point of theoretical departure for the reanalysis of culture and identity.

The present debate draws its urgency also from a remarkable shift in the political rhetorics of exclusion: the move is towards a 'cultural fundamentalism' that endows cultural differences with a new kind of divisive force (Stolcke 1995). Such a culture-bound political rhetoric of exclusion is increasingly gaining prominence in popular discourses. Hence culture has become a key semantic terrain of political contestation (Stolcke 1995: 2).

In the face of this developing political rhetoric, the critical reassessment of essentialist notions of culture is clearly important. One route is to stress the centrality of hybridising processes that undermine both the closure of 'culture' and the binary logic informing models of assimilation–resistance. In this chapter, however, my aim is to re-examine critically the adequacy of concepts such as 'hybridity', and to ask whether they successfully contend with the tendency in the discipline to reify culture. What are the limits of the challenge that creolisation or hybridisation models pose to the previous holistic constructs of culture?

The question of whether hybridisation, creolisation or hyphenation can break with the ontological premises underlying essentialist notions of culture is discussed first. Second, I analyse the subversive potential of political and social programmes such as multiculturalism that introduce a new politics of identity grounded in notions of cultural 'community'. I then go on to ask what the methodological starting point for a project of writing against culture might be. Finally, I suggest that we might find such a starting point in the study of object–person relations.

Creolisation, hybridity and hyphenated identities

Creolisation and hybridisation are the most celebrated concepts used in critiques of cultures as homogeneous, bounded, continuous and incommensurable wholes. Creolisation, a metaphor derived from linguistics, places the emphasis on internal heterogeneity, cultural mixtures and new positions of identification (Drummond 1980; Hannerz 1987; Fabian 1978; Parkin 1993). It refers to a process in which elements from disparate cultural origins are fully synthesised without their contradictions and differences being eroded (Parkin 1993: 84). Like creolisation, hybridisation refers to 'the ways in which forms become separated from existing practices and recombine with new forms in new practices' (Pieterse 1995: 49). Either way, these concepts draw attention to the processes that generate an interpenetration of diverse 'logics', producing new forms of boundary crossing that allegedly destabilise or subvert the hierarchies imposed on differences. Contrary to the dualistic logic of resistance–assimilation that characterised modernisation theory, here 'no single mode has a necessary overall priority' (Pieterse 1995: 51). Relations between cultures are conceptualised as flows that not only widen the field of identities but endow identities with a degree of fluidity.

Creolisation and hybridisation are thus conceived of as revolutionary antidotes to essentialist constructs of culture, identity and ethnicity. Yet these concepts are in danger of embracing the very reifications they seek to overcome. Above all, they fail to question some of the basic assumptions informing the critique of cultural holism. Here this danger looms especially large because hyphenation is anchored in ethnicity which could easily shift to an essential category, having continuity in time and space and thus undermining its relational character (see also Werbner 1997). Furthermore, this term limits the heterogeneity of German-Turks' cultural formations to two cultural wholes, namely to 'Turkish' and 'German' culture.[2]

Pieterse (1995), who conceives the globalisation process as one of hybridisation, urges us to theorise hybridity instead of simply celebrating it. As all cultures are creole, he says, we need to rework the notions of cultural hybridity.[3] He attempts to systematise hybridity in organisational terms, according to its functions, politics and structure, and proposes a continuum of hybridities in which hegemony refigures this 'melange'.

Although he acknowledges the weaknesses of hybridity as a perspective still informed by notions of culture and territory, he nevertheless regards it as a 'counterweight to the introverted notion of culture' (Pieterse 1995: 64) and is thus reluctant to discard it. Its potential to challenge 'a sociology confined within the framework of nations/societies' (Pieterse 1995: 63) enables it to produce a counter-history to that of imperial narratives and to develop a 'sociology from the interstices' (Pieterse 1995: 64). The problem, however, is that he fails to reflect on the limits of this potential in transcending frameworks founded on nations/societies.

Friedman (1995; 1996) is clearly not that merciful, arguing that such notions as creolisation and hybridisation 'museumise' culture as a thing. They are a 'confused essentialism' (Friedman 1995: 82) because, he says, they remain 'logically predicated on the notion of culture as text, as substance that has properties that can be mixed or blended with other cultures'. This is because they hinge on a recognition of disparate origins (or 'cultures'). Objectification is what endows the category of the 'creole' with 'validity over time' (Friedman 1995: 83). So, he concludes, instead of breaking with the basic tool of constructing the 'other', creolisation and hybridisation serve merely as 'another means of anthropological textual-isation of otherness', in which mixture is inscribed as essence.

My own view accords with that of Friedman, namely, that if the entities constituting hybrid constructs necessarily entail diverse cultural logics and rationalities, then this presumes a prior ontological difference between cultures. Moreover, such differences are often implicitly constituted by closed cultures and bounded ethnicities and territories. The interchangeable use of 'hybrid' and 'hyphenated' identities within such approaches illus-trates this unproblematised relationship between territory, culture and ethnicity. In such a perspective, the boundary-setting process fails to be endowed with a real processual character. Although hybridity ascribes cultures and identities with 'fluidity', they remain anchored in territorial ideas, whether national or transnational. Hence, despite these celebrations of 'difference', hybridity discourses set limits to these 'differences'. The 'sources of diversity' are pre-given rather than being practice-bound. Otherwise, it would not have been possible to treat culture as a code or as a substance.

Moreover, it is not at all clear why creolised forms and identities should necessary destabilise existing hierarchies. Even if they strike against the dualisms of minority–majority, this does not necessarily imply that creol-isation will overcome a hierarchical segregation between groups that is founded on unequal power relations. Subversion at one level may produce segregation at another level (Caglar 1995b). These theoretical weaknesses make it difficult to celebrate hybridity and/or creolisation as a real break from essentialist notions of culture.

The trope of community

Conceptualised as a crossover between bounded entities, notions of hybrid/creolised/hyphenated identities hinge not only on an original separation, but also on commonsense ideas of the existence of *a priori* spatialised *communities* (Gupta and Ferguson 1992; Stolcke 1995). The latter assumption is particularly apparent when notions of hybrid, multiple identities and multilocale attachments are used interchangeably with notions of hyphenated identities. There are good reasons why anthropologists have tended to conflate culture and spatiality. The people we study anchor their sociality in the landscape they inhabit and from which (if they are agriculturalists) they draw their subsistence. Popular discourses of nationalism and ethnicity evoke ideas of 'roots', of attachments to the soil, of the national homeland as mother or father. Urban living involves issues of collective consumption in which local residents must organise *vis-à-vis* the state and local state. The ecology of the city reflects class, status and power. In all these respects, commonsense ideas map culture on space. In their definitions of collective selves people position themselves in space and time, evolving topographies of space and sociality that generate topographies of what is home and foreign, 'us' and 'them'.

All this means that trying to disassociate culture from territory is in an important sense 'writing against culture'. Yet much of the literature takes the conjunction of cultured spaces for granted (see Gupta and Ferguson 1992: 7). The assumption is that 'the members of a locality form ... a distinctive community with its own unique culture' (Featherstone 1995: 103). Such a position operates not only with a holistic notion of community, but also with a taken-for-granted isomorphism of culture, place and people (Gupta and Ferguson 1992: 17). There is a 'pre-given world of separate and discrete "peoples" and "cultures"'. In this way, cultures are not only territorialised by the people we study, but this spatialisation is also naturalised in scholarly discourses. Cultural differences become the correlate of a world of 'peoples' (Gupta and Ferguson 1992: 17). Our ontology of spatialised cultural differences compels us to define 'people', *a priori*, as a community, understood here as a bounded and unified cultural entity. Images of spatialised locality as *Gemeinschaft*, an integrated and organic community, underpin our research designs on immigrants, revealing this theoretical bias.

From the primary communities that are thought to be intrinsically attached to these cultured territories, we isolate different groups of varied size, standing in a metonymic relation to each other and to the primary community. On the basis of such an ontology, a continuity is posited, for example between Turks and 'Turkish culture' in Turkey, the 'Turkish community' in Germany, and 'second-or-third-generation "German-Turks" in Germany'. The notion of *Gemeinschaft* mediates the immutable relationship between culture and place. And with this comes a bias in our research practices.

In migration studies the further tendency is to ethnicise cultural differences and spaces, as marking the boundaries between people of common stock or origin. This goes along with a more general 'multi-cultural' discourse which sees culture as 'the reified possession of ethnic groups or communities' (Baumann 1997: 209). Hence in popular and administrative European discourses, culture is merged with ethnic community and ethnic identity so that differences of 'culture' are imagined to be homologous with differences between 'ethnic' communities. The other side of this conflation is that the 'native' of Europe is similarly construed as having an immutable relation to a place and culture (Appadurai 1993). In Europe the 'natives' carry their cultural 'substance' into the hybridisation process, which means, in effect, that immigrants are defined permanently as beyond the pale, fundamentally alien, because their 'roots' lie elsewhere.[4]

Clearly, hyphenated identities – German-Turks, British-Pakistanis, French-Algerians, European-Muslims – equate 'culture', 'nation' and 'community'. Behind this commonsense usage, there is not only a spatialisation of ethnicities but an assumption that such conjunctions are potentially conflictual and problematic; that dual cultural 'membership' is a source of dual 'loyalties'. Implicitly, then, culture posits a commitment and a loyalty to a 'people' and 'territory'. Such loyalties in popular parlance are incapable of true hybridisation. Cultures (spaces) are thus in some deep sense incommensurable. Ethnicity becomes here the naturalised marker of an immutable cultural difference. Hyphenation privileges nationality or territorialised religion over other identifications. Ethnic (national or religious) identities are treated as the most basic identities that people possess. Subjectivities, 'disjunct' or not, are defined in common sense discourses as *ethnic* subjectivities.[5] The only other identification that is sometimes deemed relevant is that of gender.

The notion of a 'hyphenated' identity, instead of resolving cultural essentialism, tends thus to highlight the *problematic* nature of collective attachments: the clash of interests experienced by translocal groups which arise from their multiple and multilocale attachments and commitments. It is assumed, for example, that German-Turks share common predicaments and aspirations regarding their status in German society. The stress is always on the hyphenation of ethnic (national and religious) identities to the exclusion of other forms of identification. Yet the latter may potentially cut across ethnic attachments and generate quite different forms of sociality and alliance, based, for example, on class, gender, lifestyle, religious zeal, political tendency, and so forth.

The commonsense privileging of ethnicity often underpins anthropological research designs as well. By defining our object of study as an 'ethnic' group we are in danger of prioritising one form of identification over all others. We can avoid this by writing 'against' culture; that is, against the popular tendency to freeze cultural differences between groups of people on ethnic lines, to assume that each culture is internally homogeneous and that multiple loyalties imply potentially conflictual ethnic/national loyalties.

Of course, this is not to deny that the people we study often explicitly prioritise national and religious identifications. Popular discourses of cultural holism are not simply invented; they are invented dialogically, in interactions between self-defined cultural collectivities in the public sphere. In writing 'against' culture (or ethnicity) we thus seek to discover more hidden forms of identification and to highlight the arguments of identity *within* ethnic collectivities about who 'they' are and thus who may legitimately represent 'them' and 'their' interests or loyalties in the public arena (see Werbner 1997).

In underlining the imaginedness and constructedness of ethnic and national communities, we need, then, to draw attention to the fact that ethnic identity is only one kind of order of cultural or social difference. Our ethnographic practices must correspondingly abandon implicit ethnic-isations and spatialisations of cultural differences, or assumptions that such differences are automatically reproduced between generations.

The notion of crossover or even 'halfies' that Abu-Lughod introduces continues to rest on an original separation.[6] In such formulations, the assumption of an intrinsic discontinuity between cultures and societies persists. Ironically, hyphenated identities are mostly applied to second- and third-generation 'ethnic minorities'. Without an *a priori* spatialisation of cultures and the mediation of this separation via ethnic community versus 'natives', such a usage makes little sense, except as a technicality of dual citizenship. Clearly, however, much more is at stake than formal citizenship in these scholarly debates.

It seems to be difficult to use the notion of hybrid and/or hyphenated identities without reifying cultures as spatialised. According to Clifford, this is the dilemma evident in Gilroy's work, that

refuse[s] to let go of a 'changing same', something endlessly hybridised and in process, but persistently *there* – memories and practices of collective identity maintained over long stretches of time. Gilroy attempts to conceive the continuity of a 'people' without recourse to land, race, or kinship as primary 'grounds' of [that] continuity. (1994: 320, my emphasis)

If this is so, Clifford asks, '[w]hat then, is the persistent object of this history? How to circumscribe this "changing same"?' The dilemma is especially pertinent since Gilroy is aware of the dangers of reification associated with attempts to ground the unity of people in land, race or ethnic origin.

As long as we fail to couple our critique of the bounded, homogenised and organic concept of 'culture' with a similar critique of ethnic communities as spatialised and in some sense unified, we cannot develop adequate strategies for ethnographic research and representation that safeguard against the reproduction of the very entities our theories deny. We need to develop, simultaneously, research designs that work *against* taken-for-granted topos of spatialised cultural differences, that question implicit assumptions of a coincidence of identity, culture and community, and that question the reification of immigrants' practices and identities, albeit as more complicated 'hybridised' or 'hyphenated' cultural configurations. By conceiving of cultured spaces as necessary sources of collective identities and practices, we restrict the horizons of their actual heterogeneity.

This is not to deny that immigrants and other transnationals make 'new' spaces in their adopted places of settlement, or that notions of 'home' and 'alien' spaces dominate their moral universes (see the contributions to Metcalf 1996). The temples, mosques, ghettos and small businesses of post-1945 immigrants to Europe are the visible evidence of their presence, often grasped as an aggressive threat by European 'natives' who see the changing landscape of their homeland 'invaded' by 'races' and 'cultures' alien to Christianity and local traditions. Nor do I wish to deny that citizenship in the modern world remains tied to territorially bounded and culturally marked spaces. People live in space and thus space is an important parameter of their cognitive social maps and political commitments. My point is that this evident visibility comes to dominate our own theoretical horizons as anthropologists and sociologists almost as much as it does those of the racists, ethnic brokers or politicians who seek to control, resist and domesticate the spatialising process itself. To 'write against culture' in this context, in which space is a powerful metaphor for sociality, is to locate other, more invisible, processes that go towards the creation of culture and identity.

Multiculturalism and the burden of communities

The change of terminology to a stress on hybridity in discourses on ethnic 'minorities' clearly brings to the fore the issue of multiple attachments (loyalties) that challenge the hegemony of the modern nation-state. The shift in terminology thus allegedly has political implications. Hybridisation and the hyphenation of identities are said to draw attention to the crisis of the nation-state and to challenge its homogenising logic (Clifford 1994: 306–7). Clifford argues that 'positive articulations of diaspora identity reach outside the *normative* territory and temporality (myth/history) of the nation-state' (Clifford 1994: 306–7, emphasis added).

The collectivities that define themselves under the rubric of 'hybrid' or 'hyphenated' may arguably be said to challenge the normative foundation of the European nation-states above all others, since it is in Europe that 'nations' demanded popular sovereignty by claiming shared ethno-cultural roots. The public discussions centred around dual citizenship in Germany (especially with regard to 'German-Turks'), and that stress the potential dangers of multiple loyalties, are good illustrations of this linking of 'ethnicity' and 'nation'. Yet European nations are at present in the process of deprivileging cultural nationalism for the sake of a broader 'unity in diversity'(see McDonald 1996). What will be the place of hybridity and multiculturalism in this new multinational, multilingual constellation?

According to Clifford, 'transnational connections break the binary relation of minority communities with majority societies – a dependency that structures projects of both assimilation and resistance' (1994: 311). This leads to an advocacy of policies of 'pluralism'. Multiculturalism is the most important of such policies and their associated discourses. But what will be the shape of minority policies in the new Europe of nation-states, struggling to define itself 'against culture'?

The debate on multiculturalism may be conceived of as a discussion of democracy that highlights the tension between equality and difference (Taylor 1994). At issue is the reconciliation of the right to be different with the right to be equal, and the definition of the limits of these rights. Multiculturalism implies a decentralisation of the political community. It calls for a reformulation of the relations between its cultural collectivities, in order to create new forms of identity politics (Turner 1993: 411). This introduction of a new politics of *community* fails, however, to problematise the grounds on which different collectivities are recognised. Culture is the 'locus of collective rights to self-determination in multiculturalism' (Turner 1993: 422). Hence, multiculturalism takes the form of a political movement for cultural empowerment. Culture becomes the idiom for resistance. Yet what culture is, or who 'owns' it, is left unanswered.

Terence Turner acknowledges the risks of essentialism when we take culture as the source of collective rights, but he nevertheless sees a potential in multiculturalism for the equalisation of relations among existing cultural groups. He distinguishes between 'difference' and 'critical' multiculturalism. 'Difference multiculturalism'

> risks essentialising the idea of culture as the property of an ethnic group or race, ... [of] reifying cultures as separate entities by overemphasising their boundedness and mutual distinctness; ... [and of] overemphasising the internal homogeneity of cultures in terms that potentially legitimise repressive demands for communal conformity. (1993: 412)

By contrast, 'critical' or 'polycentric' multiculturalism (in which the self is construed as polycentric, multiple, unstable and unsituated) gives culture a new meaning. It becomes dynamic and open instead of the fixed property of particular ethnic groups (Turner 1993: 419). In critical multiculturalism, the internal nature of cultural communities is supposedly reformulated to allow space for the creation of new groups. Critical multiculturalism is flexible, 'setting no limits to the kind of social groups, networks, or relations that can guarantee a cultural identity of their own' (Turner 1993: 426).

The potential for polycentric multiculturalism to introduce a new politics of community lies in the 'infinite plasticity' of culture. At this point Turner's argument comes close to that of Baumann, who also sees a potential in the plasticity of culture for forging 'communities of action' out of 'communities of reified cultures in multi-ethnic alliances' (Baumann 1997). In being open to the formation of new cultural groups, polycentric or critical multiculturalism claims to avoid an identity politics that merges culture with ethnic origin.

So far, however, multicultural policies and discourses have failed to break away from the 'spatial symbolism of multiculturalism' (Soysal 1993), tending instead to maintain and reproduce spatialised cultures and communities. Can 'polycentric multiculturalism', perhaps, challenge and overcome the implicitly taken-for-granted immutable relationship between territory, culture and identity? The trouble is that multiculturalism not only posits membership in collectivities that are defined by their 'cultures', but also construes such membership to be the basis of collective rights. These collectivities and collective identities must therefore inevitably become sources of restrictive limitations and constraints (Appiah 1994: 163). For multiculturalism does not involve merely a recognition of collective cultural differences but the need to guarantee politically the *survival* of the cultural communities bearing these differences. This implies an institutionalisation of cultures in the public sphere, a freezing of cultural differences and a reifying of cultural 'communities'. Moreover, as the assertion of rights is based on the identity of groups recognised within the multicultural framework, only those group identities will be publicly endowed and given 'rights'.

It is this that Appiah (1994) regards as the real danger of multiculturalism. He argues that the collective dimensions of identity provide people with narratives of personhood – with life scripts of how a proper subject of that collectivity ought to behave (Appiah 1994: 169). Life scripts may be reshaped in positive ways, but if we accord rights to communities, these will limit the inherent potential for such changes. Community may very well become in such circumstances a site of oppression. A politics based on the recognition of community as the source of rights is thus in danger of leading to a politics of compulsion. This is clearly evident in the case of religious communities, which may demand conformity even from secular members. Islamists and Tabligh-i-Jamaat activists in Europe not only proselytise among non-Muslims; much of their cultural work aims to 'reconvert' 'lapsed' 'Muslims' to the 'true' Islam. The ethical life scripts they promote are grasped by these movements as binding on all Muslims. Such life scripts and the assumption of their binding nature are likely to dominate communal agendas within a multicultural framework, leaving in reality little room for 'hybridised' discourses and identities. The restrictive tendency of multicultural identity politics is deeply embedded in the idea of an integrated community, one that possesses a simple, homogenous 'culture' – as the necessary basis for rights and identity claims.

The potential of consumption studies

Writing against culture means breaking away from tropes that we, as anthropologists or sociologists, share with the people whom we study. One of these is that culture is always spatialised. Another is that people may be 'defined ontologically before they are described as doing anything' (Parkin 1993: 91). These commonsense ideas about culture and collective selfhood can no longer be taken for granted. There is no community defined *a priori* that constitutes the pregiven object of our investigations.

But if this is so, what could possibly serve as the methodological starting point of our ethnographic research? One option is to begin our study by exploring person–object relations as these exist in space and time. By plotting the networks of interconnected practices surrounding objects, and the sentiments, desires and images these practices evoke, we can avoid the need to define collectivities in advance. A concrete social practice centred on an object locates analysis at the level of situated, contextualised action.[7] By focusing on commodities, ceremonial gifts and consumption acts we avoid the need to define what is valued in advance of our investigations.

Commodities, defined generically as the objects of consumption and exchange, carry not only economic but cultural value, and are thus the locus around which several value-creating processes intersect. The material and symbolic dimensions of goods, their economic value and social meanings stand in an insoluble relationship in the activity of consumption (Miller 1995b). As value is not an inherent property of objects but is something created, an analysis at the level of commodities requires an analysis of how value is created. This, in turn, requires an analysis of the immediate context of transaction as well as of the macro factors operating on this context.

Economic value, like cultural value, is socially negotiated in specific social situations. Demand, desire, and power all intersect in the creation of economic value and all these are socially construed (Appadurai 1986: 4). The source of demand lies neither within the individual nor in the realm of economics, but in the definitions negotiated by collectivities operating in historically specific social and cultural contexts (on the latter see Friedman 1990: 102). Appadurai follows Simmel in arguing that exchange sets the parameters of economic value and that it is a politically mediated project because of the strategies (both individual and institutional) involved in it. It is a project subject to social control and political redefinition (Appadurai 1986: 6). This is true in the case of immigrants too for whom, as Werbner for example shows (Werbner 1990), the value and control of the goods exchanged is subject to continuous redefinition according to gendered and class interests, and at different phases of the migration process.

Desires and fantasies play an important role in the formation of strategies of consumption, and thus in the creation of demand. These are also constituted in a socially specific way, so that their sources do not lie solely within the individual. Commodities carry social meanings and are always consumed symbolically both as cultural good and as sign-value (Lee 1993: 17–24). However, both the sign-value and the fantasies of consumers construed around these commodities are embedded in a wider web of images that come to be attached to the commodities, to the lifestyles signified by these commodities and to the social groups which come to be imagined by means of these consumer goods and lifestyles. 'Objects are *categories of objects* which quite tyrannically induce *categories of persons*, they undertake policing of social meanings, and the significations they engender are controlled' (Baudrillard quoted in Lee 1993: 24). Thus commodities embody a wider social and symbolic framework and it is not possible to study person–object relationships outside the contexts in which these are socially embedded. For this reason, the practice of consumption is always socially specific, while at the same time it requires an analysis of the wider context in which it is constituted.

To sum up, then, relations between people and commodities are neither isolated nor idiosyncratic. Although consumption is a social activity often realised by individuals making personal choices, it remains fundamentally collective and its analysis requires an understanding of the macro projects of commerce, industry and state policy, as well as of the cultural images that construe sign-values.

All this seems to imply a return to notions of spatialised collective culture. The symbolic and expressive functions of consumer goods as markers of social prestige and status (Douglas and Isherwood 1979), and their symbolic utility in the maintenance of difference and in the social positioning strategies of different social groups in the society (Bourdieu 1984), are well demonstrated in the consumption literature.[8] These studies illustrate how lifestyles, mediated through consumer goods, play a central role in the reproduction of social groups and inequalities in the society. In our attempt to find a way to study and write against culture, what makes consumption a crucial topic is, however, its constitutive role in the formation of identities and social relations.

Consumption, as a process of incorporation and embodiment, is by nature transformative and constitutive. It refers to a process of redefinition by means of recontextualisation. This is a creative process as objects become the idiom of something completely different, depending on the localised context. The recontextualisation points to the way 'people construct themselves as social beings in the same process by which they construct their world' (Miller 1995a: 54). Hence, consumption is defined as a process of both subjective and collective objectification and re-objectification (Miller 1995a: 30). It is a social practice that serves as an important site for identification.

Through commodities and their consumption we construct our perceptions of our selfhood, our relationships to the world and hence also our relationship to the Other. Consumption refers to a signifying practice in which belongingness and membership are both constructed and asserted (Caglar, 1995a; 1995c; Miller 1987; Werbner 1990).[9] If we accept this, then we can explore the processual formation of these identities and collectivities in their changing historical and social specificity. This means analysing the extent to which certain object–person relations form the arena for the production and reproduction of groups as culturally distinct – that is, as 'communities', and how they interact to create particular discursive, aesthetic and 'ethnic' or 'cultural' genres.

Given the stress on the symbolic and cultural meanings of goods and the way in which they create 'worlds', 'selves' and 'subjects' in context, it seems odd for Miller (1995a; 1995b) to argue that consumption studies in anthropology could only develop once the discipline was no longer dominated by the concept of 'culture'. He finds the development of an anthropology of consumption particularly important, indeed transformative, because it marks 'a fundamental coming to maturity of anthropology – a final expunging of latent primitivism' (sic!) (Miller 1995b: 269). The irony is that Miller, rather than opening up new theoretical vistas, recommends a return to a 'grand narrative' tradition with consumption now elevated instead of 'culture' or 'civilisation' as 'the vanguard of history', and the bourgeois female as its progressive force (Miller 1995a).

We seemed to have reached a new impasse, a return to 'culture' in space. In the debate about multiculturalism, however, there is an advantage to taking object–person relations as our starting point. It relates to the dynamic nature of consumption networks, their responsiveness to change and to cumulative individual choices, and their ability to span new spaces and create new places. A multiculturalism of consumption is a multiculturalism of the market, in which consumers are left to define for themselves who they are, away from top-down constructions by the state or by fictive 'communities'. But this implies, as Anthias and Yuval-Davis propose (1992), that 'culture' and 'religion' must be kept entirely out of the public sphere and that citizens should be free to negotiate their own cultural self-definitions through exchange and collective consumption. Such a divorce between community and culture would need to apply as much to the majority group as to minorities within the nation.

What significantly underlines the importance of person–object relations in the study of multiculturalism is a curious feature of the European Union's cultural politics. Whereas linguistic or high-cultural differences are accorded the greatest respect in Brussels, the thrust of bureaucratic control is towards a homogenisation of goods and their modes of marketing. The intensity of the battles fought over the *cultural* packaging of commodities in the European Union is countered by the resistance of national communities who object to what they see as panoptic control methods, deployed by 'Europe' to destroy their national, 'traditional' goods (McDonald 1996). Hence, official multiculturalist policies are subverted by the counterimpulse of a centralised administration to create a single, 'standardised' 'market'.

The example reveals how a study of person–object relations may uncover the 'hidden side' of culture. It highlights the argument put here that, as anthropologists and social ethnographers, we need to find ways not only to *write* against culture but to *research* against culture. This would allow us to unmask the inherently fluid, changing and negotiated dimensions of national and translocal cultures and identities, hidden behind self-proclaimed collective spatialisations or official declarations of multiculturalism.

Notes

1. An earlier version of this chapter was presented at the International Centre for Contemporary Cultural Research conference 'Culture, Communication and Discourse: Negotiating Difference in Multi-Ethnic Alliances' held in December 1994 in Manchester. I would like to thank Gerd Baumann and Pnina Werbner for their constructive criticism during the conference. I am also grateful to George Elwert for his comments on an earlier version of this chapter.

2. Interestingly, the discussion of this heterogeneity is mostly confined to cultural syncretism. While syncretism in culture is welcomed and celebrated as creative and enriching, syncretic processes in religion are highly contested and identified as undesirable by German Turks as well as by the German public. In contrast to cultural boundaries, religious boundaries are vehemently protected against any kind of trespassing. For an interesting discussion of how the analytical and discursive boundaries of religion and culture are kept distinct see Yalçin-Heckmann 1994.

3. There is a consensus at this level that all cultures are creole (Drummond 1980; Clifford 1994; Hannerz 1987; Friedman 1995). However, this theoretical recognition is not always translated into practice, and most often these concepts are employed almost exclusively in relation to immigrants and ethnic minorities, usually within the framework of displacement and diaspora.

4. Here it is noteworthy that there is an asymmetry between the natives so that while some 'natives' are conceived to be immutably bonded to a place and culture, in the case of some 'natives' such an immutable relation is never an issue. The contrast between Germany and the United States is instructive in this sense.

5. For a counter position formulated against Barth's view of ethnic identity see Rousseau 1979.

6. Abu-Lughod defines 'halfies' as 'people whose *national or cultural* identity is mixed by virtue of migration, overseas education, or parentage' (1993: 131, emphasis added).

7. Such a position has some resemblance with the 'situational method'. For a new evaluation of this method see Rogers and Vertovec 1995.

8. Although Douglas and Isherwood, as well as Bourdieu, draw attention to important aspects of consumption and consumer goods, their approaches nevertheless entail problems. For critiques see Miller 1987; Friedman 1990; Lee 1993.

9. My own work has focused on such processes of identity and ethnic genre formation around consumption among German Turks.

References

Abu-Lughod, Lila (1993) 'Writing Against Culture', in R. G. Fox (ed.) *Recapturing Anthropology*, School of American Research Press, Santa Fe.

Anthias, Floya and Nira Yuval-Davis (1992) *Racialized Boundaries*, Routledge, London and New York.

Appadurai, Arjun (1986) 'Introduction: Commodities and the Politics of Value', in A. Appadurai, *The Social Life of Things*, Cambridge University Press, Cambridge.

— (1993) 'Patriotism and Its Futures', *Public Culture*, 5: 411–29.

Appiah, Kwame (1994) 'Identity, Authenticity, Survival: Multicultural Societies and Social Reproduction', in Amy Gutmann (ed.) *Multiculturalism*, Princeton University Press, Princeton.

Baumann, Gerd (1997) 'Dominant and Demotic Discourses of "Culture"', in Pnina Werbner and Tariq Modood (eds) *Debating Cultural Hybridity: Multi-Cultural Identities and the Politics of Anti-Racism*, Zed Books, London.

Bourdieu, Pierre (1984) *Distinction: A Social Critique of the Judgement of Taste*, Routledge and Kegan Paul, London.

Caglar, Ayse S. (1995a) 'McDöner: Döner Kebap and the Social Positioning Struggle of German Turks', in J. A. Costa and G. J. Bamossy (eds) *Marketing in a Multicultural World*, Sage, London.

— (1995b) 'Segregation in a Creolised World', paper presented at the Second Theory, Culture and Society Conference – 'Culture and Identity: City, Nation, World' – 11–13 August, Berlin.

— (1995c) 'German Turks in Berlin: Social Exclusion and Strategies for Social Mobility', *New Community*, 21(3): 309–24.

Clifford, James (1994) 'Diasporas', *Cultural Anthropology*, 9(3): 302–38.

Douglas, M. and G. Isherwood (1979) *The World of Goods*, Basic Books, New York.

Drummond, L. (1980) 'The Cultural Continuum: a Theory of Intersystems', *Man* (n.s.), 15: 352–74.

Eriksen, T. H. (1993) *Ethnicity and Nationalism*, Pluto Press, London.

Fabian, Johannes (1978) 'Popular Culture in Africa: Findings and Conjectures', *Africa*, 48: 315–31.

Featherstone, M (1995) *Undoing Culture*, Sage, London.

Friedman, Jonathan (1990) 'The Political Economy of Elegance', *Culture and History*, 7: 101–25.

— (1995) 'Global System, Globalisation and the Parameters of Modernity', in M. Featherstone and S. Lash (eds) *Global Modernities*, Sage, London.

— (1997) 'Global Crises, the Struggle for Cultural Identity and Intellectual Pork-barreling: Cosmopolitans vs. Locals, Ethnics and Nationals in an Era of De-Hegemonisation', in Pnina Werbner and Tariq Modood (eds) *Debating Cultural*

Hybridity: Multi-Cultural Identities and the Politics of Anti-Racism, Zed Books, London.

Gupta, A. (1992) 'The Song of the Nonaligned World: Transnational Identities and the Reinscription of Space in Late Capitalism', *Cultural Anthropology*, 7(1): 63–76.

Gupta, A. and Ferguson, J. (1992) 'Beyond "Culture": Space, Identity and the Politics of Difference', *Cultural Anthropology*, 7(1): 6–23.

Hannerz, Ulf (1987) 'The World in Creolisation', *Africa*, 57: 546–59.

Keesing, Roger (1994) 'Theories of Culture Revisited', in R. Borofsky (ed.), *Assessing Cultural Anthropology*, McGraw Hill, New York.

Lee, J. L. (1993) *Consumer Culture Reborn*, Routledge, London.

McDonald, Maryon (1996) 'Unity in Diversities: Some Tensions in the Construction of Europe', *Social Anthropology* 4(1): 47–60.

Metcalf, B. R. (1996) *Making Muslim Space in North America and Europe*, University of California Press.

Miller, Daniel (1987) *Material Culture and Mass Consumption*, Basil Blackwell, Oxford.

— (1995a) 'Consumption as the Vanguard of History', in Daniel Miller (ed.) *Acknowledging Consumption*, Routledge, London.

— (1995b) 'Consumption Studies as the Transformation of Anthropology', in Daniel Miller (ed.) *Acknowledging Consumption*, Routledge, London.

Parkin, David (1993) 'Nemi in the Modern World', *Man*, 28(1): 79–99.

Pieterse, J. N. (1995) 'Globalisation as Hybridisation', in M. Featherstone and S. Lash (eds) *Global Modernities*, Sage, London.

Rogers, Alisdair and Steven Vertovec (1995) 'Introduction', in *The Urban Context*, Berg, Oxford.

Rousseau, J. (1979) 'Classe et ethnicité', *Anthropologie et Sociétés*, 2(1): 61–9.

Soysal, Yasmin (1993) 'Boundaries and Identity: Immigrants in Europe', paper presented at the conference 'European Identity and Its Conceptual Roots', May 1993, Boston.

Stolcke, V. (1995) 'Talking Culture', *Current Anthropology*, 36(1): 1–13.

Taylor, Charles (1994) *Multiculturalism and 'The Politics of Recognition'*, Princeton University Press, Princeton.

Turner, Terence (1993) 'Anthropology and Multiculturalism: What is Anthropology that Multiculturalists Should be Mindful of It?' *Cultural Anthropology*, 8(4): 411–29.

Werbner, Pnina (1990) *The Migration Process: Capital, Gifts and Offerings Among British Pakistanis*, Berg, Oxford.

— (1997) 'Essentialising Essentialism, Essentialising Silence: Ambivalence and Multiplicity in the Constructions of Racism and Ethnicity', in Pnina Werbner and Tariq Modood (eds) *Debating Cultural Hybridity: Multi-Cultural Identities and the Politics of Anti-Racism*, Zed Books, London.

Yalçin-Heckmann, Lale (1994) 'Are Fireworks Islamic? Towards an Understanding of Turkish Migrants and Islam in Germany', in Charles Stewart and Rosalind Shaw (eds) *Syncretism/Anti-Syncretism: The Politics of Religious Synthesis*, Routledge, London, pp. 178–95.

CHAPTER 10

Defining Ethnicity: Another Way of Being British

Wenonah Lyon

'Ethnicity is like family or marriage; everybody knows what it means but nobody can define it' (Smith, quoted in Alonso 1994: 379). It has been argued that what is unique to ethnicity is the kind of tie binding members of the group, that 'the essence of a purely ethnic tie is that it is based upon a sense of sameness with one's fellow-ethnics and distinction from those who do not share the same observable characteristics' (Rex 1991: 11). Gordon describes it as an 'inalienable ascription from cradle to grave ... incorporated into self' (1978: 73). Ethnicity becomes a kind of psychological structure or attitude rather than a part of social or political organisation.

Ethnicity, as the term is generally used in the social sciences as well as common speech, is used as a classification for what appear to be dissimilar situations: distinctive and different patterns of social organisation and multiple attitudes towards that classification labelled as 'ethnic'. Psychologically, as well as organisationally, the importance of ethnicity is variable (Handelman 1977). As Abner Cohen says, 'there is ethnicity and there is ethnicity ... the collectivity that manifests itself ... to perform a dance is different from the ethnicity manifested by, say, the Catholics in Northern Ireland' (Cohen 1974: xiv). Whatever ethnicity is, it is widespread: Cohen, in a footnote in a 1993 article, gives the results of a survey of 132 states: only 9 per cent were ethnically homogeneous; indeed, 30 per cent had no single ethnic group comprising 50 per cent of its population (Cohen 1993: 256).

One resolution to such complexity is to define ethnicity for the purposes of scientific discussion as a particular sort of structure or classification. Smith objects to this:

> Phenomena like ethnicity or national sentiment are so largely bound up with expressions of attitude and feelings (even if they involve so much more) that purely structural approaches will inevitably seem remote from the objects of their explanations, even when they do not mislead. (Smith 1986: 7)

It is in precisely these circumstances that a structural approach is most useful, and precisely because it does not incorporate experienced complexity into the model describing or explaining the data set. If a model is not more simple than the data it describes, it is of no theoretical and very little practical use. A model should accommodate complexity, not reproduce it.

' The critical feature of ethnicity is 'the characteristic of self-ascription and ascription by others' (Barth 1969a: 13). Ethnicity, then, is most basically a way of classifying one's self and others, and my examination is based on ethnographic material: how do people actually classify themselves? I investigate 'self-ascription and ascription by others' by detailing the use of labels in a multiethnic community in the UK. Much of the ethnographic information was collected while I was working with a multiethnic theatre group in Oldham, a town near Manchester, in the northwest of England.[1] Members of the group are predominately of South Asian descent. Multiple terms are used by them to refer to themselves and other people, and the choice of terms is contextually dictated, incorporating and excluding others (and other groups) as the situation requires. Some of the terms reflect both political and cultural status: for example, 'British'. Others reflect cultural status and (or) area of origin: 'Pakistani', 'Bangladeshi', 'Indian'. Still others reflect specific political alliances – 'black', 'Asian'.

What seems crucial in this labelling is the acknowledgement of two boundaries. 'Ethnicity' then, involves a classification based on duality. Logically, ethnicity expresses relationships of both inclusion and exclusion. It is a classification involving a set and its subset. An ethnic group, then, is an acknowledged subset of an acknowledged set; all members of A are also members of B; some members of B are also members of A.

The ethnographic example: Peshkar

While working with Peshkar, a multiethnic community theatre group in Oldham, my fellow Peshkar members identified themselves in a number of ways: as Asians, British, black, white, by area of origin (India, Bangladesh, Pakistan, England), by subregion within the area of origin (Punjab, Kashmir, Bengal), by religion (Hindu, Muslim, Sikh), or language (Punjabi, Bangla, Hindi–Urdu, English, Marathi). Occasionally, in talking to me, an American whose permanent home is in Kent, in the southeast of England, they were 'we northerners' in contrast to the wicked south. They are also people who are part of the Greater Manchester area, and have more local identities as residents of Rochdale, Failsworth, Oldham – or even neighbourhoods: Coppice.

Members of Peshkar differ in age, in education, in income and in their command of English. They even differ in their support for football teams. We are about equally divided between Manchester United and Liverpool.

Football team support is the only loyalty within Peshkar that is not potentially divisive.

Each of the four religions represented in Peshkar – Christianity, Islam, Hinduism, Sikhism – has, on occasion, slaughtered the adherents of the other three – and continues to do so. The governments and citizens of each of the four nation-states represented – Britain, Pakistan, India and Bangladesh – have, at the very least, behaved badly (and, in some cases, savagely and brutally) in their treatment of citizens of the others. The important dates in South Asia – 1857, 1947, 1971 – are blood-drenched. Wars, border skirmishes, pogroms, massacres, police brutality are the stuff of the daily newspaper as well as the history books. Sectarian, national and ethnic violence are current affairs, not just a bloody past.

In this, South Asia does not differ from North or South America, Africa or Europe or Australia. However, the savagery of the human species touches my friends of South Asian descent in Peshkar more personally and closely than it touches me. If they themselves did not lose a relative during Partition or the dismemberment of the east and west wings of Pakistan, they know someone who did. In a multiethnic community – whether Peshkar or Oldham itself – identifications related to religion or national origin outside the specific community concerned are a sensitive topic.

In the UK, racism, and racist attacks, are part of British life. Peshkar is a multiracial, as well as a multiethnic, group.

Flexibility in self-identification is extremely useful in Peshkar. Some identifications could potentially lead to conflict (or at the least unpleasantness) in the group: so we label ourselves (and each other) carefully. The multiple identities assumed in Peshkar are assumed pragmatically.

Peshkar has about thirty members, most of whom are of South Asian descent. We have workshops on Sunday afternoon, and about ten members come regularly. The rest come less often. For the last two years, Peshkar has presented one major production each year. Basic funding is supplied by Oldham Leisure Services, while the Manchester Year of Drama and the Northwest Arts Council provided the funding to hire an administrator, writer, director and technical staff to put on Peshkar's most recent production, *Chapatis and Chips*. Peshkar is immensely welcoming: white as well as South Asian members are accepted with great friendliness, and lack of dramatic talent is no bar to full acceptance by the group. If you come regularly, they take you in and you are a member of the group.

Three members dominate the group, largely because of their age: a man in his early forties, Hindu, originally from Africa by way of India, a Gujarati speaker, a university graduate; a woman in her mid-thirties, Muslim, a Punjabi speaker born in Pakistan and brought up in the northwest of England; a woman in her mid-thirties, of English descent, working-class, Christian. The great majority of Peshkar's members are male, Bangladeshi, Muslim, between about seventeen and twenty-three. There are three or four other boys who are Muslims, of Pakistani descent, and we had several young male Sikhs until one of them got a car. They then abandoned us to spend their Sunday afternoons driving around. Most of the boys are in college, two study Performing Arts. Almost all have part-time jobs as well, working as waiters or in small corner shops within their communities.

About half the members of Peshkar, including the two older women, would like a career in theatre. Some have agents, and five or six have appeared in walk-on roles in Granada television productions. Three children, one nine, two twelve, accompany relatives to the Sunday workshops and were in the play. The cast of *Chapatis and Chips*, included a number of people who had not belonged to Peshkar and probably will not continue working with the group. These people were of both South Asian and English descent.

Citizenship and community

Everyone in Peshkar but me is British. Some of the boys have never been to the subcontinent; others have come to the UK relatively recently. One young man had come from Bangladesh less than a year before he appeared in *Chapatis and Chips*. Most speak at least one South Asian language in addition to English – but several do not speak it very well. (Most of the younger members of the group who are of Bangladeshi descent speak Bangla well; those of Pakistani descent speak Punjabi, Urdu or Kashmiri. Younger people of Pakistani descent say they do not 'really' speak the language – they 'get by'.) The older members of the group, and a few of the boys, read and write a South Asian language in addition to English. They all, however, have British citizenship and they all intend to remain in the UK. They are culturally as well as legally Britons of South Asian descent.

The South Asian members of Peshkar are definitely British; but they are also definitely members of a specific community within Britain. Ties to the subcontinent are somewhat tenuous: they have relatives there, they enjoy going for a holiday, they are proud of their histories and their cultures. Ties to the local Bangladeshi or Pakistani or Indian community, however, are not at all tenuous. These communities are extremely important to them. They take part in religious, cultural and national celebrations, and do not see this as involving any contradiction with being British. They are both British and of Pakistani, Indian or Bangladeshi descent.

The UK has had immigrants from South Asia since the days of the East India Company. Seamen and soldiers from South Asia fought for the British in both the First and Second World Wars, and some remained in the country. After the Second World War, South Asians came to the UK to take low-paying jobs that the members of the indigenous population were unwilling to do. Major immigration from the South Asian subcontinent came in the late 1960s and early 1970s. South Asian immigration followed a chain pattern, with early immigrants joined by kin and neighbours, which led to a concentration of immigrants within certain areas of Britain and within certain industries (Robinson 1990). Initially, young males immigrated (often intending to remain a short time) and were only followed much later by their wives and children. (Immigrants from Africa of South Asian origin were an exception to this – families immigrated from Kenya and Uganda.) Early immigrants to the UK often intended to return to their country of origin. Their children, and now often they themselves, rarely discuss returning to Pakistan or Bangladesh or India. They are, and describe themselves as, British.

While I was waiting in line at the hardware store in my predominantly Pakistani neighbourhood in Oldham, one of the men in the queue, of Pakistani descent, told me about his job at the mill. He liked his job, and described the fine work they did: 'Beautiful stuff. ... You can get this cheap foreign stuff, but if you want quality, you have to buy British. Always buy British.'

His companion, also of Pakistani descent, added, 'And support the British working man.'

My neighbour lamented his sons' lack of interest in cricket: 'They love the football – they say cricket is a toff's game. I could understand it if they supported Oldham, they're our team, but they like Manchester United.'

Attitudes of the indigenous population are mixed. The British National Party is quite straightforward: there ain't no black in the Union Jack. My neighbour in Canterbury, in his eighties, a retired carpenter, is equally straightforward: people are people, good and bad as individuals, and Bangladeshis are just like any other British citizen. Racist remarks, racist jokes, are wrong. Discrimination of any sort is wrong. Immigration laws are necessary, because otherwise we would have too many people coming here. But anyone who becomes a citizen, anyone who is born here, is just as British as he is and should be treated in exactly the same way.[2] These probably represent the extremes of opinion, and most Britons of English descent are somewhat more ambivalent.

Another neighbour, also in Kent, who was in the armed services in the Second World War, described a monument to American airforce personnel who died during the war. I described a monument that I saw in Delhi to South Asians who died during the two world wars.

He said, 'I don't much like blackies, but I have to admit they have a right to be here. They fought for us in two world wars, and they have the right ... '

Other Britons of English descent might disagree with the right of abode of members of the New Commonwealth regardless of war records, but would agree that anyone born here is British. This view has been challenged, of course: Bernard Manning, a British comedian, in a show for Greater Manchester police detectives, said 'They actually think they're English 'cos they're f(bleep) born here. That means if a dog's born in a stable it's a f(bleep) horse' (quoted in a television review in the *Guardian*, Herbert 1995: 4).

Culture, rather than race, may be offered as a justification for denying the right of those of South Asian descent to be considered British. In 1985, when I first came to the UK, I worked as a typist in an insurance agency. My colleagues wanted to explain the UK to me: 'The Welsh are sly, sneaky, they lie ... never trust the Welsh. The Irish are good fellows, always a joke and a laugh. The Scottish are clannish, stick together, always in a fight ... but if you're down in the town, and there's a fight, six Jocks [Scots] from the barracks will be right there covering your back.' (The stereotypes were integrated with the experience gained by my informants during National Service.) They talked about New Commonwealth immigrants: 'The blacks are all right. They're just like us – you can go down the pub, have a drink and a laugh, maybe get in a fight but there's no hard feelings. After twenty or thirty years, the blacks will just be English. The colour of the skin may be different, but they're like us. The Pakis, though, the Pakis will never fit in. They keep themselves to themselves, they are just too different, and they'll never fit in and they don't want to.'

People of South Asian descent, like the English, examine cultural differences. Sometimes they describe the boundary separating the English and the Pakistani (or Bangladeshi or Indian) in terms of culture, using food, clothing, language. Large-scale immigration from the South Asian subcontinent is relatively recent, and the second generation, particularly, are examining differences. Which are important, which can be changed? Sometimes these differences are seen as differences in morality and religion.

Across cultures: on being British

People in Peshkar in general, whether they grew up in the UK or abroad, are aware of values and attitudes in Britain and within their local community. Often these are the same, and when they differ people make individual choices rather than automatically supporting either tradition. In many cases, it seems that people try to establish a position that is acceptable to both communities.

When we began discussing the play we put on, the writer who had been hired asked Peshkar what they wanted the play to be about. She made half a dozen suggestions. One was a play about arranged marriages.

The boys rejected this immediately. 'The only thing English people know about Asians is that they have arranged marriages, and they are usually wrong about what they know.'

One boy, a Muslim of Bangladeshi descent, commented, 'Sometimes when I come home, my mother says, have you met a nice girl yet? When I say no, she says if you don't find one soon I'll find one for you. This is how we arrange marriages in our family.'[3]

Arranged marriages were a sensitive topic for the boys. They knew how their classmates of English descent viewed such marriages; they, like everyone else, watch television and go to the cinema. Their attitudes seemed to be that a marriage involves selecting a partner acceptable to one's parents. Generally this means someone from the same ethnic, religious, economic and linguistic background. Whether your parents introduce you to the girl or you introduce the girl to your parents is not the crucial issue. The boys have taken a conception of marriage as involving families, and a value important in South Asia, the requirement that young people be guided by older kin in most matters, including marriage, and have combined these with an important value among young people in the UK: young people should be free to make decisions that affect their own lives independently of the wishes of their parents. Independence is a sign of adulthood and a strong individual. However, if you choose to follow your parents' wishes, you are behaving as independently and with the same degree of freedom (and maturity) as any classmate of English descent.

The behaviour of women, and the control of women, is an important cultural marker distinguishing the South Asian, the South Asian British and the English communities. Segregation of the sexes is more rigid, with often draconian sanctions against its disregard, in South Asia than in the UK. Proper behaviour for men and women is redefined in the British context. The role of women in paid employment and as students is differently perceived by the South Asian community, the English community, and the South Asian community in the UK. Some aspects of gender roles are modified – daughters are expected to work and do well in school – others aspects are not – young women are far more constrained and checked than their brothers (Lyon 1995). In drawing the dividing line between being British and South Asian, some things are negotiable. Some things are not, and those that are not are often described as elements of religion rather than culture.

A part of the gender construction of women's roles is perceived as being based on religion rather than culture, and thus civic rights and civic obligations are differently defined. Family law and education are areas of potential conflict. During fieldwork, I met several women who were 'second wives'. I heard of others. These women are not protected by British law. There are several situations in which this occurs. A middle-aged, well-off Muslim of South Asian descent marries a young and attractive woman in a religious ceremony while legally remaining married to his wife. While there are immediate financial advantages to the young woman he marries, she is dependent on the man's honour and good will for continuing support. My female informants who discussed this condemned the practice – not for any moral reasons; religion justified the practice – but because the woman is in a completely unprotected position. (I am tempted, like my female informants, to see this less as a conflict of culture and religion with British law than as a case of a few males taking advantage of a situation. If they were really supporting their culture and their religion, they would also support their second wives.)

Other cases of second wives involved women married in the country of origin and later brought to Britain. In one case, a middle-aged woman and her children joined her husband and his first wife and children in the UK. He died a few months after she arrived. The government not only moved to deport her and her children, but used her existence to deny his first wife (a long-time resident and citizen of the UK) pension rights, arguing that the existence of another wife invalidated her claim to be married. (Here the government seems to be having its cake and eating it too.)

Members of Peshkar saw no conflict in being British and of Pakistani descent: nationality and ethnicity coexisted comfortably. Older informants, who immigrated to the UK as adults, sometimes asked me if the English would ever accept their children. Those who grew up here never considered that. They were British and they were Pakistani, and being Pakistani is just another way of being British, in the same way that one is English and British or Scottish and British or Irish and British or Welsh and British.

Disagreements became important, and non-negotiable, precisely when ethnicity and nationality were denied, when the subject of disagreement was defined as moral. 'Culture' (and 'ethnicity') and 'religion' are conceptually distinct. Religion can, however, have an important role in the survival of ethnic groups. Smith, using detailed comparative historical and ethnographic material, specifies instances in which religion has been a 'pivotal element' in 'crystallizing and maintaining ethnic identities' (Smith 1986: 109–25). In considering how important religion will be in the maintenance of an ethnic group, he says that 'the social aspects of religion are more crucial for ethnic survival than the purely doctrinal and ethical' (Smith 1986: 124). Ethnicity is sustained by religion; ethnicity sustains religion. Some of my informants were privately sceptical of some of the doctrinaire requirements outlined by their religious leaders, but would not publicly question these leaders.

One of the actors imported for the play, not a member of Peshkar, was a woman in her early thirties, Muslim, of Pakistani descent. She is very attractive, and an intelligent and talented actress. She said that her drama teacher had offered to lend her the money to go to drama school when she finished her A levels. Her parents were pleased, and agreed to her studying drama. Leaders in her parents' local community came and talked to her father: actresses are whores, he was told. Was he sending his daughter out to be a whore? Her father told her to do what she wanted to do. She said she thought about it, and knew that her father would be ostracised if she went to drama school. So she took a student grant, and studied pharmacy at university.

Young women who do not wear *shalwar kameez* (the South Asian traditional trousers and long top) may be criticised for being 'Westernised' and thus ignoring an important boundary marker, without being seen as immoral. Young women in my neighbourhood could wear jeans and thick long sweatshirts or sweaters – modest dress. Wearing skirts was not acceptable – that was seen as immodest, and thus offending the require-ments of religion rather than simply culture. Jean-wearing girls might be suspected of potentially 'getting out of hand', and doom might be foretold, but many of the young women I knew did have a pair of jeans that they wore in particular circumstances. Their mothers grumbled about the jeans, but paid for them and washed them; these same mothers grumbled about their children demanding chips with everything, and said their children were becoming very English, but they frequently cooked the chips. They would not have accepted non-halal meat or wine with meals.

Many people are willing to distinguish between culture (private), and civic status (public). Taxation, traffic regulations, crimes against property are not generally controversial areas: these are matters for the law of the land and accepted, more or less, as such. Governmental proscriptions involving family law, education, immigration, and some crimes against the person are sometimes disputed. Generally speaking, moral law – as religion, or natural justice, or fairness – is given as a basis for an argument rather than culture or citizenship. This conception of morality can become part of the legal system – as in anti-racist legislation, or laws governing marriage. Such matters, it is argued, are not a part of the particularity of law or culture but universal. Paying tax on a meal in a restaurant is a matter of law, eating chicken korma rather than chicken cacciatori is a matter of culture, and eating halal chicken is a matter of morality: a religious requirement.

Being 'Pakistani', being 'Muslim', are self-ascriptions in addition to being ascriptions assigned by outsiders. Taking pride in one's culture and prac-tising one's religion with devotion involve individual values as well as outside perceptions of one's self. Being 'black' and being 'Asian' seem rather different.

On being black and Asian: race and racism

People refer to themselves as 'Asian' in particular tactical situations, usually in dealing with the non-Asian community and in situations involving members from different areas of origin. 'Asian' was a useful term to

Peshkar. It was also a useful term to Peshkar's administrators. It appealed to fund givers: we were a predominantly Asian multiethnic theatre group. What community arts project in the Labour-dominated northwest could resist giving us at least a little money? Organising 'Asian' cultural groups avoids competition between the different communities that make up 'Asian'; given the limited funds available, this is probably useful. (It also, of course, provides community spokespeople with a larger constituency.)

Using 'Asian' as a common designation for the members of Peshkar conceals some real problems within the organisation as well as allowing members to avoid external conflicts that would divide members. There are differences in culture and language within the group.

The play presented was based on *Chapatis and Chips*, a novel written by Almas Khan, a woman living in Bradford who grew up in the UK and is of Pakistani descent. The book (and the play) take place in Pakistan and the northwest of England. The play was advertised as 'multilingual' before the text was written or the play was cast. The most commonly spoken language in the group other than English was Bangla. We had one native speaker of Punjabi, and the majority of the cast spoke no Punjabi and little Urdu. The writer suggested shifting the scene of the play to Bangladesh. The Bangla speakers protested: Bangladeshis do not eat chapatis, they eat rice. The name of the play would have to be changed – and the name could not be changed. *Chapatis and Chips*, presented by Peshkar, had been publicised as a part of the Manchester Year of Drama. In addition the director, of Punjabi descent, raised in the northwest of England, objected that most of our audience would not understand non-English dialogue. Urdu was chosen as the major non-English language, and speeches in a language other than English were limited, with the information contained in these speeches immediately repeated in English.

Peshkar presents itself as 'multiethnic'. Individuals, of whatever ethnic origin – including English and American – are welcomed. But the older members of the group, and decision makers within Oldham Leisure Services, are non-Bangladeshis. 'Asian' allows the 'Asia' presented to be Pakistan and northern India – a Hindi–Urdu-speaking group of chapati eaters – which, coincidentally, is a pretty good description of the people within the group who make decisions. Younger, Bangla-speaking members of the group expressed resentment at this representation of 'Asian'. They felt that their culture and their language were not properly represented by the generic term and discussed forming a separate theatrical group. 'Asian' is a useful designation – but it is useful socially, politically and economically. It cannot represent the disparities of culture, religion and language that it is intended to mask.

'Asian', like the term 'black', seemed to be used to describe currently contextually useful political positions that challenge racism, as the following discussion illustrates.

I listened to an argument between one of the boys, an eighteen-year-old Muslim of Bangladeshi descent, and one of the children in the play, a 12–year-old girl, Hindu, of Indian descent.

Him: Which school do you go to?
Her: A.
Him: That's a rubbish school, where they send all the Asians. You're Asian and they send you to two schools, rubbish schools.
Her: It was my first choice. They send you to the school nearest your house, unless you have a brother or a sister in another school.
Him: All the Asians go to those two schools.
Her: There's only five Asians in my class.
Him: B is the school I went to, and it's much better. It's got 98 per cent GSCE pass rates. You should have gone there.
Her: A is a good school.
Him: The headmistress is a racist.
Her: No she's not. She's very nice. It's a good school …
Him: They only have the Christian celebrations, and most of the kids are Asian …
Her: They have other celebrations too, not just Christian ones … we have them in my class, we had Eid.
Him: They just have Eid celebrations in the classroom … for Christian things, they go into the halls too.

This is, most obviously, two young people arguing about which school is better – they both like, and support, their own schools. The girl is bright, self-confident. She reads well, and complains because her father is too busy to take her to the Oldham Public Library every week. She uses the library at school, but the public library has a wider selection of the teenage science fiction, horror and murder mysteries that she enjoys. She likes her school and her teachers. During the play, both of her teachers came to see her performance. She intends to go to university, and both home and school encourage this. From knowing the girl, I think she probably goes to a reasonably good school. She, at any rate, thinks it is a good school and not a racist one.

The two young people arguing about their schools both accepted the designation 'Asian'. The girl commented that they had celebrated Eid in her classroom, seeing it as representative of South Asian culture as well as a Muslim holy day. In this case, 'Asian' was contrasted with 'Christian' quite specifically because of racism: the English discriminate against both Indian Hindus and Bangladeshi Muslims and for the purposes of discussing this the children accepted a common identity as 'Asian'. This common designation masked some quite important issues in the community as well as in Peshkar: real differences, and hostility, between the groups concerned.

A few days before this conversation, I went with the girl to a Diwali celebration at her temple, a few blocks from my house. Young Muslim men in the neighbourhood had harassed people coming to the temple, and some cars were vandalised.

Throughout the Diwali celebrations, people were harassed by these young men. Someone turned in false alarms to the fire department every night, and the fire department stopped responding. The back of the temple was set on fire.

At the Diwali celebration at the Queen Elizabeth Hall in the Oldham Civic Centre, I noticed a large crowd of men across the hall. Older men and the bouncers were separating young men who were fighting. I heard several stories about what happened:

1. A group of Muslims had got tickets, had come to the celebration and caused trouble.
2. A youth gang from Coppice, Pakistani Muslims, had invaded the hall and caused trouble.
3. Two young women, Hindus, had bought tickets for two male friends, Muslims, from the college. Some Hindu boys had seen the boys, recognised them as Muslims, and attacked them. The person who told me this is on the board of the temple. He commented, young people from different communities meet in college – they want to go to each other's celebrations … we are going to have to get used to that.

When I repeated the last comment to another Hindu of Indian descent that I know, he said, exasperated: 'They only come to look at our women. Go to the Muslim areas – you'll see the women have to use the alleys. They don't even let them walk on the streets there. They don't let them come to their mosques … why should we let those people come in and stare at the women in the community?' Women in Muslim neighbourhoods do not, incidentally, use the alleys. Stereotypes about each other thrive in all three communities of Asian descent as well as among their English neighbours.

The second comment came from a Muslim of Bangladeshi descent. He was complaining about the use of the term 'Asian' in newspaper reports of trouble in Oldham, and brought up the fight in the Queen Elizabeth Hall. He said that there are three Asian communities in Oldham, and only one ever causes any trouble, and we know which one that is … the Pakistanis. He said that there had been some trouble with Bangladeshi boys a few years ago, and everyone in the community was very upset. Bangladeshi leaders had gone and talked to the parents of the boys, they had organised projects, everyone had been concerned, and there had been no problems since.

'Asian' is used to incorporate for a particular purpose; it is also used to establish distance, again for a particular purpose. Within each community, people rarely described themselves, or others, as 'Asian'. When I first moved to Oldham, I talked to the hardware store owner. He praised our neighbourhood, talked of how well people got on, how safe it was. He warned me not to go a few blocks away – there were bad gangs there.

'What kind of gangs?' I asked.

He looked embarrassed. 'Asian gangs.'

He was of Pakistani origin, and the gang members are of Pakistani descent. It is less embarrassing to describe them as 'Asian' than as 'Pakistani'.

One can use the term 'Asian' to disavow responsibility for a member of the community; it is more than this, however. It provides a common label to unite around a common cause, that of challenging white racism. 'Black' serves the same purpose, emphasising the common experiences that those of Afro-Caribbean and Asian descent encounter in contact with English society. Most of the members of Peshkar, at different times, referred to themselves as 'Asian'. 'Black' was far less commonly used. Within Peshkar, the university graduate, the young man working for the council as a community relations officer and the director – a professional, a Sikh of Punjabi descent – were the only people who ever used the term 'black' unselfconsciously, as if they felt it described them themselves. The others, instead, talked about 'whites' and 'Asians'. Those members of the group who described themselves as 'black' were also those members of the group that worked in predominantly non-Asian situations and thus had the most experience of structural, as opposed to experiential, racism.

We can choose to look at racism in an institutional, sociological kind of way: differential access to education, employment, housing, city services based on culturally recognised differences seen to have a biological basis. Or we can look at racism at a much more personal level: the contemptuous attitude of a teacher, the half-dozen young men in the town centre who jeer and call out racist slogans. At the personal level, racism hurts. It is humiliating and diminishing. If you are an eighteen-year-old boy in the town centre, and six half-drunken louts push you around and call you a 'Paki bastard', you feel you ought to be able to wipe the sneer off their faces. And you really can't – outside a movie. Some people in Peshkar were comfortable in working against institutionalised racism; niggling personalised racism was a different matter.

None of the boys ever initiated an improvisation that involved racism or cultural difference.

In one of the first improvisations I did at our Sunday workshops, we were supposed to present an argument. I suggested to my partner (male, eighteen, Muslim, of Bangladeshi descent) that we have a racist argument. I would be a newsagent, he a customer, I would give him the wrong change and we would argue over it. I would make racist remarks. We started rehearsing this, and he seemed very uncomfortable. I stopped, and asked him why. He said that he hated racist speech; even when we were playing he didn't want to hear a friend say things like that, or use words like that. I said fine, and instead I played his mother and made him eat cabbage ...

We did not improvise using racism; but it was important in the play. I asked the writer about this. She said that she thought the boys were very sensitive about racism, very uncomfortable with it. She had presented racists as fools, buffoons, cleverly defeated on every front, because she thought it might be useful to the boys. In the play the 'Asian' became the classical trickster, fooling (and making fools of) the powerful.

At the cast party, one of the older members of the group came over to me. The cast member commented that he had never told the writer any of the real stories ... the real stories you don't talk about. He said when he had first come to the UK, he had known a man that ran a post office. This man had TB, and claimed he had got it from counting Paki money. The actor mimed licking his thumb, riffling through an imaginary stack of paper currency. Things like that, he said, things like that hurt you and you don't talk about them.

Racism was not just a middle-class liberal preoccupation shared by the writer and anthropologist. It was real, and the boys had to deal with it. Several times, members of Peshkar of South Asian descent came in with stories of being attacked in the town centre. Everyone knew stories of relatives or friends who had been physically attacked by racists.

I live in Oldham, in one of the two-up two-down terrace houses built for mill workers. Some of my neighbours work in the mills. It is an ethnically mixed neighbourhood, and its residents are predominantly of Pakistani origin and descent. We are civil, we nod and smile on the street, and we chat in queues at the hardware store and grocer's. An Irish tinker's four-and-a-half-ton flatbed truck broke down in the street in front of my house. Two Irish, one German, one American, one Punjabi and two Kashmiris managed to move the truck.

We are not about to have block parties or communal barbies in the back yard, but ethnic differences and individuals are respected in public. People are pleasant. I have no idea what people say in their kitchens. People in Oldham who are not of South Asian descent are aware that some comments involving colour, religion or national origin are not universally acceptable. I was known in the neighbourhood to have friends of South Asian descent, and neighbours who disliked South Asians either avoided me or the topics of racial/cultural difference and immigration.

There is racist graffiti in the neighbourhood: a swastika painted on a local building, with BNP written under it. I read the graffiti written on the underpass going into the town centre: 'BNP = Bastard National Party'. 'Stand Up for the White Race' and 'Black Bastards we are watching you', 'White dickheads stay out of Coppice', 'Show Respect for the Coppice Boyz'.

Racism is obvious in its day-to-day manifestations. However, the member of Peshkar who suffered the most physical damage in a street fight was the woman of English descent, in her early thirties. It involved white-on-white violence. The northwest of England seems to me to be a fairly violent place in general, where people beat up on each other a fair amount. So perhaps the South Asian youth gangs reported in Oldham are simply more acculturated than the others.

Labels and identities

The way people identify themselves involves, most importantly, labels. They are ways of identifying oneself, rather than an identity. A transference from the sense of 'identity-as-a-label' to 'identity-as-a-psychological-construct' seems to me unacceptable.

Even if we wish to assume that self-ascribed ethnicity results in a particular construction of self, it is difficult to see such a construct as universally similar at either the individual or the group level. Such an assumption at the individual level would involve a psychological, individual state – one that is presumed to be highly significant – without individual, psychological investigation. In considering the ethnic group, such an assumption also ignores the importance of both internal differences between ethnic groups and differences in external perceptions (and ranking and evaluations) of such groups. Does belonging to an elite ethnic group create the same sort of psychological tie as belonging to a pariah group? What about multiple possible identities? Tambiah reports a conversation between Abdul Wali Khan, the son of Abdulla Ghaffar Khan, founder of the National Awami Party, and a reporter: 'Are you a Pakistani, a Muslim, or a Pathan?' He said that he was all three. 'The reporter pressed him as to his primary identity. Wali Khan replied that he had been a Pakistani for thirty years, a Muslim for 1,400 years, and a Pathan for 5,000 years, (Tambiah 1990: 742).

Among some of the people I talked to, the label 'Pakistani' itself is rejected. When I was investigating women's groups with members of South Asian descent, one young woman, of Pakistani descent, who belonged to an Islamic group, objected to my use of the term 'British-Pakistani' or 'British-Asian': she and her friends said I should call them 'Muslims' or 'British Muslims'.

Alonso discusses replacing the term 'ethnicity' as an analytical category with peoplehood, race, or nationalist ideology. She says that although she 'agrees with these critiques of ethnicity, I remain convinced that drawing analytical distinctions between different forms of imagining peoplehood is methodologically useful' (Alonso 1994: 390–91). I share her reservations, but, like her, think the term is useful. It should probably refer to something other than a form of community bigger than the breadbox of the local and smaller than the elephant of the nation. It also needs to be something other than a deeply felt, individually perceived, sense of belonging. Geertz, discussing cultural (rather than specifically ethnic) groups, proposes a kind of 'primordial attachment' that is the result of 'being born into a particular ... community ... following particular social practices. These congruities of blood, speech, custom and so on are seen to have an ineffable, and at times overpowering, coerciveness in and of themselves' (Geertz 1973: 259). Smith looks at such an attachment in the case of ethnic groups and argues that

> the sense of ethnic identity emanates from a commitment and attachment to the shared elements which unite the members of a group rather than from the differences which debar outsiders ... we cannot regard the various collective symbols and values that so visibly differentiate communities as mere 'boundary mechanisms' or 'cultural markers' which divide 'us' from 'them'. (Smith 1986: 49)

Yet such divisions are certainly significant historically and currently.

Is there a quality then, an emotional attitude, peculiar to ethnicity (and nationalism) that leads to violence? 'Thirty-five of the thirty-seven major armed conflicts in the world in 1991 were internal conflicts – and most of them, from Sri Lanka to Northern Ireland – could plausibly be described as ethnic conflicts' (Erikson: 1993: 2). Cohen examines ethnic conflict:

> the forces involved, and the stakes at risk are so deeply felt, so much a major feature of life that the interethnic conflict becomes part of the culture, almost of normalcy for the groups involved. In many instances ... the price is often high in human suffering and sacrifice but for those involved, often the vast majority, the goals are worth it. So the struggle goes on. (Cohen 1993: 232)

Smith points out that while immediate political and economic causes are important in intensifying divisions between ethnic groups, specifically those involving ethnic nationalism, they 'rarely account for the depth of feeling involved' (Smith 1986: 224). Is there a direct, or indirect, link leading to an association of ethnicity and violence? A direct association between ethnicity and violence would appear to support arguments that ethnicity involves a particular sense of one's self and identity, an 'overpowering coerciveness'. This violence is, however, more satisfactorily explained by factors other than ethnicity *per se*.

Wallerstein points out that 'constructed "peoples" – the races, the nations, the ethnic groups – correlate ... heavily, albeit imperfectly, with "objective class". The consequence has been that a very high proportion of class-based political activity in the modern world has taken the form of people-based political activity' (Wallerstein 1993: 84). What ethnic groups do can be explained by nonethnic causes; why groups based on ethnicity do them is less easy to explain.

Tambiah examined serious interethnic rioting in Pakistan, Sri Lanka and India. He pointed out common factors: the riots occurred in urban situations, they were part of a larger incidence of violence (including state violence) in a wide range of social contexts and political circumstances, and those entrusted with maintaining law and order (the police, army, security forces) did not remain neutral during the riots. He argued that democracy as it is practised in South Asia stimulates violence: 'ethnicity is the most potent energizer, embodying and radiating religious, linguistic, territorial and class identities and interests; it is also an umbrella under which personal, familial, commercial and other local scores are sought to be settled' (Tambiah 1990: 759; see also Burgher 1993 on government manipulation of ethnic membership in the security forces in Sri Lanka, India and Pakistan).

Other writers insist that ethnicity has less to do with social and cultural division in itself than with the expression of power relationships. Ethnicity, and ethnic groups, must be seen in a wider context, that of inequality (Wirth: 1961) and/or colonialism and a hierarchy of access to resources (Alonso 1994; Vincent 1993; O'Brian 1986).

While Cohen agrees that interethnic relations can frequently involve differences in power (Cohen 1979: 402), he also insists that they can be between relative equals (Cohen 1979: 392). Cohen looks more generally at ethnicity and political activity: ethnicity is a 'means of asserting one's rights in a political community in which ethnicity is a recognised element' (Cohen 1979: 402). The form that asserting one's rights takes can be block voting, ethnic associations, or rioting. If, on the other hand, ethnicity is not a recognised element of the political community, then political organisation will occur based on other factors, such as race or class. The importance of ethnic groups, then, appears to be directly related to how rewards are distributed in a society: if group access determines reward, then groups will gain in importance – including those we describe as ethnic. Ethnicity itself can be described in other terms – in differences in status, history or language groupings, for example.

'Pakistani', 'Bangladeshi', 'Indian' could be defined in terms of history – unique myths and constructed versions of the past, a kind of symbolic representation of one's perceived uniqueness useful in the northwest of England. But a 'Pakistani' who came to the UK before 1947 is not an 'Indian', a 'Bangladeshi' who came to the UK before 1971 is not a 'Pakistani'. History is selective: to be 'Pakistani' or 'Indian' is to ignore most of what makes up one's history.

It is important to remember, in this context, that Pakistan, India and Bangladesh have all experienced serious ethnic violence, and there is no reason to think that the divisions that this represents are not represented among the immigrant communities in the UK. It seems that it is only in certain situations that one becomes a 'Pakistani' rather than a Punjabi or

Pathan, just as one is Bengali or Bihari rather than 'Indian' in some contexts. These terms select, as criteria for inclusion, an area of origin identified with a present political state.

The differences between Asians are even greater. A Muslim Kashmiri-speaking mill worker born in Pakistan and a Hindu Marathi-speaking architect born in East Africa are as culturally different as the differences between either and someone of English descent in Oldham. 'Asian', like 'black', is a boundary with few markers enclosing other, very highly marked groups. The terms 'black' and 'Asian' ignore cultural stuff, the stuff within the boundary, almost completely.

If 'Pakistani' and 'Indian' seem somewhat artificial, then 'black' and 'Asian' seem entirely so. 'Black' and 'Asian' form tactical groups in dealing with the non-black, non-Asian population of Britain. In this particular case, we have an aggregation of non-similar peoples constructed for mutual convenience: the convenience of government, who do not wish to satisfy individual groups, and the convenience of these individual groups them-selves, who gain strength in numbers in dealing with government at local, regional and state level as well as with non-blacks, non-Asians. 'Pakistani' and 'Indian' become less artificial as time goes by in the northwest; the same may be true of 'Asian' and 'black'. As Cohen and Barth both point out, ethnic labels change in response to circumstances (Cohen 1979; Barth 1969b).

Conclusions

Ethnicity is a social classification that is not immediately based on territory, ideology, class or interest, although these factors may determine the importance and function of ethnicity. As a social classification, ethnicity is potentially politically and economically important. It becomes important as 'a cultural construction within empires ... political empires, such as that of the Habsburgs, Great Britain or the Soviet Union; [and] economic empires, such as that of modern, global capitalism' (Vincent 1993: 128). It is likely to become increasingly significant in the New Europe – a con-glomeration of culturally distinct nation-states. 'Ethnicity', then, provides a way of group organising that originates in both inclusion, as a part of such an empire, and exclusion, as a distinct acknowledged part of such an empire. It involves a manipulation of logical (as well as group) relationships.

Multiculturalism, like ethnicity, involves a set and its subset: an acknow-ledged subset of an acknowledged set; all members of A (an ethnic group) are also members of B (a larger, bounded group); some members of B are also members of A. Its distinguishing feature as a social classification is that it can be rewritten as two subordinate social classifications logically related by inclusion (both classifications belong to the same set) and exclusion (one set is a subset of the other).

These classifications indicate, or describe, a boundary and what it separates without specifying the reasons for the boundary or the areas separated – much as Barth asserted in his original 1969 article. (Bartha 1969a). However, an assumption of two boundaries rather than one is required.

Concentrating on these boundaries rather than on the cultural stuff they enclose allows us to understand the shifting, flexible politics of multiculturalism and ethnicity. Ethnicity is defined by its form rather than its content. People have to choose to invoke ethnic boundaries. Highly marked groups ignore these markings for some purposes, and see themselves as the same, establishing a boundary to distinguish themselves from others who, by other criteria, are seen as the same. Ethnicity is a way of imagining peoplehood that ignores everything that makes a people – asserting a boundary that asserts only uniqueness.

Notes

I would like to thank Professor Chris Hann and Dr Michael Fischer for comments on earlier versions of this chapter. I am also grateful for comments made at a seminar at the Free University of Berlin.

1. Fieldwork was conducted from 1 February 1994 to 1 February 1995 in Manchester and Oldham as part of an ESRC funded research project on 'South Asian Popular Culture: Gender, Generation and Identity' at International Centre for Contemporary Cultural Research, Keele and Manchester, directed by Pnina Werbner. I am grateful to the ESRC for its generous support.

2. This was a spontaneously offered speech: my neighbour came by for a cup of tea. I started to tell him a Scottish joke I had read in the *Guardian*. He interrupted me and gave a speech, which I paraphrased. He himself used the example of Bangladeshis. The speech was well-rehearsed, and he had probably given it at assorted pubs and labour clubs in the southeast of England. He found it embarrassing, but necessary, to give. He finished by saying he knew I hadn't meant any harm, but jokes like that were a bad idea.

3. A proportion of marriages, probably a large proportion, among Asians in Oldham are arranged, where parents look among relatives and friends for a spouse for their child. The boys are objecting to the notion that they are bullied into marriage by their parents.

References

Alonso, Ana Maria (1994) 'The Politics of Space, Time and Substance: State Formation, Nationalism and Ethnicity', *Annual Review of Anthropology*, 23: 379–405.

Barth, Fredrik (1969a) 'Introduction', in F. Barth (ed.) *Ethnic Groups and Boundaries*, Little, Brown & Co, Boston, pp. 9–38.

— (1969b) 'Pathan Identity and Its Maintenance', in F. Barth (ed.) *Ethnic Groups and Boundaries*, Little, Brown & Co, Boston, pp. 117–34.

Burgher, Angela S. (1993). 'Ethnicity and the Security Forces of the State: The South Asian Experience', in Judith Toland (ed.) *Ethnicity and the State*, Transaction Publishers, London, pp. 79–102.

Cohen, Abner (1974) 'Introduction: The Lesson of Ethnicity', in Abner Cohen (ed.) *Urban Ethnicity*, Tavistock, London.

Cohen, Ronald (1979) 'Ethnicity: Problem and Focus in Anthropology', *Annual Review of Anthropology*, 7: 379–403.

— (1993) 'Conclusion: Ethnicity, the State, and Moral Order', in Judith Toland (ed.) *Ethnicity and the State*, Transaction Publishers, London, pp. 231–58.

Erikson, Thomas (1993) *Ethnicity and Nationalism: Anthropological Perspectives*, Pluto Press, London.

Geertz, Clifford (1973 [1963]) 'The Integrative Revolution: Primordial Sentiments and Civil Politics in New States', in *The Interpretation of Cultures: Selected Essays by Clifford Geertz*, Basic Books, New York.

Gordon, Milton (1978) *Human Nature, Class and Ethnicity*, Oxford University Press, New York.

Handelman, Don (1977) 'The Organization of Ethnicity', *Ethnic Groups*, 1: 187–200.

Herbert, Hugh (1995) 'Engaged, Vacant', *Guardian*, 25 April, p. 4.

Lyon, Wenonah (1995) 'Islam and Islamic Women in Britain', *Women: A Cultural Review*, 6(1): 46–56.

O'Brian, Jay (1986) 'Towards a Reconstitution of Ethnicity: Capitalist Expansion and Cultural Dynamics in Sudan', *American Anthropologist*, 88: 898–906.

Rex, John (1991) *Ethnic Identity and Ethnic Mobilisation in Britain*, Centre for Research in Ethnic Relations, Coventry.

Robinson, V. (1990) 'Boom and Gloom: The Success and Failure of South Asians in Britain', in Colin Clarke, Ceri Peach, Steven Vertovec (eds) *South Asians Overseas*, Cambridge University Press, Cambridge.

Smith, Anthony (1986) *The Ethnic Origin of Nations*, Blackwell, Oxford.

Tambiah, Stanley (1990) 'Presidential Address: Reflections on Communal Violence in South Asia', *The Journal of Asian Studies*, 49(4): 741–60.

Vincent, Joan (1993) 'Ethnicity and the State in Northern Ireland', in Judith Toland (ed.) *Ethnicity and the State*, Transaction Publishers, London, pp. 123–46.

Wallerstein, Immanuel (1993) 'The Construction of Peoplehood: Racism, Nationalism, Ethnicity', in E. Balibar and I. Wallerstein *Race, Nation, Class: Ambiguous Identities*, Verso, London, pp. 75–85.

Wirth, Louis (1961) 'The Problem of Minority Groups', in Talcott Parsons, Edward Shils, K. Naegele, J. Pitts (eds) *Theories of Society*, Free Press, New York, pp. 301–5.

PART FOUR

Plural Polities: Instituting Multiculturalism

CHAPTER 11

Why 'Positive Action' is 'Politically Correct'

Gideon Ben-Tovim

Many commentators have recently acknowledged that, in the new world disorder following on from the break-up of the Soviet empire and the satellite communist regimes, the spectre that is haunting Europe, and indeed most parts of the world, is the resurgence of racist, nationalist and neo-fascist movements and the recrudescence of apparently deep-seated ethnic conflicts (Rattansi and Westwood 1994).

Yet within mainstream Western political discourse, a new consensus has been gathering strength that suggests that the major threat to individual freedom lies in the authoritarianism not of the racist and nationalist right but of the anti-racist liberal left and the racially egalitarian state.

It is an urgent task, then, to try to reconstruct a 'common language of anti-racism' within Europe if not beyond, before the gains of the last three decades of civil rights legislation, anti-racist politics, multiculturalism and equal opportunity policies are completely extinguished.

The key argument of this chapter, which draws on evidence from local political struggles for racial equality in Liverpool, is that 'positive action' or its equivalent formulation 'affirmative action' needs to be acknowledged and vigorously defended as a core strategic concept in the struggle for racial equality.

The attack on anti-racism

In recent years in the USA and subsequently in Britain, the construction of a mythological discourse of so-called 'political correctness' (Dunant 1994) has been used by the 'anti-anti-racist' (Gordon 1990) forces of both the right and the liberal centre to undermine the validity of positive action as a necessary (albeit as we shall argue not sufficient) ingredient of the race relations policy agenda.

This 'political correctness' discourse operates by exaggerating and ridiculing all anti-racist initiatives as authoritarian, illiberal, dogmatic or absurd. Further, it has been used in an even broader context to undermine other egalitarian progressive movements, particularly feminism. Hence the reclaiming of 'positive action' is an important strand of a larger struggle that needs to be waged at the ideological and political levels – and in terms of social policy – to recapture the initiative and the moral high ground on issues of equality and equal opportunity.

In recent years, then, powerful forces have been attempting to push back the political, legislative and social gains achieved by women and racial/ethnic minorities, particularly in the USA and in Britain. Arguably, the New Right has used the 'threat' of 'positive discrimination' on behalf of women and minorities as the crucial ideological cement for their free-market, tax-cutting, anti-welfare, anti-state-intervention agenda that continues to be a dominant political force in Europe and the USA (Gordon and Klug 1986).

Meanwhile, in the light of apparently intractable problems of minority-group exclusion, marginalisation and impoverishment, some of the left have abandoned 'affirmative action' and 'equal opportunities' for a restatement of the primacy of class interests and the state of the economy, which draws them close to the economic determinism of neo-liberalism in seeing economic growth and the market, rather than the state's intervention through civil rights legislation and government action, as the key to racial equality (see Wilson 1987); some liberals have retreated from their commitment to race and gender equality by prioritising individual 'freedom' against the sometimes bruising effects of the exercise of group rights and power (see Edwards 1987); and finally the anti-racist movement has itself been weakened by deep internal ideological, strategic and tactical differences, including own goals scored by the excesses of zealotry and personalised vendettas on the part of some of its own advocates (see Gilroy 1990; Macdonald 1989).

The case for 'positive action'

Thus reaffirmation of the significance and legitimacy of 'positive action' as a crucial element of social policy may help contribute to the broader realignment of forces that is needed to strengthen the relative weakness, defensiveness and division within much of the centre-left in Europe and the USA; and to provide a robust counter-offensive to the 'political correctness' mythology which has been used so successfully to help marginalise a key focus for progressive social intervention.

Interestingly, whilst 'affirmative action' or 'positive action' has come under sustained ideological attack in the USA and in Britain, the new South Africa has actually begun to introduce forms of 'affirmative action' as a key component of its social reconstruction programme; in recent years the affirmative action dimension of anti-discrimination legislation in Northern Ireland has actually been strengthened (Knox and Hughes 1994);

and, despite political opposition, the USA and Britain both retain 'positive' or 'affirmative' action within their repertoire for legitimate state action to combat racial, ethnic, religious or sex discrimination. This range of developments shows the potential widespread application of this measure (for a recent comparative survey, see *New Community* 1994).

We are, then, talking about a deeply contradictory situation, highlighted by recent examples from Britain. On the one hand, a mild, legally sound attempt by the BBC to establish a positive action regional news training scheme targeted at minorities is attacked by a Conservative MP as a 'nonsensical example of political correctness' (*Guardian* 13 June 1994); by contrast, in Liverpool with a blaze of publicity Conservative minister David Hunt opens a 'Retail Initiative' scheme aiming to attract black and ethnic minorities to work with Royal Insurance, saying 'the initiative helps break the cycle of unemployment through positive action' (*Daily Post* 1 July 1994).

The confusion of language between 'positive action' and 'positive discrimination' is of course one important element in the 'political correctness' discourse, which translates what are frequently limited attempts to target educational and training initiatives for under-represented groups into deeply threatening attacks on the rights of others.

Thus in Britain's equalities legislation so-called 'positive discrimination' is in fact confined to those few exceptional contexts in which people are allowed to be appointed to employment positions on the basis of ethnicity or gender; 'positive action', the weaker version of American 'affirmative action', is concerned with measures taken to encourage under-represented groups to apply for employment, measures to provide race- or gender-specific educational and training opportunities that enable ethnic minorities or women to compete on more equal terms, measures to encourage employers to seek actively to make their workforces more representative at all levels of their local communities; and measures to enable services to be provided to meet the particular needs of minority groups and of women (Burney 1987).

By contrast, in the case of Northern Ireland, employers are now under a greater statutory obligation to monitor their workforce and implement fair employment practices to make up for historical patterns of discrimination (in this case upon religious grounds) than in Britain, where positive action and equal opportunity policies are normally only a voluntary, exhortative, 'good practice' option, despite attempts by the Commission for Racial Equality to make them a requirement on all employers (Commission for Racial Equality 1992).

At the most elaborate end of the affirmative action spectrum in the USA, the Reagan and Bush presidencies encouraged the weakening of the civil rights legislative framework, which has historically had considerable success in opening up areas of previous exclusion and under-representation of minorities and women, through a significant array of legal powers and economic sanctions to enforce and monitor changes in employment practices, to enhance access to service opportunities such as in the education field, and to strengthen minority businesses (Weir 1993).

This attack is continuing under the Clinton administration with the growing dominance of newly resurgent Republicanism, which has the clawing back of affirmative action policies and minority business set-asides as a central policy aim, to reward the 'angry white men' who form its key electoral constituency.

There are undoubtedly major debates to be had to clarify the terminology and scope of the positive or affirmative action agenda and to draw out the best practice from current international comparisons. At the heart of such practice, however, can be identified a key underlying premise that could be elevated into an axiom of international salience, as relevant in South Africa, Northern Ireland, France, Germany, and the United States as in Britain: where a racial, ethnic or national minority has suffered from historic and systematic patterns of discrimination, exclusion, under-representation or marginalisation, then targeted, group-specific initiatives to redress the balance are an essential component of social policy that aims to achieve their 'inclusion' or 'integration' on the basis of social equality and justice.

Players of the 'politically correct' card frequently use misleading characterisations of the unholy trinity of 'anti-racism, feminism and multiculturalism' to oppose 'positive action' in the name of 'equal opportunity' (for white men in particular). But positive action needs to be seen as a crucial strand of equal opportunity policy because it argues that removing formal discriminatory or exclusionary barriers to competition or eligibility for resources and services, whilst being an essential component of anti-discrimination policy, does not necessarily translate into the reality of equality of access, equality of treatment, and especially equality of outcome (Ouseley 1990; Mason 1990).

Hence the proactive use of 'targets', 'earmarking', 'set-asides' and 'quotas', and the implementation of measures to monitor actual progress in meeting targets are, to varying degrees, allowed and formally encouraged in the anti-discrimination legislation of the USA, Britain and Northern Ireland, and should be seen as essential to the European Commission's anti-discrimination legislation that will be developed in future years.

This argument is in line with some of the conclusions of the important International Symposium on Anti-Discrimination Law held in Edinburgh in 1993, which agreed that a powerful case had been made for greater use of positive action (particularly in terms of conditions for public tenders and contracts) and offered 'general support for the stronger line advocated by the Commission for Racial Equality to require employers and service providers to adopt equal opportunity policies, to set targets, to monitor their performance, to publish reports annually' (New Community 1994: 350).

The links with social exclusion

On an even broader field of social policy, it can be argued that parallel practical targeted measures of social intervention and redress are necessary to benefit any group in danger of exclusion, marginalisation and discrimination by the free play of market forces, whether it be women, people with disabilities, the elderly, young people or the long-term unemployed.

Thus European Commission social policy has been pressing for a range of measures to achieve the integration of excluded groups, as can be exemplified in the recently agreed Objective One programme for Merseyside, which involves a range of targeted or focused initiatives aimed at encouraging particular 'priority groups' excluded from the labour market to enter various 'pathways to integration' (in the areas of education, skills acquisition, training and job creation). The assumption here is that previous urban regeneration initiatives have failed because benefits do not automatically trickle down from infrastructural improvements to groups in greatest need, or from prestige flagship projects to residents in nearby areas; hence the targeting of disadvantaged groups and their active involvement in partnership structures with the public and private sectors is necessary. But this framework also acknowledges that targeted community, educational or training projects do not necessarily lead to permanent employment advance unless they are followed through and linked to sustained economic opportunities (Merseyside 2000, 1994; see also Ben-Tovim 1987).

This debate over exclusion is in fact a reworking of the debates over the limits and potential of 'positive action', albeit in terms of a different organising concept. However, there is a danger in the principle of 'positive action' being extended to cover the full range of groups at risk of 'exclusion' and 'marginalisation': the *specific* disadvantages, discrimination and oppression facing racial/ethnic minorities may be diluted within a broader framework concerned with the problems of *all* groups facing patterns of structural or institutionalised inequality. On the other hand, an acknowledgement of the underlying shared principles that straddle actions potentially encompassing a wide range of social groups could help to promote broad-based alliances and provide a degree of unifying consensus around concepts of positive action and equal opportunities.

The transnational potential of the positive action agenda was reflected at a recent meeting of the Council of Europe Working Party on Cities and Education, in which senior educational colleagues from Western and Eastern Europe agreed, after lively controversy and debate, that a legal and social policy framework that outlaws acts of overt discrimination has to be accompanied by an approach that helps to compensate for the particular disadvantages and levels of exclusion facing ethnic minorities in their societies. This necessitates:

> Bold and clear forms of 'positive action' or 'affirmative action', which may be transitional measures to provide additional support in or after school, extra resources and additional training and recruitment measures (e.g. to recruit minority teachers) in the context of broader political interventions to combat disadvantage, inequality and exclusion and to meet particular social needs. (Council of Europe 1995)

The struggle for positive action in Liverpool

The recent history of racial politics in Liverpool provides evidence for the controversy and bitterness that the debate around positive action can generate. But this example also points to the possibility of achieving a constructive resolution of the issue, enabling anti-racist measures to remain a legitimate strand of a broader local agenda to combat social exclusion (see Nelson and Ben-Tovim 1996).

Liverpool's black community has had a historically marginalised position for many generations, encountering deep-seated personal and cultural racism (embodied in prejudices and myths concerning the community with its tradition of black–white intermarriage); systematic institutionalised racism in the field of employment, housing, education, social welfare and the criminal justice system; and the structural racism involved in the interplay of race and class in the context of Liverpool's industrial, urban and fiscal decline (see Gifford et al. 1989; Connolly et al. 1992; Ben-Tovim 1980; 1986; Ben-Tovim and Law 1984). This long-standing exclusion has been perpetuated by a range of political administrations in the city where universalistic, colour-blind ideologies of right, centre and left have traditionally refused to adopt targeted measures in terms of training, employment or service provision to improve the disadvantaged position of the black population (see Ben-Tovim et al. 1986).

During the 1970s and 1980s, Liverpool's black and anti-racist organisations mounted a series of protracted struggles to gain local official acknowledgement of the problem of racism, and to carve out a space for black-led, race-specific initiatives. These conflicts were particularly bitter during the period of the Militant left-wing administration (1983–87), whose dogmatic, class-only approach ruled out the possibility of its supporting any form of positive action policy or autonomous black initiative (see Liverpool Black Caucus 1986).

However, the replacement of Militant by a more pragmatic Labour administration in Liverpool has opened the way to a consensus, sustained across all mainstream parties, that specific positive action measures are necessary to redress the particular disadvantages facing Liverpool's black community (Nelson and Ben-Tovim 1997).

As a consequence of this current shift towards consensus, there has been little negative politicisation of a range of race equality initiatives that have been adopted by Liverpool City Council in partnership with other local institutions – for example, an ambitious, multi-million-pound 'positive action' training programme designed to recruit six hundred black people for training (and eventual employment) within Liverpool City Council; a substantial enhancement of black Access to Higher Education courses; introduction of widespread ethnic record-keeping and monitoring procedures; establishment of race equality management teams in education, housing, leisure and social services departments; support for a wide range of black and ethnic minority voluntary organisations; a comprehensive set of guidelines for anti-racist, multicultural, and multilingual approaches to education; a radical new multifaith religious education syllabus; a relaunched supplementary school targeted at black pupils; 'job link' and 'construction charter' initiatives aimed to boost black job recruitment; support for minority housing associations; outreach education guidance schemes targeted at black adult returners; establishment of a 'black parents group' as a formal part of the local education structure; and sheltered accommodation and a residential care centre targeted at black and ethnic minority elders (Ben-Tovim et al. 1993; 1995).

Each of these measures was initially resisted by local administrations, of whatever political colour, but interestingly these programmes have actually been enhanced in Liverpool in recent years at a time when municipal anti-racism has been in retreat across the rest of the country; this flourishing was a consequence perhaps of the strength in Liverpool of the 1981 street disturbances or 'uprisings', the sharpness of the ideological and political struggle in the mid-1980s, and the relative solidity of the broad-based, non-sectarian, cross-party alliances forged during this period by the local anti-racist and black community organisations. The consistent production of objective research evidence concerning the disproportionate and specific inequalities facing black people and ethnic minorities in Liverpool, much of which was gathered in association with the local university, also made an important contribution to the process of shifting the parameters of local debate (and indicating the potential value of alliances between community activists and researchers in this area).

These measures have been developed in a climate which has supported complementary initiatives aimed at improving the position of women and people with disabilities (the refurbishment, for example, under the City Challenge initiative of a high-quality education centre for women specialising in new technology training), and which acknowledges the range of local 'priority groups' at risk of exclusion from the labour market who need additional support and targeting in programmes of local intervention (as in the various 'partnership' areas across Liverpool, which contain the most significant pockets of poverty and unemployment).

Towards a strategic approach

Of course, 'affirmative action' or 'positive action' programmes cannot of themselves resolve all the issues of exclusion, marginalisation, disadvantage and inequality; they need to be linked with more general socioeconomic strategies, structural policies and political alliances that are designed to boost the economy, create jobs and training opportunities, invest in education and skills enhancement, improve welfare services, reduce poverty and ill health, redistribute wealth, and create genuine partnerships between the central and local government as well as the private and voluntary sectors.

Equal opportunity measures need also to be linked to a legislative, political and ideological framework which is concerned across Europe with the following:

- outlawing direct and indirect racism in employment and service delivery;
- combating the growth of far-right political organisations (racist, fascist, neo-Nazi, anti-Semitic, and ultra-nationalist groups and parties);
- protecting minorities from the growing problems of racial harassment, violence and attack;
- ensuring that minorities enjoy full civic, cultural, and political rights and freedoms;
- acknowledging and celebrating the multicultural, multiethnic, multifaith and multilingual nature of our national and global societies;
- counteracting the xenophobia of harsh and exclusionary immigration, nationality and asylum policies.

The relative weakness of the anti-racist movement has in part been located in the frequent failure to acknowledge the need to work in a united and non-sectarian way on all these fronts. The unnecessary polarisation in Britain of 'anti-racism' and 'multiculturalism' in education, for example, was arguably an absurdly wasteful, self-indulgent battle that left a gaping, confused hole in the middle ground, enabling the New Right to dominate the divided opposition with the reassertion of 'English' and 'Christian' values in the National Curriculum, and in the area of religious education and collective worship (but see overviews by Rattansi 1992; Troyna 1992).

Predictably, perhaps, the tide of sociological fashion seems to have swung from the early focus on 'ethnicity', 'multiculturalism' and 'prejudice' towards a more radical concern with 'anti-racism' and 'black perspectives', then away from 'anti-racism' and a unitary 'black' identity (Modood 1994; Modood et al. 1994) to the reworked multiculturalism of postmodernist 'new ethnicities' (Hall 1988) and 'multiple identities' (Rex 1991), and once again back to an acknowledgement that a focus on the discourse of shifting, contingent, subjective 'identity' cannot be a substitute for facing up to the harsh objective realities of racism and its more oppressive and intolerant strands of 'fundamentalist' identity politics.

A common language of anti-racism?

It is perhaps timely, then, to suggest a number of staged arguments to help the attainment of a 'common language of anti-racism' for Europe.

All our societies are 'global' – all our national states *are* 'plural', multicultural, multiethnic, multilingual, multifaith (Goldberg 1994). 'Multi-culturalism' therefore is not really a matter of choice, of dogma, of 'political correctness' but of an acknowledgement of the material nature of our communities: the young man of Algerian origin born in Paris in a rundown suburb may be categorised as a 'Muslim' or an 'Arab' – as 'other' – or may identify himself in a number of complex and varied ways, but he is also French – France is a Muslim, Jewish and Christian society, not simply the secular, assimilated, post-Jacobin state its establishment likes to claim to be; German 'Turks' are German, even if deprived of full citizenship and a German identity by a legislative framework that grants automatic franchise or citizenship to ethnic Germans on the basis of an ideology of 'German blood' and limits it in the case of migrant workers and their families; Britain's active worshippers include a significant Muslim population whose leaders claim the same rights as other religious minorities (including the same access to voluntary-aided school status as is enjoyed by Christian and Jewish groups, and revision of Britain's ethnocentric blasphemy laws).

One strand of 'anti-racism', then, has to be the struggle for parity of esteem, or status, political, civil, religious, cultural and linguistic rights for all minorities: the opposition of 'multiculturalism' is not 'anti-racism' but 'monoculturalism' which is an important ideological component of racism, the Eurocentric, colonial assertion of the inferiority, primitiveness or invisibility of cultural minorities. This cultural imperialism (Said 1993) is one defining strand, along with anti-Semitism, of the European racist heritage, with variants seen in French colour-blind cultural assimilationism, Germany's denial of its own ethnic diversity, and the recent reassertion of English 'core values' in the National Curriculum.

Ideological racialisation has profound real-life effects: thus the protection of minority rights has to include as a bottom line the robust outlawing of hostile acts of aggression, exclusion and discrimination, and broad-based, high-profile opposition to racist ultra-right mobilisation against minorities and to the harsh and racist immigration, nationality and asylum policies of mainstream 'Fortress Europe' (Sivanandan 1990).

But in addition, acknowledgement of the validity of a group's allegiance to a 'different' culture, religion and language has to encompass positive measures to enable minorities to define, protect or enhance their own identities on as equal as possible a footing with members of the majority culture: in other words, multiculturalism has to address the issue of *power* if it is to overcome the sense of cultural oppression, injustice and exclusion that may propel minorities into support for ultra-nationalist or fundamentalist movements.

However, minority communities are themselves not homogeneous and are stratified by class and gender – they contain complex divisions, a fluidity and diversity of ethnic identity and allegiance, contradictions, struggles and fragmentation which cannot be reduced to a single ethnic or cultural 'essence' – the hallmark perhaps of more simplistic multicultural, anti-racist and indeed some minority perspectives (see Gilroy 1987; hooks 1991; Yuval-Davis 1992; Gabriel 1994).

Social policy, then, which is anti-racist, multicultural and egalitarian has to grapple with the dilemmas of *pluralism* (Goulbourne 1991) – the concern, particularly sharpened in recent debates over 'Islam' and in the wake of the apparently 'ethnic' conflicts in former Yugoslavia and Rwanda, that active support for the rights of minorities or the political mobilisation of ethnicity may conflict with the maintenance of broader national unity, women's rights and civil liberties of the individual; may encourage secessionist or ethnically exclusivist movements; may strengthen the patriarchal and conservative underpinnings of some ethnic minority organisations and nationalist movements; and may even lead to the ultimate barbarism of 'ethnic cleansing' and genocide (Hobsbawm 1994).

Such justifiable fears, however, have to be set against the broad principles that democratic, egalitarian, multicultural societies have to find ways to acknowledge, not suppress, their diversity, that is to say they have to provide space for the institutional expression of the ethnic identities and the differences of all groups, whilst holding on to the other safeguards of a secular, liberal, nonauthoritarian, nonsexist civil society, and building a reconstructed, progressive national culture and identity from all its component parts.

The aim, then, is to create a 'seamless pluralism' rather than to encourage an absolutist and reactionary cultural nationalism, so that individuals are not coerced into a monolithic, imposed, ethnic straitjacket and so that boundaries between groups are as fluid and nonexclusive as the multiple identities many people are actually constructing in our 'postmodern' societies.

The same principle of moving beyond non-discrimination and 'equality of opportunity' to ensure 'equality of access', 'equality of treatment' and 'equality of outcome', lies behind the notion of 'positive action': specific, targeted actions and initiatives are required in the fields of education, training, employment and service provision to ensure that members of historically discriminated-against, excluded and disadvantaged minority groups are able to move towards equal representation within the workforce and in receipt of services, and to receive a level of redress for past inequalities.

The ultimate analytical justification for this interventionist approach to 'equal opportunities' lies in the approach to racism that sees racial inequalities as stemming as much from the unconscious, routine policies, rules, practices and procedures of *institutions* ('institutionalised' or 'indirect' racism) as from the subjective, personal intent of *individuals* ('direct racism') or from the operation of macro-level, socioeconomic *structures* ('structural racism') – (see Ginsborg 1992). Hence a moralistic emphasis on the racist individual, a class-based structural emphasis on capitalist economic processes, an orientation that stops at the elimination of acts of direct discrimination, a definition of racism that is limited to the expression or effect of racialised discourse (Miles 1993), a formalistic and passive commitment to equal opportunity – none of these necessarily tackles the actual day-to-day mechanisms that reproduce patterns of racial inequality, subordination and exclusion; hence the need for forms of interventionist 'positive' or 'affirmative' action.

These principles do not need to be counterpoised against other complementary social policies; indeed, they should be seen as aspects of a broader political strategy. Affirmative action and equal opportunity policies point to the need for targeted interventions to combat the exclusion of a range of socially disadvantaged groups; the need for broader structural changes and policies to deal with endemic problems of unemployment, poverty and economic decline; the need for a measure of redistribution of resources to benefit the more marginalised and impoverished strata of society; and the need for a broader democratisation of the work process and of central and local state political structures.

But such broader policies have to incorporate targeted race- (or ethnically) specific measures, or else the particular needs and disadvantages facing ethnic minorities will be overlooked, and the balance of discrimination will not be redressed. Alliances and unity on the broadest fronts of social intervention and change can only be constructed successfully on the basis of respect for the autonomy of constituent groups and the irreducibility of specific oppressions.

Conclusion

Through the steps of the arguments in this chapter, I hope to have presented the case for a European-wide 'common language of anti-racism'. This needs to involve, in the first place, what is frequently referred to as 'anti-racism', that is, the outlawing of explicit acts of direct discrimination; opposition to extremist racist, anti-Semitic, fascist and ultra-nationalist groups; the protection of minorities against the oppression of racial harassment and violence; and opposition to exclusionary immigration, nationality and asylum policies – the sharp edge of anti-racist movements and alliances.

All this has to be complemented by a positive action strategy which tackles the accumulated and frequently indirect discrimination of historical and institutionalised policies and practices, and goes on to provide a legislative framework to enable and promote targeted affirmative actions in education, training, employment and services as part of proactive, outcome-oriented equal opportunity policies.

To underpin this framework in ideological terms, a radical pluralism or multiculturalism has to be reinstated that dispenses with the colour-blind, universalist and nationalist discourses of left, centre and right (which conspire to deny rights of religious and cultural expression, civic enfranchisement, and nationality status to minorities across Europe) and instead advocates the acknowledgement and celebration of the diverse, fluid, multiethnic nature of our modern societies.

But to prevent the fragmentation, authoritarianism, patriarchy, group closure, sectarianism and ultra-nationalism that an exclusivist politics of ethnic identity can encourage, multiculturalism needs to be seen not as an end in itself, but as a component of the struggle for social equality, justice and freedom which has to be pursued within the non-relativistic framework of secular liberal and social democracy, but which seeks to build alliances and unity through the recognition rather than the suppression of diversity and difference.

Our 'common language of anti-racism', then, has to be inclusive, to help the broadest possible alliances both to overcome the forces of racism, fascism and ultra-nationalism and to reconstruct a progressive, critical agenda of social intervention and social change for the left of centre. 'Positive action' or 'affirmative action' has enormous potential to link anti-racism and multiculturalism with feminism and wider struggles for social equality and justice; that is why it has been so bitterly opposed, and that is why we have to argue that it *is* politically correct.

References

Ben-Tovim, Gideon S. (ed.) (1980) *Racial Disadvantage in Liverpool*, University of Liverpool, Department of Sociology, Liverpool.

— (1986) *Racial Discrimination and Disadvantage in Employment in Liverpool*, Merseyside Community Relations Council, Liverpool.

— (1987) 'Race, Local Politics and Urban Regeneration Strategy – Lessons from Liverpool', in B. Foley et al. (eds) *Regenerating the Cities*, Manchester University Press, Manchester, pp. 145–55.

Ben-Tovim, Gideon S. and F. Cogley (1993) 'Vocational Education for Special Groups in Liverpool', in *Combating Unemployment Through Vocational Training –*

The Role of the City, CLRAE Studies and Texts No. 33, Council of Europe Press, Strasbourg, pp. 55–65.

— (1995) 'The Role of Parental Participation in Supporting the Education of Children from Minority Groups in Liverpool', in *The City's Approach to the Education of its Multi-cultural Population (Migrants and Minorities)*, CLRAE Studies and Texts No. 37, Council of Europe Press, Strasbourg, pp. 75–89.

Ben-Tovim, Gideon S. and I. G. Law (1984) *Race and Housing in Liverpool*, Commission for Racial Equality, London.

Ben-Tovim, Gideon S., J. Gabriel, I. G. Law and K. Stredder (1986) *The Local Politics of Race*, Macmillan, London.

Burney, E. (1987) *Positive Action in a Cold Climate*, Runnymede Trust, London.

Commission for Racial Equality (1992) *Second Review of the Race Relations Act 1976*, CRE, London.

Connolly, M., K. Roberts, Gideon S. Ben-Tovim and P. Torkington (1992) *Black Youth in Liverpool*, Giordano Bruno, Culemborg.

Council of Europe (1995) *The City's Approach to the Education of its Multi-cultural Population* – CLRAE Studies and Texts No. 37, Council of Europe Press, Strasbourg.

Dunant, S. (1994) *The War of the Words: The Political Correctness Debate*, Virago, London.

Edwards, J. (1987) *Positive Discrimination, Social Justice and Social Policy*, Tavistock, London.

Gabriel, John (1994) *Racism, Culture, Markets*, Routledge, London.

Gifford, Lord, W. Brown and R. Bundey (1989) *Loosen the Shackles*, Karia Press, London.

Gilroy, Paul (1987) *There Ain't no Black in the Union Jack*, Hutchinson, London.

— (1990) 'The End of Anti-racism', in W. Ball and John Solomos (eds) *Race and Local Politics*, Macmillan, London, pp. 191–209.

Ginsborg, N. (1992) 'Racism and Housing: Concepts and Reality', in P. Braham et al. (eds) *Racism and Anti-Racism*, Sage for the Open University, London.

Goldberg, David T. (ed.) (1994) *Multi-culturalism – a Critical Reader*, Blackwell, Oxford.

Gordon, Paul (1990) 'A Dirty War – the New Right and Local Authority Anti-racism', in W. Ball and John Solomos (eds) *Race and Local Politics*, Macmillan, London.

Gordon, Paul and F. Klug (1986) *New Right, New Racism*, Searchlight, London.

Goulbourne, Harry (1991) 'Varieties of Pluralism: the Notion of a Pluralist, Post-Imperial Britain', *New Community* 17(2): 211–22.

Hall, Stuart (1988) 'New Ethnicities', in *Black Film: British Cinema*, ICA London Documents 7, ICA, London.

Hobsbawm, Eric (1994) *Age of Extremes*, Michael Joseph, London.

hooks, bell (1991) *Yearning – Race, Gender and Cultural Politics*, Turnaround, London.

Knox, C. and J. Hughes (1994) 'Equality and Equity: An Emerging Government Policy in Northern Ireland', *New Community* 20(2): 207–25.

Liverpool Black Caucus (1986) *The Racial Politics of Militant* (edited by Gideon Ben-Tovim), Runnymede Trust, London.

Macdonald, I., R. Bhavnani, L. Khan and Gus John (1989) *Murder in the Playground*, Longsight Press, London.

Mason, David (1990) 'Competing Conceptions of "Fairness" and the Formulation and Implementation of Equal Opportunity Policies', in W. Ball and John Solomos (eds) *Race and Local Politics*, Macmillan, London, pp. 45–61.

Merseyside 2000 (1994) *Programming Document for Objective One*, European Commission, Brussels.

Miles, Robert (1993) *Racism After 'Race Relations'*, Routledge, London.

Modood, Tariq (1988) '"Black", Racial Equality and Asian Identity', *New Community*, 14(3).

— (1994) 'Political Blackness and British Asians', *Sociology*, 28(4): 859–76.

Modood, Tariq, S. Beishon and S. Virdee (1994) *Changing Ethnic Identities*, Policy Studies Institute, London.

Nelson, W. E. and Gideon S. Ben-Tovim (1997) 'Race, Class, Equal Opportunity Policies and Local Government: the Case of Liverpool', *National Political Science Review*, 6: Special Edition on 'Race and Ethnicity in Europe'.

New Community (1994) *Comparative Approaches to Anti-Discrimination Law*, 20(3).

Ouseley, H. (1990) 'Resisting Institutional Change', in W. Ball and John Solomos (eds) *Race and Local Politics*, Macmillan, London, 132–52.

Rattansi, Ali (1992) 'Changing the Subject? Racism, Culture and Education', in J. Donald and A. Rattansi (eds), *Race, Culture and Difference*, Sage for the Open University, London, pp. 11–48.

Rattansi, Ali and Sallie Westwood (1994) *Racism, Modernity and Identity*, Polity Press, Cambridge.

Rex, John (1991) *Ethnic Identity and Political Mobilisation in Britain*, Centre for Research in Ethnic Relations, University of Warwick, Coventry.

Said, Edward W. (1993) *Culture and Imperialism*, Chatto and Windus, London.

Sivanandan, A. (1990) *Communities of Resistance*, Verso, London and New York.

Troyna, Barry (1992) 'Can You See the Join? An Historical Analysis of Multicultural and Anti-racist Education Policies', in D. Gill et al. (eds) *Racism and Education*, Sage for the Open University, London, pp. 63–91.

Weir, M. (1993) 'From Equal Opportunity to "the New Social Contract"' in Malcolm Cross and Michael Keith (eds) *Racism, the City and the State*, Routledge, London, pp. 93–107.

Wilson, W. J. (1987) *The Truly Disadvantaged*, University of Chicago Press, Chicago and London.

Yuval-Davis, Nira (1992) 'Fundamentalism, Multi-culturalism and Women in Britain' in J. Donald and Ali Rattansi (eds) *Race, Culture and Difference*, Sage for the Open University Press, London, pp. 278–91.

CHAPTER 12

Society as a Kind of Community: Communitarian Voting with Equal Rights for Individuals in the European Union

Christopher Brewin

Creating a new political order in Europe includes what in North America has been well called the politics of recognition. Charles Taylor, in his Princeton lecture on multiculturalism, argued that since the eighteenth century our individual identities have been formed in 'a continuing dialogue and struggle with significant others' (Taylor 1994: 36). Part of our entitlement to equal dignity is a public recognition of the uniqueness of individuals and groups (Taylor 1994: 38). If as Gypsies, or immigrants, or females, or believers, our sense of ourselves as having these identities is that we are therefore considered inferior to commuters, or natives, or males, or unbelievers, this is as illiberal as any other form of exploitation or injustice (Taylor 1994: 64).

I begin by discussing the American 'debate' on Taylor's lecture contained in the 1992 volume edited by Amy Gutmann. However, there are significant differences between multiculturalism in the American context of a strong state that actively promotes a constitutional conception of citizenship, and multiculturalism in Europe, the subject of Section Two of this chapter. One of these differences is the new respectability in western as well as post-communist eastern Europe of Tönnies' 1887 conception of community as *Gemeinschaft*, which Habermas and Dahrendorf had tried to demolish as incompatible with 'modernity' (Habermas 1987; Dahrendorf 1968). I return to R. G. Collingwood's 1942 attack on '*Gemeinschaft*' thinking in fascism (and Marxism). I try to revive his rival liberal definition of society as a community of a particular kind. Collingwood argues that what makes society different is that it is a community ruling itself (Collingwood 1942, 20.36) and in perpetual tension with the nonsocial communities out of which society emerges and back into which it constantly threatens to relapse. This distinction is particularly useful where communities have been brought together in order to survive in the face of an external threat, or to take advantage of an external opportunity.

In the third section of this chapter, I shall focus on the multicultural aspect of the vacuous citizenship provisions in the Treaty of Maastricht. The most threatened groups in Europe, whether immigrants or other minorities, would be more secure if the area were stabilised by reasonable expectations of financial and military aid, organised on a pan-European basis, whether by German hegemony, confederal actions or a federal state. This raises questions of what is meant by rule that I shall not discuss in this chapter. Instead I shall attempt a critique of the Maastricht provisions on citizenship on various grounds highlighted by transposing them into the North American context. Among the possible solutions to this question of rights, I shall argue that a more equal recognition of nonterritorial communities would follow from two reforms. The first would ground the right to vote in European elections on stable residency rather than national citizenship. The second would copy the Israeli model of proportional representation in which Europe would form a single constituency. Communities could, if they wished, organise themselves to participate electorally on a nonterritorial or alternatively, as now, on a territorial basis, trading the purity of smaller parties against the efficacy of larger parties. The principle of equality of rights under the law would thereby be reconciled with the (self-)recognition of minority and majority cultures and ideologies to an extent that is not possible at present.

Section One: The North American debate

In North America, the idea that citizens are equal members of a multicultural society has led liberal political thought in contradictory directions. One school holds that in a multicultural society, where people by definition have different ways of life, the state must avoid identification with any single culture, putting the emphasis on judicial defence of individuals' rights to act as each sees fit, emphasising procedures rather than substance. Jürgen Habermas, the only contributor to this debate carrying a European passport, cites Dworkin and Rawls in support of this state 'neutrality'. In contrast, he adds, 'communitarians like Taylor and Walzer dispute the ethical neutrality of the law and thus can expect the constitutional state, if need be, actively to advance specific conceptions of the good life' (Habermas 1994: 111).

Taylor's example of the 'procedural' response to multiculturalism is the Canadian adoption of a Charter of Rights in 1982. The contrary demand for 'substantive' support from the state for a threatened culture is illustrated by 'Quebeckers, *on the one hand, and aboriginal peoples on the other*' (Taylor 1992: 52, my emphasis). It is worth drawing attention to the way that Taylor does not bracket the two communities together, but by his use of two hands differentiates between the Québécois and the aboriginal peoples.

As with Gypsies in Europe, the aboriginal peoples are not politically on a par with Quebeckers, as it seems for Taylor. They are to be well treated as dependants, or compensated as native communities for past injustice, but are not expected to participate fully in electoral (majority) politics.

As for Quebec, some of its characteristics are different from most of the immigrant communities of North America. It is long-established. It is located in a territorially distinct province which makes secession a possibility. Its French-speaking culture is threatened by the dominance of Anglo-Saxon commerce, and its views on the role of women, the size of families and the nature of work are distinctly old-fashioned. Whilst laws requiring all but the smallest firms to use French as the working language may appear to sacrifice inward investment for the romance of community survival, these laws do give an immediately tangible advantage to French-speaking job seekers. Feelings of *Gemeinschaft* are reinforced by individual interest in ways that could be easily replicated in parts of Europe – Wallonia, Croatia, the Basque region, Northern Ireland, the Baltic states, Slovenia, Slovakia, Georgia, Greenland, Scotland.

Michael Walzer is more representative of the 'hyphenated identities' of North America. Jewish-Americans are scattered throughout the USA even if they are more powerful in some areas than others, and wield electoral influence on national policies towards the Middle East for example. Walzer's contribution to the debate was to soften the impact of divided liberalisms. In his comment he suggests that in the context of what Americans with historical memories call an 'immigrant society', communitarians like himself would nevertheless support a neutral state that was not identified with any particular community, and which protected individual rights without naming any communities. He similarly uses numerals rather than emotive labels in setting out the difference between the two perspectives.

> The first kind of liberalism ('Liberalism 1') is committed in the strongest possible way to individual rights and, almost as a deduction from this, to a rigorously neutral state, that is, a state without cultural or religious projects or, indeed, any sort of collective goals beyond the personal freedom and the physical security, welfare, and safety of its *citizens*. The second kind of liberalism ('Liberalism 2') allows for a state committed to the survival and flourishing of a particular nation, cultures and religions – so long as the basic rights of *citizens* who have different commitments or no such commitments at all are protected. (Walzer 1992: 99, my emphasis)

I highlight the repeated use of the word 'citizen' because to my European eyes, this serves to make the point that in North America the two liberal perspectives are held together within the powerful context of constitutional union. Anybody who has seen the ferocity with which US schoolteachers teach the Constitution, or with which the US army demands respect for the flag, can have no doubts that the 'neutral state' does have its own project. The USA and Canada may not be based on the single culture that justified German and Italian demands for self-determination and unification. There is no sense of ethnic territorial community in North America comparable to that of '*Gemeinschaft*' in Austria or of '*narod*' in Russia. Nevertheless it is precisely the institutionalised *Bildung* of citizenship in America and Canada that accounts for the intensity of the multicultural debate about which authors should be included as textbooks in American courses on Western civilisation.

Similarly, it is relevant that the Quebekers' demands for recognition are contained within a strong state, a pervasive civic conception of citizenship and considerable economic redistribution. It is inconceivable that Canadians would have tolerated the seizing of farms, murder and rape that post-Maastricht Europeans have tolerated in Bosnia.

It may therefore seem at first sight odd that Habermas criticises other authors in the North American debate for not being strong enough on citizenship:

> Once we take this internal connection between democracy and the constitutional state seriously, it becomes clear that the system of [individual] rights is blind neither to unequal social conditions *nor to cultural differences*. (Habermas 1994: 113)

His point is derived from the longstanding division between utilitarian liberals and Kantians. If I have understood him aright, the American concept is too passive, looking to citizenship as a useful bundle of rights: civil rights dating from the eighteenth century, political rights dating from the nineteenth century and the welfare rights of the twentieth century (Marshall 1950). Habermas explicitly prefers the Kantian view that we should obey laws we have given, or could have given, ourselves (Habermas 1994: 111–12). On this view of citizenship as protecting autonomy, we may well decide that the way to protect our autonomy is to link up with others – Scots, Germans, Quakers, Turks. On the model of conscientious objection for Quakers, the laws have to be framed to allow autonomy for communities as the Swiss have done for centuries.

Habermas's emphasis on democratic *rule* rather than *rights* ties in with his sharp distinctions between 'oppressed ethnic and cultural minorities' and the 'nationalism of peoples'.

> The struggle of *oppressed ethnic and cultural minorities* for the recognition of their collective identities … differs from the *nationalism of peoples* who see themselves as ethnically and linguistically homogeneous groups against the background of a common historical fate and who want to protect their identity not only as an ethnic community but as a people forming a nation with the capacity for political action. (Habermas 1994: 117–18).

He locates Quebec on the boundary that might lead either to sovereignty, like Croatia, or to the kind of protection for minorities that is preferred in Switzerland to majority rule. Habermas here takes explicitly a European nation-state perspective that is at odds with the neutral state of Liberalism 1; at the same time he maintains, against Liberalism 2, that the law is ethically neutral.

It is the nation, the *Kulturnation* of the German middle classes, that has a substance, a project, a capacity for political action, a historically specific political culture and 'a kind of constitutional patriotism':

> At the same time, the ethical substance of a constitutional patriotism cannot detract from the legal system's neutrality vis-à-vis communities that are ethically integrated at a sub-political level. (Habermas 1994: 134; see also 127)

These pre-political communities are not on the same level as political societies:

> ... a collectivity that thinks of itself as a community with its own identity *attains a new level of recognition* by taking the step of becoming a nation in its own right. It cannot reach this level as a *pre-political* linguistic and ethnic community, or even as an incorporated or a fragmented 'cultural nation'. (Habermas 1994: 127, my emphasis)

European states are now mostly multicultural. The German self-image of being unlike the USA and Canada in not being an immigrant culture is inconsistent with the empirical observation that 'nearly one-third of the West-German population has resulted from immigration movements since World War II' (Habermas 1994: 145). He argues that it is a corollary of the fact that first-generation immigrants to Germany can only be expected to conform outwardly that the state should be 'procedurally neutral' towards all minorities. Habermas does not see it as a duty to keep cultures alive in the way that endangered species might deserve to be protected. And he excludes fundamentalist sects on what seem to me illiberal grounds. He excludes fundamentalists because they cannot admit the possibility of being wrong: 'In multicultural societies, the national constitution can tolerate only forms of life articulated within the medium of such non-fundamentalist traditions' (Habermas 1994: 133).

This assumption that only nonfundamentalists are right is hard on sects like the Quakers. The better rule is to tolerate all unless to do so would mean that liberty itself is thereby put seriously at risk, as may be the case in Algeria. The example of Quakers is interesting because by the twentieth century their views on war could be accommodated by allowing conscientious objection to universal conscription, precisely because their numbers were predictably small and static.

Finally, Habermas sees Europe not as a federal state in the making, nor as a union of states capable of protecting its state-members, minorities and individuals against the states of which they are citizens. His frequent references to Europe are consistently contextual. For example, Europe is the geographical area in which countries 'will individually and jointly use all means at their disposal to stem the tide' of immigration (Habermas 1994: 136 and n.).

I have cited Habermas's contribution to the Princeton debate at length to show that a distinctively European voice can be detected. In particular I have underlined his emphasis on the 'substantive' state produced by its painful past. It is the nation-state that, after democratic debate, is to set the procedures for dealing with the pre-political communities to be found within its territory. It is time to turn more specifically to Europe to establish how it differs from the North American debate in its use of society and community, and especially the renewed respectability of community in the sense of *Gemeinschaft*, a revival on which Habermas's silence is deafening.

Section Two: Society and community in Europe

In Europe since 1989 the sense of territorial community or *Gemeinschaft* has returned as a major issue in the multicultural debate. Lacking both a strong economy and a strong state, people in the former communist states of Eastern Europe have sought identity in terms of their loyalties to ethnic, religious and cultural communities. The new states of Slovakia, Slovenia, Serbia, Bosnia, Croatia, Estonia, Georgia, have all been created to enable a community to rule itself, with consequent new minority problems (see Kurti, this volume). The Russian tradition of *narod* is given credit for holding Russia together through its political upheavals.

What is as significant is the return to respectability in Western Europe of a *Gemeinschaft* thinking that until recently had been treated as anachronistic by theorists of modernity. Among the many 'Quebecs' on the agenda are the longstanding two *de facto* states in Cyprus, the demands of Walloons and Flemings, of Ulstermen and of Basques, and of Scottish separatists. On reading a draft of this chapter, a historian wrote to me that *Gemeinschaft* will win over *Gesellschaft* every time. Claus Offe contrasts the modernist and 'identity' reactions of Western intellectuals:

> Large parts of the Western public in general and liberal intellectuals in particular are dismayed by the outbursts of nationalist politics and ethnic strife that have emerged in the post-Communist societies. Moral condemnation of nationalist values, attitudes, behaviours for their *pre-modern* and 'obscurantist' character is one of the two reactions we observe in the Western public. The other, and opposite, reaction considers the resurgence of nationalisms and ethnic movements – which it also condemns in many of its manifestations – as *the proof that modernity has not eliminated, but instead presupposes and is founded upon, national identities.* (Offe 1995: 2, my emphasis)

The debate goes deep. Some date it from Tönnies' 1887 book. It can be traced back to Hobbes. (Hobbes' 'Leviathan' makes much more sense as a 'modern' tract in the context of an English nationalism unknown in the Middle Ages but exemplified in Shakespeare's 'patriotic' plays. Adding in patriotism is as necessary as adding in the modern concept of possessive individualism highlighted by C. B. Macpherson.)

I mention Hobbes mainly because the most sustained attack on *Gemeinschaft* thinking is to be found in the updating of Hobbes, the 1942 'New Leviathan' written by the philosopher and historian, R. G. Collingwood. If one can discount his wartime English chauvinism in attacking German barbarism and Marx, there are two aspects of Collingwood's account of community and society that are worth reviving.

The first is that participation by citizens in ruling themselves is the criterion that differentiates liberal thinking about community and society from *Gemeinschaft* thinking.

> 20.12 By a community I shall mean a state of affairs in which something is divided or shared by a number of human beings.
> 20.36 A society is a self-ruling community.
> 37.22 Civilisation is the process of converting a non-social community into a society. (Collingwood 1942)

Let us be clear what this means, first in the example of loyalty to my football club, and then in denying the title of citizen to those who fought for Stalin and Hitler but could not remove them by their votes.

Members of a local community often identify with its football club. It gives them a sense of pride when it is winning, but can also command deep loyalties even when it is losing. For example, Crewe Alexandra supporters share many things – a past, expectations of the future, a ground where they assemble and shout the same language, the rights conferred by buying a ticket. However, they do not count as a society until what they share is rule, which in liberal thought should include the right to elect the club's directors.

In the case of the Germans who resembled each other in having German descent, who voted with their rifles in supporting Hitler's bid to rule non-German communities, who had expectations of a future entitlement to a Volkswagen car in peacetime, they were not a society in the sense propounded by Collingwood because they could not remove their leaders. They did not share rule.

Similar arguments are used to deny that *Gesellschaft*, in the sense of a contractual relationship between workers and employers, constitutes a society in this sense of sharing rule. Collingwood supports his thesis by tracing the origin of the word *societas* in Roman law. He argues that in the parts of Europe influenced by Roman as opposed to Germanic law, the members of a society must have free will and, moreover, the partnership must be in the personal interests of each individual agent.

19.94 The words society, social, contain a reference to free will ... the words *Gesellschaft, gesellschaftlich*, do not.

The second interesting aspect of Collingwood's unusually precise distinction between community and society is his stress on the dialectic between them.

37.28 You may work as hard as you like to turn a non-social community into a society; but you can never finish the job. Every particular society has about it a trace of the non-social community out of which it has emerged.

Here he invokes history to point up what is different about modern, egalitarian, participatory society. In the European Middle Ages, a body politic was a 'collective name for people born in a certain place'. It was both static and characterised by the unequal rights of the different estates (status groups). In the classical *polis*, citizenship was an exclusive category, excluding slaves, metics, foreigners and usually the female members of a citizen's household. By contrast, the modern relationship between a society and the community or, better, the communities out of which it emerges, and back into which it may relapse, is dialectical.

This is true at the level of the family. In the nuclear family, the children are brought up to participate in more and more decisions as they grow older, and then they leave – unlike the households of classical and medieval times. At another level, political societies are formed out of one or, usually, several communities. Instead of the nationalist assumption that every community deserves its own state, this conception makes possible the notion that the process of ruling has to be in the interests of the communities out of which it has been composed. For example, it has often been necessary for communities to come together if they are to survive by meeting an external threat at its own level. The state, in other words, does not need to be in a one-to-one relationship with a single historically formed community. The safeguarding of communities, and especially of territorially dispersed minorities, is a normal feature of their joint rule. Correspondingly, as the external economic and military threat, say, diminishes, it may again become possible for the component communities to seek to become societies in their own right.

Until recently, Collingwood was in tune with current usage throughout Europe in his hostility to Tönnies' 1887 *Gemeinschaft/Gesellschaft* dichotomy. One of the legacies of the war between Hitler and Stalin, and their respective attempts to exterminate internal enemies as embodied by all Jews and some Poles and Ukrainians, has been to induce scepticism about '*Volksgemeinschaft*' and the Russian '*narod*'. Hitler's action at Stalingrad in elevating von Paulus to the rank of field marshal to prevent his 'rational' surrender of his defeated army exemplifies the irrational scale of suffering for country that was accepted in the Great Patriotic War. Before Bosnia, obligations to the state comparable to the supposed limitless love between mothers and sons were no longer trumpeted from public platforms. The German sociologist Dahrendorf (1968: 128) accused Tönnies of 'cultural pessimism', of having promoted an ideology that 'contributed to hindering the advent of modernity in Germany'.

In today's more heterogeneous Europe the crisis of governance may be seen as a reflection of two simultaneous dialectics. The first has established a neo-federalism since 1945 in which both national societies and individuals are better safeguarded by continental military cooperation and economic integration, conventions, and institutions than in 1939. Here the use of the word 'community', as in the European or the North Atlantic Community, implies a sharing of interests and arguably rule in specified sectors limited by the need for each to agree to what is proposed. The other dialectic is related to the first in that the lessening of fears of external dragons, both German and Soviet, has removed some of the cement that kept communities together in nation-states. Minorities and multiculturalism are intimately involved in both dialectics. On the one hand, the best hope for threatened groups is often to obtain money, military protection and legal intervention in defence of individual human rights from a politically organised Europe. On the other hand, many territorial communities see no reason to continue in national states that, as in the cases of the Basques and Walloons, do not offer sufficient recognition for them within consociational, decentralised or centralised nation-states.

In Europe strong national conceptions of citizenship comparable to those in North America used to be the norm, but have become much less secure. Herr Brunner complained to the German Constitutional Court in Frankfurt that once the Treaty of Maastricht was ratified, his right to vote as guaranteed by the German Basic Law would be lost. He would no longer be voting for the real government. The Swiss government tried unsuccessfully to persuade its electors that it could only influence European legislation, by which in practice it had to abide, from within the European Economic Area. In military terms, the withdrawal of US leadership has shown that the national interests of individual states are not a sufficient basis for deterring even Serb aggression. In eastern Europe, the nationalism (*Gemeinschaft*) that has replaced communism is an attempt to shore up weak states and compensate for weak economies. The stress on history in the UK National Curriculum was intended both to integrate immigrants and to restore a pride in Britain that the government found wanting. If the current size and wealth of unified Germany make it possible for it to take over the USA's leadership role in Europe, Habermas is not alone in wondering whether it will still be inhibited by the past:

> Discussion and clarification of the ethical–political self-understanding of the citizens of the two states [of East and West Germany] with widely divergent

historical fates is urgently needed but has not yet taken place. (Habermas 1994: 146–7)

Another sign of the weaker concept of national citizenship in Europe is that the historical differences in the bases of citizenship have narrowed.

> In France national consciousness could develop within the framework of a territorial state, while in Germany it was originally linked with the romantically inspired educated middle-class notion of a *kulturnation*, a nation defined by its culture. (Habermas 1994: 146)

While the basis of German citizenship remains blood descent from a German, with an automatic right of return for *Volksdeutscher*, German law now allows those who have been educated in Germany for fifteen years to apply for citizenship. While the basis of British citizenship remains birth on British territory, the 1981 British Nationality Act introduced *jus sanguinis* in that a child born in Britain is not thereby entitled to citizenship unless one parent has permanent residency rights (Koslowski 1994: 37). In all European countries, citizens enjoy remarkably similar bundles of rights. Moreover, they can apply on human rights grounds for judgments against their own states, and be supported by states other than their own, a *de facto* federalism.

The most remarkable instance of this new federalism has been the institution of European citizenship in the Treaty of Maastricht. It is not based on any strong sense of *Gemeinschaft* comparable to that which brought the German states into one empire, or since 1989 into one state. It is not based on a constitutional contract comparable to a *Gesellschaft*, even though in 1983 the European Court of Justice could characterise its fifteen treaties as a 'Constitutional Charter'. The German Constitutional Court in the Brunner Judgment can continue to assign the right of final judgment on constitutionality to itself and to the German parliament, remarking that Germany remains a sovereign state under the UN Charter. Since the EU lacks sovereignty in the sense of the original right to legislate in accordance with a constitution accepted by its citizens, there is a real question whether European citizenship as instituted by the Maastricht Treaty is an empty, 'Alice in Wonderland' notion. It adds no new duties or rights of legislation, taxation or conscription. Therefore the attribution of the right to vote to nationals of member states living in another member state in local and European, but not national, elections seems to disappear before our eyes, like the Cheshire cat, ending with the grin.

Citizenship in the Maastricht Treaty

The provision for European citizenship in the Maastricht Treaty is innovative. It marks the acceptance of the doctrine that the European treaties apply to all citizens of member states, not just to workers. In proposing European citizenship, the Spanish saw it as of equal importance to economic and monetary union and to a common foreign and security policy (Agence Europe 1990).

Let us return to Herr Brunner's complaint that in consequence of ratification of the Maastricht Treaty he would lose his right as a German citizen to vote for the real government. In reply, the German Constitutional Court developed three different lines of argument.

The first might be called the national constitutionalist argument. The court agreed with Herr Brunner that 'It is fundamental to the democratic process that the exercise of state functions and powers be *derived from and answerable to* the people of the state' (Karlsruhe Court 1994: 64). The court argued that, after Maastricht, the Federal Republic of Germany remained a sovereign state as defined by the UN Charter, that the two houses of the German parliament could decide whether or not to go ahead with monetary union, and that the German courts would have the final say in whether EU acts were in accordance with the German Basic Law. I take the implication of this to be that the German government remains the real government. This accords with the fact that only nationals, and not nationals of other member states resident in Germany, have the right to vote in national elections for national governments. In contrast to the USA, the nationality principle applies to the member states and not to the European Union.

I do not know if Habermas approves of this answer, but it would seem to accord with his definition of citizens in the American debate as 'the totality of *persons* who live together in a territory and are bound by the constitution. ... Their descendants have implicitly (and as naturalised citizens even explicitly) agreed to continue a preexisting constitutional project' (Habermas 1994: 126, my emphasis). The first element of this definition is that the right to vote should be restricted to persons living together in a territory – thus excluding persons of Germanic descent who live in France or, say, Poland and who may by the German Law of Return at present claim citizenship. The second element restricts this right to those who have implicitly or explicitly accepted a past project, like the Basic Law. By implicit acceptance, Habermas does not intend to include those who by their residency obey German law and pay German taxes, nor to exclude those who before 1945 had a different project. The theorist of modernity is embarrassed to draw attention to the 'implicit' acceptance that descent is on racial or tribal grounds. Moreover, he is thinking of a past project like the German 1948 Basic Law, not a future project such as a European Union, as the justification 'in modern natural law according to which citizens come together voluntarily to form a legal community of free and equal consociates' (Habermas 1994: 107).

The court's second line of argument might be called future-oriented or federalist. It told Herr Brunner that *if* the European Parliament developed its powers, then his right as a German national to vote for the 'real' government at a European level would accord with democratic principles. Taken together with the principle of 'subsidiarity' in the devolutionary sense in which it is interpreted by the German *länder*, European citizenship is regarded by federalists as a new if still territorially based understanding of citizenship. In this perspective, Maastricht is seen as progress towards the election of European, national and regional governments and legislatures, each answerable to its constituents at the appropriate territorial level. The German court does not discuss whether a system of hierarchically ordered federal courts will be necessary to secure rights for individuals, or communities, or national societies, in a federation. Nor does it say at what point it would allow the final say (principle of finality) to lie with the Court of Justice in Luxembourg, asserted by that rival court in claiming to be the arbiter of consistency in accordance with treaties interpreted as equivalent to a constitution.

The court's third line of argument might be called communitarian in the peculiar international relations sense that societies may share rule, transferring rights of sovereignty but not sovereignty itself to the whole of which they are parts. I have quoted above from that part of the Brunner judgment that stresses that state functions must be answerable to the people. It goes on immediately to say that *'democratic legitimation is differently produced in a Community of States'* (Karlsruhe Court 1994: 64). In international relations, democratic governments are entitled to agree policies, make treaties and, in the Council of the European Union, make regulations and directives in secret, by consensus, and often with explicit exemptions for named national societies. However, such methods do not meet the principles of publicity, generality, or universality required of democratic lawmaking or the continuous policy-making characteristic of the present European Union. What is as bad is that it is not efficacious, not at the level of events. To rely on a consensus among the national interests of states, each treated as a separate society, is a recipe for inaction, even when confronted with blatant territorial aggression and slaughter of communities on ethnic grounds. Perhaps a hypothetical example would make the point better. We can all imagine the separate replies of our national societies in Council when faced with a Russian attack on Estonia in defence of the 30 per cent of inhabitants who are Russians. The Swedes will say they are too small and also neutral; the Germans will say that memories of 1941 are too recent; the French will offer to threaten the *force de frappe*; and the British will want to consult the USA.

However, the critique I want to make of the Maastricht Treaty is not that Europe is not as efficacious as it could ideally be in protecting communities and societies at risk, but that its voting provisions are less democratic than they might be.

My first argument is that nationals of member states who exercise their rights to work and live in another member state thereby disenfranchise themselves. They sacrifice in practice their right to be electors in a democracy. The 34,454 British expatriates who nominated proxies to vote on their behalf in the 1992 election constituted a tiny proportion of the worldwide total. Even those who have voted in the UK have no right to participate by voting for the government that makes the laws they have to obey and levies the taxes they have to pay. They are second-class citizens in that while they enjoy the civil protection of the courts, and rights of welfare and education for themselves and their families, and pay full taxes, they do not have the right to vote or the duty to be conscripted. The numbers affected are not trivial: 1.2 million Spaniards, 1.2 million Italians, 0.84 million Portuguese, 0.63 million Irish and 0.4 million Britons are not allowed to vote in the elections that at present matter, the national elections in the country where they work (European Parliament, October 1994). The lack of entitlement to stand for election and to vote at the subnational and supernational levels, for municipalities, for regions, and for a European Parliament that cannot levy taxes, change any government or make laws, might seem almost to be calculated to bring democracy into disrepute.

The oddity of this provision can be illustrated by transposing it to the US context. It is as if an American who moved from Boston to Los Angeles was told that he could vote for the Mayor of Los Angeles because that is a municipal election – and for the senators and representatives sent by California to Washington, for that is a continental matter. However he could not vote for the governor or legislature of California because for those purposes he must continue to vote in Massachusetts!

My second argument concerns the implications for new settlers from beyond the European Union of restricting the right to vote to nationals and of restricting the exercise of that right within the historical territorial constituencies. This means that individuals from non-member states are not recognised as entitled to participate in electing those who make the rules under which they live and work. *A fortiori*, this inhibits their capacity to seek recognition as communities by political self-organisation. It particularly discriminates against the estimated 13 million Muslims resident in the EU, of whom probably over 10 million have no rights as nationals. From a human rights perspective, this seems as unnecessary as it is regrettable.

It may be objected that this does not matter because most member states are composed largely of nationals, with a relatively small proportion of residents coming either from other member states, or from non-member states. For example, 98 per cent of those resident in Spain are Spanish nationals. My reply is that nationals have little to fear and something to gain by reducing the marginalisation of aliens.

It may also be objected that states such as Turkey and Morocco have been keen to stop their nationals from assimilating to the cultures where they have 'temporarily' found work. Both states want to maintain their nationals' allegiance to their countries of origin, which results in massive transfers of hard currency to families in these countries. It may be further objected that nationals from other member states have a freedom not open to those who are, say, Germans by descent, in that they may live and work without having to be subject to obligations like conscription which are the counterparts to voting rights.

I admit that these are genuine difficulties. However, they are not adequate reasons for denying to residents the right in the modern, highly mobile Europe to vote for the government that actually orders their lives. The right to vote in the country where one legally resides could be treated as on a par with the right to welfare benefits and education for children. In other words, the right to vote need not entail either giving up one's nationality of origin or entitling one to stay beyond the term of legal residency.

The proposal that has inspired the writing of this chapter is therefore the following: the European Union is unlike the United States or the Europe of nation-states; it includes a variety of established communities, including those that rule themselves on the inadequate nation-state level, which together are currently forming a society capable of ruling itself on the scale required to be on the level of events. Recognition of those internal communities would best be done by breaking the link with territory and weakening the link with nationality exemplified by the criteria for European citizenship established at Maastricht. This proposal presupposes that obligations and rights at the level of European government will be uniform.

The idea is that political power in Europe should be responsive to its inhabitants, irrespective of nationality, *Staatsangehörigkeit*, or citizenship. Let us assume that in a European Union of 365 million inhabitants, members of the European Parliament would each represent 500–750,000 voters, depending on the relationship between the size of the European Parliament and the size of the EU.

Communities that could muster multiples of the requisite number of votes could organise themselves to secure sufficient votes *on any basis they chose*. Turks scattered throughout the European Union might choose to vote for a Turkish candidate, or for a Muslim slate of candidates. Christian Democrats and Socialists might well have several hundred candidates on single lists, transnationally constituted. Bavarians and Catalans, Orangemen or Frenchmen might choose to assert their territorial identities by voting for the candidates of their ethno-nation, or, more sophisticatedly, for a trans-European 'Green' or a socialist or a single-issue slate that included sufficient candidates from their nation to secure their approval. I would guess that in Europe territorial communities would feature strongly as a focus of electoral appeal. Unlike the USA, linguistic communities in

Europe, long-settled communities, and entrenched job security provisions all combine to give strong territorial identities. The system would reward sophisticated political organisational ability as well as representing the mass solidarities actually given priority by voters. Gypsies might therefore remain, unfortunately, unrepresented.

Eligibility

The novelty here would be giving the vote to all adults who could demonstrate a legal residency qualification of at least three months. This provision would exclude tourists, illegal migrants, and EU nationals who had chosen to live outside the territories of the EU. On 30 January 1995 Agence Europe reported that the Migrant Forum asked that:

> The Treaty of Maastricht should be amended to grant EU citizenship to all non-Community citizens residing legally in the union and who wish to apply without having to request naturalisation in one or another Member State. They should be given the status of European resident as a transitional measure for a renewable ten-year period.

Single constituency and transferable vote

As in Israel, the whole territory of the EU would constitute one constituency. As in the USA, balloting would be computerised to enable voters to vote for any candidate in a list. As in the Irish Republic, once a candidate had received the votes needed for election, the surplus could be transferred to others on the same list, or as nominated by the elector under the transferable vote system.

If it could be demonstrated that proportional representation on a continental scale would increase the danger of anti-democratic parties – racist, fascist or fundamentalist – holding coalition politics to ransom, this could be met by a combination of the devices familiar from national political systems. Parties might be required to commit themselves to democratic practices, to acceptance of secular legislation, to abjure racist rhetoric, or to meet a threshold comparable to the 5 per cent threshold in Germany. My own view is that these precautions are unnecessary, or if necessary they would be insufficient to contain a widespread antipathy to democratic values. In themselves, they would be inimical to opening the way for the representation of self-conscious communities seeking to participate in joint rule on a European scale.

Conclusion

The liberal project in Europe differs from that in the USA and Canada in important ways. In the North American debate, both Liberalism 1 and

Liberalism 2 assume a strong constitutional state, an army, an educational system teaching the virtues of the constitution and promoting an American or Canadian identity in more ferocious terms than the 'European dimension' taught in European schools, and a system of federal courts enforcing a bill or charter of rights. There is therefore a substantial framework capable of protecting individuals and responding to demands for recognition from minorities. Moreover, there are relatively few territorially based *Gemeinschaften* such as that of the Quebeckers.

In Europe, the states have been weakened in that since the Depression of the 1930s they have been too small on their own to act on the continental scale of modern economic production and military deployment. From the perspective of communities and cultures under threat, even before Bosnia the weakness of the liberal project was shown by the Western states' toleration of ethnic cleansing in Northern Ireland and by both Greeks and Turks in Cyprus. It was in no individual state's national interest to intervene decisively when the weak economies and weak states of post-communist Eastern Europe became the scenes of territorial aggression and ethnically motivated destruction.

In comparison with the 1930s, it is something of an achievement that the major states of Europe have kept themselves together diplomatically, have provided militarily protected aid to warring communities struggling to establish their exclusive rule in Bosnia, and hope to societies 'in transition', and that their publics cannot plead ignorance. It is possible that on the international relations model, European states as a league can protect 'minorities' through conditionality of aid, and through the procedures of a consensus behind closed doors. It is conceivable that communities and the human rights of individuals could be protected on the alternative international relations model of substituting German for US leadership.

In addition, in relation to the concept of citizenship in the European Union, I suggest that some of the shortcomings of the Maastricht provisions on voting could be avoided by treating the EU as a single constituency, and allowing all who live and work within its borders to vote. This would enable individuals to organise themselves according to the criteria that they find most fit – national, ideological, religious or regional. A stronger version of the Maastrict Treaty provisions would look to a federal structure in which the ghosts of Hitler and Stalin would be exorcised by making European government answerable to its citizens, a more demanding criterion than either US-style legitimation or identification with one's own pre-political community.

References

Agence Europe, (1990) 'Spanish Proposal on "European Citizenship"' *AE Doc. 1653*, 2 October 1990.

Anderson, M. (1994) with Monica den Boer and Gary Miller, 'Citizenship', in Duff, A. et al. (eds) *Maastricht and Beyond*, Routledge, London.

Collingwood, R. (1942 [1947]) *The New Leviathan*, Clarendon Press, Oxford.

Dahrendorf, R. (1968) *Society and Democracy in Germany*, Weidenfeld and Nicolson, London.

Gutmann, A. (ed.) (1994) *Multiculturalism and 'The Politics of Recognition'*, Princeton University Press, Princeton.

Habermas, J. (1987) *The Philosophical Discourse of Modernity*, MIT Press, Cambridge, MA.

— (1994) 'Struggles for Recognition in the Democratic Constitutional State', in A Gutmann (ed.).

Karlsruhe Court (1994) 'Brunner vs Treaty of European Union', *Common Market Law Report* 69: 2, 11 January 1994.

Koslowski, R. (1994) 'Intra-EU Migration, Citizenship and Political Union', *Journal of Common Market Studies*, 32: 3 September 1994.

Macpherson, C. B. (1964) *The Political Theory of Possessive Individualism*, Oxford University Press, Oxford.

Marshall, T. H. (1950 [1992]) *Citizenship and Social Class*, Pluto Press, London.

Offe, C. (1995) 'On the "Rationality" of Ethnic Politics in Post-Communist Societies', *RUSEL* 2, Exeter University Department of Politics, Exeter.

Taylor. C. (1994) 'Multiculturalism and the Politics of Recognition', in A. Gutmann (ed.).

Tönnies, F. (1887 [1955]) *Community and Association*, trans. P. Loomis, Routledge and Kegan Paul, London.

Walzer, M. (1992) 'Comment', in A. Gutmann (ed.) *Multiculturalism and 'The Politics of Recognition'*, Princeton University Press, Princeton.

CHAPTER 13

The Plural Guises of Multiculturalism: Conceptualising a Fragmented Paradigm

Yunas Samad

Introduction: globalisation of multiculturalism

Processes of globalisation have led to planetary flows not only of ideas and images but also of people, finance and commodities (Appadurai 1990). Along with these has come an increasingly pervasive acceptance of multiculturalism as the true paradigm for a postmodern global age. The deterritorialisation of multiculturalism from any particular place has thus resulted, as Schierup argues, in the concept becoming the hegemonic credo of the late twentieth century, invoked as a global solution to national practices of education, science, politics and social policy (Schierup 1995).

Charles Taylor identifies a normative conception of multiculturalism as a discourse that codifies the procedural as well as the substantive principles around which multicultural societies are organised (see Taylor 1994; Goldberg 1994: 7). Hence, the argument goes, identity politics are shaped by the recognition, absence or misrecognition of multicultural principles. The absence of recognition, or misrecognition, perpetrates oppressively imposed identities and thus sets the stage for identity politics to redress this imposition (Taylor 1994). Yet this definition begs an important question: why is it that multiculturalism appears in so many different and contrasting forms? It seems that the hegemonic ascendancy of the concept as a slogan or paradigm has simultaneously resulted also in its fragmentation. This chapter proposes that multiculturalism has different implications and meanings depending on its social, political and disciplinary location. Multiculturalism can be conservative or radical, and social policy based upon it can have different implications and outcomes depending on the context in which cultural difference is negotiated. This emphasis on the 'multi' part of multiculturalism is partly, at least, a consequence of the uneven geometry of globalisation. Varying in its impact geographically, it is further modified by pre-existing political and civic structures that are already in place in specific locales. The global–local nexus is the interface where global processes are reconfigured by the structural contours that are predominant in a locale. Such structures represent national characteristics as well as local variations. Thus, this chapter argues that what has come to be invoked as a globalised multicultural paradigm is, in reality, re-interpreted in each locale, and that this process varies from locale to locale, even within the same nation-state, let alone in Europe, an emergent confederation of culturally distinct nation-states.

Pluralism

The structural typology that profoundly influences and modifies multi-culturalism is the existing forms of culturally plural practice already prevalent in particular contexts. Political, social and cultural pluralism are precursors of multiculturalism, and may all be regarded as variations of pluralism. But what is significant, for our purpose, is that the furrows of political, social and cultural pluralism have had an influence on the shape of particular multiculturalisms. These different forms of pluralism were an important factor that contextualised the newly heralded multiculturalism, which is thus the unique product of local pluralistic variations.

I propose, therefore, that the type of political pluralism already prevalent in a locale acts to bound and delimit the space for politico-cultural agency. To illustrate this I want to consider here two models of political pluralism: the Anglo-American tradition and the continental European.

Common to all forms of political pluralism is their emergence in opposition to unitary conceptions of authority prevalent in the *ancien régime*. Such pluralism created a dispersal of power among all associations and interests in civil society, rather than their being concentrated in the state. This was seen as conducive to democratic norms, allowing for mutual adjustments and thus avoiding group conflicts. There were, however, differences between the different traditions. Pluralism's 'groupist' character in North American politics was seen as a negative but necessary feature of democratic politics. The contending groups balanced each other out and the ensuing equilibrium thus allowed the system to harmonise the conflictual tendencies associated with interest-group politics. The less organised British system, by contrast, perceived pluralism to be a beneficial feature of a healthy democracy. It was thought to act as an important counterbalance to the centralisation of power by the state. Both forms of pluralism assumed that the formation of associations in civil society would influence public policy, but they were mainly concerned with *political* pluralism (Goulbourne 1991: 216–17).

Another form of pluralism was evident in the consociational demo-cracies of Switzerland, Belgium and the Netherlands, where incorporation of various groupings in the political realm was conditioned by equivalence (Lijphart 1968). 'Pillarisation' in the case of Holland meant that Catholics, Protestants and humanists built separate organisational networks in the public domain. This form of compartmentalised society was governed by the elites of each pillar, who formed coalition governments. 'Pillarisation' was a functional feature of Dutch society in the 1950s and early 1960s, and persisted in the institutional sphere despite increasing secularisation and individualisation of the society. This form of political pluralism was closely associated with social and cultural pluralism.

The notion of social and cultural pluralism was first formulated by F. S. Furnival and later elaborated by several other scholars. Furnival used the concept of pluralism with reference to colonial Indonesia which was ethnically segmented. Intercourse between tightly bound and separate communities only occurred, he argued, in the marketplace. Groups of people mixed for purposes of economic exchange in the marketplace without interacting socially and culturally. Thus, the plural society was segmented by differences of language, kinship, religion, or culture (Furnival 1956: 304–5). M. G. Smith's contribution to the concept of plural society was to insist that such societies were held together by political power; that is, by the state. Influenced by Malinowski's notion of society as a set of interrelated institutions, Smith argued that British West Indian society was composed of discrete groups of people, each with an almost complete set of institutions, bound to each other by a single political system, based on domination by a ruling group (Smith 1974: 75–91).

The controversy provoked by Smith's theory of social and cultural pluralism forced him, in the late 1960s, to integrate Weberian ideas regarding the corporate nature of society into his approach. This led him to identify three variants of pluralism: cultural, structural and social. Structural pluralism, he proposed, is marked by differential political incorporation of cultural sections, and presupposes cultural and social pluralism 'by prescribing sectional access to the common public domain, and by establishing differing contexts and conditions of sectional co-existence, segregation and subordination' (Kuper and Smith 1971: 440). Such a system can be instituted in two ways. In the first, subordinate groups are formally excluded from the public domain, which remains a formal monopoly of the ruling group; this is exemplified by what was the apartheid system in South Africa. The second way involves the institution of substantial and sufficient inequalities of sectional participation in, and access to, this sector of the societal 'organisation', exemplified by African-Americans in the USA. Smith's second type of schema, social pluralism, 'is the condition [in] which such institutional differentiations coincide with the corporate division of a given society into a series of sharply demarcated and virtually closed social sections or segments' (Kuper and Smith 1971: 440). This form of pluralism was evident in the consociational democracies of Switzerland, Belgium and the Netherlands, where incorporation of a number of groupings in various spheres, including the political realm, was conditioned by equivalence. 'Cultural pluralism consists in variable institutional diversity without corresponding collective segregation' (Kuper and

Smith 1971: 444). In the United States and Britain, by contrast, the incorporation of social and cultural differences was restricted to the private domain. Such differences were considered to have personal importance but were excluded from the public domain where incorporation was based on universal principles, and hence these differences did not, in theory, have structural implications. The reality was, of course, very different, since different groups had *de facto* greater access to the state, the economy and the public sphere.

Hybrid multiculturalisms

As John Rex has pointed out, there were a number of difficulties with social and cultural pluralism which mean that advocates of multiculturalism are unlikely to construct the type of pluralist society that Smith and others described. Multiculturalism only avoids the pitfalls associated with social and cultural pluralism when linked with some notion of equal opportunities. For the fundamental issue at stake is not merely that of cultural *recognition* (the point stressed by Taylor), but the political terms that serve to improve or restrict access to all forms of life chances (Rex 1987: 219–20).

In reality, however, I argue, multiculturalism does not displace various forms of pluralism but *encapsulates* them in a hybrid amalgam. This accounts for the wide variations in multiculturalism from one locale to another. The form of political, social and cultural pluralism that exists in a society modifies multiculturalism, meaning that the policy, despite its apparently singular banner, does not have the same consequences in different societies or even part-societies. The German variation of multiculturalism was premised on the fact that ethnic minorities had restricted political rights. Hence the German example (as well as that of Austria and Switzerland), was closer to a structural rather than a social or cultural pluralism. Political voting rights in national elections, and hence also the electoral power inherent in cultural-cum-ethnic mobilisation, are not, however, on their own a panacea for social disadvantage. This is indicated by the fact that differences between the British and US conceptions of pluralism have produced results that in certain important areas are dissimilar. The civil rights movement and black militancy in the USA, which were essentially located in the political sphere, have, through positive action and multi-culturalism, arguably transformed structural differentiation into social and cultural representative pluralism at state and federal levels. This cannot be said to be happening in Britain. The demand for Black Sections within the Labour Party and the call to create an Islamic Party were essentially marginal to the popular concerns of ethnic minorities, the majority of whom participate in mainstream politics, which continues to be dominated by the majority.

Furthermore, multicultural debates in the USA were focused upon tertiary education, especially over course content (the argument over 'the canon'), and over the need for positive action in university minority appointments. In Britain, there was rather little positive discrimination (see Chapter 11 of this volume), the stress being mainly on equal opportunities, while the discourse of multiculturalism primarily surrounded school curricula, both primary and secondary, and was symbolised by relatively small local authority grants for cultural and welfare voluntary activities. The most that could be made out of this situation was to present minorities in a sensitive manner. The scope for originality in educational matters was greatly restricted by the introduction of the Education Reform Act.

In the case of consociational forms of democracy as in the Netherlands and Belgium there are other differences. 'Pillarisation' has incorporated religious minorities and retarded xenophobic and defensive developments among them. The Islam versus secularism debates, graphically represented by the vitriolic controversy around *The Satanic Verses* in Britain and the headscarves affair in France, are nonissues in the Netherlands, as Muslims there are already covered by blasphemy laws, allowed to have state-funded Muslim schools, and have access to the media in the form of an Islamic television channel. Clearly, then, the issues are not just about secularism versus religion, but about forms of political activity that are deemed by a national society to be legitimate in the light of existing social structures.

Irrespective of the variations in multiculturalism, as a political ideology it has stirred up a fierce debate, both among radicals and conservatives, in the academic and in the political and public spheres. Some feel multiculturalism has led to an ethnic tower of Babel. Franz-Olaf Radtke argues forcefully that in the case of Germany, minorities are excluded from the public sphere and encouraged to form apolitical communal groups. Multiculturalism, accompanied with a clientalism associated with the welfare state, has resulted, he claims, in a self-ethnicisation of minorities and 'inevitably ends up in folklorism' (Radtke 1994: 36–7; see also Chapters 5 and 9 of this volume). Multiculturalism translates the concept of 'plurality of interests' into a concept of 'plurality of descent', and this becomes, he proposes, fertile ground for cultural or religious 'fundamentalisms'.

The tendency towards reification of ethnic identity is an aspect of multiculturalist policies that also reverberates throughout the North American controversy about its virtues and faults. The debate there over canonical cultural diversity has become so highly contentious and polarised that opponents have accused protagonists of multiculturalism in education of falsifying history and of disuniting the USA. Arthur Schlesinger takes up this point, arguing passionately and sharply that multiculturalism drives wedges between 'races', leading to self-ghettoisation and to fears that a common American identity will be fragmented (Schlesinger 1992). Yet, in defending America's European legacy, he feels compelled to denigrate the cultural legacy of black people, thus casting in doubt his underlying motives as an impartial universalist.

Similar fears of disintegration were voiced on this side of the Atlantic by Ray Honeyford and Norman Tebbit, who revived the assimilationist project (Honeyford 1988: 301). Ronald Takaki exposes the political agenda that underpins the conservative opposition to multiculturalism. The debate, he proposes, is over power and privilege. The battlefield is society's collective memory of what should be remembered or not and, by implication, what makes and constitutes the national identity. Education as a defence of monolingual, monocultural and European views lies at the core of this ideological agenda. The war against multiculturalism by the likes of Schlesinger and Honeyford has threatened to impose an orthodoxy that divides 'them' from 'us' – where 'we' are located at the centre and 'they' are marginalised (Takaki 1993: 117–20). In reality, it also reflects an identity crisis among indigenous white Anglo-Americans, who have become increasingly nervous about the changing racial and cultural composition of their nations.

It needs to be recognised, however, that the so-called multiculturalist policies that are so reviled by the conservatives are not the product of a misplaced magnanimity on the part of the Establishment. In Britain and the USA, social policies specifically designed to deal with racial discrimination were implemented as a result of social upheaval and political protest. Political mobilisation, particularly in the USA, along with the impact of the Watts and Chicago riots in the 1960s, and, in Britain, the riots of the 1980s in Brixton, Toxteth and Handsworth, *forced* the authorities to act.

Despite the structural differences between the two sides of the Atlantic, multiculturalism does appear to generate a general problem: the tendency to reify identity. Echoing others, Steven Vertovec argues that this is primarily a consequence of the commonsense prevalence of notions of 'culture' as a collection of fixed, discrete, unchanging collective traits transmitted from generation to generation. Values, behaviour and social relations are seen to be imbued with essential, intrinsic qualities (Vertovec 1996: 51; see also Caglar's discussion in Chapter 9). Both heterophiliac and heterophobic rhetorics are premised on irreducible and impermeable differences between 'cultures' (al-Azmeh 1993: 4). These separate uni-cultures are imbued with further significance as they are referred to as 'communities', possessing essential and overdetermined values. Al-Azmeh goes on to argue that cultural pluralism with universal political and civil incorporation, which most discourses on multiculturalism envisage, has channelled developments in the direction of *de facto* structural pluralism. This is primarily a consequence of the underlying 'culturalism' of the multicultural discourses (Vertovec 1996: 51, 56–7).

Multiculturalism in the locale: Bradford

The issues that have been raised need to be examined empirically in particular locales and the first question that needs to be addressed is why multiculturalism seems to lead to the reification of identity. As Husband suggests,

> The interface between the pursuit of the narrow self-interest of the politics of difference and the state's strategies in managing diversity has promoted divisiveness within territorially defined urban communities and competition between the marginalised communities of interest defined through their exclusive claims as communities of identity. (Husband 1996: 41)

For example, a common argument is that local authorities' management of ethnic minorities for political purposes reinforces exclusive identities. However, by the same token, the local state's strategies are themselves influenced by discourses of 'race', ethnicity and multiculturalism. Local politicians are concerned not to offend white voters, on the one hand, by introducing policies that are perceived to be advantageous to ethnic minorities. Simultaneously, they are under pressure from ethnic minorities to redress disadvantage and discrimination. Consequently, municipal authorities only introduce such policies when under pressure. A kneejerk response has been to institutionalise ethnic minority leadership, nominated as 'representatives' of the 'community' (see Werbner 1991: 21).

Any study of policy strategies concerning the ethnic minorities in Bradford has to take account of the fact that 72 per cent of the ethnic minorities are Pakistani, and that over 80 per cent of Pakistanis are from Mirpur. Common origin gives an element of social cohesion that translates into a degree of political solidarity which is rare. The Pakistanis are able to exert, or at least try to exert in conjunction with other ethnic minorities, a significant input into the political debate in the local arena. By 1990, there were thirteen ethnic-minority councillors out of sixty-seven on the city council (Rex and Samad 1996).

Our study of Bradford shows that Bradford City Council's policy vis-à-vis ethnic minorities has been reactive rather than proactive, subject to influence from groups hostile to ethnic minorities, and lacking any clear implementation procedure. In the late 1970s, Bradford was witnessing a policy shift away from assimilationist strategies towards a bipartisan position on integration. The 1960s approach of bussing school children from inner-city schools, and spreading them evenly within the city's other schools, gave way under pressure from ethnic minorities. The local authority experimented in the late 1970s with mother-tongue teaching in the schools and this, along with other activities, brought it acclaim as a leader in multiculturalism.

It was the inner-city riots of 1981 that convulsed Brixton, Toxteth and

Handsworth, however, that forced the local authority in Bradford to engage seriously with the issues of multiculturalism, equal opportunities and anti-racism. Tensions within the city were rising, and the case of the Bradford Twelve exemplified the polarisation taking place. Members of the United Black League and the Asian Youth Movement were arrested after being found in possession of petrol bombs. At their trial (in which they were acquitted) they argued that they had prepared the petrol bombs as a means of self-defence, in anticipation of racial attack by far-right extremists.

In this context, Bradford City Council produced its blueprint for harmonious race relations. The document, *Turning Point*, elaborated a twelve-point equal opportunity, multicultural and anti-racist strategy (see also Chapter 7). To oversee these policy initiatives the All-Party Race Relations Group, the Race Relations Subject Committee and the Multi-cultural Education Support Group were established. They represented communication nodes where political parties and representatives of ethnic minorities could meet and influence policy at a developmental stage. These were consultative bodies set up with the aim of transforming ideas into policies, but implementation was still very much dependent on political will. No independent procedure was established to ensure that council practices conformed to policies.

On an *ad hoc* basis, various initiatives were taken. The most significant was the institutionalisation of the Bradford Council of Mosques (BCM). It included twenty-two organisations, not all mosques. Several programmes funded by the Manpower Services Commission were run from the BCM's headquarters. Mohammed Ajeeb, former chair of the Community Relations Council, was appointed to run these projects which included two centres for the elderly, advice workers (both male and female) working from the mosques, and religious services for women in hospitals and clinics (Rex and Samad 1996). The religious leaders were encouraged to unite on a single platform institutionalised by Bradford City Council. This appeared to be a deliberate ploy to reinforce first-generational control over the younger generation, and to prevent the breakdown of law and order, as was happening in other cities in the early 1980s. Of course, the local council wanted a tame BCM and could not possibly have anticipated that they had set in motion forces that would become quite independent of their control, as exemplified by the BCM's role in the Rushdie agitation.

As the city council began to implement various multicultural, equal opportunities and anti-racist procedures, these attempts provoked a white backlash, polarising race relations and weakening the city council's commit-ment. The first of these issues was the controversy over providing halal meat to schools. The BCM, led by Sher Azam, had rallied the Muslim population into organising a series of demonstrations and school boycotts on this issue. The granting of this concession provoked a counter-agitation, however, led by animal rights groups infiltrated by National Front activists. This conflict was followed by a controversy over Race Awareness Training (RAT) programmes run by members of two organisations, Checkpoint and Al-Falah. Allegations were made in the press that brainwashing exercises were held in the Lake District at the city council's expense. These programmes were also unpopular among council employees and teaching staff at schools. Other, less controversial, initiatives, involving the establishment of supplementary schools, relaxation of uniform regulations for girls, and toleration of extended leave to the Indian subcontinent, were introduced, and mother-tongue teaching was extended.

The entire multicultural and anti-racist edifice was attacked by Ray Honeyford in a series of articles in the *Salisbury Review*, a New Right journal, and the *Times Higher Education Supplement*. His defence of British culture and family values from dilution by an anti-racist, multicultural discourse turned him into an icon of the New Right and into the *bête noire* of the anti-racist movement. His critiques were littered with negative racial stereotypes of Afro-Caribbeans and Asians, and his fiercest barbs were reserved for the Mirpuris, the overwhelming majority of whom locally were parents of pupils in his school. The anti-Honeyford campaign was led by the Drummonds Parents Action Committee. It included the Asian Youth Movement, Bradford Council of Mosques (BCM), the Asian Workers Support Group, the Azad Kashmir Muslim Association, and various left-wing groups that tried to intervene. The campaign engaged in a long-drawn-out struggle for the dismissal of Honeyford, which was partially successful in that he was encouraged (by a substantial golden handshake) to take early retirement.

The BCM was again in the media spotlight when it played a prominent role in the anti-Rushdie agitation. Unlike over the Honeyford affair, it found itself isolated this time, and its demands were rejected by secular organisations. However, importantly for the BCM, it was solidly backed by the Mirpuri community in Bradford. The lingering feeling of injury resulting from the Honeyford affair was intensified by the perceived insults perpetrated on Muslims by Rushdie. The sense of humiliation was compounded by the escalation in racial violence in the city as homes, businesses and individuals were subjected to daily threats and insults. The city council's response to the BCM's demonstrations was quietly to disassociate itself from it and to cut its funding.

The city council's strategy of co-opting the religious leadership at the expense of secular organisations was based on an understanding that it was religious institutions that were best placed to control the younger generation and to stop them from rioting on the streets. This rather simplistic understanding of 'the community' was based on a political rationale. Out of all the possible identifications that could be recognised and legitimated, such as 'black', 'Asian', 'Pakistani' and 'Mirpuri', the council sages selected Islam, and then built it up so that it could have more influence over the community. Once it became apparent that all this policy had achieved was mobilisation on the basis of religious identity, the municipal authorities quickly distanced themselves from the BCM (see also Philip Lewis's discussion in Chapter 7).

Birmingham: trans-ethnic mobilisation

The type of political response that Birmingham's ethnic minorities were able to produce was quite different from that which occurred in Bradford. Patently, an important factor influencing this divergence was the variegated character of Birmingham's minorities. Figures show that 32 per cent are from Pakistan (half from Mirpur), 28 per cent are African and Caribbean, and 40 per cent consist of other Asians, including Bangladeshis, Indians (Sikhs and Hindus), East Africans, Yemenis, Vietnamese and Chinese. Moreover, the term 'Caribbean' does not indicate a homogeneous group but instead is a collective label for people originating from various islands, often separated from one another by thousands of miles. With this kind of diversity, ethnic mobilisation and transethnic mobilisation have always been difficult exercises in Birmingham. The fact that in 1985 Birmingham was convulsed by riots (a spontaneous social upheaval and hence the antithesis of ethnic mobilisation) only reinforces this point.

Birmingham was a late starter in multiculturalism. This seems to have been a result of the early mobilisation of whites on race issues. Enoch Powell's 'rivers of blood' speech and the defeat of a Labour minister, Patrick Gordon Walker, in Smethwick were warnings to politicians of all hues of the electoral significance of white hostility to ethnic minorities. Birmingham was only prodded into implementing multicultural policies by the riots of the early 1980s, and by the Scarman Report which followed the riots in Brixton in 1981. Political activity in Birmingham was initially directed towards Afro-Caribbeans. This was due, primarily, to the fact that they had settled in the city earlier than other minorities. Two organisations, Harambee and the Afro-Caribbean Self-Help Organisation, were active in the late 1960s. Influenced by the emergence of black consciousness in the USA, they attempted to educate black youth in the city and established political contacts with Africa, for example with the Pan-African Congress. Birmingham escaped the riots of 1981 as a consequence of moderate community policing, but a subsequent change in police tactics led to a deterioration in relations, so that a minor traffic incident detonated a very vigorous response from minorities in 1985. It resulted in the burning and looting of shops in Handsworth, the deaths of two Asians (for which two white men were convicted), and millions of pounds' worth of damage.

The social upheavals were caused by the combination of social discontent, unemployment and oppressive policing. The main element that was behind what was called, in popular parlance, the 'uprising' were the youth, both black and white. The media and the government, however, reduced the riots to a black problem, and helped reinforce the demonisation of black immigrants as 'black devils'. In its usual, Janus-faced manner, the government vehemently denied that socioeconomic factors might be behind the social upheavals, and yet poured millions into the riot-torn areas.

A short-lived bipartisan approach did emerge in the council in reaction to the developments on the ground, but this intra-party consensus broke down when the Race Relations Unit was formed in 1984 by the Labour council. In the post-Scarman atmosphere, the funding of the black voluntary sector increased significantly. Coinciding with a number of black campaigns on specific issues, the funding exercise was moved by mixed motives. Organisations received grants because they were led by highly prominent individuals as a way of buying off troublemakers or of placing nominees in important positions. The black voluntary sector was dominated by Afro-Caribbeans and two thirds of the grants were allocated to them. The main focus of Asian activity in this period was on constructing temples, mosques and *gurdwaras*, which were ineligible for council funding. Some of the prominent ethnic organisations were Handsworth Employment Services (it had 360 trainees and job placements of which 5 per cent were Asians), ACAFESS (it had 300 trainees and job placements and a higher percentage of Asians), and Harambee which, among its various social and political functions, had established a black housing association for the mentally disabled (Rex and Samad 1996).

The consequence of institutionalising black identity seems to have been the reinforcement of a 'black' essentialism. Such essentialist notions were vividly illustrated by the debate over transracial adoption, in which black social workers argued that trans-racial adoption led to identity confusion and was a new form of slave trade. Black children needed a 'positive black identity' which could only be provided by a black family; it was better that a child remain in care, raised by black social workers, if a suitable black adoptive family could not be found (Gilroy 1987: 65).

There was the inevitable backlash from the white electorate, and under this threat the multicultural, equal opportunity and anti-racist initiatives were given a lower profile. The Race Relations Unit was merged with the Women's Unit and located in the Personnel Department. With this more anodyne profile, the Race Relations Unit continued to formulate and monitor multiculturalist policy implementation.

The council at first ignored ethnic minorities, in deference to the white electorate. However, when this was no longer possible it institutionalised individuals and organisations, primarily Afro-Caribbeans, as a means to buy off the opposition. The consequence was, primarily, the reification of a 'black' identity. This stress was in line with the labour stress on class oppression. It ran the danger, however, of encouraging the glorification of Afro-centricity, an ideological tendency that has been criticised by Gilroy as a volkish preoccupation with descent: 'Its political counterpart is a variety of black cultural nationalism, which relies on mystical and essentialist ideas of a transcendental blackness' (Gilroy 1987: 65).

Return to social policy

The criticisms of multicultural policy have led to suggestions of alternative routes towards integration. Some argue for the wholesale jettisoning of multiculturalism in its entirety (see Caglar, in Chapter 9). Others emphasise agency, while some consider new forms of incorporation. Al-Azmeh insists that 'structural and spatial segregation and social involution and ghetto formation' lie at the basis of a culturalism that was now becoming the prevalent mode of discourse for ethnic minorities. He, along with others, argues vigorously for a return to a class-based social policy, which is unequivocally anti-culturalist and anti-essentialist (al-Azmeh 1993: 2).

This recommendation, although culturally motivated by an anti-essentialist stress on openness, turns out to be naïve in practice. Bradford offers an interesting example of the consequences of a *de facto* return to a culture- and colour-blind social policy by the city authorities. Post-Honeyford, the commitment of political parties to the programme of multiculturalism, equal opportunities and anti-racism was significantly weakened. It was primarily seen as an electoral liability, and Peter Gilmour lost his seat because of his personal association with its various initiatives. Compounding the situation was the breakdown of the bipartisan consensus. In 1986, a newly elected Labour council disbanded the Race Awareness Training programme, absorbing it into the council's training programme, in order to take the sting out of the criticism of its earlier multicultural and anti-racist policies. Although this was followed by a report by the Race Relations Advisory Group which suggested further innovations, this only led to a breakdown in the all-party consensus on race.

When the Tories captured power in 1988, they scrapped the Race Relations Subcommittee; more important, in line with Tory policies they introduced cuts in the budget totalling £5 million and a contracting-out of council functions (*Yorkshire Post* 2 January 1989; *Telegraph and Argus* 3 July 1989).

Decentralisation had a profound impact on an organisation that never had a strong centre to begin with. The directors of the service departments were always very independent, and this development only reinforced their autonomy (Carr 1993: 40). When Labour was returned to power, it was so sensitive to the possibilities of a white backlash, particularly after the Rushdie affair, that it did not return to the *status quo ante*. The only concern it demonstrated for its policies on multiculturalism, equal opportunities and anti-racism was to establish a general committee dealing with disadvantaged groups, that included women and disabled as well as ethnic minorities.

Another trend which had been developing in the background surfaced to embarrass Labour deeply, exposing the lack of policy implementation procedures in the areas of multiculturalism, anti-racism and equal opportunities. The council had lost five cases in six years in industrial tribunals, on the grounds of racial discrimination. In the Ellington case, aggravated damages were awarded and another four cases were settled out of court. These cases were only the tip of an iceberg, and the Race Equality Council prompted the Commission for Racial Equality to initiate legal action under Section 62 of the Race Relations Act; eventually there was an out-of-court settlement. Bradford City Council was the first ever organisation to be charged with being a persistent discriminator, and it has lost more cases on racial grounds than any other employer in the UK (Carr 1993: 10–13)! Further embarrassment was to arise when the council's Education Department was accused of discrimination for failing to include Manningham in the catchment area of any school. It survived the High Court action but the case left its image tarnished.

Prompted by the Commission for Racial Equality's legal action and the negative publicity, the city council ordered an inquiry by an independent consultant. As a consequence of John Carr's report, it appointed an outside adviser, Tim Whitfield, to assist in the changes that were needed to ensure that council policies were implemented. One of the major findings of the inquiry was that decentralisation had led to a situation where the Chief Executive Office had no executive authority, only an advisory role, over the various directorates. What is evident is that with a weak centre, multiculturalism, equal opportunities and anti-racism may slip between departments. Aggravating the situation in Bradford were the policy changes emanating from Whitehall, mainly in education and social services. These implicitly, and, in the case of education, explicitly, demoted the significance of multiculturalism, anti-racism and equal opportunities. It must be added that some senior personnel in the directorates still do not attach significance to the results of the legal actions, arguing that 'old scores were being settled over Honeyford', that the 'cases were a by-product of liberalisation', or falling back on 'I don't think it's as bad as it seems' (Carr 1993: 22, 40). For the Chief Executive Office, however, the message was very clear: equal opportunity was cost-effective and less embarrassing than involvement in expensive litigation.

Bradford City Council's policy on multiculturalism, equal opportunities and anti-racism went through several phases. First, there was an initially bipartisan approach to these issues which was essentially reactive to social upheavals taking place nationally. In this new atmosphere of integration and toleration of difference, the council made minor concessions under pressure from Muslims, only to be faced with a white backlash. In this downward spiral of deteriorating race relations, the political resolve that had brought multiculturalism, equal opportunities and anti-racism on to the council's agenda was severely weakened. Once the commitment was undermined and compounded by the breakdown of bipartisan under-standing on this issue, then both political parties placed it low on their list of priorities. The combination of Tory cuts to Bradford's budget with policy changes emanating from the centre exposed the weakness in the council's commitment to multiculturalism and equal opportunities. The spate of legal action, some of it successful, exposed the fact that policy implementation procedures were rudimentary at best, forcing the council to re-evaluate policies and procedures in the light of the changes emanating from central government and demonstrating that a *de facto* return to a colour- and culture-blind social policy was damaging to the interest of ethnic minorities in Britain.

Alternative forms of incorporation

Against the equation of multiculturalism with cultural essentialism, others argue that the way forward is through new forms of incorporation (see Philip Lewis in Chapter 7). The relationship between 'public space' and multiculturalism has usually been posed in terms of 'the two domain thesis' elaborated by John Rex, which divides British society into the communal, private, familial domain and the common public domain of shared political culture. However, the controversy over polygamy, female genital mutilation and Islamic opposition over *The Satanic Verses* has highlighted the interpenetration and potential conflicts between the two domains. It pointed to the need to increase the emphasis on a broader, shared public culture. Bhikhu Parekh sees the granting of funds and nomination of communal ethnic 'leaders' as a disguised way of regulating these groups' agendas in the public domain. Against this imputed policy, he argues that if minorities were to become an integral part of British society 'they would be entitled to have a say in shaping its shared public culture'. This is something they are unlikely to develop if they feel that the public culture is an alien imposition. Multiculturalism is, Parekh argues, not simply about the acknowledgement of a plurality of cultures, but also about creating space for communities to grow at their own pace. It means a dialogue that enriches the common culture and creates new hybridities. Parekh suggests that new forms of incorporation that do not simply amount to communal co-opting would transform the public sphere (Parekh 1990: 70). Steven Vertovec argues that such new modes, facilitating the incorporation of multiple and cross-cutting forms of group engagement, are emerging. He cites developments among Muslims in Leicester as an example: the Leicester Federation of Muslim Organisations is an entirely grassroots development that has represented Muslim interests in the city without leading to isolation

(Vertovec 1996: 56–7; see also Diop, in Chapter 6 of this volume, on France). However, the resources, both capital and human, available to Leicester's Gujarati Muslims, the majority of whom originate from East Africa, are not available to other Muslims from a less privileged background, and make this strategy a difficult road to follow, particularly in the more depressed areas of Britain such as Bradford or Birmingham.

In the case of Birmingham, however, there is some evidence suggesting that dialogues between ethnic groups are making headway. The first attempt at incorporation, mainly at the urging of Councillor James Hunte, was of the Birmingham Community Advisory Liaison Committee. It failed as a result of political rivalries, which led to a boycott by nominees of James Hunte. With only partial participation from Afro-Caribbean organisations, it was doomed to failure. The committee limped along for a couple of years before being replaced by the Standing Consultative Forum. With the exception of secular Afro-Caribbean umbrella organisations, the representatives of the other ethnic minorities became the basic units of the Standing Consultative Forum.

The Standing Consultative Forum is an umbrella organisation consisting of federations and not of individual organisations or individuals. What differentiates this form of incorporation from the earlier method of nominating ethnic 'representatives' is that a broad range of ethnic minority groups and associations have a substantial input into how and who will represent them, and what will be put on the agenda. The Afro-Caribbean community, however, refused to be represented by a single umbrella organisation. A clear cleavage emerged in this community between secular and religious groups, and consequently two umbrella organisations were formed. In the case of Muslims, it was the Bangladeshis who rejected the option of forming a single federation and demanded a separate representative body, while among the Pakistanis there was a vigorous and vitriolic debate on whether they should call themselves Pakistanis or Kashmiris. Today, the joint forum consists of the Pakistan Forum, Bangladeshi Islamic Project, Sikh Gurdwara Council, Hindu Temple Council, Afro-Caribbean Peoples Movement, Council of Black-led Churches, Vietnamese and Chinese Forum, and the Irish Forum, while two new bodies, one for Yemenis and the other for black women, are on the drawing board. These umbrella organisations between them represent 500 organisations, which include 88 supplementary schools, 60 mosques, 116 Churches, 13 *gurdwaras* and eight temples. They have been promised, and some have received, £5,000 start-up grants, and two officers to help administer individual forums. The development worker was funded directly by the council and the education worker was funded by the state under Section 11. Besides these facilities, the elected representatives of the individual forums and the Standing Consultative Forum have direct access to the directors of the various council departments, to the Chief Executive Officer, the Chief

Constable and other important functionaries who have responsibilities that influence, affect, or concern ethnic minorities (Rex and Samad 1992; Annual General Meeting of the Standing Consultative Forum, Summary Report: 6–7, 12; ibid. Appendix I).

The Race Relations Unit, with its budget of £1,000,000, has ensured that policy initiatives dealing with equal opportunities (the council has met its target of employing 20 per cent ethnic minorities in its work force), multiculturalism and anti-racism have been implemented. The Race Relations Unit has thrown out a web which has developed along with decentralisation. As council service operations are devolved to the local level, the Race Relations Unit ensures that ethnic minority needs are not neglected. Birmingham's race initiatives, however, are based on weak electoral foundations. The Tories have made clear that on coming to power (a clear possibility) they will disband the Race Relations Unit and relocate the Standing Consultative Forum and subsidiary forums in the Race Equality Council (Interview 29 September 1993).

This development is still unfolding and it is too early to conclude how effective the means of empowerment it hopes to provide will be in practice. All the officers have not yet been appointed, and even where they have, they require a period of research before community development plans can be drawn up. The important thing is that the 'communities' are being allowed to decide what their priorities are. As for the education officers, the ones in place are channelling their energies into informing parents of the changes to education introduced by the government, and how they could get more involved, for example by becoming parent-governors. The council's magnanimity should not overshadow the fact that political considerations have informed the initiative. Elected officials implicitly expect a payback in the form of the binding of the electoral loyalties of the ethnic minorities to Labour's mast. This could be crucial as in some wards the party's majority has been slim. As for the ethnic minorities themselves, they are perfectly aware of these electoral considerations and attempt to turn them to their advantage by threatening to de-select any candidate or even abstain from voting in marginal seats if promises are not fulfilled. Despite such caveats, ethnic minorities are being given the choice of how to incorporate and develop their own agendas. This appears to be a possible example of how multiculturalism can be fine-tuned according to the specific conditions in a particular locale.

Transethnic agency

Schierup and Gilroy both argue, but with different emphases, that new forms of *trans*ethnic agency are the way forward. Gilroy sees the future entirely in terms of a syncretic and hybrid youth culture. This leads him to argue that there is a need to conceptualise new forms of agency emerging among ethnic minorities. 'These are mediated by cultural forms that amalgamate past and present experiences into complex processes of identity work and social strategies' (Gilroy 1987). The formation of anti-racist social movements of urban youth, Gilroy argues, extends the boundaries of politics into a 'powerful cultural formation and an alternative public sphere with the potential of offering alternatives to the urban powerlessness and misery of hard drugs' (cited in Schierup 1994: 43–5). Schierup feels that Gilroy offers an exciting and novel alternative but that 'the strategic horizon of his political discourse appears … . limited to that of … "rebellious mini-politics", constantly in the danger of being mar-ginalised and sectarianised'. What is missing, he proposes, is greater attention to the role of the state. He feels that 'new ethnically-mixed youth cultures' lack the public space to become significant so long as ethnicity is regulated by the welfare state. In this context, ethnicity is standardised, selected and classified, and transethnic identities are thus treated as aberrations and not as authentic expressions of the popular will. Only increasing decentralisation and decomposition of the political and administrative system could allow for the emergence of new hybrid and syncretic formations along the lines argued by Gilroy (Schierup 1994: 43–5; see also Caglar in Chapter 9).

If we look at the evidence from Birmingham and Bradford we find certain paradoxes. Hybrid identities are open-ended in the sense that they can be either progressive or conservative. There has been the development of fusions of Caribbean and South Asian music in Birmingham and elsewhere, represented by singers such as Apache Indian, Bally Sagoo and Johnny Z and an emergence of Bhangra as a form of pan-Asian music, attracting youth from various parts of the subcontinent. This is not, however, the only influence found among the youth. In Bradford, where ethnic spatial segregation makes transethnic formations difficult, hybridity has resulted in a stress on an Islamic identity among Asian youth who have been either predominantly or entirely educated in Britain. This exclusionist Islamic identification is as alien and distant from the rural cultural practices of the older generations of Mirpuris as are the youthful identifications produced by South Asian popular culture.

In Bradford, these youth identities became a major force in the anti-Rushdie agitation and in the opposition to the Gulf War (Samad 1992). The Bradford Council of Mosques was a bastion of powerful male elders, and yet during the agitation against *The Satanic Verses* Muslim youths swelled the meetings, demanding that a tough stance be taken even when the leaders were prepared to compromise. The pressure from these youths was reinforced by attempts made by small numbers of young men to rampage through the city centre. The message was clear: failure to grasp the nettle would lose the religious leadership its influence over the youths to more radical Islamic organisations attempting to make inroads among them. The same division resurfaced during the Gulf War, despite the fact that the BCM had by then lost its institutional recognition. Its leadership was again subjected to vigorous popular pressure from the younger generation. This was epitomised by a crucial meeting which took a resolution from the floor, probably proposed by Palestinian students, that the BCM should declare *jihad* against the Western Alliance. This suicidal resolution (given the enormous support for the war in Britain and the vulnerable position of Muslim minorities) was quashed only after vigorous intervention by Councillor Mohammed Ajeeb. He reminded the proposers that they would eventually return home, but local Muslims would bear the brunt of any hostile reaction from the white community. It was a close vote, and the issue only became critical because of the support it had received from more militant youths.

The matter is not so simple, however. When riots broke out in Bradford in the summer of 1995, there was evidence of collaboration along trans-ethnic lines and the emergence of a 'black' identity. The frustration and militancy of the youths, which had so far been headed off by the first generation of leaders, finally boiled over. They simply bypassed the leadership to become involved in direct action against those they perceived to be oppressing and discriminating against them: the police and mainstream society. After initial indiscriminate acts of looting, gangs of youths targeted specifically white establishments. Their aborted attempt to loot the city centre left a trail of destruction on a route in which only an Afro-Caribbean pub was left deliberately untouched.

What is thus emerging in Britain is a fractured and disarticulated politics of marginality which is relatively autonomous of municipal strategies. The intensity of sectarian hybrid identities is reinforced by the persistent perception among Muslims that they are being deliberately discriminated against and excluded from a variety of political arenas and centres of power. The lack of Muslim parliamentary representation at the national level, in the civil service and in the judiciary is perceived as denying Muslims a voice through which to modify and act upon the public sphere and be accommodated by it (Samad forthcoming). Attempts to redress this situation through public action have on the whole been unsophisticated and have not had the desired result. The disaffiliation of Muslim members of local Labour Party constituencies in Manchester and Birmingham, and the suspension of local constituencies in Bradford for using what were, in effect, merely the same tactics deployed by the 'white Mafia' that runs the local party machinery, reinforces this sense of alienation and exclusion (Solomos and Back 1994: 157; 1995: 107–12). Now that a Muslim, Mohammed Sarwar, has been elected to Parliament in a Glasgow constituency, the question arises as to whose voice such a Muslim MP will represent, and what possible effect could s/he have on the course of parliamentary democracy in Britain. Clearly, what is needed to effect change in the public sphere are more sophisticated lobby and pressure-group tactics than have so far been developed by any of the immigrant groups in the UK. Unless visible signs of public influence emerge, it is hard to see why the imagining of an exclusive 'English' identity in the UK will not continue to dominate.

Conclusion

Although, as I have argued here, multiculturalism has become a global credo, it has different implications and impacts in different locales. Different forms of pluralism – political, social and cultural – direct and modify the impact of multiculturalism on these locales. Consequently, there are significant variations between multiculturalisms. Nevertheless, multiculturalist policies do seem to generate also a common thrust towards the reification of cultural and religious identities, irrespective of location. The comparison of multicultural policy implementation in Bradford and Birmingham suggests that attempts by local authorities to manage ethnic minorities politically by incorporating or institutionalising them have on the whole tended to further this process. What it is equally important to recognise, however, is that the specific development of such institutionalisation varies from place to place: in the case of Bradford, it has been Islam that has loomed high on the agenda, while in Birmingham black consciousness has dominated. Nevertheless we have seen also that sophisticated procedures for representation, such as the Standing Consultative Forum in Birmingham, do open up spaces for dialogue without a top-down imposition of agendas, and do allow 'communities' to be represented in these broader forums. Multiculturalisation here creates a framework for dialogue that takes politics off the streets.

Given its reificatory tendencies, however, should multiculturalism be abandoned perhaps in favour of a colour-blind, culture-blind, social policy? Such a solution has been shown to be fraught with danger for ethnic minorities. In the case of Bradford, the *de facto* abandonment of multiculturalism for fear of a backlash from the white electorate resulted in issues concerning ethnic minorities being downgraded to a low priority. When this was combined with decentralisation and competitive tendering, multicultural issues dropped to the bottom of the agenda. The point was brought home by a series of industrial tribunal cases that the council lost, and the threat of legal action by the Commission for Racial Equality. Clearly social policy on its own could not address the specific needs of ethnic minorities.

The alternative forms of incorporation in Birmingham, not quite self-incorporation and not mere nomination, seem to have gone some way towards addressing the concerns of the ethnic minorities, without falling into the trap of earlier reificatory policies. At present, we cannot be sure that this will not become just another example of managing ethnic minorities. The newly instituted Standing Consultative Forum does seem to be flexible enough, however, to allow ethnic minorities to decide their own agendas, and it attempts to fine-tune differences by focusing on women as a separate interest group. Nor does it ignore white 'minorities', but one evident lacuna not yet addressed seems to be that of youths, especially of young men who so far have no representation in the forum.

The Bradford evidence suggested that even with the deinstitutional-isation of religious leaders, youths gravitated towards exclusive Islamic identities in certain situations, and alternated by moving in others towards transethnic identifications. Hence, it is particularly among youths that a disarticulated and fractured politics is emerging on the ground, outside the influence of local state strategies. It is in this context that exclusive identities and a sense of alienation from the state and the society at large are being imagined in response to perceived discrimination and exclusion.

The real question is whether organised forums such as the Standing Consultative Forum in Birmingham can ever hope to 'represent' such disaffected youths? The problem is not restricted to Britain alone. In the politics of multiculturalism in the New Europe it is states, regions and large-scale federated organisations that lobby for the rights of 'cultures'. Youth culture cuts across these large-scale collectivities, or forms enclaves within them. Either way, young people's lifestyles are often perceived by established politicians to be a threat to the social order, becoming the subject of periodic moral panics. The youths, for their part, demonstrate their dissatisfaction in rallies, riots and demonstrations that undermine any neat and orderly politics of multiculturalism.

References

Appadurai, Arjun (1990) 'Disjuncture and Difference in the Global Cultural Eco-nomy', in Mike Featherstone (ed.) *Global Culture: Nationalism, Globalization and Modernity*, Sage, London, pp. 295–310.

Azmeh, Aziz al- (1993) *Islams and Modernities*, Verso, London.

Carr, John (1993) '"Alibis for Inaction": A Report on Aspects of the City of Bradford Metropolitan Council's Procedures for Handling Complaints of Dis-crimination', City of Bradford Metropolitan Council, February.

Furnival, John Sydenham (1956) *Colonial Policy and Practice: A Comparative Study of Burma and Netherlands India*, New York University Press, New York.

Gilroy, Paul (1987) *There Ain't no Black in the Union Jack*, Hutchinson, London.

Goldberg, David Theo (ed.) (1994) *Multiculturalism: A Critical Reader.* Blackwell, Cambridge, MA.

Goulbourne, Harry (1991) 'Varieties of Pluralism: The Notion of a Pluralist Post-imperial Britain', *New Community*, 17(2): 211–27.

Honeyford, Ray (1988) *Integration or Disintegration? Towards a Non-racist Society*, The Claridge Press, London.

Husband, C. (1996) 'Defining and Containing Diversity: Community, Ethnicity and

Citizenship' in W. I. U. Ahmad and K. Atkin (eds) *'Race' and Community Care*, Open University Press, Buckingham.

Kuper, Leo and Michael Gorfield Smith (eds) (1971) *Pluralism in Africa*, University of California Press, Berkeley and Los Angeles.

Lijphart, Arend (1968) *The Politics of Accommodation: Pluralism and Democracy in the Netherlands*, University of California Press, Berkeley.

Parekh, Bhikhu (1990) 'Britain and the Social Logic of Pluralism', in *Britain and Plural Society*, Commission for Racial Equality and the Runnymede Trust Discussion Paper 3, London.

Radtke, Frank-Olaf (1994) 'The Formation of Ethnic Minorities and the Transformation of Social into Ethnic Conflicts in a So-called Multi-cultural Society: The Case of Germany', in John Rex and Beatrice Drury (eds) *Ethnic Mobilisation in a Multi-cultural Europe*, Avebury, Aldershot.

Rex, John (1987) 'The Concept of a Multi-cultural Society', *New Community*, 14(1/2): 218–29.

Rex, John and Yunas Samad (1996) 'Multiculturalism and Political Integration in Birmingham and Bradford', *Innovation: European Journal of Social Sciences*, 9(1).

Samad, Yunas (1992) 'Book Burning and Race Relations: Political Mobilisation of Bradford Muslims', *New Community*, 18(4): 507–19.

— (forthcoming) 'Imagining a British Muslim Identification', in Steven Vertovec (ed.) *Muslims, Europe, Youth: Reproducing, Religion, Culture and Ethnicity*, Avebury, Aldershot.

Schierup, Carl-Ulrik (1994) 'Multi-culturalism and Ethnic Mobilisation: Some Theoretical Considerations', in John Rex and Beatrice Drury (eds) *Ethnic Mobilisation in a Multi-cultural Europe*, Avebury, Aldershot, pp. 43–5.

— (1995) 'Multiculturalism and Universalism in the United States and Europe', paper presented at the COST-A2 Workshop on Nationalism and Ethnicity, 2–4 March, Bern.

Schlesinger, Arthur M. Jr (1992) *The Disuniting of America: Reflections on a Multicultural Society*, Norton, New York.

Smith, M. G. (1974) *The Plural Society in the British West Indies*, University of California Press, Berkeley and Los Angeles.

Solomos, John and Leo Back (1994) 'Conceptualising Racisms: Social Theory, Politics and Research', *Sociology*, 28(1).

— (1995) *Race, Politics and Social Change*, Routledge, London.

Standing Consultative Forum (1992) 'The 1992 Annual General Meeting of the Standing Consultative Forum (SCF) for Black and Ethnic Minority Communities', Summary Report, and Appendix I 'The Context for Understanding Community Issues' (unpublished report).

Takaki, Ronald (1993) 'Multiculturalism: Battleground or Meeting Ground?' *The Annals*, Vol. 530, November: 109–21.

Taylor, Charles (1994) 'The Politics of Recognition', in David Theo Goldberg (ed.) *Multiculturalism: A Critical Reader*, Blackwell, Cambridge.

Vertovec, Steven (1996) 'Multiculturalism, Culturalism and Public Incorporation', *Ethnic and Racial Studies*, 19(1).

Werbner, Pnina (1991) 'Black and Ethnic Leaderships in Britain: A Theoretical Overview', in Pnina Werbner and Muhammad Anwar (eds) *Black and Ethnic Leaderships: The Cultural Dimensions of Political Action*, Routledge, London.

CHAPTER 14

Afterword: Writing Multiculturalism and Politics in the New Europe

Pnina Werbner

This book has taken as its starting point not multiculturalism *per se* but the way that cultural differences may be negotiated and transcended politically. The political theatre in which these cultural, ethnic, national and ideological differences must be negotiated is that of the so-called New Europe, a mass of land delimited by cultural and historical enmities and exclusions, frequently of the most barbaric kind. The Europe of 'civilisation' which Eurobureaucrats in Brussels try unsuccessfully to evoke (McDonald 1996; Shore 1995; Shore and Black 1994; Pieterse 1991) is sutured irretrievably to an anti-history: a past to be remembered only as a lesson of what should never recur, in Renan's terms (Anderson 1991: 201). It is in this sense that Europe is 'new', a suprastate oriented away from its distopic past towards a utopian future. But unlike the old universalist ideals that animated the founding fathers of the modern nation-state, today's architects of the New Europe confront the political fact that the past cannot be *made* to die; that they must somehow contain the divisive power not only of old enmities but of deeply held ethical and political traditions, and the languages and rituals in which these traditions are cast. At the same time, what is irrevocably shattered is the illusion that cultural purity and authenticity, the nation or *Volk* unto itself, is ever possible as a political reality. Every new territorial unit, however small, generates its own minorities (Hobsbawm 1990: 33, 155, 174, 185–6) as eastern Europe has so tragically demonstrated. Not only that. Europe today, as we show in this volume, is the product of postcoloniality: a continent of immigrants and their descendants.

But can the 'new' Europe, in the words of Derrida, escape its own created monstrosities of xenophobia, racism, anti-Semitism, religious or nationalist fanaticism (Derrida 1992/1991: 6)?

What philosophy of translation will dominate in Europe? In a Europe that from now on should avoid both the nationalistic tensions of linguistic difference and the violent homogenization of languages through the neutrality of a translating medium that would claim to be transparent, metalinguistic, and universal? (Derrida 1992/1991: 58)

The path between the Scylla of homogenising universalism and the Charybdis of xenophobic cultural nationalism is increasingly being called 'multiculturalism', a word plucked out of educational debates about school curricula to confront the larger world of what Soysal calls 'postnational politics' (Soysal 1994). Critics of multiculturalism have argued, as Caglar does in Chapter 9, that the 'culture' of multiculturalism is not the vital, gradually changing, creative, mimetic, unreflective, unbounded and hybrid culture that anthropologists study.[1] It is a far more reified and politicised imagined entity, the object of representation by elected and self-appointed group spokespersons who stress its inviolability as a sacred domain of collective sovereignty. This assumption is what makes the negotiation of difference so difficult: finding common cultural and political grounds requires the pooling not only of political but also of cultural sovereignty, embodied in public respect for the symbols and values of the 'other', the incoming 'stranger'. The challenge is not, however, impossible. The democratic political arena is inherently one in which collective differences are both exaggerated and transcended. Despite clarion calls to amity, even members of nations that represent themselves as culturally unitary do not share 'the same substantive conception of the good life', as Kymlicka recognises (1995: 86). Conversely, citizens whose cultures differ may share certain ethical premises (such as liberalism, religious humanism or social-ism) which divide them from others within their own cultures. The aporia disadvantaged groups (women, ethnic minorities) face in the political arena relates to the definition of citizenship as the duty, *qua citizen*, to aim 'towards a politics in which people will transcend their localised and partial concerns' (Phillips 1995: 290). Particularistic claims for measures to compensate for historical underprivilege are often constructed as narrow, selfish and divisive. Hence the challenge of the new multicultural or 'transversal' politics, as we argued in *Debating Cultural Hybridity*, the first volume in this pair (Werbner and Modood 1997), is how to transcend these constructions, how to eliminate current subordinations while still recognising the validity of 'difference'. In Quebec's multicultural 'minority circuit', for example, activists are selected who 'show themselves capable of operating on a broader transethnic basis ... adopting a generic minority rights rhetoric as an occupational vernacular' (Amit-Talai 1996: 106). The real question is whether, in suppressing their particularist cultural claims, these activists fail in the task of challenging the hegemonic culture of the majority. Despite its morally grounded claims to separate cultural sover-eignty, Quebec remains a deeply racist society (Knowles 1996).

Indeed, we argue in this book, multiculturalism without anti-racism does not make sense as a radical political programme. The outstanding contributions by Taylor and others to the liberal theory of multiculturalism (Taylor 1994; Kymlicka 1995) are marred, as Blum cogently argues, by a failure to recognise sufficiently this complementary duality (1994: 187, 190). Racism denies universal human commonalities beyond culture and thus presumes a licence to violate the symbolic and physical integrity of individuals and groups (Werbner 1996; Balibar 1991: 18). As Blum argues, the need is to stage a dual struggle for the universal *and* the particular: 'We value each other *both* because of our commonalities *and* because of our differences' (Blum 1994: 190). In Europe, we argue here even more strongly, multiculturalism without anti-racism or anti-racism without multiculturalism cannot withstand the forces of repression or regression. In Europe 'culture' easily gets linked to discourses of origins and innate mentalities (Barker 1981). As theorists of nationalism such as Anderson and Hobsbawm demonstrate, in reality, nationalism is always historically conjunctural: it joins with liberalism, human rights, socialism, fascism. In itself 'the call of ethnicity or language provides no guidance for the future' beyond xenophobia and exclusion (Hobsbawm 1990: 176; also 130, 145). In this respect, Stolcke's (1995) argument that nationalism as 'cultural fundamentalism' may be detached from racism fails entirely to come to grips with the intrinsically conjunctural nature of nationalism.

A central advocacy of this book is thus for a multiculturalism that aims not only to allow national, ethnic and immigrant minorities a voice, but to protect them from offensive symbolic as well as civic and material exclusions and violations (Asad 1993, Chapter 7; Turner 1993: 412). This advocacy comes with an insistence, however, that individual human rights must be observed by these minorities. Sovereignty must be pooled; otherwise as Kymlicka, an advocate of this duality, lamely admits, it is almost impossible to 'impose liberalism' once groups are granted full autonomy (1995: 165). Claims to full political autonomy or nationhood in a post-national era, in which even the larger nation-states in Europe are in the process of pooling sovereignty, and are signatories to international and transnational charters, in any case seem empty and delusionary. What a critical multiculturalism recognises is the rights of minorities to demand restitution for historical racialisations which disempowered them and suppressed their voice in the national sphere.

The other key aim of multiculturalism, grounded theoretically in the work of Homi Bhabha (1994: Chapter 8), is ideological: continuously to remind 'Europe', as it negotiates its internal differences, that the continent is fundamentally incomplete, a postcolonial locus of multiple diasporas; and by doing so to 'interrupt' or 'disrupt' singular narratives of nation and supranation; to demand 'the decentring of culture(s) from the political system ... [and deny the idea of] a unitary hegemonic culture as the indispensable consensual basis of national political institutions' (Turner 1993: 425; see also Tilly 1992: 717).

Third, majoritarian democracies need protection from themselves. Here the right of the individual to take action *against* the state in the name of, and protected by, overarching principles of justice is crucial (Hall and Held 1989: 186). The European Court of Justice is currently taking on just such a role. Hence, we need to strike 'a new balance between the individual and social dimensions of citizenship rights' (Hall and Held 1989: 179), between 'narrow universalism' and 'narrow particularism' (Parekh 1995a: 148). The point is that these are not necessarily contradictory.

What this volume shows, however, is that multiculturalism is ultimately not a matter of theory, even critical theory, but of real politics; there are as many multiculturalisms as there are political arenas for collective action. The argument over the canon in the USA seems arcane and remote in Europe. What seems axiomatic in one democracy (for example, the separation of religion and state) is contravened by another (for example, pillarisation in the Netherlands). Contributors to this volume highlight the intricate interrelations of multicultural politics at different levels: the local, the national, the supranational, and different domains, from the orientalist construction of Eastern Europe (Kurti) and racism (Bjørgo), to migration (Melotti), ethnicity (Lyon), hyphenated identities (Caglar), religion (Lewis and Diop), local politics (Samad and Yalçin-Heckmann), education (Schif-fauer), affirmative action (Ben-Tovim) and European citizenship (Brewin). If status in a community mediates citizenship rights, determining notions of caring and mutual responsibility, as T. H. Marshall recognised, this implies that social citizenship in the nation-state is 'tiered' (Yuval Davis n.d.). In the new Europe citizenship is *multi-tiered*. The issue is not simply one of contrasting national cultures but of recognising the power of historically and contingently evolved political cultures, the habits and expectations in different countries that grow out of rule-governed be-haviour in conducting political business (Weale 1995: 216). Immigrants and ethnic minorities in Europe are subject to differential 'incorporative regimes' at different levels, as Soysal (1994) argues. But our case studies in this book show that Soysal's gross typologies cannot capture the full complexity of multicultural struggles in different European arenas. Multi-culturalism is always a specific negotiated order and no amount of abstract philosophical or legal reasoning can prescribe a single 'just' model.

Thus in Europe we need what Charles Taylor has called a theory of 'deep diversity' (Taylor 1991: 75), a vocabulary allowing us to analyse the complex interplay of cultures and belongings at different levels and in different domains, as seen by Europeans *meroscopically*, through partial perspectives or visions.[2] Such a theory would have to take account of alliances and cross-cutting ties across and within ethnicities and nations. The supranational identity of Europe will necessarily always be the product of such partial perspectives (Parekh 1995b: 267). Endemic racism and racial violence in Western Europe of the kind Bjørgo and Kurti discuss here, and regional nationalisms (MacDonald 1993) seem to confirm a sceptical view of the impossibility of the European Union transcending our deeply felt ethnic or national identities (Smith 1995: 111). But there is also an explicit and public counter-movement, led by feminists and minority activists, to recognise that all identities are partial, multiple and fractured by cross-cutting alliances. The politics of multiculturalism in Europe is leading *de facto*, as the contributions to this book show, towards the creation of a *heterogeneous European community*, one modelled, perhaps, on the cosmopolitan city (Young 1990; 1995). Such a politics cannot fix and reify groups as permanent and closed; it is always oppositional or 'critical', combined with rather than antithetical to anti-racism. It is deeply embedded in broader political processes. This means that for minorities to gain dignity and voice requires strong *majoritarian* backing, beyond normal politics. It is naïve to suppose, with Habermas (1994), that ordinary democratic politics will suffice to guarantee cultural recognition. At the same time Habermas is undoubtedly right that the challenge for minority activists and anti-racists is also, as we show in this volume, one of negotiating *internal* differences – of consolidating alliances and formulating agendas beyond divisive identity politics. Only these will ultimately compel Europe to address real issues of distributive justice and symbolic equality.

Acknowledgement

I am grateful to Richard Werbner for his immensely helpful comments.

Notes

1. For this tension with anthropology see Roseberry 1992; Turner 1993; Amit-Talai 1995.
2. My neologism 'meroscopic' (of or with partial perspective), builds on Strathern's 'merographic connections' (a mode of exposition of partial relations), which itself draws on Thornton's 'mereology' (the science of part to whole) (see Strathern 1992: 72–81).

References

Amit-Talai, Vered (1995) 'Anthropology, Multiculturalism and the Concept of Culture', *FOLK, Journal of the Danish Ethnographic Society*, 37: 135–44.
— (1996) 'The Minority Circuit: Kashtin, the Media and the Oka Crisis', in Vered Amit-Talai and Caroline Knowles (eds) *Re-situating Identities: the Politics of Race, Ethnicity, Culture*, Broadview Press, Ontario, pp. 89–114.
Anderson, Benedict (1991 [1983]) *Imagined Communities: Reflections on the Origin and Spread of Nationalism*, 2nd edn, Verso, London.
Asad, Talal (1993) *Genealogies of Religion*, Johns Hopkins University Press, Baltimore.
Balibar, Etienne and Immanuel Wallerstein (1991) *Race, Nation, Class: Ambiguous Identities*, Verso, London.

Barker, M. (1981) *The New Racism*, Junction Books, London.

Bhabha, Homi (1994) *The Location of Culture*, Routledge, London.

Blum, Lawrence (1994) 'Multiculturalism, Racial Justice and Community: Reflections on Charles Taylor's "Politics of Recognition"', in Lawrence Foster and Patricia Herzog (eds) *Defending Diversity*, University of Massachusetts Press, Amherst, pp. 175–206.

Derrida, Jacques (1992) [1991]) *The Other Heading: Reflections on Today's Europe*, trans. Pascale-Anne Brault and Michael B. Naas, Indiana University Press, Bloomington.

Habermas, Jürgen (1994) 'Struggles for Recognition in the Democratic Constitutional State', in Amy Gutmann (ed.) *Multiculturalism*, Princeton University Press, Princeton, pp. 107–48.

Hall, Stuart and David Held (1989) 'Citizens and Citizenship', in Stuart Hall and Martin Jacques (eds) *New Times: The Changing Face of Politics in the 1990s*, Lawrence and Wishart in association with *Marxism Today*, London, pp. 173–88.

Hobsbawm, E. J. (1990) *Nations and Nationalism Since 1780: Programme, Myth, Reality*, Cambridge University Press, Cambridge.

Knowles, Caroline (1996) 'Racism, Biography, and Psychiatry', in Vered Amit-Talai and Caroline Knowles (eds) *Re-situating Identities: The Politics of Race, Ethnicity, Culture*, Broadview Press, Ontario, pp. 47–67.

Kymlicka, Will (1995) *Multicultural Citizenship: A Liberal Theory of Minority Rights*, Clarendon Press, Oxford.

McDonald, Maryon (1996) 'Unity in Diversities: Some Tensions in the Construction of Europe', *Social Anthropology*, 4(1): 33–46.

MacDonald, Sharon (ed.) (1993) *Inside European Identities*, Berg, Oxford.

Parekh, Bhikhu (1995a) 'Introduction', *British National Identity in a European Context*, special issue of *New Community*, 21(2): 147–52.

— (1995b) 'The Concept of National Identity', *New Community*, 21(2): 255–68.

Phillips, Anne (1995) 'Democracy and Difference: Some Problems for Feminist Theory', in Will Kymlicka (ed.) *The Rights of Minority Cultures*, Oxford University Press, Oxford, pp. 288–99.

Pieterse, Jan N. (1991) 'Fictions of Europe', in *Europe: Variations on a Theme of Racism*, special issue of *Race and Class*, 32(3): 3–10.

Roseberry, William (1992) 'Multiculturalism and the Challenge of Anthropology', *Social Research*, 59(4): 841–58.

Shore, Cris (1995) 'Usurpers or Pioneers? European Commission Bureaucrats and the Question of European Consciousness', in Anthony P. Cohen and Nigel Rapport (eds) *Questions of Consciousness*, Asa Monograph 33, Routledge, London, pp. 217–36.

Shore, Cris and Annabel Black (1994) 'Citizens' Europe and the Construction of European Identity', in Victoria Goddard, Josep R. Llobera and Cris Shore (eds) *The Anthropology of Europe*, Berg, Oxford: pp. 275–98.

Smith, Anthony D. (1995) *Nations and Nationalism in a Global Era*, Polity Press, Cambridge.

Soysal, Yasmeen N. (1994) *Limits of Citizenship: Migrants and Postnational Membership in Europe*, University of Chicago Press, Chicago.

Stolcke, Verena (1995) 'Talking Culture: New Boundaries, New Rhetorics of Exclusion in Europe', *Current Anthropology*, 36(1): 1–22.

Strathern, Marilyn (1992) *After Nature: English Kinship in the Late Twentieth Century*, Cambridge University Press, Cambridge.

Taylor, Charles (1991) 'Shared and Divergent Values', in Ronald Watts and D. Brown (eds) *Options for a New Canada*, University of Toronto Press, Toronto, pp. 53–76.

— (1994) 'Examining the Politics of Recognition', in Amy Gutmann (ed.) *Multiculturism*, Princeton University Press, Princeton, pp. 25–74.

Tilly, Charles (1992) 'Futures of European States', *Social Research*, 52(4): 705–17.

Turner, Terence (1993) 'Anthropology and Multiculturalism: What is Anthropology That Multiculturalists Should be Mindful of It?', *Cultural Anthropology*, 8(4): 411–29.

Weale, Albert (1995) 'From Little England to Democratic Europe?', *New Community*, 21(2): 215–26.

Werbner, Pnina (1997) 'Essentialising Essentialism, Essentialising Silence: Ambivalence and Multiplicity in the Constructions of Racism and Ethnicity', in Pnina Werbner and Tariq Modood (eds) *Debating Cultural Hybridity: Multi-cultural Identities and the Politics of Anti-Racism*, Zed Books, London.

Werbner, Pnina and Tariq Modood (eds) (1997) *Debating Cultural Hybridity: Multicultural Identities and the Politics of Anti-Racism*, Zed Books, London.

Young, Iris M. (1990) 'The Ideal of Community and the Politics of Difference', in Linda J. Nicholson (ed.) *Feminism/Postmodernism*, Routledge, London, pp. 300–23.

— (1995) 'Togetherness in Difference: Transforming the Logic of Group Political Conflict', in Will Kymlicka (ed.) *The Rights of Minority Cultures*, Oxford University Press, Oxford, pp. 155–76.

Yuval-Davis, Nira (n.d.) 'Women, Citizenship and Difference', background paper for the conference on 'Women, Citizenship and Difference', University of Greenwich, 16–18 July 1996.

Index